Civvies

MANCHESTER
1824

Manchester University Press

Cultural History of Modern War

Series editors

Ana Carden-Coyne, Peter Gatrell, Max Jones, Penny Summerfield and Bertrand Taithe

Already published

Julie Anderson *War, disability and rehabilitation in Britain: soul of a nation*

Rachel Duffett *The stomach for fighting: food and the soldiers of the First World War*

Christine E. Hallett *Containing trauma: nursing work in the First World War*

Jo Laycock *Imagining Armenia: Orientalism, ambiguity and intervention*

Chris Millington *From victory to Vichy: Veterans in inter-war France*

Juliette Pattinson *Behind enemy lines: gender, passing and the Special Operations Executive in the Second World War*

Chris Pearson *Mobilizing nature: The environmental history of war and militarization in Modern France*

Jeffrey S. Reznick *Healing the nation: soldiers and the culture of caregiving in Britain during the Great War*

Jeffrey S. Reznick *John Galsworthy and disabled soldiers of the Great War: with an illustrated selection of his writings*

Michael Roper *The secret battle: emotional survival in the Great War*

Penny Summerfield and Corinna Peniston-Bird *Contesting home defence: men, women and the Home Guard in the Second World War*

Wendy Ugolini *Experiencing war as the 'enemy other': Italian Scottish experience in World War II*

Colette Wilson *Paris and the Commune, 1871–78: the politics of forgetting*

http://www.arts.manchester.ac.uk/subjectareas/history/research/cchw/

Centre for the Cultural History of War

Civvies

Middle-class men on the English Home Front, 1914–18

LAURA UGOLINI

Manchester University Press

Published by Manchester University Press
Altrincham Street, Manchester M1 7JA, UK
www.manchesteruniversitypress.co.uk

British Library Cataloguing-in-Publication Data is available

ISBN 978 1 5261 1666 6 *paperback*

First published by Manchester University Press in hardback 2013

This edition first published 2017

Printed by Lightning Source

Contents

Illustrations

Acknowledgements

My first thanks are due to those scholars who provided help and encouragement, particularly when the research for this book was at its earliest stages: many thanks especially to Joanna Bourke and Jessica Meyer. I am also very grateful to the staff of the archives where I undertook most of the research for this book, especially the Imperial War Museum and the Brotherton Library's Special Collections. Particularly warm thanks are due to the staff of the Bodleian Library's Special Collections and especially to Colin Harris, the Superintendent of the Reading Rooms, for pointing me towards documents I would otherwise no doubt have ignored. Thank you also to the British Academy, for generously supporting the research for this book with a small grant.

Thanks are also due to Philip for his help with Chapter 4. I am very grateful to Stephen and Helen for their hospitality while I was undertaking research in Leeds, to Carol 'la mamma' while I worked in Norwich and to Sarah for the many lunches while I was working at the Imperial War Museum – although I should say that I have not chosen the archives on the basis of the availability of three-course meals – and to Lisa, Maurizio and Giacomo while I didn't do any work at all.

Introduction: Middle-class men and the First World War

Decades after the end of the conflict, F. W. M. Drew recalled that in 1917, at the age of thirteen, he had entered 'HMS Conway, the naval training base near Liverpool'. He had 'fully expected to be able to take an active part in the war, but the following year it was all over. Still, several of my fellow trainees, lads of sixteen and seventeen who had graduated and gone to sea, never returned'. He added that 'the toll had been so terrible that no one dared speak of their experiences. Only those like myself who had no part of it could afford the luxury of recollection'.[1] In a way, of course, he was right. As a number of historians have observed, many returning combatants wished for nothing better than to retreat to their old civilian lives, to home and family, and put their wartime experiences behind them: 'the average man thought fondly of stepping back into civvies and resuming his original job, with the sole difference that he would no longer be "b … d" about by people in authority'.[2] In another way, however, Drew was quite wrong: not only did many ex-servicemen prove determined to recall and publish accounts of their experiences, but those men 'who had no part of' the war were in fact granted little 'luxury of recollection'.

Few civilian memoirs were published in the aftermath of war to parallel the large number of combatant autobiographical accounts, and hardly any that were authored by men.[3] Writing in 1938, Macleod Yearsley observed that there were many people who, like himself, had been 'compelled by circumstances to pass those four years of stress at home, and it is curious that few, if any, have left behind any record of their experiences'.[4] Civilian men – including middle-class men – seem to have taken the view that their experiences would be of little interest to the reading public, either in the immediate post-war period, or in subsequent decades.[5] Perhaps they were right. It is certainly the case that in the hundred years since the outbreak of the First World War, the British Expeditionary Force and the battle fronts, particularly the Western Front, have attracted a good deal more attention than the British home front, not only in academia, but also in literature, drama, visual arts and popular culture.

This is not to say that civilian men, and especially middle-class and middle-aged men, were entirely excluded from the process of remembering the war. In the decades following the end of the conflict, for example, many became involved in the creation of public monuments and rituals to commemorate the war and the war dead. According to Stefan Goebel, in Britain, unlike Germany, 'memory work was by and large in the hands of middle-aged civilians who ... lacked first-hand army experience ... as well as military socialisation in peacetime'. The result was that 'agents of remembrance failed to translate the experience of combat into a public discourse', adopting instead tried and tested chivalric themes, already well-established parts of the public cultural repertoire, with their emphasis on 'courage, duty, honour, fairness and faith'.[6] But whether they used themes and motifs drawn from a mythical medieval chivalric past or from the classical canon,[7] British war monuments focused overwhelmingly on servicemen, on their conduct, courage and sacrifice: civilian men may have been central to their creation, but public memorials did not portray *their* experiences of war.[8] Indeed, any attempt to do so would no doubt have received short shrift, as an absurd and offensive attempt to compare the suffering of civilian men with that of combatants.[9] But while understandable, this absence has contributed further to the dominance of the figure of the soldier-hero in the history and collective memory of the First World War.

That said, although academic and popular interest in the military side of the First World War remains strong, civilian experiences have in recent years begun to attract welcome attention, both in Britain and beyond.[10] In 2007, when dealer Shaun Sewell brought the hand-written and illustrated diaries of Thomas Cairns Livingstone, a Glasgow clerk, to the BBC television programme *Antiques Roadshow*, they immediately caused a stir. Although the diaries covered the period between 1913 and 1933, it was the wartime sections that aroused the greatest attention; after a 'bidding war' they were published by Harper Collins in 2008, becoming one of the best-sellers of the year. As many of the reviewers pointed out, part of the diaries' fascination lay in the fact that they provided insights into wartime experiences that had little to do with the more common accounts of soldiering, trench warfare and mud, but focused instead on domestic, family and personal details. As the *Daily Mail* put it, this was 'the missing piece of the wartime jigsaw puzzle'.[11]

This is an exaggeration. There is no doubt that military matters and combat continue to dominate narratives of the First World War. However, the suggestion that *Tommy's War* is 'the' missing piece of a puzzle underestimates existing research on the British home front.[12] We now know a great deal about wartime economic, administrative and labour policies, about culture, leisure and sport, as well as about the impact of the war on issues such as health, housing and standards of living.[13] Efforts have also been made to record, particularly through the use of oral history, the 'everyday' experiences of individuals and of towns and communities during the war.[14] At the same time, there still remain significant gaps in our knowledge: in particular, we know more about women's experiences on the home front than about men's,[15] and we know more about working-class than about middle-class men.[16] It is this latter group that is the subject of this book: focusing particularly on the English home front, its aim is to explore civilian middle-class men's wartime experiences, questioning how the war affected lives and identities, as well as the extent and ways in which 'normal' practices were disrupted and relationships renegotiated.

Attempting to argue that middle-class men have been neglected and 'hidden from history',[17] even if only for the relatively short period of just over four years, is an awkward business. Although there were concerns about the financial and social hardships endured by many struggling white-collar workers and their families, Edwardian middle-class men as a whole can more properly be described as prosperous, well-educated and most importantly, powerful, especially if compared to the bulk of the working-class population or, indeed, women.[18] It is striking, for example, that 'the average wage for the male industrial worker on the eve of war was about £75 per annum, whereas the average annual income of the salaried class was £340'.[19] From a different perspective, and yet equally telling, is the estimate that the daily calorific intake of the Edwardian working class was only 76 per cent of the national average, from which it can be inferred that the middle (and upper) classes were proportionately doing – and eating – a good deal better.[20] As the 'great self-recording class', furthermore, with its abundance of diaries, letters and other writings, middle-class experiences and attitudes are far from hidden from the historical record.[21] In short, middle-class men hardly fit into the mould of 'losers' who need historians to rescue them from 'the enormous condescension of posterity'.[22]

And yet, soldiers have – understandably – cast a long shadow over the history of the First World War. Not only does there continue to be an insatiable appetite for accounts that focus on the experiences of 'ordinary' servicemen, as well as on the decision-making of the 'top brass',[23] but in recent years historians of gender have shed much new light on the often ambivalent relationship between Edwardian notions of manliness and military values, as well as on the varied impact of military service on masculine identities and understandings of what it meant to 'be a man'.[24] Although the personal and political impact of the war on elite literary and political figures on the home front – most notably, perhaps, Herbert Asquith and Rudyard Kipling, both of whom lost sons in the conflict – has been relatively well documented,[25] we know far less about the wartime experiences of the 50 per cent of 'ordinary' men of military age[26] who did not fit the 'hegemonic' military mould, and did not enlist and were not conscripted into the armed forces.[27] As T. G. Ashplant, Graham Dawson and Michael Roper point out, 'in the context of national imaginaries, dominant memory' of war 'is often centred around the idealized figure of the masculine soldier', leaving little space for other memories, and effectively silencing 'others – women especially, but also non-combatants and the older generation – who together made up the home front'.[28] It is this silencing of a section of the population that was normally vocal and (relatively) powerful, which provides the point of departure for this book, as it seeks to explore how civilian middle-class men dealt with their threatened relegation to the subordinate status of non-military, potentially unmanly, 'other'.

The English home front, gender and masculinity

In July 1916 *Punch* published a cartoon depicting a seaside pier as 'An Adamless Eden-on-Sea', where the smartly-dressed young 'nuts' of pre-war days were replaced by smiling but lifeless tailors' dummies (Figure 1).

The image of the home front as denuded of its men – and of its young men in particular – was a powerful and evocative one, particularly so soon after the start of the battle of the Somme. It was not, of course, the literal truth, certainly as far as the country as a whole was concerned, but was suggestive of the heavy demands made by the war machine on men and manpower over the four years of conflict: it has been estimated that there were '5.7 million men in the army at one time or another, approximating to 22.1 per cent of the male population of the United Kingdom'.[29]

Around 50 per cent of boys and men aged between fifteen and forty-nine were mobilised in the course of the war.[30]

Images of an 'Adamless Eden' also resonated with civilians' own perceptions of the reality around them. In July 1916 the journalist and editor of the *Daily Express* R. D. Blumenfeld observed that 'conscription has completely skinned the countryside of its young men. They have all gone'.[31] Two years later, Andrew Clark described the rural parish of Great Leighs in Essex as 'absolutely empty of young men'.[32] Women, it was widely noted in the final years of war, had taken men's place in a variety of spheres that had previously been overwhelmingly, if not entirely, masculine. Not only did many engineering shops and ordnance factories seem, at least if one was to judge by official photographs or press and propaganda images, almost entirely populated by women, but other bastions of masculinity appeared similarly changed in character. According to journalist Charles Sheridan Jones, for example, in 1917 one could see in many City of London banks 'three earnest young women struggling

AN ADAMLESS EDEN-ON-SEA.

THANKS TO A CUNNING ARRANGEMENT OF DUMMIES THE PROMENADE RETAINS SOMETHING OF ITS SPICE;

1 'An Adamless Eden-on-Sea', *Punch*, 5 July 1916. Reproduced with permission of Punch Limited.

with the task once performed with careless ease by an imperturbable bank clerk … flappers now sit in the places where lounged the youths of the pale faces and radiant socks – youths that the war has turned into men!'[33] Evidence of the continued presence of men, especially men of military age, in such supposedly feminised spaces, could thus take people by surprise. In March 1916 Harold Cossins, a company secretary working for a London firm, was 'much struck' by 'the crowds of young men trooping out of the munitions works, as shown in the "Britain Prepared" film yesterday'.[34]

Arguably, perceptions of grief and loss also contributed to the creation of an image of the home front as a feminine space. Carol Acton suggests that 'the gendered division of wartime behaviour excludes women's voices from speaking war when it is defined as combat, and at the same time privileges grief and mourning as the province of women on the home front'.[35] The reality of bereavement was of course a great deal more complex than this simple division of labour might suggest, and yet the belief in a link between grief, femininity and the home front was a widely held one. 'Widows and mothers', Adrian Gregory points out, 'were the archetypal bereaved in public rhetoric'.[36] It is telling that after the war the Liberal politician and journalist C. F. G. Masterman should observe of the Unknown Soldier in Westminster Abbey, that 'we were burying every boy's father, and every woman's lover, and every mother's child', overlooking adult men's own wartime losses.[37] Mothers' suffering, according to Michael Roper, was a central preoccupation of those individuals – often, as mentioned above, middle-class men – seeking to create post-war memorials to the dead. By the end of the war, then, the home front had become strongly identified with grieving women, and more specifically with grieving mothers.[38]

Middle-class men, furthermore, seem to have disappeared from the home front at a faster rate and in higher proportions than other sections of the male population. On the eve of the war, it has been argued, the middle classes were more likely to favour intervention than other social groups,[39] while public school-educated 'young middle- and upper-class men were the most conventionally patriotic component of the population',[40] and were thus proportionately more likely to enlist.[41] By February 1916, according to surveys carried out by the Board of Trade, 28.3 per cent of men employed in industry had enlisted, while the proportion for commerce and finance was 40.1 per cent and 41.7 per cent for the professions.[42] Middle-class men – especially junior officers – were also more likely to become casualties: 'in broad statistical terms, Scotland aside, the population was being killed in order of social precedence. By the second half of the war these losses were reaching deep into the lower middle class'.[43]

However, such figures should not obscure the fact that the British home front was hardly entirely stripped of its middle-class (or other) men. Apart from the men who were over (and, of course, boys who were under) military age and the men of military age who for a variety of reasons did not enlist (as mentioned above, roughly half the men aged between fifteen and forty-nine in England and Wales), there were also plenty of men who were conscripted after 1916, but experienced the first two years of war – and often longer – as civilians.[44] It is such men who are the focus of this book: not the relatively small number of pacifists and conscientious objectors who refused to serve for political, ethical or religious reasons,[45] but those who did not enlist, or did not enlist *immediately* for (much more common) reasons, which might include age, physical unfitness, family and others responsibilities, or, indeed, a simple reluctance to enter the armed forces, with all its attendant inconveniences and dangers.

That said, although the home front was hardly an entirely feminised space, in a context where enlistment was viewed as the 'norm' for most men, and where servicemen were thought to embody the highest qualities of patriotic manliness, the continued presence of civilian men cannot have been unproblematic. According to Stephen Garton, writing about Australia, but with obvious parallels with Britain, 'war represented the attainment of an ideal of manliness, physical action, bravery, self-control, courage and more importantly for many, male comradeship … the point of contrast, of otherness … was home, the place of women, domesticity, constrained masculinity and the shirker – the non-man'.[46] At the very least, as Lois Bibbings points out, 'all men who were not in the military were, to varying degrees, excluded from exemplary notions of maleness'.[47] If, furthermore, middle-class men were perceived as especially keen to enlist, it is at least conceivable that those who did not, would have had the most to explain. This book, then, seeks to find out how middle-class civilian men negotiated their presence on the home front, explores their changing experiences over the four years of war, and questions whether they were able to construct identities for themselves as manly civilians, avoiding being reduced to the status of 'non-men'.

Middle-class men and manliness

Historians of the First World War often seem to have a very clear idea of who middle-class men were and how they reacted to the outbreak of the conflict. Gerald DeGroot, for example, makes a (no doubt slightly provocative) distinction between 'those from the public schools' and 'those from the rest of society'. The former, 'most of whom became officers', belonged to a generation that had been 'raised to believe in manly, chivalric values, yet had little opportunity to test their relevance to their real world'. Now they had their chance.[48] On the other hand, historians who focus on the nature and development of the nineteenth and twentieth-century English (or, indeed, British) middle class, rarely share such confidence. As Alan Kidd and David Nicholls point out, 'some historians have been inclined to despair at reaching any satisfactory definition of the middle class. How can millionaire financiers, millocrats, farmers, shopkeepers and the like possibly be lumped together in one social category?'[49]

They have a point. Of the men who feature in this book, for example, it would be difficult to find too many points of commonalty between Holcombe Ingleby, a well-to-do solicitor, Conservative MP for King's Lynn and keen hunting man and golfer, who divided his time between London and his house in Norfolk, and Frank Lockwood, the son of a weaver and a trainee lithographic artist, who lived with his parents near Huddersfield. In terms of income,[50] education, age, social milieu and family background, it would be difficult to imagine two more different men, despite the fact that they were both among the approximately 20 per cent of the working population employed in 'non-manual' occupations[51] and shared a liking for musical comedy and 'shows'.[52]

That said, there were also 'common and unifying characteristics' that make it possible to explore the First World War experiences of – however widely defined – 'middle-class' civilian men. Such unifying characteristics included their 'engagement in broadly the same enterprise, the capitalist enterprise of accumulation and improvement', as well as a set of 'social and cultural practices and mores' that helped to bridge the gap 'between the propertied capitalists … and the intermediate groups of professionals and managers'. Perhaps most importantly, at least as far as the present book is concerned, a middle-class identity was built in a 'dialectical relationship with other social classes'.[53] Indeed, the men who are the focus of this book would have felt a kinship with each other not simply on the basis of comparable (if by no means identical) economic, educational and social backgrounds, or shared values and aspirations – although these were far from irrelevant – but also on an awareness that they were separate and different from 'others', both the upper class and, increasingly importantly as the war dragged on, the working class.

Indeed, as mentioned above, it is not difficult to find evidence of middle-class power, prestige and well-being on the eve of war, setting it apart from the bulk of the working class.[54] Not only were middle-class incomes on average a good deal higher than those of much of the working-class population,[55] but financial instruments such as fixed-interest securities had been developed to ensure that the benefits of such incomes could be optimised further.[56] 'Income inequalities', together with factors such as 'unequal patterns of consumption and differential access to health care'[57] meant that the Edwardian middle classes tended to live longer and enjoy better health than their working-class counterparts. It has been suggested, for example, that between 1910 and 1912 the infant mortality rate among children of unskilled workers was twice that endured by professional families,[58] while unskilled men aged between twenty and sixty-four suffered from a death rate approximately 50 per cent higher than men in non-manual occupations.[59] The physical manifestation of inequality was made clear by the fact that 'between 1880 and 1913 thirteen-year-old working-class boys in London and Glasgow were on average 2½ inches shorter than their middle-income group contemporaries'.[60]

Historians have long debated the timing and nature of the 'rise' or the 'making' of the British middle class, but there seems to be little doubt that the process had taken place by 1914.[61] In his sweeping history of the middle class, for example, Lawrence James describes the period between 1832 and 1914 as marked by 'the triumph of the middle classes'.[62] It can be argued, furthermore, that middle-class notions of manliness, with their emphasis on self-control, courage, independence and 'fair play', had achieved 'hegemonic' status in Edwardian society.[63] Not only did middle-class men enjoy political and economic power closed off to – and perhaps at the expense of – women and working-class men, while their prosperity ensured that they benefited from a greater material well-being and physical fitness than most other sections of the population. In addition, cultural and gender norms also enshrined their authority and power within the home and the workplace, as well as in the political, military and imperial spheres. As Simon Gunn and Rachel Bell point out, 'one of the important attributes of middle-class status was the ability to wield power over others, whether immediately, in the form of employees, servants or tradespeople, or more widely … through institutions such as voluntary associations, political parties and parliament'.[64] Such attributes were gendered: not only did middle-class men wield a good deal more power than women, but their continued authority over women should also not be underestimated.[65]

Of course, it is not difficult to think of groups of middle-class men who were excluded from dominant notions of manliness. Homosexual men have attracted the most scholarly attention, but the manliness of swathes of lower middle-class, white-collar workers, from clerks to 'counter-jumpers' was also thought to be at the very least doubtful. The nature of their work, their relative poverty, their supposedly unadventurous nature, over-dependence on home and family, as well as their neglected physiques, were all thought to undermine their claims to manliness.[66] Wartime images of inoffensive little clerks galvanised into action by the outbreak of hostilities, demonstrating their patriotic manliness firstly by volunteering and then by showing an unexpected mettle on the field of battle, returning home as 'new men', proved popular ones.[67] This book, however, focuses on those middle-class men who, either through choice or necessity, did not thus 'prove' their manliness. It explores the experiences of those middle-class men who before the war may or may not have enjoyed to the full the power and privileges that came with prosperous, authoritative middle-class masculinity, but who at the outbreak of war definitely missed out on the ultimate manly identity of 'soldier-hero'.

Home front memories

Whatever their reticence in subsequent years, at the outbreak of war many middle-class men seem to have had little doubt that the impact of the war on the home front was a subject worth writing about: it is these personal writings, together with collections of correspondence, that provide the main sources for this book. Unsurprisingly, the nature of these documents means that their interpretation is not always entirely straightforward. It is important to note, for example, that a significant number of diaries were conceived not as personal, private accounts of experiences and emotions, but as records of what were recognised as important historical events. Horace Joseph, a middle-aged philosophy tutor and bursar of New College, Oxford, began his diary in August 1914 'because hereafter any account of the way in which an ordinary citizen was affected by a war of such a huge extent, the first in which aircraft, submarines and great steel navies have been used, may prove interesting'.[68] Like other diarists, he did not anticipate the eventual scale and duration of the war, but in August or September 1914 few believed that the conflict would be a small one or of short duration: there were no references to it being 'over by Christmas'. Ernest Cooper, a solicitor and town clerk of the seaside town of Southwold in Suffolk, opened his diary by stating that 'this being the greatest war the world has ever known it may be of some interest in years to come, if we survive it, to have a few notes of local events in this little Frontier Coast Town of Southwold lying at this moment within eighty miles from the Front in Belgium and not more than two hundred and fifty from the great War Harbours of Germany'.[69]

Recording the effect of such significant events on the home front was thus considered worthwhile. It was for this reason that Andrew Clark, the vicar of the rural parish of Great Leighs in Essex, began compiling a diary at the outbreak of war. As he explained in his 'Introductory Notes', he had decided to record 'from day to day, such echoes of the Great War as reached the Rectory from outside, ignoring … all information directly or indirectly drawn from newspapers, but giving authentic written scraps of genuine village opinion'. Indeed, 'it had always been a deep regret to me that I had not kept a village record of this sort throughout the Boer war'.[70] Thus, Clark sought to compile a record of local events and opinion as they were affected by the conflict, positioning himself as an impartial scribe and providing insights into the attitudes and opinions of a range of individuals, including farmers, businessmen and men employed in various middle-class professions.[71]

Of course, even Clark was never able to maintain an entirely impartial view of the events he described, and his opinions were frequently made clear: for example, on the topic of 'the senseless futility of the nightly patrols asked of special constables in this out-of-the-way corner' of the country.[72] That said, his diary, like many others kept by middle-class civilians, is perhaps best understood as a 'public', rather than an entirely 'private' document. Personal matters unconnected to the war were excluded: most notably, neither his wife's long illness nor her eventual death in October 1916 were mentioned.[73] The inclusion of apparently superfluous material had to be justified by making reference to the war: in November 1916 Clark explained that he had been providing details of the weather in order 'to record the weather-conditions under which the men billeted in the neighbourhood or under canvas here and at Terling, lived. As the two camps … are now broken up, weather-notes will … be discontinued'.[74]

Men like Clark assumed that their diaries would be read by others, not only members of their family, friends and acquaintances, but also future generations. Towards the end of September 1914 Reginald Gibbs, a thirty-five year-old science teacher at a public school near Aldershot, Hampshire, reflected that 'there is such an immense number of sidelights on, and points of view of the war, that it is very difficult to decide what to include and what to omit'. He acknowledged that:

> these notes and memoirs cannot of course pretend to be a history … My object is merely to record the passage of events, and to present the point of view at the time, as it appears to me, to record my sensations and impressions … If in future years these notes are ever read they will by many be considered the egotistical vapourings of a shallow, one-sided, mediocre man. But even so, they will yet present a picture, a record of sensations as the horrible drama opens out.[75]

Readers, furthermore, were not always passive in their relationship with diaries. In August 1917 Gibbs noted that a Mr Braisher was reading his diary and told him that he would be happy if he were to add comments, as long as he dated and initialled them.[76] Braisher does not seem to have taken advantage of the offer, but he did briefly take over the writing of the diary when Gibbs was called up in November 1917.[77]

More 'personal' matters were of course not entirely excluded from wartime diaries. Cossins, for example, decided to start a diary in August 1914 in order to record 'the effect of … war on the community at large and private individuals'.[78] However, alongside careful accounts of the most significant military and political events, he also wrote a good deal about his family, particularly his wife's poor health, their leisure activities and daily life, as well as about personal matters that had little to do with the war. Thus, in August 1916 he noted that 'I had a couple of tooth stumps out this morning. An injection of novocaine made the extraction quite painless and I felt no unpleasant aftereffects and had a splendid afternoon's tennis'.[79] Other diaries were of a more 'private' nature still. Between February and December 1917, for example, E. W. Hewish kept a record of his time as an officer of the 4th Battalion Duke of Cornwall's Light Infantry, while stationed in Herne Bay. Here he confided his ambivalence about his prolonged stay on the home front, his mood veering between happiness at setting up house with his new wife Wendy, and disappointment at not being able to take a more active part in the war, particularly in the knowledge that his brother was serving on the Western Front. In October 1917, for example, he noted that he had passed up on a chance to go to America to train US troops. He explained that 'I have so far escaped being thrown into the Hell of warfare in France, and I should feel a perfect skunk(?) if I got sent to America and perhaps miss the chance of ever seeing any real fighting. I feel most unhappy at times to be still here'. He hoped that 'my chance may come soon'.[80]

Even so, most of the diaries consulted in the course of the research for this book were conceived primarily as records of significant events, both on the battle and home fronts, rather than as an opportunity to express intimate feelings and impressions. But whatever their aims, individuals did not always find the task an easy one. According to Yearsley, 'my original intent was to put on record for possible posterity the feelings of a private citizen during one of the most stirring periods of modern history'. However, he found in February 1915 that 'so far it has become a mixture of imperfectly recorded fragments, with trivial jokes and notes. I have found it impossible to keep pace with the enormously varying happenings in all parts of Europe'.[81] In some cases, keeping a diary took on the nature of a self-imposed duty. In September 1917 Gibbs admitted to being bored, but stressed that 'I shall not shrink from my self-appointed task'.[82] Four days after the Armistice Frederick Robinson, a businessman living in Cobham, Surrey, added a 'Prefatory note' to his diaries. He stated that with the end of the war, 'it is an intense relief to feel that this daily self-imposed task, I might almost say, this daily penance, is finished. I feel like the man must have felt who took off the hair shirt he wore for his soul's sake'.[83] He had started the diary 'in the form of a few brief notes, for an entirely different purpose, and upon an entirely different subject', the Irish Home Rule crisis, but it had grown into a much bigger enterprise, chronicling the main events of the conflict.[84] This became an increasing burden: by January 1918 he was finding it 'almost more than flesh and blood can stand' to maintain such a 'dreary record' of the war. 'Can I keep it up', he wondered, 'and if I do will there be anyone foolish enough to read it?'[85] He made his last entry in the almost 3,500 pages-long diary the day after the Armistice.

In reality, of course, diaries were a good deal more than lists or 'dreary records' of significant events. Not only were 'personal' details included, but opinions were expressed, often quite forcibly, and neither the government's nor the armed forces' conduct of the war was accepted uncritically: diarists were both frightened and horrified by the ever growing loss of life and treasure that the war entailed. Robinson, for example, expressed his feelings clearly by marking 25 March 1916 as 'the 600th day of Armageddon'.[86] That said, there was little outright questioning of the pros and cons of the conflict, or of the justice of Britain's cause. In December 1916 Lockwood asserted that 'the war has developed into a trade war of the worst description',[87] but such comments were very rare.

The notable exception to the *de facto* acceptance of the war can be found in Gibbs's diaries. In the early months of the conflict he reflected on the nature of warfare, questioning whether this was, as was widely stated, 'a noble and beautiful thing'. He admitted that 'war provides the opportunity for the display of the highest manly virtues', although 'also for the display of all the vilest qualities of man', adding that 'in its concrete aspect, war is unspeakably frightful'.[88] He initially wavered between a desire to believe the government's arguments for entering the conflict, and his abhorrence of warfare.[89] In July 1915 he thus refused to glory 'in deeds of war, and at the same time to be allowed the right to feel glad when the enemy, when attacking, is repulsed'.[90] However, by the end of the year his attitude had hardened: the war, he believed, was being fought 'to sneak as much more land as possible for our cursed double-damned empire'.[91] He did not think of himself as a 'pacifist', who would refuse to fight even in self-defence, but rather described himself as a 'semi-pacifist', somebody 'keenly averse to warfare where it can possibly be avoided' and opposed to 'any policy of aggression at the expense of weaker peoples', but 'prepared to fight in defence of our country'.[92] The present war, he believed, was not being fought in self-defence. In July 1917 he thus noted approvingly 'the remarkably lucid letter from a young officer at the front … complaining … that the war had become one of "aggression and conquest"'.[93]

In working out his ideas about the war, Gibbs – and other diarists like him – were influenced by the thought of a future, often unknown, readership. Letters, on the other hand, were generally written with a specific, well-known, and often beloved, recipient in mind.[94] In one sense, then, wartime letters were the more 'private' documents, filled with many of those very intimate, mundane, everyday matters and news that were often not considered suitable for diaries. Clark, for example, was much more open about his unhappy personal circumstances in his correspondence than in his diaries. Writing to his friend William Redman in April 1916, a year after the latter had left Great Leighs, he confided that he was 'in great troubles'. His wife was 'in the grip of a fatal disease … and has to be dazed with drugs day and night to keep away the pain', while he too had 'for some four months been subject to a wasting illness … as well as a feeling of weariness which it is difficult to fight against'. He stressed that 'I miss you in everything, but especially because we have in Lyons Hall park … a canvas town of almost six hundred Scots gunners, for whom your influence would have been most helpful'.[95]

It would be inaccurate to suggest that middle-class civilians were always less reticent about expressing emotions and feelings in letters than they were diaries. Indeed, the identity and circumstances of the recipient were important in determining the content and tone of a letter. The letters written by Walter Goodwin's parents in November 1915, for example, were filled with joy and relief at finally receiving news of their son after five weeks of silence: Walter, a private in the London Regiment, was in hospital in Egypt with an infected hand, which he had contracted at Gallipoli. The letters thus included news intended to interest and amuse him, such as his father's efforts at digging a trench in the garden, 'preparing to plant a climber on the trellis'. Working with another man, they had come 'across an obstacle and went at it with might and main when we discovered it was a water pipe and when my pick went through it … we had soon a nice little pond … if this had been in Gallipoli I daresay it would have been very welcome'.[96] Presumably Walter would have been able to picture the trellis and the garden, as well as the damage done by the water and his father's embarrassed and horrified reaction.

Letters were often based on such reserves of shared memories, knowledge and experiences, which gave meaning to the news they contained. Thus, in his letters to his son in Canada, Robert Saunders was able to make reference to various people and places, including in August 1915 the names of men who had joined the local Volunteer Training Corps, sure in the knowledge that his son would recognise and remember them.[97] Similarly, a few months later Ingleby wrote to his son Clement, then a Lieutenant in the Royal Naval Volunteer Reserve, that he had just received a telephone call from George Tyrrell 'to ask me for a game of Bridge to-night, so you see we carry on the same old game'.[98] At the same time, there were matters that were thought to be of no interest to a correspondent, and thus best avoided. In January 1916 Ingleby organised a joint shoot in Norfolk with a Sir Edward Green. As he wrote to his son: 'you can imagine the sort of thing: an army of beaters divided into two parts, a dozen guns … general disputes … negativated to some extent by an excellent lunch'. However, he concluded, 'this is very small beer to you, and of no particular interest'.[99]

Often, then, letters were written in order to maintain an existing relationship, and could be used not only to communicate the latest news, but also to guide, nurture, as well as to reprimand and criticise the recipient. Ingleby's letters to his son thus saw him enacting what clearly was his long-established role as adviser and ultimate authority within the family. His determination to give Clement the benefit of his experience could sometimes be taken to extraordinarily tactless lengths. On the eve of the birth of Clement's first son, for example, Holcombe warned him that 'a first baby is always more of a trouble to bring to birth and to rear than subsequent arrivals. I should have had an elder sister, but she was stillborn. Eustace Rolfe had an elder brother … who died an infant'.[100] Ingleby's intention was not, it seems, to frighten his son, but rather to reassert his own superior knowledge and experience. Such reassertions punctuated the men's correspondence throughout the war, shedding light not only on the relationship between father and son, but also with other family members. In March 1916, for example, Holcombe wrote to his son that 'we are not entirely happy with the baby … he won't put on weight'. He added that 'you need not worry over this. The baby is well … he takes his grub all right and sleeps well and is satisfactory in every way except that he persists in remaining thin. I daresay Muriel [Clement's wife] has told you all this'. However, women could not be trusted to impart news in a judicious and balanced way: 'as the women, bless them, sometimes suffer from over-anxiety and have larger imaginations than our more cold-blooded sex, I thought I would give you a plain statement of fact'.[101]

Civvies: middle-class men on the English home front

In reality, despite Ingleby's assertion to the contrary, few letters or diaries simply provided 'plain statement[s] of fact'.[102] His own certainly did not. Diarists and letter-writers reflected and commented on the main events of the war, shedding light on experiences and attitudes on the home front as the conflict progressed, while at the same time providing clues about the nature of relationships in wartime, whether between family members, friends or acquaintances. The first three chapters of this book, then, follow in middle-class men's own steps, as they used their writings to try to understand and explain how the war was affecting both their own lives and those of the people around them. The emphasis here was on evidence and expectation of change, as men looked about themselves and assessed the extent and nature of the impact of war on the home front. Chapter 1 focuses on the first twelve months or so of war, a period when many middle-class men assumed that the war could hardly fail to affect them, and yet were often made to feel their distance from any real action and their relegation to the role of passive spectators. This, Chapter 2 argues, changed in mid-1915, as the war began to affect middle-class lives in very clear, sometimes unexpected and often unpleasant ways. Chapter 3 then moves from experiences to the realm of ideas and attitudes, as it delves deeper into middle-class men's understandings of civilians' appropriate behaviour in wartime. It suggests that the notion of a national (and to a lesser extent, imperial) community united against a common enemy played a central part in their thinking, although fear and hatred of an external enemy – strongly identified with Germany – proved less important than anger against those sections of the national community who were felt not to be pulling their weight or shouldering their fair share of the burden of war.

In her study of *Experience, Memory and the First World War in Britain*, Janet Watson points out that although historians frequently confuse the two, the ways in which the war was experienced between 1914 and 1918 were different to how it was remembered afterwards: consequently, she suggests, these should be studied separately.[103] In fact, the present book is concerned primarily with wartime experiences, while most of the sources on which it is based were written as the war unfolded, without the benefit of hindsight. Gibbs made the point as he addressed the future reader: 'You who read know quite well what happened tomorrow, what happened next week. The writer does not'.[104] Of course, despite the lack of published civilian autobiographies, there do exist manuscript memoirs[105] and oral history recordings[106] focusing on civilian experiences, which are influenced both by hindsight and by the ways in which the war has been memorialised in the decades since the Armistice. For this reason, they have to be approached with care. But perhaps most importantly, the sources used in the writing of this book also make clear that experience and memory are not always as easy to disentangle as one might expect.

Diaries, for example, were not always quite as steeped in current events as they might appear at first glance. Like other civilian men, Cooper tidied up and copied out his diary after the war, probably towards the end of 1919, including both extracts from the original diary and comments written with the benefit of hindsight. In February 1917, for example, he noted that 'we are just starting on the Voluntary Rationing and I think it must make a lot of difference if carried out properly'. However, he added subsequently: 'writing later it seems that there is a difficulty in carrying out voluntary rationing, the servants resent it and generally the poorer people do not realise any necessity for it so long as they can buy all they want'.[107] This interplay between experience and memory is especially important in relation to the issue of war service, which is explored in Chapters 4 and 5. Unsurprisingly, this aroused strong feelings during the conflict and continued to do so in the years following its conclusion, gaining new layers of meaning as most memories and memorials of the war focused on the figure of the brave, yet tragic, front-line soldier. Chapter 4 thus explores middle-class men's reasons for not conforming to dominant norms of manly conduct by enlisting, considers individuals' experiences of 'non-enlistment' and assesses the extent to which the decision to remain a civilian in wartime was viewed as acceptable and justifiable. Chapter 5 then shifts the focus onto middle-class men's involvement in volunteer activities on the home front, including service in organised, 'public' bodies such as Volunteer Training Corps and special constables, and 'private' activities like allotment keeping and vegetable growing: did they provide adequate substitutes for military service, enabling the formulation of a specifically civilian manly identity?

Both the 'problems' of military service and of patriotic activities on the home front loomed large in civilian wartime writings, and continued to do so in post-war accounts and oral history interviews. Indeed, it is the preoccupations and concerns expressed by middle-class men in their diaries, letters and other documents, that dictate the topics and issues covered by this book. Inevitably, this means that there are some omissions, including some that are perhaps rather surprising. The most notable, no doubt, is religion. This is not to suggest that religious beliefs and practices were not a part of many middle-class men's lives: the fact that church (or chapel) attendance or other religious activities were rarely written about may simply mean that they were so deeply ingrained in daily lives that they did not merit special mention. Indeed, occasions of special significance brought to the fore the continued importance of faith and of religious ceremony. In July 1918, for example, Saunders, whose own three sons were serving in the armed forces, attended 'an impressive Memorial Service'. The church 'was simply packed, and the whole atmosphere … was full of feeling. There were special Hymns, Psalms, Lessons, then Chopin's Funeral March, and The Last Post sounded by trumpeters from the camp, followed the reading of the names of those who had fallen'.[108]

Despite such occasions, however, religious sentiments and language featured little in middle-class men's writings.[109] The aim of Reverend Hugh Chapman's booklet *Home Truths about the War*, published in 1917, was 'to insist on the fact that at this moment the combination of patriotism and piety is the one lesson of the war'.[110] In reality, most middle-class civilian men did not respond to the war by developing a new 'piety', and the relationship between faith and the conflict does not seem to have been a matter of general discussion. In August 1916, in his role as Town Clerk to the Southwold town council, Cooper 'attended in State an Intercession Service' to mark the second anniversary of war, 'although it seems to me God has very little to say to this War'.[111] Most middle-class men would probably have bridled at such bluntness. Indeed, rather than a denial of its relevance, or even a crisis of faith, it seems likely that for most civilians the war simply did not bring about a major shake-up of existing religious (or, as Chapter 3 suggests, political) beliefs: it was in other areas of life that the conflict entailed the greatest changes and challenges. The second part of this book thus concentrates on three of these areas: work, consumption and relationships.

Chapter 6 focuses on middle-class men's working lives, paying particular attention to those aspects of work that were most affected by the war, and where they experienced the greatest difficulties – most notably, those caused by shortages of labour. The chapter then explores the impact of widely held notions of work appropriate to a society at war, and considers civilian men's responses to the new ambivalence towards profit-making, as well as to the doubts cast on the 'value' of much middle-class, white-collar work in wartime. Chapter 7 moves on to consider consumption and leisure, paying attention not only to continuities, but also to changes in middle-class practices, both those self-imposed as a patriotic duty, and those dictated by wartime shortages and high prices. The chapter then assesses the ways in which middle-class men negotiated their roles as wartime consumers and suggests that consumption provided one of the main arenas where they sought to define themselves as responsible, patriotic citizens, in contrast to 'others' condemned as selfish, heedless and unpatriotic. Finally, Chapter 8 concludes the book by exploring the impact of war on middle-class relationships. It considers the nature of wartime links between civilians and servicemen, as well as the role of the paterfamilias within the middle-class family, before turning to focus on the relationship between civilian fathers and combatant sons, seeking to shed light on the extent to which paternal authority and ties were challenged and perhaps even overset by the experience of war.

In the workplace, the marketplace and the home, middle-class civilian men felt that their lives and place in society were being changed fundamentally by the war. They thus sought to develop strategies to cope with wartime challenges that could range from shortages of labour, to the difficulties of maintaining their own or their families' standard of living, to the problems of keeping meaningful links with servicemen sons. It is the aim of this book to try and find out how successful they were, and the extent to which by November 1918 they had been able to construct viable roles and identities for themselves as 'manly' civilians.

Notes

1 F. W. M. Drew, Recollections, not dated, DF148, Liddle Collection (1914–18), Special Collections, Brotherton Library, Leeds University (hereafter Liddle Collection), Leeds.

2 R. Graves and A. Hodge, *The Long Weekend: A Social History of Great Britain* (Abacus, London, 1995, first published 1940), p. 16. See also A. Carden-Coyne, *Reconstructing the Body: Classicism, Modernism and the First World War* (Oxford University Press, Oxford, 2009), p. 2; H. McCartney, *Citizen Soldiers: The Liverpool Territorials in the First World War* (Cambridge University Press, Cambridge, 2005), especially pp. 89–103.

3 The creation of 'a vision of the war centred on the trench and therefore exclusive of all other experiences' is explored in J. S. K. Watson, *Fighting Different Wars: Experience, Memory and the First World War in Britain* (Cambridge University Press, Cambridge, 2004), p. 239. See also Chapter 6. Published autobiographies, furthermore, 'formed only a fraction of the total number of written records' of men's military experiences. J. Meyer, *Men of War: Masculinity and the First World War in Britain* (Palgrave Macmillan, Basingstoke, 2009), p. 128. For women's literary responses to war and combat see C. M. Tylee, *The Great War and Women's Consciousness: Images of Militarism and Womanhood in Women's Writings, 1914–64* (Macmillan, Basingstoke, 1990).

4 Macleod Yearsley was a middle-aged London ear surgeon. He married and had his first child during the war. M. Yearsley ('Eyewitness'), 'The Home Front, 1914–18', p. 1, DS/MISC/17, Department of Documents, Imperial War Museum (hereafter IWM Documents), London.

5 Even civilian autobiographies that cover a longer time-span, encompassing the 1914–18 period, tend to deal with the war only in passing, as I discovered when working on a book on the sale and consumption of menswear in Britain between 1880 and 1939, which made considerable use of published autobiographies. L. Ugolini, *Men and Menswear: Sartorial Consumption in Britain, 1880–1939* (Ashgate, Aldershot, 2007). There are some exceptions. See, for example, R. Roberts, *The Classic Slum: Salford Life in the First Quarter of the Century* (Penguin, Harmondsworth, 1974, first published 1971); P. McGeown, *Heat the Furnace Seven Times More* (Hutchinson, London, 1967); J. Gray, *Gin and Bitters* (Jarrold Publishers, London, not dated, *c.* 1938). All these focus on working-class communities.

6 S. Goebel, *The Great War and Medieval Memory: War, Remembrance and Medievalism in Britain and Germany, 1914–1940* (Cambridge University Press, Cambridge, 2007), pp. 188–9, 194. The irony of civilians' involvement in setting up war memorials was not lost on contemporaries. Conflict over such involvement is at the heart, for example, of George Blake's 1931 novel *Returned Empty* (Faber and Faber, London, 1931).

7 Carden-Coyne, *Reconstructing the Body*, especially Chapter 3.

8 Only women and children, for example, appear to bid farewell to husbands and fathers on their way to the front in 'The Response', Goscombe John's monument in Newcastle-upon-Tyne. G. Robb, *British Culture and the First World War* (Palgrave, Basingstoke, 2002), p. 215. For the imagery of war

memorials, see also A. King, *Memorials of the Great War in Britain: The Symbolism and Politics of Remembrance* (Berg, Oxford, 1998), especially pp. 128–41.

9 These were, after all, intended as memorials to the dead. In the course of the war an estimated 1,266 British civilians were killed by air and sea bombardments, while there were over 15,000 deaths among passengers and crews of merchant and fishing vessels. J. M. Winter, *The Great War and the British People* (Palgrave Macmillan, Basingstoke, 2003, first published 1985), p. 71. On the other hand, the number of British servicemen killed has been estimated at between approximately 723,000 and 772,000. Winter, *The Great War and the British People*, pp. 70–1. See also P. Dewey, *War and Progress in Britain 1914–1918* (Longman, Harlow, 1997), p. 23.

10 See, for example, recent works by A. G. V. Simmonds, *Britain and World War One* (Routledge, Abingdon, 2011); A. Gregory, *The Last Great War: British Society and the First World War* (Cambridge University Press, Cambridge, 2008) and I. F. W. Beckett, *Home Front 1914–1918: How Britain Survived the Great War* (The National Archives, London, 2006). Beyond Britain, see for example, J. Winter and J.-L. Robert (eds), *Capital Cities at War: Paris, London, Berlin 1914–1919 Volume 2: A Cultural History* (Cambridge University Press, Cambridge, 2007). B. Davis, *Home Fires Burning: Food, Politics and Everyday Life in World War One Berlin* (University of North Carolina Press, Chapel Hill, NC, 2000); H. McPhail, *The Long Silence: Civilian Life under the German Occupation of Northern France, 1914–1918* (I. B. Tauris, London, 1999); J. Winter and J.-L. Robert (eds), *Capital Cities at War: Paris, London, Berlin 1914–1919* (Cambridge University Press, Cambridge, 1997). A very useful overview of the literature on home fronts is J. Winter and A. Prost, *The Great War in History: Debates and Controversies, 1914 to the Present* (Cambridge University Press, Cambridge, 2005), Chapter 7.

11 T. Livingstone, *Tommy's War: The Diaries of a Wartime Nobody* (HarperPress, London, 2008), front cover. See also the Introduction by Shaun Sewell and the Foreword by Andrew Marr, especially p. xii.

12 And overstates the importance of the diaries, unique and fascinating as they are.

13 Gregory, *The Last Great War*; Beckett, *Home Front*; Winter, *The Great War and the British People*; Winter and Robert (eds), *Capital Cities at War*; G. J. DeGroot, *Blighty: British Society in the Era of the Great War* (Longman, Harlow, 1998, first published 1996); S. Constantine, M. W. Kirby and M. M. Rose (eds), *The First World War in British History* (Edward Arnold, London, 1995); J. Turner, *British Politics and the Great War: Coalition and Conflict, 1915–1918* (Yale University Press, New Haven, CT, 1992); J. M. Bourne, *Britain and the Great War 1914–1918* (Edward Arnold, London, 1989); B. Waites, *A Class Society at War: England 1914–1918* (Berg, Leamington Spa, 1987); T. Wilson, *The Myriad Faces of War: Britain and the Great War, 1914–*

1918 (Polity Press, Cambridge, 1986); J. Williams, *The Home Fronts: Britain, France and Germany, 1914–1918* (Constable, London, 1972); A. Marwick, *The Deluge: British Society and the First World War* (Palgrave Macmillan, Basingstoke, second edition, 2006, first published 1965).

14 See, for example, K. Grieves (ed.), *Sussex in the First World War*, Sussex Record Society vol. 84 (Sussex Record Society, Lewes, 2004); F. Meeres, *Norfolk in the First World War* (Phillimore, Chichester, 2004); R. Van Emden and S. Humphries, *All Quiet on the Home Front: An Oral History of Life in Britain during the First World War* (Headline, London, 2003). Photographic archives are at the basis of P. H. Liddle, *Voices of War: Front Line and Home Front* (Leo Cooper, London, 1988), while Adrian Gregory makes effective use of a range of civic histories in *The Last Great War*. See, for example, the account of wartime Preston in H. Cartmell, *For Remembrance: An Account of some Fateful Years* (George Toulmin & sons, Preston, 1919).

15 Watson, *Fighting Different Wars*, especially Chapters 2 and 3; S. R. Grayzel, *Women's Identities at War: Gender, Motherhood, and Politics in Britain and France during the First World War* (University of North Carolina Press, Chapel Hill, NC, 1999); D. Thom, *Nice Girls and Rude Girls: Women Workers in World War I* (I. B. Tauris, London, 1998); S. Pedersen, *Family, Dependence, and the Origins of the Welfare State: Britain and France, 1914–1945* (Cambridge University Press, Cambridge, 1993); A. Woollacott, *On Her Their Lives Depend: Munitions Workers in the Great War* (University of California Press, Berkeley, CA, 1994); G. Braybon, *Women Workers in the First World War* (Routledge, London, 1989); D. Beddoe, *Back to Home and Duty* (Pandora, London, 1989).

16 D. Silbey, *The British Working Class and Enthusiasm for War, 1914–1916* (Frank Cass, London, 2005); Winter, *The Great War and the British People*; C. Wrigley (ed.), *Challenges of Labour: Central and Western Europe 1917–1920* (Routledge, London, 1993); J. N. Horne, *Labour at War: France and Britain 1914–1918* (Clarendon Press, Oxford, 1991); A. Reid, 'The impact of the war on British workers', in R. Wall and J. Winter (eds), *The Upheaval of War: Family, Work and Welfare in Europe, 1914–1918* (Cambridge University Press, Cambridge, 1988), pp. 221–33; Waites, *A Class Society at War*; J. Bush, *Behind the Lines: East End Labour 1914–1919* (Merlin Press, London, 1984). It is worth noting that the experiences of 'labour' have attracted more attention than those of working-class men.

17 The terms are taken from the title of the influential feminist history by S. Rowbotham, *Hidden from History: 300 Years of Women's Oppression and the Fight Against it* (Pluto, London, 1973).

18 It has been estimated that the Edwardian middle classes represented between 10 and 18 per cent of the British population, while the working class comprised roughly 80 per cent. Marwick, *The Deluge*, p. 63.

19 Marwick, *The Deluge*, p. 63. Judges and some barristers could earn up to £5,000 a year, but most middle-class men could expect annual incomes of up to £500. See A. A. Jackson, *The Middle Classes 1900–1950* (David St John Thomas Publisher, Nairn, 1991), p. 24.

20 From estimates by Derek Oddy, in P. E. Dewey, 'Nutrition and living standards in wartime Britain', in Wall and Winter (eds), *The Upheaval of War*, pp. 199–200.

21 S. L. Hynes, *The Soldiers' Tale: Bearing Witness to Modern War* (Pimlico, London, 1998), p. 32.

22 E. P. Thompson, *The Making of the English Working Class* (Penguin Books, London, 1988, first published 1963), p. 12.

23 Don Todman notes the 'persistent undercurrent of emotional investment' that throughout the twentieth century 'has dragged Britons back to the war, to revisit, reconsider and refight its battles, whether they experienced them at first hand or not'. D. Todman, *The Great War: Myth and Memory* (Hambledon, London, 2005), p. 221.

24 See, for example, M. Roper, *The Secret Battle: Emotional Survival in the Great War* (Manchester University Press, Manchester, 2009); Meyer, *Men of War*; S. Das, *Touch and Intimacy in First World War Literature* (Cambridge University Press, Cambridge, 2005); S. Dudnik, K. Hagemann and J. Tosh (eds), *Masculinities in Politics and War: Gendering Modern History* (Manchester University Press, Manchester, 2004); N. F. Gullace, *'The Blood of our Sons': Men, Women and the Renegotiation of British Citizenship during the First World War* (Palgrave Macmillan, Basingstoke, 2002), especially Chapters 2 and 5; G. L. Mosse, *The Image of Man: The Creation of Modern Masculinity* (Oxford University Press, Oxford, 1998), especially Chapter 6; S. M. Cullen, 'Gender and the Great War: British Combatants, Masculinity and Perceptions of Women, 1918–1939' (Unpublished DPhil, University of Oxford, 1998). Earlier works remain important, especially J. Bourke, *Dismembering the Male: Men's Bodies, Britain and the Great War* (Reaktion Books, London, 1996); G. Dawson, *Soldier Heroes: British Adventure, Empire and the Imagining of Masculinities* (Routledge, London, 1994); S. M. Gilbert, 'Soldier's heart: literary men, literary women, and the Great War', in M. Randolph Higgonet, J. Jenson, S. Michel and M. Collins Weitz (eds), *Behind the Lines: Gender and the Two World Wars* (Yale University Press, New Haven, CT, 1987), pp. 197–226; E. Leed, *No Man's Land: Combat and Identity in World War One* (Cambridge University Press, Cambridge, 1979).

25 Gregory, *The Last Great War*, p. 152; T. and V. Holt, *'My Boy Jack?' The Search for Kipling's Only Son* (Leo Cooper, Barnsley, 1998); A. Gregory, *The Silence of Memory: Armistice Day 1919–1946* (Berg, Oxford, 1994), pp. 22–3; Wilson, *The Myriad Faces of War*, pp. 753–5. D. Cannadine, 'War and death, grief and mourning in modern Britain', in J. Whaley (ed.), *Mirrors*

of Mortality: Studies in the Social History of Death (Europa Publications, London, 1981), pp. 187–242. Insights into well-connected, elite political opinion can be found, for example, in S. Gwynn (ed.), *The Anvil of War: Letters between F. S. Oliver and his Brother 1914–1918* (Macmillan and Co., London, 1936) and H. Lucy, *The Diary of a Journalist*, vol. 1 (J. Murray, London, 1920).

26 It has been calculated that 46.2 per cent of men aged between fifteen and forty-nine in England and Wales (there do not seem to be separate figures for the two countries) served in the armed forces during the war. This represented 24 per cent of *all* males in England and 21.5 per cent in Wales. Of the men who enlisted in England, roughly half (a little over two million) volunteered and half (just under two million) were conscripted. I. F. W. Beckett, 'The nation in arms, 1914–18', in I. F. W. Beckett and K. Simpson (eds), *A Nation in Arms: A Social History of the British Army in the First World War* (Manchester University Press, Manchester, 1985), p. 11; Winter, *The Great War and the British People*, p. 28. Marwick suggests that 'one in three of the adult male population' experienced 'the horrors of war', although he does not explain who is included in the definition of 'adult', and whether the figure refers to Britain or the United Kingdom as a whole. Marwick, *The Deluge*, p. 120.

27 The concept of 'hegemonic masculinity' as a system of masculine power has been developed by the sociologist Raewyn Connell. See, for example, R. Connell, *Masculinities* (Polity, Cambridge, second edition, 2005, first published 1995) and *Gender and Power: Society, the Person and Sexual Politics* (Polity Press, Cambridge, 1987). For the challenges of applying this concept to historical studies of masculinity, see J. Tosh, 'Hegemonic masculinity and the history of gender', in Dudnik, Hagemann and Tosh (eds), *Masculinities in Politics and War*, pp. 41–58.

28 T. G. Ashplant, G. Dawson and M. Roper, 'The politics of war memory and commemoration: contexts, structures and dynamics', in T. G. Ashplant, G. Dawson and M. Roper (eds), *The Politics of War Memory and Commemoration* (Routledge, London, 2000), p. 21.

29 I. F. W. Beckett, *The Great War 1914–1918* (Pearson Education, Harlow, 2001), p. 210. The total population of the United Kingdom was approximately forty-five million. Robb, *British Culture*, p. 12.

30 Beckett, 'The nation in arms', p. 11. See also note 26 above. The figures for France (79 per cent) and for Germany (81 per cent) were significantly higher. A. Gregory, 'Lost generations: the impact of military casualties on Paris, London, and Berlin', in Winter and Robert (eds), *Capital Cities at War*, p. 59.

31 R. D. Blumenfeld, *All in a Lifetime* (Ernest Benn, London, 1931), p. 58.

32 A. Clark to F. Madan, A. Clark War Diary, 'Echoes of the 1914 War in an Essex Village' (hereafter Clark Diary), 25 November 1918, Ms Eng. Hist.

e.171, Special Collections, Bodleian Library, University of Oxford (hereafter Bodleian Special Collections), Oxford.

33 C. Sheridan Jones, *London in War-Time* (Grafton, London, 1917), p. 70. For 'the great feminine takeover', see also Williams, *The Home Fronts*, pp. 60, 181.

34 H. C. Cossins Diary, 1914–18 (hereafter Cossins Diary), 11 March 1916, PP/MCR/371, IWM Documents. It has been calculated that 'the war produced a leap in women's employment from twenty-six per cent of the workforce in 1914 to thirty-six per cent by 1918'. Robb, *British Culture*, p. 40. This is, of course, a striking change. However, it also suggests that by the end of the war 64 per cent of the workforce was still male.

35 C. Acton, *Grief in Wartime: Private Pain, Public Discourse* (Palgrave Macmillan, Basingstoke, 2007), p. 105. See also P. Jalland, *Australian Ways of Death: A Social and Cultural History 1840–1918* (Oxford University Press, Melbourne, 2002), p. 7.

36 Gregory, *The Last Great War*, p. 255. See also Gregory, *The Silence of Memory*, pp. 10, 41.

37 Quoted in P. Jalland, *Death in the Victorian Family* (Oxford University Press, Oxford, 1996), p. 379.

38 Roper, *The Secret Battle*, pp. 221–32. Also Grayzel, *Women's Identities at War*, especially pp. 228–9.

39 Gregory, *The Last Great War*, p. 25.

40 *Ibid.*, p. 289; J. A. Mangan, '"Muscular, militaristic and manly": the British middle-class hero as moral messenger', *The International Journal of the History of Sport*, vol. 13, no. 1 (1996), pp. 28–47. See also L. S. Bibbings, *Telling Tales about Men: Conceptions of Conscientious Objectors to Military Service during the First World War* (Manchester University Press, Manchester, 2009), p. 93; DeGroot, *Blighty*, pp. 44–6.

41 Gregory, *The Last Great War*, pp. 317, 244. A view that is refuted, for example, by Silbey, *The British Working Class*, especially pp. 42–5.

42 Gregory, *The Last Great War*, p. 289; Winter, *The Great War and the British People*, p. 36. Ian Beckett cautions that these surveys were 'not entirely reliable'. Beckett, *The Great War*, p. 213. See also Beckett, 'The nation in arms', p. 9. Owing to the concentration of exemption among working-class trades, the middle classes were seemingly also over-represented in the conscripted army. Gregory, *The Last Great War*, p. 244; Winter, *The Great War and the British People*, pp. 37, 42.

43 Gregory, *The Last Great War*, pp. 130–1. See also Winter, *The Great War and the British People*, Chapter 3, especially pp. 83–99. Of course, it is worth keeping in mind that almost 94 per cent of the dead were in 'other ranks', while 96 per cent of 'men who died in the infantry … did not have commissions'. Bourne, *Britain and the Great War*, p. 205 and Winter, *The Great War and the British People*, p. 84.

44 Approximately 22 per cent of boys and men aged between fifteen and forty-nine in England and Wales enlisted after the introduction of conscription in January 1916. Beckett, 'The nation in arms', p. 11. Of course, as Chapter 2 will point out, there were also plenty of men in uniform on the home front.

45 Conscientious objectors are considered, for example, in Bibbings, *Telling Tales about Men*. Approximately 16,500 men applied for exemption from combat duties on the grounds of conscience. Beckett, *The Great War*, p. 214.

46 S. Garton, 'Return home: war, masculinity and repatriation', in J. Damousi and M. Lake (eds), *Gender and War: Australians at War in the Twentieth Century* (Cambridge University Press, Cambridge, 1995), p. 191. See also T. Tate (ed.), *Women, Men and the Great War: An Anthology of Stories* (Manchester University Press, Manchester, 1995), pp. 5–6. Gullace, '*The Blood of our Sons*', p. 105.

47 'However', Bibbings adds, 'the conscientious objector was a particularly marginalised figure … as he became the antithesis of the iconic figure of the soldier'. Bibbings, *Telling Tales about Men*, pp. 95, 96.

48 DeGroot, *Blighty*, p. 44. Also p. 31.

49 A. Kidd and D. Nicholls, 'Introduction: the making of the British middle class?', in A. Kidd and D. Nicholls (eds), *The Making of the British Middle Class? Studies of Regional and Cultural Diversity since the Eighteenth Century* (Sutton Publishing, Stroud, 1998), p. xxvii. See also S. Gunn and R. Bell, *Middle Classes: Their Rise and Sprawl* (Phoenix, London, 2003, first published 2002), pp. 4–8.

50 It is worth noting that while well-to-do Ingleby complained of money troubles during the war, Lockwood did not.

51 The 1911 census included under the heading of 'non-manual' occupations the professions, business proprietors, managers and clerical workers. A. J. McIvor, *A History of Work in Britain, 1880–1950* (Palgrave Macmillan, Basingstoke, 2008, first published 2001), pp. 33, 34, 40. Earlier censuses do not provide comparable data.

52 See, for example, Holcombe Ingleby to Clement, 11 June 1915, The First World War Letters of Holcombe Ingleby MP (hereafter Ingleby Letters), P.343, IWM Documents and F. T. Lockwood, 'Notes Written by F. T. Lockwood', 19 February 1916, 96/52/1, IWM Documents. After the war Lockwood made his career as a commercial artist for Cadbury at Bournville, Birmingham.

53 Kidd and Nicholls, 'Introduction', p. xxvii.

54 While not necessarily aspiring to upper-class status.

55 Middle-class men's incomes, furthermore, were a good deal higher than women's. In 1913–14, for example, the wages of women in the 'lower' professions were on average 57 per cent of men's, while those of women clerks

were only 42 per cent. M. Daunton, *Wealth and Welfare: An Economic and Social History of Britain 1851–1951* (Oxford University Press, Oxford, 2007), p. 387.

56 J. Benson, *Affluence and Authority: A Social History of Twentieth-Century Britain* (Hodder Arnold, London, 2005), p. 45. Not until much later in the twentieth century did financial instutions develop similar investment opportunities aimed at small working-class savers. Benson, *Affluence and Authority*, pp. 45–6.

57 *Ibid.*, p. 81.

58 Winter, *The Great War and the British People*, p. 9.

59 Benson, *Affluence and Authority*, p. 77.

60 They were also four inches shorter than upper-class boys. H. Perkin, *The Rise of Professional Society: England since 1880* (Routledge, London, revised edition, 2002, first published 1989), p. 35.

61 See, for example, Gunn and Bell, *Middle Classes*, especially pp. 8–20; D. Wahrman, *Imagining the Middle Class: The Political Representation of Class in Britain, c. 1780–1840* (Cambridge University Press, Cambridge, 1995); R. J. Morris, *Class, Sect and Party: The Making of the British Middle Class, Leeds, 1820–1850* (Manchester University Press, Manchester, 1990); T. Koditschek, *Class Formation and Urban Industrial Society: Bradford, 1750–1850* (Cambridge University Press, Cambridge, 1990); L. Davidoff and C. Hall, *Family Fortunes: Men and Women of the English Middle Class, 1780–1850* (Hutchinson, London, 1987).

62 L. James, *The Middle Class: A History* (Little, Brown, London, 2006), pp. 229–407.

63 The link between normative modern masculinity and the 'moral universe of the middle classes' is emphasised, for example, in Mosse, *The Image of Man*, especially p. 79. In reality, middle-class men's behaviour was not always as 'serious' or as conventionally respectable as it is often portrayed. M. J. Huggins, 'More sinful pleasures? Leisure, respectability and the male middle classes in Victorian England', *Journal of Social History*, vol. 33, no. 3 (2000), pp. 585–600.

64 Gunn and Bell, *Middle Classes*, p. 7.

65 J. Tosh, *A Man's Place: Masculinity and the Middle-Class Home in Victorian England* (Yale University Press, New Haven, CT, 1999).

66 Ugolini, *Men and Menswear*, Chapter 5; A. J. Hammerton, 'The English weakness? Gender, satire and "moral manliness" in the lower middle class, 1870–1920', in A. Kidd and D. Nicholls (eds), *Gender, Civic Culture and Consumerism: Middle-Class Identity in Britain, 1800–1940* (Manchester University Press, Manchester, 1999), pp. 164–82; C. Hosgood, 'Mrs Pooter's purchase: lower middle-class consumerism and the sales, 1870–1914', in Kidd and Nicholls (eds), *Gender, Civic Culture and Consumerism*, pp. 146–63; C. P. Hosgood, '"Mercantile monasteries": shops, shop assistants and shop life in

late-Victorian and Edwardian Britain', *Journal of British Studies*, vol. 38, no. 3 (1999), pp. 322–52.

67 C. F. G. Masterman, *England after War: A Study* (Hodder and Stoughton, London, 1923), p. 72. See also J. Wild, '"A merciful, heaven-sent release"? The clerk and the First World War in British literary culture', *Cultural and Social History*, vol. 4, no. 1 (2007), pp. 73–94.

68 Wartime Diaries of H. W. B. Joseph 1914–18 (hereafter Joseph Diaries), 4 August 1914, Ms. Top. Oxon. e.288, Bodleian Special Collections. For Joseph, see also the pamphlet *H. W. B. Joseph 1867–1943: An Address Delivered in Chapel by the Sub-warden of New College (A. H. Smith) 23 November 1943* (University Press, Oxford, not dated).

69 The Diary of Ernest R. Cooper, 'Nineteen Hundred and War Time', 28 July 1914 – 3 December 1918 (hereafter Cooper Diary), not dated, P.121, IWM Documents. This entry is not dated, but is marked '1914' and seems to have been written in the early months of the war. Cooper was married with one small child and although his age was not stated, he was clearly over military age.

70 Clark Diary, 'Introductory Notes. Occasion of this Diary', Ms Eng. Hist. e.88, Bodleian Special Collections. A selection of diary entries have been published as J. Munson (ed.), *Echoes of the Great War: The Diary of the Reverend Andrew Clark 1914–1919* (Oxford University Press, Oxford, 1985). Clark was married with two grown-up daughters, and in 1914 was in his late fifties. A keen historian, Clark also collected ephemera relating to the war, including advertisements and official circulars, and made a study of changes in 'English words in war time', which he deposited, together with his wartime diaries, in the Bodleian Library. See, for example, A. Clark, 'Scrapbooks of leaflets, newspaper cuttings etc., illustrating aspects of the Great War', Bodleian Library, University of Oxford, Oxford.

71 Clark's interlocutors were for the most part, but by no means exclusively, other men. His daughters, for example, were also important sources of information, particularly his youngest daughter Mildred, a medical student at St Andrews University. His eldest, Mary Alice, lived at home. See, for example, Clark Diary, 3 July 1915, Ms Eng. Hist. e.106, Bodleian Special Collections.

72 *Ibid.*, 21 January 1915, Ms Eng. Hist. e.96.

73 Munson (ed.), *Echoes of the Great War*, pp. 164, 167.

74 Clark Diary, 3 November 1916, Ms Eng. Hist. e.137, Bodleian Special Collections. In fact he continued to include detailed information about the weather throughout the war years.

75 Diary of R. W. M. Gibbs, 1914–20 (hereafter Gibbs Diary), 24 September 1914, Ms Eng. misc. c.159, Bodleian Special Collections. The school, Holmdale, was a preparatory school for young men intending to enter Sandhurst. Gibbs was married and by the end of the war was the father of six children.

76 *Ibid.*, 28 August 1917, Ms Eng. misc. c.192.

77 *Ibid.*, 21 November 1917; 22 November 1917, Ms Eng. misc. c.195; 3 December 1917, Ms Eng. misc. c.196. Gibbs continued to keep a diary until he was demobilised in April 1920.

78 Cossins Diary, introduction, 1919, PP/MCR/371, IWM Documents. Cossins was born in Sicily on 19 January 1878. His father had been the manager of 'Ingham, Whitaker's wine establishment' in Marsala 'and subsequently British Vice-Consul'. In 1889 the family returned to Britain and Cossins was educated at Marlborough and subsequently Oxford. After a short spell as a schoolmaster, which he had disliked, he trained for secretarial work and in 1906 became Secretary to the Alberta Land Company. He married Marjorie Badcock in 1908 and their son John was born in 1909. At the outbreak of war the family lived in St Albans, from where Cossins commuted daily to work in London. He was called up in March 1917, and continued to keep a diary until 1919.

79 *Ibid.*, 12 August 1916. Individuals who continued a pre-war practice of keeping a diary were perhaps the most likely to record 'personal' matters. See, for example, Frank Lockwood's diary, which begins in January 1914. Lockwood, 'Notes', 96/52/1, IWM Documents.

80 E. W. Hewish, 1917 Dairy and Accounts (hereafter Hewish Diary), 29 October 1917, 02/43/1, IWM Documents.

81 Yearsley, 'The Home Front', p. 57, DS/MISC/17, IWM Documents.

82 Gibbs Diary, 16 September 1917, Ms Eng. misc. c.193, Bodleian Special Collections.

83 F. A. Robinson, 'Diary of the Great War', 'Prefatory note', 15 November 1918, vol. 1, P.401, IWM Documents. Robinson was married with two grown-up children still living at home.

84 *Ibid.*

85 *Ibid.*, 1 January 1918, vol. 4, P.402.

86 *Ibid.*, 25 March 1916, vol. 2, P.401. Caroline Playne believed that not everyone was horrified by the war: there were 'not a few … who … not completely satisfied with all the cruelties there were … gloated in imagination over the next big offensive'. C. E. Playne, *Britain Holds on 1917, 1918* (George Allen & Unwin, London, 1933).

87 Lockwood, 'Notes', 11 December 1916, 96/52/1, IWM Documents.

88 Gibbs Diary, 27 September 1914, Ms Eng. misc. c.159, Bodleian Special Collections.

89 *Ibid.*, 1 October 1914, Ms Eng. misc. c.160; 7 November 1914, Ms Eng. misc. c.161.

90 *Ibid.*, 7 July 1915, Ms Eng. misc. c.169.

91 *Ibid.*, 23 November 1915, Ms Eng. misc. c.172.

92 *Ibid.*, 11 March 1916, Ms Eng. misc. c.175.

93 *Ibid.*, 31 July 1917, Ms Eng. misc. c.191. The 'young officer' was the poet Siegfried Sassoon. M. Egremont, *Siegfried Sassoon: A Biography* (Picador,

London, 2005), pp. 143–4.

94 This was of course not always the case. See, for example, the letters addressed to Edwin Yates in response to his call for potential volunteers to join a special 'bantam' battalion of men under regulation height. E. Yates, Correspondence, 1914, DF146, Liddle Collection. See also the letters of condolence examined in Meyer, *Men of War*, Chapter 3, whose recipients were often strangers.

95 Munson (ed.), *Echoes of the Great War*, p. 147.

96 'Dadd' to 'Wallie', 7 November 1915, W. A. Goodwin Collection, Con Shelf, IWM Documents. Before the war Walter Goodwin had been employed as a clerk.

97 R. Saunders to son, 7 August 1915, R. Saunders, Letters to Son in Canada, 1914–18 (hereafter Saunders Letters), 79/15/1, IWM Documents. Saunders was the headmaster of a National School in Fletching, Sussex. He and his wife had thirteen children, of whom three were in the armed forces.

98 Holcombe Ingleby to Clement, 23 November 1915, Ingleby Letters, P.343, IWM Documents.

99 *Ibid.*, 7 January 1916.

100 *Ibid.*, 21 January 1916.

101 *Ibid.*, 19 March 1916.

102 *Ibid.*

103 Watson, *Fighting Different Wars*, pp. 1–13.

104 Gibbs Diary, 24 September 1914, Ms Eng. misc. c.159, Bodleian Special Collections.

105 Many of these were collected by Peter Liddle in the late 1970s and early 1980s, and are now part of the Liddle Collection (1914–18), Special Collections, Brotherton Library, Leeds University, Leeds.

106 A number are held by the Department of Sound, Imperial War Museum, London.

107 Cooper Diary, 16 February 1917, P.121, IWM Documents. In 1938 Yearsley typed up and edited selected entries drawn from 1056 pages of manuscript diaries. Yearsley, 'The Home Front', p. 1, DS/MISC/17, IWM Documents.

108 R. Saunders to son, 20 July 1918, Saunders Letters, 79/15/1, IWM Documents. Mark Connelly stresses the importance of churches and other places of worship in providing community-based spaces for commemoration and solace, both during and in the aftermath of war. M. Connelly, *The Great War, Memory and Ritual: Commemoration in the City and East London, 1916–1939* (The Boydell Press for the Royal Historical Society, Woodbridge, 2002), Chapter 7.

109 Including, it is worth noting, those of Reverend Andrew Clark. He frequently dealt with church matters, but not issues of faith or doctrine, presumably because he considered these unsuited to a 'war diary'. Of course, there were exceptions to the lack of reference to faith. See, for example, the letters

written to H. Carter by his parents in H. Carter Collection, 86/8/1, IWM Documents.

110 H. B. Chapman, *Home Truths about the War* (George Allen & Unwin, London, 1917), front cover.

111 Cooper Diary, 4 August 1916, P.121, IWM Documents.

1

The impact of war, *c.* 1914–15

Introduction

In February 1916 Harold Cossins noted in his diary that the Prime Minister had recently 'said that the effects of the war would continue to be felt for at least a generation'. Cossins added, rather disconsolately: 'there is not much chance of my experiencing normal peacetime conditions again'.[1] Some servicemen may have believed that civilians were hardly touched by the war, but this sentiment was not widely shared on the home front. On the contrary, even in the early months of the conflict, there was a strong feeling that the war would change lives fundamentally and perhaps irrevocably. This chapter and the next will thus explore some of the changes experienced by middle-class men as they went about their 'everyday' lives in wartime. Focusing particularly on the first twelve months or so of the war, this chapter will suggest that although middle-class men were physically distanced from the actual fighting, the war intruded in their lives in a variety of ways. Indeed, it was generally felt right that it should: few believed that people should continue their normal activities as though nothing was happening. Middle-class men were thus often deeply interested in news of the war, trying to follow events as best they could, although it was not long before many became convinced that much information, both about events on the battle and on the home fronts, was being withheld from the civilian population. The rumours and 'scares' that flourished in the space created by the lack of credible official information presented middle-class civilian men with a problem: how should rational, well-educated individuals navigate their way between what seemed credible and what seemed fantastic? What, in other words, were they to believe?

This chapter will suggest that as well-established sources of information in the press were found to provide little or no real 'news' and official communiqués were increasingly distrusted, middle-class men turned to alternative sources of information. Networks of informants, both civilians and combatants, especially those able to provide first-hand and 'eyewitness' accounts, as well as the exciting new medium of film, were increasingly used to fill the gap in knowledge created by official silence and censorship. However, the chapter will conclude, these sources did not entirely counter the feeling among many civilians that they were marginal to the war effort, their role a largely passive one: in a way, then, for many middle-class civilian men the first twelve months of war turned out to be a period of disappointed expectations.

Signs of war

In October 1914 Edward Barker, an Essex postman, paid a visit to his son in Harwich, where he was stationed with the 5th Essex. He travelled there by motorbike, taking his son's fiancée with him. When they arrived in Harwich 'a sentry challenged him, and he, not knowing what he was expected to do, just shouted out "all right" and went on. The sentry at once levelled his rifle, and fired, the bullet whistling past Barker's head. When he stopped, the sentry … searched the machine thoroughly … He then let them go on, with a warning to behave himself better in future'.[2] Rather more dramatically than was the case with most people, the incident showed Barker what would soon become clear to all: that the war required changes to everyday practices and behaviour.

Especially in the first few months of the conflict, the exact nature of these changes had not yet become clear, and individuals spent a good deal of time trying to identify 'signs' of war. Some of these signs were obvious and no doubt difficult to ignore, particularly in the larger towns and cities. Returning home to the Sussex village of Fletching after a stay in London in September 1914, Robert Saunders noted that they 'were not sorry to get back to the quiet of the country'. It was impossible to live in London 'at the present time without feeling an atmosphere of restless excitement that tells on the nerves and leaves you tired and more or less irritable and used up'. Everywhere one could 'see flags flying, appeals to enlist, men in khaki, special constables with their badges, photographs and war telegrams in shop windows and recruiting stations'.[3] The day after the declaration of war, Ernest Cooper found visitors to Southwold, a small seaside town on the Suffolk coast, 'almost in a state of panic, the newspaper shops were besieged, spymania set in badly and the old women in trousers soon began to worry the authorities'.[4] The war also manifested itself in more mundane ways: in August 1914 Cossins noted that newspapers had been reduced to six or eight pages 'owing to lack of paper. Advertisements have almost disappeared'. A fortnight later, he recorded that 'all the railways have restored cheap excursion rates which have been suspended since the beginning of the war'.[5] Other signs and incidents appeared more baffling, their significance uncertain. When war broke out, Reginald Gibbs was on holiday in Bournemouth with his wife and daughter. He noted that 'for some unknown reason the tradesmen in Bournemouth refused to part with small change'. His wife had bought him some collars, and the outfitter had 'let her have them for four pence less than their value, rather than give change'.[6] By July 1915, Cossins noted, 'there are so many evidences of war about that it is hard to realise that there is anything unusual about them'.[7]

Frequently, however, observers found themselves disappointed, being able to record few signs of the war. In September 1914 Reverend Andrew Clark travelled to Braintree from his village parish of Great Leighs. He noted that 'neither there nor on way there nor on way back was there any khaki-clad figure, or any war-wagon, or other sign of war, other than posters inviting recruits or announcing Red Cross Lectures', although the fishmonger did tell him 'that the war was having a most prejudicial effect on the fish-supply'.[8] In August 1914 Horace Joseph was on holiday at the family home in Dinder, near Wells, Somerset, where 'for now … there is nothing to show we are at war … the trains were running punctually, and though not crowded were not noticeably empty. There were no signs of excitement on the way. Here and there are some men in khaki, but not in greater numbers than often are seen in August'.[9] This lack of 'signs' of war was not limited to rural areas. Four months after his holiday, Joseph was 'struck with the slightness of the difference which war has made to the appearance of London except for the darkened streets at night, and the appeals everywhere for recruits, so much reiterated that I think one would learn to ignore them'.[10] Indeed, throughout the war years there were moments when individuals were taken aback by scenes that seemed far distanced from the conflict and from events on the battle fronts. In May 1917 Frederick Robinson attended Chestnut Sunday in Bushey Park. Despite the travel restrictions, 'the crowd of sight-seers was never greater, and the last thing that one would have thought was that we were in the midst of the greatest war the world has ever known'.[11]

Whether struck by the extent of change or remarking on its absence, few civilian men seem to have doubted that the conflict had something to do with them. Although far distanced from the actual fighting, most saw themselves as involved in the war, even if only in the limited role of spectators, rather than active participants. Great efforts, thus, were made to follow the news and obtain information about events both on battle and on home fronts. In the early months of the war, interest seems to have been at fever pitch. In August 1914 a letter from his son in Canada was for Saunders 'a welcome relief from the constant topic of war that is on every one's lips. No one seems able to settle down to work but spends a good part of the time talking matters over with anyone who comes along'. A few days later he remarked that they had experienced 'another week of excitement, everyone restless and ready to discuss war news on the slightest provocation'.[12] Looking back on the first eighteen months of war from the vantage point of January 1916, Clark noted that 'there has never been a war in which so many English men and women, who remained at home, have had so direct and personal an interest. Little was read, little was talked about, except the army and navy and other forces'.[13]

Throughout the war years, middle-class civilians attempted to follow the fortunes of the armed forces, as well as political events both at home and abroad. Thus, on 3 July 1916, two days after the start of the battle of the Somme, Robinson and his family spent 'much time in hunting out on the map the numerous places mentioned in the dispatches'.[14] During the seemingly successful German offensive of spring 1918, Cooper noted that 'we have been watching most anxiously the news from the Western Front'.[15] Certain items of news seem to have affected people particularly deeply. In June 1916 Cossins was lunching at the Oxford and Cambridge Club in London, when the news of Kitchener's death 'came over the tape machines; the effect was very marked both there and in the streets as I walked back to the office'. People, he added, looked at newspaper placards 'as if mistrusting their own eyes'.[16] According to F. Ashe Lincoln, a young boy growing up in Plymouth during the war, 'everyone … [felt] somehow that we'd lost the war, because Kitchener was an outstanding figure'.[17]

Despite their efforts to follow events, most civilian men were well aware of their distance, both physical and psychological, from the realities of the battlefields. Following the surrender of Kut to the Turks in April 1916, Cossins observed that 'the past month must have witnessed great privations and suffering among the troops. It is difficult to realise it, for there is always the tendency to regard the operations as if they were recounted in a story that was found to come right in the end'.[18] Earlier on in the war Gibbs had been struck by 'what a very stately and sedate old lady the newspaper Bellona is to be sure. Everything that happens about her is so *nice*. Wounded men sink gently to the ground like tired children ... There are no routs of terror-stricken men, nothing so vulgar, there are only *retirements* and *evacuations*'.[19] A year later, he observed that 'everybody stands agape at the picture-show of the war, till one by one is rapped smartly on the shoulder by dull reality'.[20]

That said, there is little evidence that civilian men were, or wished to be, entirely shielded from the grimmer realities of the battle fronts, lulled by a mixture of 'music-hall gaiety, Fleet-Street bluster, bellicose sermons, and military propaganda'.[21] In June 1915 Clark recorded that 'the wounded all agree that the danger of pestilence [on the front] is very great. Everywhere in Flanders you see feet and hands, legs and arms, of imperfectly buried bodies sticking out of the soil'.[22] Cold, wet or windy weather at home led many to worry about the conditions endured by soldiers 'in the trenches', while the ever growing casualty lists were a constant refrain of diaries and letters. In February 1915 a shocked Saunders asked his son: 'Have you noticed our losses so far are 104,000 nearly half of what we used to consider our whole standing army'.[23]

Unsurprisingly, middle-class men turned first and foremost to the press, still 'by far the most important medium of communication in the late nineteenth and early twentieth centuries', for information about events both at home and abroad.[24] The daily newspapers, which were thought to contain the most up-to-date news, were eagerly read, with attention paid both to reportage and to official despatches. After the war, for example, Robinson described himself as 'an ordinary individual who, for the most part, had to depend on what he read in the newspapers. Oh! Those newspapers! To "*The Times*" in particular one's thanks are due'.[25] Writing to his son in June 1915, Holcombe Ingleby lamented the fact that despite the recent destruction of two Zeppelins, 'we do not seem to be able to prevent the rascals bombing us whenever they choose'. He warned that 'I cannot send you particulars', although in fact being a member of parliament did not give him access to confidential information: 'indeed, I hardly know them myself as my information has been supplied by the papers'.[26] A day that passed without reading newspapers was worthy of note. Cossins spent the last Sunday in August 1915 tidying up his garden: 'for the first time since war began I have not seen a paper at all during the day'.[27] Almost exactly three years later, Robinson noted that 'we are cut off from the outside world and get no papers to-day – which is a relief'.[28]

However, it was not long before complaints began to be voiced about the lack of real 'news' in the press. As Robinson observed in October 1914, echoing the discontent felt by many others on the home front: 'the papers are as usual full from end to end of war "news", but they contain absolutely no news about the war'.[29] Inevitably, this led to fears that bad news was being suppressed. Early in November 1914 Cossins considered it 'evident that a great deal is being kept back from us. The Expeditionary Force has lost, it is said, at least half its numbers'.[30] Gibbs stressed how little was known of the British army in the first weeks of war, news arriving in dribs and drabs, before 'the curtain' went down again.[31] In May 1915 Clark recorded that there was a good deal of 'bitterness' in Great Leighs about the lack of firm news of the Essex Yeomanry, where many of the village's young men were serving, despite rumours that it had 'suffered terribly in a recent action'.[32] Clark himself was regularly infuriated by the 'offensively paltry' and uninformative official bulletins issued by the War Office: 'only an institution lost to all sense of shame could pretend to fulfil a solemn pledge by issuing rubbish of this sort'.[33] The worst instance, according to Clark, of the War Office's 'heartless insolence' was the bulletin published on 9 July 1916, in the early days of the battle of the Somme: 'with the guns in Flanders thundering in the ears of villagers here, whose relatives are at the front, there is not a word about our troops'.[34]

The result, Saunders wrote to his son in February 1916, was that 'there is not the feverish rush for papers as formerly owing to the absence of important news … the Censorship is so strict that much of the interest in the reading of War News has been destroyed'.[35] People began to fear the worst, worrying that official silence meant that bad news, whether of defeat in the field, of destructive air-raids at home, or of other catastrophes, was being withheld. When the papers were forbidden to publish any detail of an air-raid on London at the end of May 1915, Gibbs commented that 'the government are evidently afraid of the public and their attitude naturally gives rise to all sorts of misgivings'.[36] There was also, it seems, a growing tendency to mistrust much of the information that *was* released. In January 1917 James Caldwell, an engineer and businessman, a good friend of Andrew Clark, was sceptical about the official reports of the Silvertown munitions factory explosion. Like many others, he believed that many more had died than the sixty-nine reported by the authorities.[37] Five months later, according to Gibbs, it was widely asserted that the official figures relating to casualties during a recent air-raid on London (fewer than one hundred dead and approximately four hundred injured) 'are all moonshine', and that in reality the number of the dead was much higher.[38]

Rumours and spies

In the vacuum left by official silence, rumours flourished.[39] In March 1917 Robinson observed that little fresh news was available, 'but what is lacking in news is made up in rumours', including that the Germans had just landed in the north of England. 'Everyone is ready to believe everything, which is largely due to the fact that information as to what is happening is deliberately kept back by the Government until several days afterwards, and perhaps altogether'.[40] Certain rumours were well-known, widely reported and, it seems, generally believed. One that stood out for its ubiquity in the first three months of war concerned the alleged movement of Russian troops through Britain, on their way to the Western front: 'the East Coast trains have been commandeered to transport them rapidly south en route for the French theatre of war'.[41] Despite press rebuttals of what was described as 'pure fabrication',[42] the story proved remarkably resilient, circumstantial details adding verisimilitude.[43] Thus, in September 1914 a soldier told Gibbs that 'his pal had seen trainload after trainload go through Basingstoke', while a 'a city man' told him that 'one of his clerks had heard from his daughter in Ostend and she referred to "the difficulty of landing Russian troops"'. Understandably bewildered, Gibbs wondered: 'what is one to believe?'[44]

Other rumours were more limited to a specific time and place. Macleod Yearsley was on a golfing holiday in Kent when war broke out. His caddy told him that Dover had been placed under martial law and that civilians had been evacuated. Trenches were being built all the way to Folkestone. 'Four days later, being anxious to see all these changes I visited Dover, to find everything going on very much the same as usual. People were bathing, sitting in canvas chairs, walking, and generally amusing themselves on the front just as in the piping days of peace'.[45] Three months later, Clark heard that a sentry at the Marconi works in nearby Chelmsford had been shot dead. 'It was presumed that this was done by German agents in a motor'.[46] The following day it was discovered that the alarm had been caused by 'the accidental discharge of a revolver. No sentry was shot at'. By then, however, the rumour had 'spread like wildfire throughout the district',[47] and the incident was still the subject of speculation a week later. According to Dr Smallwood, a local doctor and one of Clark's most frequent visitors,[48] there was more to events than had been made public: 'not one shot was fired, but four. It was an officer who fired, and an English officer would not draw a revolver from his holster without substantial cause. The alarm was immediate, and the search severe', with all the cars in the vicinity stopped and carefully searched.[49]

The ways in which such rumours spread, gaining in drama as they were passed on, was vividly described by Gibbs, who on 8 September 1915 recorded in his diary that:

> A neighbour, Mrs Mason came in last night, rat-tat-tatting on the front door, like a special messenger from the king. She told us a long circumstantial yarn, which she was supposed to have heard from her husband, who is employed at the College, to the effect that all the prisoners from Frith Hill have escaped after battering down their guards with the butt-ends of rifles, and that they were roaming the countryside in armed bands. She said also that the troops at Aldershot and Deep Cut had been called out, and that even boy scouts had been armed with rifles. However it all turned out to be moonshine. *One* wretched German prisoner had escaped.[50]

While such alarms proved short-lived, other rumours cropped up again and again in the course of the war, one of the most common being that German troops had landed on British soil. Given that such an invasion seemed a very real possibility, it is not surprising that in September 1914 so many people should have fallen for a poorly judged practical joke: Cooper's nephew Noel drove round Suffolk with some friends, including one in uniform, warning people that a German aeroplane had landed and the crew were at large. Understandably, 'this created a scare and the people were about all night searching "for the airmen"'.[51] Such 'scares' recurred regularly over the next four years. In November 1914 Clark recorded a rumour that 50,000 Germans had invaded Cromer, on the Norfolk coast.[52] In June 1915 it was reported in Braintree 'that Great Leighs was in occupation of Germans, who had alighted on it from air-craft'.[53] In October 1915 it was rumoured that the Germans had landed at Yarmouth,[54] and at Harwich in March 1916.[55] For some reason, 25 March 1917 stood out as a day especially 'full of rumours', including 'that there had been an attempted German invasion … The Home defence forces had all been called up and men were even then repelling the invaders with fixed bayonets'.[56] According to Caldwell, there were 'endless reports in Chelmsford … but no one had any definite ideas. One rumour was that Germans had landed in Yorkshire. Another was that Germans had attacked Harwich'.[57]

Rumours of external threats were paralleled by fears of treachery and betrayal from within. In 1915, for example, it was widely believed that

Zeppelins on air-raid missions were being guided from the ground by cars with powerful head-lights.[58] 'It is difficult to believe', wrote Clark in August 1915, 'that these reports, coming independently from different sources, and dovetailing in with each other, are groundless'.[59] There was a good deal of speculation in Great Leighs about the identity of the cars' drivers and owners, although suspicion tended to centre on individuals who did not entirely fit in the local community, either because of their religion, ethnic background, or political beliefs. In May 1915 'a wicked and slanderous, but widely circulated, report assigns this car to an estimable local landowner, Sebag Montefiore, of Stisted Hall'.[60] Stisted Hall was a 'very fine estate' near Braintree and Montefiore 'a Jew, of reputed great wealth'. According to Clark, he was 'the beau ideal of an English squire. He has spent much money in improving the estate, especially in ways conducive to the welfare of the labourers but not productive of monetary return … he is a frank, hearty gentleman'.[61] In September the same year there were 'sensational' (and, it turned out, incorrect) reports that a Mr Seabrook, from the nearby village of Little Waltham, had been arrested for showing a 'brilliant light which guided the Zeppelin' during a recent air raid. Seabrook was 'a very hard-working, respectable man; but somewhat intolerant in his expressions of extreme anti-church and Socialist opinions'.[62]

Stories of individuals providing assistance to the crews of Zeppelins often blended with wider fears of spies and saboteurs operating on the home front.[63] Returning to London after a holiday in August 1914, Yearsley noted that 'there is no doubt that the country is infested with spies and there is cause to fear that they may do serious damage by bombs, etc.'[64] A year later, Joseph was told by a friend who worked at the War Office that 'spies were being caught and shot at the rate of about three a week: one … actually came to the War Office about a commission'.[65] Rumours abounded in 1914 and 1915 of people being unmasked as spies. In April 1915 Clark was told a 'well-ascertained … spy-story'. The family of Captain R. G. Pretyman, the MP for Chelmsford, employed a German governess 'of whom they thought highly. Her only peculiarity was a constant desire to stay in the house when all the rest of thc family was out. "She did not like walking". After the war broke out, this became suspicious … it was found that she communicated … whatever intelligence she had picked up to another spy, who stayed outside the garden waiting to receive her report'.[66] Clark was amused by anecdotes involving the unmasking of suspected spies, such as the 'delightful story of a German spy at the Boreham end of Great Leighs parish'. A man with a 'foreign accent' had been drawing plans of the roads. The two soldiers who had been called out to investigate 'had a good look at him; thought him very suspicious; arrested him as a spy … (He was probably an Ordnance Survey reviser)'.[67] Although told to amuse, such stories had a darker side, revealing the harassment suffered by outsiders who seemed to behave suspiciously, who appeared out of place, or who looked or sounded 'foreign'.[68]

As rational, educated, well-informed men, many middle-class civilians sought to distance themselves from what they saw as other people's credulity.[69] Thus, according to Joseph, in August 1914 Wells and its environs were full of 'alarms about the water supply … and stories come from several places of attempts to poison reservoirs; but in the absence of detailed evidence, or of anyone being apprehended, I feel suspicious'.[70] 'Others' were mocked for their willingness to give credence to, and then pass on, any rumour, however fanciful. Yearsley was scornful of people who believed that Kitchener's death had been due to treachery in 'high places',[71] while Clark recounted with slightly malicious glee how in October 1914 Little Waltham special constables had suspected a tramp, sheltering beside a haystack, of being a spy.[72] In September 1916 the manager of the Alberta Land Company, Mr Hatton, told Cossins 'a story now current of some new rays invented by Marconi which are directed on enemy airships and paralyse the occupants making them helpless against aeroplane attack'. Exasperated, Cossins wondered 'who starts these tales'[73] (Figure 2).

Many stories, particularly when recounted by unreliable – often female – informants, were treated with derision and scorn. Thus, in the early days of the war Yearsley was critical of 'Fat Boys (of both sexes)' who sought 'to make other people's flesh creep' by reporting exaggerated versions of rumours, including stories of supposed spies.[74] In March 1915 Clark observed that the figures in Dr Smallwood's anecdotes 'are always more reckless than reliable'.[75] A year later, he recorded 'a characteristic story of a German-spy told by a Great Leighs woman, confusedly and unintelligibly, but it is impossible to interrupt the narrator and clear up obscurities – by questioning'. The story centred on a woman (or a man disguised as a woman) with 'very large feet', who had dined at the White Hart hotel in Braintree, and had predicted that Zeppelins would soon come to Braintree and then to Scotland. 'It has all turned out as "she" said. "She" was certainly a spy. Anyone with such large feet must have been a spy'.[76]

That said, it was not always possible to maintain such a position of sceptical distance when confronted with seemingly believable rumours. Reflecting on wartime 'spy mania' from the vantage point of 1938,

2 'The rumourists: first ass and second ass', *Punch*, 4 April 1917.

Yearsley recalled that in September 1914 there had been 'a strange under-current at work which made for panic, chiefly centred on the "Army of Spies" existing largely, if not wholly, in the imagination'.[77] At the time, the existence – indeed, ubiquity – of spies was rarely questioned.[78] Thus, following a meeting of the Great Leighs special constables in January 1916, talk turned to the recent air-raids, and Caldwell stated that 'there was not a little village in England that had not an agent in it, making reports to a central German office in London'. Nobody demurred, although William Brown, Sergeant of the special constables, said that 'the village agents were not Germans but English'.[79] Even when a piece of news was received sceptically, an element of doubt often remained. Thus, in February 1916 Cossins was told 'a startling story, probably without any foundation whatever … by Mr Rhodes, who had it from his tobacconist, who heard it from a fishmonger from Billingsgate whose information came from a trawler just in. It was to the effect that a great sea fight had taken place in the North Sea, which had resulted in the sinking of four British and fourteen German battleships or cruisers. I wonder'.[80] In 1917 Robinson expressed the opinion of many, when he complained that the conflict was proving to be a 'war of *lies* as well as of *arms* and one literally does not know what to believe'.[81]

Information and news

According to Yearsley, it was only in the early months of 1915 that people on the home front really began to realise the seriousness of the war. 'Now we were all trying to do the right thing, and … groping for the right way in which to do it. Had we not been kept unnecessarily in the dark … we could have done so much better and felt so much happier'.[82] Censorship, official silence and obfuscation meant that alternative sources of information were increasingly sought out and prized. On 3 September 1916, Cossins noted that the papers were silent about a big Zeppelin raid the previous night: 'the censorship is evidently at work'. His information came via soldiers at the YMCA canteen where Mabel, the Cossins's maid, helped out: one of them claimed that he had seen Zeppelins dropping bombs while he was on guard duty.[83]

News, as well as gossip and rumours, were increasingly acquired through such word-of-mouth sources. In a letter to his father in March 1917 Joe Hollister, a city worker living in New Cross, south-east London, both sought and gave information about family members. He had received 'a line from Bert … have you heard anything of Dick since you wrote last?' He also passed on various snippets of information:

> its [*sic*] extraordinary the amount of female labour employed in the City now … there was a flutter of excitement in Gracechurch street the other day at two girls with trouser overalls cleaning the windows of shops … The Zepps made another futile attempt to pay us a visit on Friday night, but I don't think they will get as far as London again … I suppose you did not

> suffer any damage by the Munitions explosion in January, we came out alright although about a dozen houses down the road had windows broken and shop windows as far as Brixton (6 or 7 miles away) were blown in.[84]

Information was also acquired through more roundabout routes. In November 1915 Gibbs 'heard from two different sources that our men on Gallipoli are in a bad way'. One of his students told him that 'every bit of food and every drop of water had to be landed under fire … I happened to mention this to Mr Parsons, the grocer and he told me that one of his customers a Colonel Somebody had told him the same thing … he said "they are *doomed* Parsons"'.[85]

While some – particularly female – informants were scorned, others were greatly valued. Thus, servicemen's accounts of events on the battle fronts were considered an important supplement, and indeed corrective, to official information. Towards the end of September 1914 Gibbs observed that 'a feature of this war is the fact that the British Public is getting "graphic descriptions" direct from the British soldiers, the men in the trenches'.[86] He was referring to first-hand accounts published in the press, but equally valued was the information imparted by servicemen in their letters, and especially while on leave, when they were not constrained by censorship. In February 1916 Clark disapproved of the way in which in the village of Great Leighs, 'with the usual *penchant* for the horrible, and the usual proneness to exaggeration, soldiers on leave have made most harrowing descriptions of their horrible experiences, to excite sympathy and to gain notoriety … This talk has badly frightened the women-folk'.[87] However, he too valued the information and opinions provided by soldiers, 'be they right or be they wrong, because impressions of the war (as they reach us in the village) come from "official" (and therefore *ordered*) sources or from blatant newspapers'.[88]

Far from being uninterested in soldiers' experiences, civilian men seem to have taken advantage of every opportunity to find out more.[89] For example, when his brother-in-law called on him on his way to re-join his unit in December 1915, Cossins listened with interest to his account of active service and his opinions concerning the conduct of the war,[90] while Saunders tried to keep in touch with ex-pupils who had enlisted: 'I write to as many of my old boys as I can so I get a good deal of information that doesn't appear in the papers'.[91] Civilian informants who could claim to have special or 'insider' knowledge were also valued. Thus, in August 1914 Cossins had a conversation with somebody who worked for Tate 'the sugar people', who said the government had practically taken control of the industry by purchasing all raw materials.[92] A year later, a journalist told him that he believed that a 'surprise' was about to be 'sprung' at the Germans.[93] Unsurprisingly, information that could claim to originate from people with inside knowledge gained in credibility. In June 1915 Gibbs heard from William Tinniswood, his head-master, 'who has it from a General that the War Office have given up all hope of ever getting Belgium out of the claws of the German dragon'.[94]

Alongside such 'word-of-mouth' networks of information, by the end of 1915 a new – and highly valued – source had also emerged: film. In December 1915 Cossins noted that 'several series of cinematograph records have been taken of life at the front. These are to be shown throughout England very shortly and will be most interesting. An attempt will be made to keep them as a record for future generations'.[95] In March 1916 he went to see 'one of the series of official military and naval pictures', *Britain Prepared*, which 'took nearly three hours to show and covered practically all the preparations being made in this country for the war', including 'munitions making' and 'the training of the new armies'.[96] However, it was films that showed events on the battle fronts that attracted the most interest. In January 1917 'the films depicting the battle of the Ancre were shown to the public … and seem to have aroused great enthusiasm, especially the "tanks". I hope to see the pictures next week'.[97]

While increasingly sceptical of the information made public in the press and in official communiqués, middle-class civilian men do not seem to have viewed such films as propaganda, but as faithful depictions of real events; there is little evidence of any 'knowingness' about the artifice involved in certain scenes.[98] Having been to see the film of the battle of the Ancre, Cossins wrote that he had found it 'most interesting … but one had to keep reminding oneself that it was a true and not made up story. It will make any description of other battles … much more easily realisable'.[99] Yearsley thought it 'a stirring film, with a spirit of pathos in the sight of men and horses knee-deep in liquid mud, and the wounded being brought in'.[100] Picture houses may have been, in the words of the chairman of the London branch of the Cinematograph Exhibitors Association, 'emphatically the poor man's theatre',[101] but middle-class men were just as keen to view the new war films as the rest of the population. They were less happy with the other fare on offer. In September 1916 Robinson went to see the film of the battle of the Somme, which moved him deeply: 'You certainly have the realities of the war brought home to you, you feel the sacrifices which are being made by those at the front and you realise how little is your own part'. This, he thought, made it all the more scandalous that such a film should be shown sandwiched between 'screaming farces' such as 'Fickle Fatties Fall'.[102]

Despite their importance and popularity, neither word-of-mouth information nor films could entirely satisfy civilian men's desire for reliable and up-to-date news of events at home and abroad. It was this desire that may explain their increasing determination to – as far as was practical – 'see things for themselves'. The battle fronts were out of bounds for most civilians, but by the summer of 1915 many were doing their best to find out what was *really* going on at home: there were parallels here with the 'interested spectators' who in August 1914 crowded outside Buckingham Palace to witness 'the great events going on'.[103] What some condemned as a 'senseless craze for sightseeing',[104] many more saw as a way of finding out the reality behind official obfuscation and censorship. Thus, in October 1915 Rory Macleod travelled up to London from Cambridge 'to see magazine, barbed wire entangled around it'.[105] In February 1916 Cossins went to see the Brighton Pavilion, which had 'just been cleared of the Indian wounded for whom it was transformed into a hospital',[106] while a year earlier Gibbs and his sister Ethel had travelled to Farnborough 'to see the air-sheds', where he had 'noticed at least five different types' of aircraft.[107] D. B. Skinner, a London schoolboy, was impressed by an 'interesting exhibit … moored at the Embankment, Westminster … a captured German submarine',[108] while in March 1918 Yearsley and his wife 'went to Trafalgar Square to see the tank "Egbert"'.[109]

Of all the wartime 'sights', it was the aftermath of air-raids that attracted the most attention. In August 1915 Fred Lewin, one of Clark's fellow special constables in the village of Great Leighs, used some spare time in Chelmsford while waiting for a train to London to investigate 'the place where bombs had fallen on Tuesday morning'. He was 'fortunate enough to arrive' at a bomb site just 'when the specialist from Woolwich was superintending the digging out of the bomb'. Not only did 'Mr Lewin's badge as a special constable obtained him a foremost place of observation', but 'when the bomb had been removed, Mr Lewin had the curiosity to get into the hole'.[110] A month later, Saunders spent a few days' holiday in London with his daughter and her family. All the talk – he observed – was of the recent Zeppelin raids, and everyone was very nervous: 'you hear from conversation in the buses and along the streets the same Nervy ideas'. Saunders himself was curious, and 'amused' himself 'by investigating matters … first I went to Shoreditch High Street … on the route by 35 bus to Liverpool Street. On both sides of the road windows were smashed and a big hole in the road marked the spot where a bus were[?]

destroyed'. He then continued westward, observing the damage along the way.[111] The use of underhand tactics to gain access to restricted areas was not unknown: on one occasion, Yearsley managed to enter a bomb-damaged part of Lincoln's Inn that had been closed to the public by carrying conspicuously 'a bundle of documents girded by red tape', which his solicitor had lent him.[112]

By spring 1915, it had become common for crowds of sightseers to make their way to areas that had been bombed in order to see the damage. After an air-raid on Lowestoft and Southwold in April 1915, 'streams of cars came in to see what had happened'.[113] Six months later, a Zeppelin attack on London caused a good deal of destruction (as well as over 150 casualties, including fifty-five deaths), particularly in the Aldwych area. As this was quite close to his place of work, Cossins was able to see the damage at first hand. He also noted that 'the crowds this afternoon were enormous, people having come in from all parts to see what had been done'. The following day there were 'still great crowds of sightseers in London'.[114] The following spring, it was the turn of the Essex town of Braintree to be the victim of a Zeppelin attack. The next day Clark noted that 'all afternoon there has been a great race of bicyclists going past the Rectory – presumably lads from Terling, Witham, Chelmsford, to see the bomb-damage at Braintree'.[115]

The one sight that proved to be of even greater interest than scenes of destruction was the spectacle of downed enemy aircraft. In these circumstances, sightseers sought to act as more than passive spectators. In June 1917, for example, Cooper saw a Zeppelin being brought down. As Captain of the Southwold Fire Brigade 'I should at once have got a car and taken some firemen with cranes etc. when I should most likely have been employed to help with the ruins', but he had been so tired after a day working in the garden, that he went to bed instead. 'I regret I lost this opportunity … although I have no wish to have another chance'.[116] Most civilians sought to play an active part in the spectacle of destruction not by attempting to participate in the rescue work, but by picking up 'souvenirs'. Years after the end of the war, Denis Toomey thus recalled that one night his family had seen a Zeppelin being brought down: 'we went over to the place at Shenfield where it came down, though we weren't allowed near. However, we did have a bit of light twisted metal from it for many years'.[117]

In September 1916 two Zeppelins were brought down in Essex, and crowds quickly made their way there to see the remains: 'one of Major Brown's workmen went to see the Zeppelin at Billericay and brought back a cross[?]-bar of aluminium, like guttering, with four round-topped aluminium nails holding it together. Tom Hallington and the manager of Fortnam's[?] drapery shop in Braintree have brought back from Peldon, as souvenirs, bits of bedding', which were among the items the Zeppelin crew had thrown out in an unsuccessful attempt to gain height.[118] As the aluminium bar and bit of bedding suggest, most of the items picked up were not necessarily valuable, and there was nothing furtive about (most) collectors' actions: objects were shown to people back at home, discussed, and in some cases given away as gifts or sold. In October 1916, for example, Clark noted that the secretary of the YMCA 'has got what professes to be the coat of the commander of the Billericay Zeppelin. He has given a piece of it to Mrs Leslie Tritton'.[119]

A month earlier Robinson had been shown 'a small piece of the silk envelope of the [Zeppelin] brought down near Brentwood'. He had heard that the many people who had visited the scene 'got little satisfaction as soldiers with fixed bayonets kept them some half mile away – which seems a pity'.[120] In June 1917 Cooper drove to see the wreck of the Zeppelin he had seen brought down, but was disappointed: 'not allowed very close and no relics to be got'.[121] When denied the opportunity to handle and take away some of the aircraft's remains, spectators felt deeply let down. Towards the end of September 1916 Robinson went to see the remains of the Cuffley Zeppelin, which had been placed on public display in a tent on the grounds of the Honourable Artillery company in Finsbury, North London: 'the people pass round in a long queue seeing as much as they can in the extremely short time allowed', hurried on by police constables. 'You have scarcely time to read the descriptive labels attached. The whole thing is an annoyance which is not worth the trouble involved'.[122] Gilbert Hyam, interviewed many years after the event, remembered being taken to see the exhibition as a child of six. He thought it 'gory! … it showed … bits and pieces of charred uniforms … and god knows what of all the remains of the Germans who had been burnt to death!'.[123] However, as far as Robinson was concerned, goriness was not the problem with the exhibition. Rather, having been reduced to the status of a passive spectator, he felt correspondingly disappointed by the spectacle and the objects on display: 'the general impression is of a marine store dealer's, the fragments are without form, and are one mass of hopeless rubbish – or what appears to be such'.[124]

Discussion, debate and indifference

In February 1918 Clark tried to piece together the details of a recent air raid. In what had by then become established practice, he collected information from various people, some of whom he knew better than others, including W. H. Dee, the churchwarden, G. S. With, the headmaster of the Council School, as well as James Caldwell, Minnie Taylor 'at Post Office', the postman from Chelmsford, and two special constables 'out last night on road between Little Waltham and Bromfield'.[125]

Such conversations between relatives, friends, acquaintances or, indeed, strangers, were not always limited to an exchange of information, but often also led to a discussion of the latest news. In November 1915 Cossins and his family relocated temporarily to Brighton. The first morning, having left his razors at home, Cossins 'went out to get shaved … and found a sort of little club in a small saloon. We discussed the war while waiting our turns'.[126] Such discussions seem for the most part to have been quite amicable, although it is not clear whether this was because middle-class men tended to discuss 'serious' matters with individuals who were most likely to share their opinions, because of a desire to avoid arguments or, most likely, a mixture of the two. Whatever the reasons, open conflict and disagreements were rarely mentioned. That said, there were exceptions to this scenario of amicable exchange of opinions.

As discussed in the introduction, Gibbs's attitude towards the conflict was more critical than that of most (although by no means all) middle-class civilian men. His diaries show him questioning not only the way in which the war was conducted, but also its very justification: he believed that at the basis of Britain's entry into the war lay a desire to keep its imperial possessions intact, as well as to extend its sphere of influence. He was also more willing than most to contemplate the possibility of a British defeat, and to advocate the need for an immediate cease-fire. It is perhaps not surprising, then, that in May 1915 he should write that 'I seldom speak to anyone about the War and form most of my opinions from the papers'.[127] In reality, Gibbs was a good deal more willing than this suggests to express his opinions, a willingness that regularly brought him into conflict with strangers, acquaintances, colleagues and family. In November 1914 he tried to engage in conversation a Major with whom he shared a train compartment. 'Thinking of my memoirs and hoping to get something interesting out of him', he mentioned H. G. Wells's recent letter to *The Times*, in which the novelist had complained that in case of invasion, civilian men 'would not know what action to take'. The Major's curt answer was that civilians should enlist, to which Gibbs replied that he thought all the necessary men had already enlisted. 'I could see that this remark made him very angry. He made no reply. As we both got out at Camberly, he took particular care to slam the door in my face'.[128]

This was only one of the many occasions during the course of the war when his opinions brought him into conflict with his interlocutors, including not only strangers, but also friends and relatives. Gibbs's fraught relationship with his father, in particular, is revealing of the mixture of combativeness and reticence he displayed when faced with opinions about the war that differed radically from his. During a visit to his parents in December 1915 his father and he soon began to argue about the war: his father stressed 'the superiority of the English over the dirty Germans, who are the cads of Europe … I tried to make clear to him … the intricate machinations of the military clique in the pre-war days. To all this he opposed a blank solid "pooh-pooh"'. However, they agreed 'in one thing, that is, in disagreeing with everybody else. In consequence we have both acquired a sort of porcupine attitude of mind … When we meet, the air becomes tense with an electricity of suppressed individualism. There are fidgety silences, and sudden gusts of tumultuous words, conveying badly expressed ideas, hasty withdrawals and diffident pauses, a little embittered by smiles of self-deprecation, apt to be mistaken for contempt'.[129]

In January 1917 he lamented that 'with regard to the war outlook I seem to be in a minority of one'. He had tried to explain his views to several people, and 'they nearly bit my head off. One man (at the paper shop) I argued with, until he had to admit that our forcing the issue was merely a gamble. He went white with anger'.[130] Gibbs could certainly be provocative. In November 1916 he broke the lunch-time hush at his school, interrupted only by low voices asking for the mustard, salt and other similar requests, by stating that 'we are bleeding to death. There can be nothing worse for a nation, than national death'. Having made his pronouncement, he suddenly noticed the headmaster 'glaring at me round the table decoration and I was quite startled'. He said: '"There is *Dishonour*. That is worse than Death"'.[131]

It is perhaps not surprising that by May 1915 people were responding to Gibbs with phrases such as: '"Oh for goodness sake shut up about the war. We shall be all right, don't you worry – our turn is coming" and so on'.[132] However, there was more to this attitude than impatience with one individual's unorthodox and pessimistic opinions. It also marked a new reluctance to talk about the war, as the feverish interest in the conflict of the early months of war could no longer be sustained. As H. G. Wells suggested in his 1916 novel *Mr Britling Sees it Through*: 'after the jolt of the food panic and a brief financial scare, the vast inertia of everyday life in England asserted itself ... After the first impression that a universal catastrophe had happened there was an effect as if nothing had happened'.[133] In March 1915 Robinson noted that a leading article in *The Times* had recently dealt with the 'Monotony of War'. It had observed that '"when the war began we felt that a new life was beginning for us, a life terrible and tragic, but now we see there is a routine of war as of peace", especially when "nothing very decisive seems to happen"'. According to Robinson:

> our own experiences bears this out. Events which in the earlier stages created great excitement, and which stirred us to the utmost, to-day ... pass by without scarcely attracting our attention. Take for instance the first casualty list that was published, how eagerly we read it, today the publication of such lists has become a matter of routine, and therefore monotonous ... there are to-day many people who scarcely realise that a war is going on. It seems so far off, and they see nothing of the actualities of war, such as the Belgians and the French have done.[134]

In September 1917 he noted the indifference with which people met news of recent air-raids: 'all this is very sad but it makes little or no impression except upon the people immediately concerned. People are becoming so indifferent that they would hardly walk along the street to see the damage done'.[135] A year earlier, Cossins had recorded that eight steamers had been reported as sunk, 'with heavy loss of life'. He added that 'it is dreadful to think how callous one is becoming but it undoubtedly [is] a fact that these disasters are taken very philosophically now – except of course by those who are nearly concerned in them'.[136]

Conclusion

In the course of the first twelve months of war, middle-class civilians made considerable efforts to bridge the physical and psychological gap between themselves and the battle fronts, seeking a role beyond that of passive spectatorship. However, they were frustrated by what they perceived as a concerted effort on the part of the authorities to withhold information from them. The press and official communiqués were dismissed as uninformative and even misleading, and while war films were very well received, they did (and could) not provide the steady stream of up-to-date, reliable news about events at home and on the battle fronts that middle-class civilians wanted. In the vacuum left by official silence and obfuscation, rumours and 'scares' flourished, leaving even – supposedly – rational, clear-sighted and well-educated middle-class men uncertain about what to believe.

In this context, alternative sources of information were actively sought, with individuals sometimes going to considerable lengths to see things for themselves, visiting all sorts of 'sights', which might include areas affected by Zeppelin air-raids, as well as the remains of downed enemy aircraft. The practice of collecting 'souvenirs', furthermore, and subsequently selling, gifting, or simply showing them to an interested audience, arguably allowed individuals to feel that they were more than purely passive spectators to the events of the war. That said, listening to soldiers' stories, discussing the latest rumours, visiting bomb sites or collecting bits of enemy aircraft did not prove enough to counter the widespread feeling that middle-class civilian men were marginal to the war effort and distanced from 'real' events. Perhaps inevitably, then, the initial feverish interest in military and political events gradually waned. As Robinson observed in January 1915, 'lack of information soon produces lack of interest'.[137] In May 1916 Gibbs was told – only half-jokingly – that 'people in the trains are beginning to drop the war as a subject for conversation and have taken up the weather once more'.[138] However, indifference towards the war should not be overestimated. By mid-1915 the conflict had begun to intrude in new and sometimes unexpected ways in the lives of civilians, including the lives of middle-class men: it is these that will be the focus of the next chapter.

Notes

1 H. C. Cossins Diary, 1914–18 (hereafter Cossins Diary), 16 February 1916, PP/MCR/371, Department of Documents, Imperial War Museum (hereafter IWM Documents), London.

2 A. Clark War Diary, 'Echoes of the 1914 War in an Essex Village' (hereafter Clark Diary), 19 October 1914, Ms Eng. Hist. e.90, Special Collections, Bodleian Library, University of Oxford (hereafter Bodleian Special Collections), Oxford.

3 R. Saunders to son, 17 September 1914, R. Saunders, Letters to Son in Canada, 1914–18 (hereafter Saunders Letters), 79/15/1, IWM Documents. See also R. Briggs, Memoir, 1919, 01/59/1, IWM Documents.

4 The Diary of Ernest R. Cooper, 'Nineteen Hundred and War Time', 28 July 1914 – 3 December 1918 (hereafter Cooper Diary), 28 July 1914, P.121, IWM Documents.

5 Cossins Diary, 11 August 1914, 24 August 1914, PP/MCR/371, IWM Documents.
6 Diary of R. W. M. Gibbs, 1914–20 (hereafter Gibbs Diary), 18 September 1914, Ms Eng. misc. c.159, Bodleian Special Collections.
7 Cossins Diary, 18 July 1915, PP/MCR/371, IWM Documents.
8 Clark Diary, 25 September 1914, Ms Eng. Hist. e.89, Bodleian Special Collections.
9 Wartime Diaries of H. W. B. Joseph 1914–18 (hereafter Joseph Diaries), 14 August 1914, Ms. Top. Oxon. e.288, Bodleian Special Collections. See also 16 August 1914.
10 *Ibid.*, 23 December 1914.
11 F. A. Robinson, 'Diary of the Great War', 27 May 1917, vol. 3, P.402, IWM Documents.
12 R. Saunders to son, 8 August 1914, 15 August 1914, Saunders Letters, 79/15/1, IWM Documents. See also M. Yearsley ('Eyewitness'), 'The Home Front, 1914–18', p. 18, DS/MISC/17, IWM Documents.
13 A. Clark, '1915. Miscellaneous notes as to newspapers and miscellaneous periodicals and some official notices in wartime', in A. Clark, 'Scrapbooks of leaflets, newspaper cuttings etc., illustrating aspects of the Great War', Bodleian Library, University of Oxford, Oxford.
14 Robinson, 'Diary of the Great War', 3 July 1916, vol. 2, P.401, IWM Documents.
15 Cooper Diary, 20–26 March 1918, P.121, IWM Documents.
16 Cossins Diary, 6 June 1916, PP/MCR/371, IWM Documents.
17 F. Ashe Lincoln, Interview, 1993, DF148, Liddle Collection (1914–18), Special Collections, Brotherton Library, Leeds University (hereafter Liddle Collection), Leeds.
18 Cossins Diary, 29 April 1916, PP/MCR/371, IWM Documents. On the surrender of Kut see also Gibbs Diary, 30 April 1916, Ms Eng. misc. c.176, Bodleian Special Collections.
19 Gibbs Diary, 21 December 1914, Ms Eng. misc. c.162, Bodleian Special Collections. For the continued use of 'high diction' to depict the war, see P. Fussell, *The Great War and Modern Memory* (Oxford University Press, Oxford, 1977, first published 1975), pp. 21–3.
20 Gibbs Diary, 31 December 1915, Ms Eng. misc. c.173, Bodleian Special Collections. See also Robinson, 'Diary of the Great War', 8 July 1916, vol. 2, P.401, IWM Documents, for reflections on the realities behind bland newspaper reports.
21 J. M. Winter, *The Great War and the British People* (Palgrave Macmillan, Basingstoke, 2003, first published 1985), p. 290.
22 Clark Diary, 4 June 1915, Ms Eng. Hist. e.104, Bodleian Special Collections.
23 R. Saunders to son, 11 February 1915, Saunders Letters, 79/15/1, IWM Documents.

24 M. L. Sanders and P. M. Taylor, *British Propaganda during the First World War, 1914–18* (Macmillan, Basingstoke, 1982), p. 2. Six million newspapers were sold daily. G. Robb, *British Culture and the First World War* (Palgrave, Basingstoke, 2002), p. 112.
25 Robinson, 'Diary of the Great War', 'Prefatory note, 15 November 1918', vol. 1, P.401, IWM Documents.
26 Holcombe Ingleby to Clement, 11 June 1915, The First World War Letters of Holcombe Ingleby MP (hereafter Ingleby Letters), P.343, IWM Documents.
27 Cossins Diary, 29 August 1915, PP/MCR/371, IWM Documents.
28 Robinson, 'Diary of the Great War', 14 July 1918, vol. 4, P.402, IWM Documents.
29 *Ibid.*, 7 October 1914, vol. 1, P.401. Newspapers' roles as propaganda tools should not be exaggerated, but either because of censorship or self-censorship, readers' complaints about the lack of 'real' news seem to have been largely justified. Robb, *British Culture*, pp. 110–14; Sanders and Taylor, *British Propaganda*, pp. 18–32.
30 Cossins Diary, 4 November 1914, PP/MCR/371, IWM Documents.
31 Gibbs Diary, 20 September 1914, Ms Eng. misc. c.159, Bodleian Special Collections.
32 Clark Diary, 18 May 1915, 19 May 1915, 20 May 1915, Ms Eng. Hist. e.103, Bodleian Special Collections.
33 *Ibid.*, 1 November 1915, Ms Eng. Hist. e.113; 14 November 1915, Ms Eng. Hist. e.114.
34 *Ibid.*, 9 July 1916, Ms Eng. Hist. e.129.
35 R. Saunders to son, 3 February 1916, Saunders Letters, 79/15/1, IWM Documents.
36 Gibbs Diary, 1 June 1915, Ms Eng. misc. c.168, Bodleian Special Collections.
37 Clark Diary, 27 January 1917, Ms Eng. Hist. e.143, Bodleian Special Collections. James Caldwell worked for the Sun Chemical Company Ltd, based in Finsbury, London: 'Unusual ores and mineral products. Laboratory Apparatus, Porcelain, Glassware, etc. Exporters and Importers of chemicals'. Clark Diary, 17 July 1917, Ms Eng. Hist. e.150, Bodleian Special Collections.
38 Gibbs Diary, 14 June 1917, Ms Eng. misc. c.190, Bodleian Special Collections.
39 M. MacDonagh, *In London during the War: The Diary of a Journalist* (Eyre and Spottiswoode, London, 1935), p. 16. See also A. Gregory, *The Last Great War: British Society and the First World War* (Cambridge University Press, Cambridge, 2008), pp. 63–7.
40 Robinson, 'Diary of the Great War', 25 March 1917, vol. 3, P.402, IWM Documents.

41 Clark Diary, 28 August 1914, Ms Eng. Hist. e.88, Bodleian Special Collections.
42 *Ibid.*, 29 August 1914.
43 The story was mentioned, for example, in *ibid.*, 30 August 1914, Ms Eng. Hist. e.88; 14 September 1914, 3 October 1914, Ms Eng. Hist. e.89; Cossins Diary, 28 August 1914, 29 August 1914, 15 September 1914, PP/MCR/371, IWM Documents; Yearsley, 'The Home Front', p. 21, DS/MISC/17, IWM Documents.
44 Gibbs Diary, 20 September 1914, Ms Eng. misc. c.159, Bodleian Special Collections.
45 Yearsley, 'The Home Front', p. 10, DS/MISC/17, IWM Documents.
46 Clark Diary, 5 November 1914, Ms Eng. Hist. e.91, Bodleian Special Collections.
47 *Ibid.*, 6 November 1914.
48 Although this is not stated in the diary, it seems likely that the frequent visits were due to Clark's wife's illness. Dr Smallwood also spent time chatting with Clark and was one of his main sources of information on local events and opinions. Mrs Clark died in October 1916. J. Munson (ed.), *Echoes of the Great War: The Diary of the Reverend Andrew Clark 1914–1919* (Oxford University Press, Oxford, 1985), p. 164.
49 Clark Diary, 9 November 1914, Ms Eng. Hist. e.91, Bodleian Special Collections.
50 Gibbs Diary, 8 September 1915, Ms Eng. misc. c.170, Bodleian Special Collections.
51 Cooper Diary, 7 September 1914, P.121, IWM Documents. Noel was let off with a caution, while 'for weeks' his uncle 'was chaffed about this business'.
52 Clark Diary, 19 November 1914, Ms Eng. Hist. e.92, Bodleian Special Collections.
53 *Ibid.*, 3 June 1915, Ms Eng. Hist. e.104.
54 *Ibid.*, 7 October 1915, Ms Eng. Hist. e.112.
55 *Ibid.*, 19 March 1916, Ms Eng. Hist. e.122. For rumours of a German landing at Harwich in July 1915, see also Gibbs Diary, 12 July 1915, Ms Eng. misc. c.169, Bodleian Special Collections. Each spring seems to have brought renewed fears of invasion.
56 *Ibid.*, 26 March 1917, Ms Eng. misc. c.187.
57 Clark Diary, 25 March 1917, Ms Eng. Hist. e.146, Bodleian Special Collections. See also Robinson, 'Diary of the Great War', 25 March 1917, vol. 3, P.402, IWM Documents. Presumably, the 'February' revolution in Russia and the US decision to enter the war, as well as awareness of an imminent new Allied 'offensive' on the Western Front (the British offensive at Arras began on 9 April) all contributed to the climate of uncertainty and speculation. D. Stevenson, *1914–1918: The History of the First World War* (Allen Lane, London, 2004), especially chapters 6 and 13.

58 Yearsley, 'The Home Front', pp. 53, 110, DS/MISC/17, IWM Documents; Robinson, 'Diary of the Great War', 23 January 1915, vol. 1, P.401, IWM Documents.

59 Clark Diary, 20 August 1915, Ms Eng. Hist. e.108, Bodleian Special Collections. See also Robinson, 'Diary of the Great War', 20 January 1915, vol. 1, P.401, IWM Documents.

60 Clark Diary, 8 May 1915, Ms Eng. Hist. e.103, Bodleian Special Collections.

61 *Ibid.*, 7 March 1915, Ms Eng. Hist. e.99.

62 *Ibid.*, 20 September 1915, Ms Eng. Hist. e.111. Clark thought that 'the sole foundation for the report is probably only his having been summoned for refusal to darken his lights. He is quite of that obstinate type'.

63 Contemporaries acknowledged that such fears were being nurtured by press reports of the 'spy danger', although this did not make it easier to distinguish fact from fiction. Cossins Diary, 23 October 1914, PP/MCR/371, IWM Documents. The inter-play between press, public opinion and government action is explored in D. French, 'Spy fever in Britain, 1900–1915', *The Historical Journal*, vol. 21, no. 2 (1978), pp. 355–70.

64 Yearsley, 'The Home Front', p. 14, DS/MISC/17, IWM Documents.

65 Joseph Diaries, 31 August 1915, Ms. Top. Oxon. e.288, Bodleian Special Collections.

66 Clark Diary, 30 April 1915, Ms Eng. Hist. e.102, Bodleian Special Collections.

67 *Ibid.*, 20 October 1914, Ms Eng. Hist. e.90. See also, for example, 26 October 1914, Ms Eng. Hist. e.90.

68 Robb, *British Culture*, p. 10.

69 For middle-class 'claims to authority based on rational knowledge', see R. Gray, 'The platform and the pulpit: cultural networks and civic identities in industrial towns, c. 1850–70', in A. Kidd and D. Nicholls (eds), *The Making of the British Middle Class? Studies of Regional and Cultural Diversity since the Eighteenth Century* (Sutton Publishing, Stroud, 1998), p. 131. See also J. Tosh, *A Man's Place: Masculinity and the Middle-Class Home in Victorian England* (Yale University Press, New Haven, CT, 1999), p. 47.

70 Joseph Diaries, 17 August 1914, Ms. Top. Oxon. e.288, Bodleian Special Collections.

71 Yearsley, 'The Home Front', p. 171, DS/MISC/17, IWM Documents.

72 Clark Diary, 30 October 1914, Ms Eng. Hist. e.90; 'Little Waltham "Special Constables" 1914', not dated, Ms Eng. Hist. e.95; Bodleian Special Collections.

73 Cossins Diary, 5 September 1916, PP/MCR/371, IWM Documents.

74 Yearsley, 'The Home Front', p. 24, DS/MISC/17, IWM Documents.

75 Clark Diary, 3 March 1915, Ms Eng. Hist. e.98, Bodleian Special Collections.

76 *Ibid.*, 16 April 1916, Ms Eng. Hist. e.124.
77 Yearsley, 'The Home Front', p. 26, DS/MISC/17, IWM Documents.
78 According to War Office records, twenty-eight individuals were court-martialled for spying in England (two of whom were acquitted), forty were tried at a military court abroad and a further ten 'at a general court martial abroad'. Nine were executed. James Morton suggests that 'these men and women were the tip of the iceberg. Most spies were never caught'. J. Morton, *Spies of the First World War: Under Cover for King and Kaiser* (The National Archives, Richmond, 2010), pp. 134–5.
79 Clark Diary, 31 January 1916, Ms Eng. Hist. e.119, Bodleian Special Collections. Major William Brown, of 'long service in the Essex Yeomanry', was a substantial landowner and farmer. See 29 October 1914, Ms Eng. Hist. e.90; 20 January 1915, Ms Eng. Hist. e.96, Bodleian Special Collections.
80 Cossins Diary, 8 February 1916, PP/MCR/371, IWM Documents. The battle of Jutland took place three months later, in May 1916. Stevenson, *1914–1918*, pp. 250–5. According to David Stevenson, the battle 'in large measure ... resulted from a change in the German naval command ... in February 1916'. Stevenson, *1914–1918*, p. 252. Perhaps rumours of a naval battle were an echo of such changes.
81 Robinson, 'Diary of the Great War', 4 August 1917, vol. 3, P.402, IWM Documents.
82 Yearsley, 'The Home Front', p. 49, DS/MISC/17, IWM Documents.
83 Cossins Diary, 3 September 1916, PP/MCR/371, IWM Documents.
84 J. Hollister to 'dad', 19 March 1917, J. Hollister Letter, 1917, 98/10/1, IWM Documents. Joe Hollister's father lived in Romford, east London.
85 Gibbs Diary, 6 November 1915, Ms Eng. misc. c.172, Bodleian Special Collections.
86 *Ibid.*, 25 September 1914, Ms Eng. misc. c.159.
87 Clark Diary, 27 February 1916, Ms Eng. Hist. e.121, Bodleian Special Collections.
88 *Ibid.*, 12 October 1914, Ms Eng. Hist. e.90.
89 Gregory, *The Last Great War*, p. 133.
90 Cossins Diary, 15 December 1915, PP/MCR/371, IWM Documents.
91 R. Saunders to son, 14 June 1915, Saunders Letters, 79/15/1, IWM Documents.
92 Cossins Diary, 29 August 1914, PP/MCR/371, IWM Documents.
93 *Ibid.*, 7 August 1915.
94 Gibbs Diary, 14 June 1915, Ms Eng. misc. c.168, Bodleian Special Collections.
95 Cossins Diary, 2 December 1915, PP/MCR/371, IWM Documents.
96 *Ibid.*, 10 March 1916. See also 11 March 1916.
97 *Ibid.*, 16 January 1917. Ana Carden-Coyne suggests that film satisfied not only the public's 'thirst for information', but also its 'fascination with

modern technology'. A. Carden-Coyne, *Reconstructing the Body: Classicism, Modernism and the First World War* (Oxford University Press, Oxford, 2009), p. 87.

98 A. Horrall, *Popular Culture in London, c.1890–1918: The Transformation of Entertainment* (Manchester University Press, Manchester, 1991), pp. 208–10. See also N. Reeves, *Official British Film Propaganda during the First World War* (Croom Helm in association with the Imperial War Museum, London, 1986), especially pp. 239–48.

99 Cossins Diary, 25 January 1917, PP/MCR/371, IWM Documents.

100 Yearsley, 'The Home Front', p. 198, DS/MISC/17, IWM Documents.

101 Quoted in A. Marwick, *The Deluge: British Society and the First World War* (Palgrave Macmillan, Basingstoke, second edition, 2006, first published 1965), p. 181.

102 Robinson, 'Diary of the Great War', 8 September 1916, vol. 2, P.401, IWM Documents. On the film *The Battle of the Somme*, see also Yearsley, 'The Home Front', p. 178, DS/MISC/17, IWM Documents. Twenty million people saw it in the six weeks following its release. Horrall, *Popular Culture in London*, p. 208.

103 Gregory, *The Last Great War*, p. 13.

104 Clark Diary, 7 March 1916, Ms Eng. Hist. e.122, Bodleian Special Collections. The terms were used by a (female) correspondent, writing from Oxford about a recent Zeppelin alarm.

105 R. H. Macleod Diary, 7 October 1915, R.H. Macleod Papers, DF087, Liddle Collection. Having spent twenty-five years working in the Indian Civil Service, in 1914 Macleod was living in Cambridge, teaching 'Hindu and Mohammedan law'.

106 Cossins Diary, 6 February 1916, PP/MCR/371, IWM Documents.

107 Gibbs Diary, New Year Day 1915, Ms Eng. misc. c.163, Bodleian Special Collections.

108 D. B. Skinner to P. Liddle, 5–8 March 1979, DF148, Liddle Collection.

109 Yearsley, 'The Home Front', p. 259, DS/MISC/17, IWM Documents.

110 Clark Diary, 20 August 1915, Ms Eng. Hist. e.108, Bodleian Special Collections. Witnessing an air-raid first-hand was, of course, a different matter, and will be discussed in Chapter 2.

111 R. Saunders to son, 20 September 1915, Saunders Letters, 79/15/1, IWM Documents. For visits to bomb sites, see also Robinson, 'Diary of the Great War', 10 September 1915, vol. 1, P.401; 9 July 1917, vol. 3, P.402, IWM Documents.

112 Yearsley, 'The Home Front', p. 110, DS/MISC/17, IWM Documents.

113 Cooper Diary, 15–16 April 1915, P.121, IWM Documents.

114 Cossins Diary, 14 October 1915, 15 October 1915, PP/MCR/371, IWM Documents.

115 Clark Diary, 1 April 1916, Ms Eng. Hist. e.123, Bodleian Special Collections.

See also 2 April 1916, 3 April 1916.

116 Cooper Diary, 16 June 1917, P.121, IWM Documents.

117 Toomey was four at the outbreak of war. His father was an 'Army schoolmaster – a warrant officer teaching at the Duke of York's Royal Military School near Dover Castle'. His mother taught the younger children. D. Toomey, 'Recollections of the 1914–1918 War', not dated, DF148, Liddle Collection. Not everyone approved of the practice of collecting 'souvenirs'. Emma Cusson's mother had been hurt in an earlier bombardment, and told her husband that she did not want him to keep the piece of aluminium he had collected: 'I don't want it in my house, it smells of death. If you want a souvenir, look at my scars'. Quoted in R. Van Emden and S. Humphries, *All Quiet on the Home Front: An Oral History of Life in Britain during the First World War* (Headline, London, 2003), p. 170.

118 Clark Diary, 24 September 1916, Ms Eng. Hist. e.135, Bodleian Special Collections.

119 *Ibid.*, 3 October 1916, Ms Eng. Hist. e.136. This was presumably the secretary of the YMCA canteen set up in connection with the army camp in the grounds of Lyons Hall, the estate of the Great Leighs lord of the manor, J. Herbert Tritton. Mrs Leslie Tritton was his daughter-in-law. Munson (ed.), *Echoes of the Great War*, pp. xviii–xix. See also Clark Diary, 25 September 1916, Ms Eng. Hist. e.135, Bodleian Special Collections.

120 Robinson, 'Diary of the Great War', 25 September 1916, vol. 2, P.401, IWM Documents.

121 Cooper Diary, 19 June 1917, P.121, IWM Documents.

122 Robinson, 'Diary of the Great War', 27 September 1916, vol. 2, P.401, IWM Documents.

123 G. Hyam interview, 9567, reel 2, Department of Sound, Imperial War Museum (hereafter IWM Sound), London. There were instances when 'sightseeing' could turn into seeing too much. See, for example, the experiences of children who witnessed corpses being taken away from the scene of an explosion near Nottingham, in Van Emden and Humphries, *All Quiet on the Home Front*, pp. 260–1. As a *Times* journalist, in September 1916 Michael MacDonagh was allowed to see the corpses of the airmen killed near Billericay. 'The frightfully disfigured bodies … huddled together … smelling foully', proved a disturbing sight. MacDonagh, *In London during the War*, p. 133.

124 Robinson, 'Diary of the Great War', 27 September 1916, vol. 2, P.401, IWM Documents.

125 Clark Diary, 17 February 1918, Ms Eng. Hist. e.160, Bodleian Special Collections.

126 Cossins Diary, 21 November 1915, PP/MCR/371, IWM Documents.

127 Gibbs Diary, 31 May 1915, Ms Eng. misc. c.167, Bodleian Special Collections.

128 *Ibid.*, 1 November 1914, Ms Eng. misc. c.161.
129 *Ibid.*, 30 December 1915, Ms Eng. misc. c.173.
130 *Ibid.*, 1 January 1917, Ms Eng. misc. c.185. See also 12 May 1917, 20 May 1917, Ms Eng. misc. c.189.
131 *Ibid.*, 23 November 1916, Ms Eng. misc. c.183. William Tinniswood, Holmdale's headmaster, was one of Gibbs's regular interlocutors and sparring partners.
132 *Ibid.*, 10 May 1915, Ms Eng. misc. c.167.
133 H. G. Wells, *Mr Britling Sees it Through* (The Hogarth Press, London, 1985, first published 1916), p. 208.
134 Robinson, 'Diary of the Great War', 12 March 1915, vol. 1, P.401, IWM Documents.
135 *Ibid.*, 5 September 1917, vol. 3, P.402.
136 Cossins Diary, 28 February 1916, PP/MCR/371, IWM Documents. See also Gibbs Diary, 31 January 1917, Ms Eng. misc. c.185, Bodleian Special Collections.
137 Robinson, 'Diary of the Great War', 14 January 1915, vol. 1, P.401, IWM Documents.
138 Gibbs Diary, 3 May 1916, Ms Eng. misc. c.177, Bodleian Special Collections.

2

The war on the home front, *c.* 1915–18

Introduction

In mid-1915 many civilian men began to notice that the conflict was intruding in their lives in new and often unexpected ways: paradoxically, just as the feverish interest in war news of the early months was starting to fade, the conflict became increasingly difficult to ignore. In January 1918 Frederick Robinson noted the war's combination of grim monotony and ubiquity: 'we go from day to day, from week to week, from month to month, with the same old inactivity both on land and sea … the country is getting tired out, people no longer talk of the war, they are saturated with it, they live with it, they sleep with it, it enters into their every thought and action, it is part of their flesh and of their bone … When are we again to live proper lives?'[1] The war, Arthur Marwick suggests, was changing lives on the home front in important ways, and 'as 1916 passed away the community began to savour more sharply the realities of modern total war'.[2]

It is some of the most significant changes to the 'everyday' lives of middle-class men that are explored here. The chapter begins by suggesting that by the end of 1915 the relationship between civilians and soldiers had become unprecedentedly close. On the one hand, middle-class men were increasingly likely to have relatives or friends in the armed forces, giving them a newly personal stake in events on the battle fronts. On the other, men in uniform were becoming a ubiquitous presence on the home front: a pleasing and profitable presence for some, a destructive and inconvenient one for others. The chapter then assesses the rather more dramatic impact on civilian lives of enemy air-raids, before turning to the regulatory and financial demands made by the wartime state on its citizens. Demands which, many middle-class civilians complained with increasing frequency and bitterness, weighed more heavily on their shoulders than on those of any other section of society.

Civilians and soldiers

By the second year of war, most civilians could claim a newly personal interest in the fortunes of the armed forces. Of course, not everybody had a close relative – a father, son, husband or brother – in uniform. Of the men who feature prominently in this book, for example, only Robert Saunders and Holcombe Ingleby were in this position. Saunders had three sons in the armed forces, including one serving in the Infantry, while Ingleby's only son was in the Royal Naval Volunteer Reserve, later transferring to the Royal Flying Corps.[3] That said, most people had at least a friend, colleague, acquaintance or relative on active service; diaries and letters were peppered with references to such individuals. In March 1917 Joe Hollister wrote to his father that they had recently received 'a line from Bert', with the news that he had been transferred to a new ship:

> a fine ship, clean, plenty of room, and no beastly coaling … I am very glad for I think it a scandal that youngsters of 16 or 17 should be expected to coal-ship … have you heard anything of Dick since you wrote last? My understudy at the office died of pneumonia in France in January after serving in the HAC for a year and eight months without having been up to the fighting line, yet you hear of others being out and killed four months after joining up.[4]

In a small community such as the village of Great Leighs, news of local men spread fast: few were complete strangers. In September 1914 Andrew Clark heard that Joseph Rogers, a private in the Essex Regiment, had been reported as missing. A few days later he met Joseph's father, James Rogers, who told him they had not yet received official confirmation of his (only) son's fate.[5] It was not until mid-October that they heard that he was a prisoner of war in Germany, where he remained until the end of the conflict.[6] Towards the end of September 1914 news of the first deaths began to reach the village. On 25 September Clark heard that Dick Fitch, the son of a Great Leighs agricultural labourer, had died.[7] Such losses were very different from the distant, anonymous reports of newspaper casualty lists: three weeks after Dick's death, his mother Sophia came to see him 'to have their application signed for the effects of their son … killed in action … a lad of just 19, and enlisted so recently as a year ago last June'.[8] In January 1915 Clark noted in his diary that Mrs

Fitch had called once again, this time 'with the papers to claim the effects of her son Arthur Fitch, who went down … in the Formidable … Richard [Dick] Fitch, another son, was a Tommy and killed. Two other sons are at the front'.[9] Clark did not describe his feelings on hearing of these or other deaths. However, his diaries do provide some clues about his state of mind. In June 1915, when he received a request that he should resume the practice of putting up 'in the Church porch a list of those men of this parish who were serving … I said, for myself, no! It had been so painful removing the names of those who were killed that I could not force myself to do it again'.[10]

Harold Cossins was similarly unable to describe the shock and grief he experienced at the death of his brother-in-law Mervyn. In December 1915 he wrote that 'our minds are filled today with the dreadful news in a letter from Auntie that Mervyn has been killed in Flanders a week ago today. We can none of us realise it and it seems to have numbed our senses'. He found it difficult to believe that 'it was only on the previous Wednesday that [Mervyn] … had looked in at the office, the essence of cheerful confidence. The last I saw of him was when he waved at me from the District train'. Unable 'to think or write', he copied instead 'some extract from the letter in which Capt Mayhew sent the news to Auntie'.[11] Having received further details of Mervyn's death the following day, he decided 'to give plain facts and shall not attempt to describe feelings and emotions. I could not do it'.[12]

The death of young (and not so young) men was a regular wartime occurrence. By 1915, the deaths of colleagues, friends or relations at the front were regularly mentioned in letters and diaries. In May 1915 Robinson recorded 'another tragedy … in our circle of friends – Joey Farrar whom we have known since he was born was killed in action on Sunday'.[13] Reginald Gibbs noted a number of casualties among his ex-pupils. In April 1917 he heard 'that two more old pupils had been killed. It seems only yesterday they were here. One was Storey … a very nice fellow – very keen on dogs. The other was Bishop who used to be always making fun … I remember … [him] joking and saying "I don't know how I shall bayonet a man. I think I shall prick him with it first and see what he does"'.[14] In the autumn of 1915 Horace Joseph lost two colleagues in quick succession. The death of Arthur Heath, whose gentleness and 'spiritual quality' he had found particularly endearing, he felt 'a real bereavement'.[15] According to Robert Saunders, writing in October 1917, few weeks went past 'without some sad tale [of acquaintances being killed] that makes you curse all the war makers'.[16] For the Saunders family, news of deaths among their circle of friends and relatives brought additional worries about the fate of their own sons in the armed forces: 'shan't we appreciate the peace when it comes and be able to go to bed without worrying about the boys'.[17] Ron, who had enlisted in the Infantry and was soon posted to the Western Front, was a particular source of concern. In October 1915 the 'terrible lists of casualties' made them especially anxious. Hearing of others, 'you can't help feeling, sometimes that Ron's turn may come as well as others'.[18]

News that a friend, an acquaintance or a relative had been killed, wounded, taken prisoner or was 'missing', brought into sharp relief the extent to which civilians had acquired a newly personal 'stake' in the fate of the British Expeditionary Force. That said, the rapidly expanding armed forces also had a rather more mundane impact on the lives of civilian men (and, of course, women). In mid-August 1914 Joseph noted on his way to Somerset that 'here and there are some men in khaki, but not in greater numbers than often are seen in August'.[19] However, men in uniform were soon to become a much more visible and public presence on the home front. A few days before Joseph set off on his holiday to Somerset, James Butlin wrote to his friend Basil Burnett Hall that 'the war has affected Weymouth very much. The whole place is teeming with soldiers who are billeted in most private houses'.[20] In November 1914 Clark noted that the streets of Braintree were full of servicemen 'strolling up and down or standing in groups … Outside the Wheatsheaf a barrel organ was playing, a great group of Tommies standing about, a few couples of them dancing in the street'.[21] In May 1915 Saunders was struck by the extent to which London had altered since his last visit: 'Everywhere you go you see soldiers in uniform, and it is interesting to look at the badges and try to realize [*sic*] how many different regiments there must be'.[22] Two months earlier Cossins and his wife had spent a Saturday together in London, 'and we both agreed that there was an exceptional number of officers and men in khaki about'.[23]

By 1915, men in uniform had become an ubiquitous presence in most public spaces on the home front: on the street, in shops, parks, restaurants and other places devoted to sport, leisure and entertainment, as well as on trains, buses and other means of transport. They included not only fit and able-bodied men, but also war casualties: sick, wounded or disabled men. In September 1917, for example, Joseph went on a cycling holiday in the West Country: 'there were not many places where war was outwardly in evidence, except for [the] wounded, whom one saw frequently, and men in khaki'.[24] Ana Carden-Coyne suggests that the sight of disabled soldiers became a wartime 'spectacle', part of a 'pleasure culture' of war. She points out that visitors to military hospitals 'revealed an appetite for tales of wounding and overcoming, suggesting that, far from horrifying, the wounded body and the military hospital were theatrical sites'.[25] Gilbert Hyam would have agreed. Years after the end of the war, he recalled that no attempt had been made to 'hide' the wounded transported out of Charing Cross and placed into ambulances. As a young boy, he had found the sight 'pretty disturbing'. Others, however, were not so sensitive. According to Hyam, 'everybody loves a spectacle like that. Human nature. As long as they are not part of it'.[26]

There certainly is much evidence of civilians' mingled feelings of sympathy and curiosity towards wounded and maimed servicemen. In December 1914 Macleod Yearsley visited the No 1 Stationary Hospital (Territorial) at Camberwell. As he surveyed 'the poor shattered remnants that were among the five hundred in the hospital', his reaction was not that of a detached medical observer. 'In my diary that night I wrote: "If ever the country forgets them, may she be cursed"'.[27] In October 1914 Clark was told by a Colonel Egerton, of Chatham Hall, that 'the feature of Newmarket this year was the presence of batches of wounded soldiers from the Cambridge Hospital', who had been admitted to the stands for free. According to Egerton, 'there was great rivalry to provide them with smokes. Their talk was a lot more amusing than the actual racing'.[28] Casualties with psychological problems may not have been as immediately visible to civilians, but their fate was a source of discussion and worry too. In September 1915 the head-gardener of a local asylum told Cossins that they had 'two hundred cases of soldiers suffering from mental trouble and war shock there and that the whole of the accommodation of the asylum (two thousand patients) might have to be handed over to the military authorities for this purpose'.[29] A year later Clark heard from the wife of the rector of Fairsted, who had visited her son in a London hospital, that the bed next to him was occupied by a man with 'shell-shock'. She told Clark that 'his eyes were very strange, and he kept moaning all the time'.[30]

The sight of wounded and mentally disturbed servicemen attracted not only prurient curiosity, but also anger and sympathy, while uniformed men as a whole were treated with a new admiration and respect. Soldiers, including rank-and-file troops, could not longer be dismissed as 'dissolute ne'er-do-well[s]': they now represented the very epitome of manly patriotism.[31] Their 'suffering', according to Adrian Gregory, 'stood at the very centre of wartime values'.[32] Nevertheless, abstract ideas of gallant officers and brave, cheerful Tommies did not always prepare civilians for the realities of servicemen's actual – and often troublesome – physical presence on the home front. Unsurprisingly, there were ambivalent reactions to the growing number of soldiers who needed accommodation before being posted overseas, particularly when such soldiers intruded into the private sphere of the home.[33] Shortages of barracks accommodation meant that in the winter of 1914–15 approximately 800,000 soldiers had to be billeted with civilians, 'bringing the nation face to face with its army to an unprecedented degree'.[34]

Towards the end of September 1914 Clark noted that a number of Berkshire Territorials had just marched from Chelmsford to new quarters in nearby Broomfield and Little Waltham.[35] Reactions varied. In November 1914 Clark was told that the soldiers billeted in Bocking were 'very gentlemanly fellows and give no trouble'.[36] Over a year later, Chelmsford people declared themselves 'very pleased with the "Scotties". Instead of doing nothing, like the previous troops, they turned out and swept the snow off the streets'.[37] The financial benefits of having a large body of young men stationed in a town or village could be considerable. In December 1914 it was calculated that 'expenditure on account of the troops in Chelmsford, in the Chelmsford shops, is quite £1,000 a day'.[38] Two months earlier, Cossins had observed that the decision to station two thousand Territorials in Minehead would 'offer much needed employment to many who are out of work in the neighbourhood owing to the cessation of hunting and also to the closing down of the brickworks'.[39] In March 1915 the 22nd Londons left St Albans, after being stationed there for some time. According to Cossins, they would be 'missed by many, some by their girls, others by the women of the houses where they have been billeted who have mothered them and incidentally had the most prosperous period of their career owing to the billet money and that which the troops have spent'.[40]

However, experiences of living in close contact with troops were not always so positive. While the Berkshires stationed in Little Waltham in October 1914 had 'behaved themselves in an exemplary manner',[41] a few miles away in Chelmsford, the Warwickshires were said to 'have behaved themselves in a most disgraceful manner. Men, *and officers*, have been seen, drunk night after night'.[42] While it was acknowledged that many of 'the men of the new army are gentlemanly fellows … [and expect] gentlemanly treatment',[43] it was also noted that this was not the case with all recruits. According to James Caldwell, the men quartered at Little Waltham in December 1914 'are a nasty set. They are carters and carmen and dockhands (from Bristol and Avonmouth), who held a beano for Christmas after their own fashion. They generally return drunk to their quarters in the drill hall'.[44] There were bitter complaints not only about drunkenness and rough behaviour, but also slovenliness and carelessness towards private property. In Broomfield 'things are smashed about anyhow. Windows in commandeered houses are broken … Gates are torn off their hinges and thrown aside. Side-roads and yards are littered disgracefully'.[45] In Chelmsford, many 'householders' complained about the behaviour of the officers quartered with them, who would, for example, tear 'carpets by unnecessary roughness such as no one would use in a house of his own', and then responded with 'sulky, or even uncivil, looks and language when it was suggested that more care might be taken'.[46]

In Southwold, Ernest Cooper's experiences of dealing with the troops billeted in the town were overwhelmingly negative. In October 1914 he had arranged for a detachment of Lincolnshire Yeomanry to make use of a section of the Common, 'where they made a most horrible mess, damaged the fence, gave my men a lot of trouble and then refused to pay the modest sum of 10/- asked for water and accommodation of forty-four horses for two nights'.[47] Five months later, almost seven hundred men of the 2/6th Battalion Royal Sussex Cyclists 'were billeted in empty houses', where 'they caused us a lot of trouble by overcrowding the houses, damaging property and hatching infectious diseases'.[48] In October 1918 he noted that the Quartering Committee had taken over a new building 'for use as an officers' mess, it is a great shame they do this as the late mess, Southwold House, was so badly treated by other officers that the owners will not let it again, so they take a fresh house and proceed to damage that'.[49] As Town Clerk, Cooper was forced to deal with the military's destructiveness, high-handed behaviour and 'shuffling over payment'.[50] He and his family also suffered more personal inconvenience. For about three months during the spring and summer of 1915 they had a troop of Sussex men billeted near their house. This meant the presence of 'a sentry outside our house day and night and after ten everyone was challenged, hands up and who goes there, so there was not much peace with night alarms and football on the Green by day. One day the football came through our window and covered the room with glass'.[51] A year later, he found four 'West Riding Tommies' spending the weekend on his yacht, moored in a quiet creek. 'They had made her in a beastly state', but he had to admit that 'it was rather amusing as we rowed up quietly and I jumped on board and looked down the skylight giving them quite a shock'.[52]

Bombardments and air raids

In May 1918 Saunders observed in a letter to his son that 'we can't get away from the war even on the most peaceful day, Aeroplanes or Airships passing over, distant guns rumbling, or the nearer practice of Bombs, Mines and Machine Guns at Maresfield'.[53] According to Ingleby, writing to his son in June 1916, the Norfolk village of 'Sedgeford is now alive with aeroplanes, and their incessant droning does not add to the peace and comfort of what was once a pleasant home'.[54] By then, the noise associated with war had become an everyday presence in many parts of the home front. So much so that 13 September 1916 was noted by Clark as 'quite singular, for the total absence of rifle- or cannon-shooting. No rifles at Witham, Terling or Boreham butts. No cannon at Shoeburyness or Southchurch or Danbury'.[55] Such noise could come as quite a shock to those unused to it. Having just moved to Crowborough, Sussex, in May 1916, the Cossins were suddenly woken up in the night by loud explosions. They eventually found out that the noise had been caused by bomb practice at a nearby military camp: 'the noise was very loud in the still air and I cannot imagine what real firing must be like'.[56] Especially during the summer months, echoes of explosions on the battle fronts could be heard on the south and south-east coasts. According to Cooper, during the last week of August 1915 'there were some hot still breathless nights [on the Norfolk coast] and I distinctly heard the big guns booming away in Belgium'.[57] On 1 July 1916 Cossins, at the time still living in Sussex, recorded in his diary that 'our offensive has begun. We have been hearing the guns almost incessantly, and they seemed to be firing all last night'.[58] For the Saunders family, living in Fletching, Sussex, hearing the noise of the battle of the Somme was particularly distressing: 'since the big offensive started we hear the guns all day sometimes, and can't forget that Ron is there. And we are dreading the telegram that so many have received lately'.[59]

For many civilians, the noise of bomb and gun practice, of aeroplanes flying overhead, even of explosions on the Western Front, had by 1916 become part of everyday life. In September 1917, for example, Clark noted the 'commingled sounds of peace and war. Pleasant whirr of reaping-machines in the barley fields. Very loud explosions … in regular succession, only a few seconds between each. Probably bomb practice at Witham'.[60] Far more noteworthy – and alarming – than such wartime noises, were those associated with enemy air raids. In October 1915 St Albans experienced its first aerial incursion: the Zeppelin, which passed over the town without dropping any bombs, was audible, although not visible, and 'everyone has been very excited'.[61] That same night, Cooper was woken up by the sound of a Zeppelin flying down the coast. It had headed out to sea before reaching Southwold 'and with the greatest relief we heard the sound of the propellers die away at sea, in the morning we heard lurid rumours of the damage on London'.[62] In May 1918 the Robinsons had gone to bed 'with the sound of distant guns in our ears, knowing that an air-raid is in progress in London'.[63] There were occasions when (distant) air-raids could be enjoyed as a spectacle, rather than feared as a threat. In 1987 Frank Dawkins recalled that during air-raids in London, 'unless there was intense gunfire … we would hang about the streets and watch the bursting shrapnel'.[64] One evening in October 1917 groups of Great Leighs people 'stood … on the road, listening to the cannonade and watching the ceaseless ascent of star-shells (which was really a wonderful sight)'. The local policeman asked people to return indoors, given the danger of falling shrapnel, but 'they were not … to be denied the grand fireworks and pooh-poohed him'.[65]

It was not always possible to maintain such a position of detached spectatorship. The frightening nature of air-raids should not be underestimated, nor the extent to which civilians (including the great majority who never experienced them) felt under threat. Advertisements for services and commodities such as insurance against air-raid damage, fire-extinguishers, face masks and respirators, tonic wines and a variety of other restoratives for 'frayed nerves', provide an insight into the prevailing atmosphere of fear.[66] There was a widespread perception, furthermore, that worse was yet to come. In May 1915 Cossins wrote that 'it is felt that the spasmodic raids made hitherto have been trial trips and that the real thing when it comes will be very different and that gas bombs will be among those that will be dropped'.[67] Less than a month later, he 'invested in five respirators at cost of 1s 6d each, one for each member of our household'.[68]

Even when not threatened themselves, people were aware of the dangers to loved ones. In September 1917 Saunders complained of 'a trying week what with school and Air Raids three during the week. The guns are going again as I write … Of course we feel safe enough here but it is disquieting to know Win and her family may be in danger'.[69] At around the same time Robinson could also 'hear the guns defending London from the air-raiders, and we see numberless shells exploding over London although we are twenty miles in the country. It is an impressive spectacle'. While up until then the war had 'seemed so far off;

to have actual hostilities going on within earshot and within sight seems to bring it home as nothing hitherto has done'. He worried: 'shall we hear that friends, or perhaps relatives, have perished or been maimed?'[70] The noise and destructiveness of air-raids could also affect civilians rather more closely and directly. In August 1916 Gibbs had just gone to bed when he 'heard some fool, as I thought banging the front door … Suddenly I became aware of a series of flashes just like summer lightning'. He jumped out of bed and went to the window, where he 'saw flash after flash and something like a big red-hot spark fall out of the sky and I heard the deep boom boom boom of the guns at Dover, and the searchlights swept the sky'.[71]

Sixteen months earlier, Southwold had experienced its first aerial bombardment. The Coopers were woken up 'by a terrific explosion and immediately heard the loud whirring of the engines apparently over the West part of the town, very quickly another explosion occurred and shook the whole place'. They (Cooper, his wife, nurse and baby) took refuge in the dining room, with 'the horrid noise of the Zeppelin going on all the time and the soldiers running about'. Eventually Cooper, who was the captain of the Southwold Fire Brigade, 'dressed and went round to the Fire Station in case the engines should be wanted'. They all went to bed at around 2.30, when things had quietened down, and 'woke very tired'. It turned out that very little damage had been done, although the following morning the town's citizens were in a considerable state of agitation, with 'many rumours and tales … flying about'.[72]

Most middle-class civilian men were reluctant to admit that they were frightened for their own, rather than others' safety, but it is clear that many who witnessed air-raids first-hand were deeply shaken by the experience.[73] In April 1915 the Copeman family experienced a Zeppelin raid during a stay in Caister, Norfolk. Writing to his son Tom a few days later, Charles Copeman tried, not entirely successfully, to down-play the incident: 'I don't suppose any of us are any the worse for our experiences, what surprised me was how matter of fact it all was, the worst for the nerves were the Zeppelin bombs as you could not tell when the next was coming … The firing was terrific, I hardly noticed the shells, what struck me was the vicious quickness of the guns, hellish is the word without a doubt'.[74] In June 1917 Caldwell was caught up in a daylight Gotha air-raid on London. He later told Clark that the experience had been 'really very alarming. Major Caldwell thinks he is fairly cool but has to confess to a sort of indescribable discomfort at the time'. He added that 'one of the causes of unpleasantness was the anti-air craft gun high up on the tops of the roofs. These guns have a very sharp report and the shell comes out of them with the strange whizz'.[75] A year earlier, neither George Wilkinson nor his brother acknowledged feeling any fear when they realised that the nearby works were being attacked by Zeppelins. It was their sisters who got 'out of bed all in a panic'.[76] Fear – in middle-class men's accounts – was overwhelmingly the preserve of women. In March 1917 there was a Zeppelin scare in Fletching, Sussex, when firing was heard in the distance. Saunders wrote to his son: 'it seems odd to me I felt so much more nervy than I had done [during an earlier raid] in London, I suppose it was having Ma and the others here and seeing their terror'.[77]

In January 1917 the Cooper family was once again woken up by explosions, followed by gunfire and shelling: 'I told the Missis to hurry and get the baby down as the Germans were upon us'. The attack only lasted five minutes or so, and 'some of the papers called it a comic bombardment or silly raid … but to those who were in it there was nothing comic or silly but a very present danger'.[78] A few weeks later very heavy firing could be heard out at sea and according to Cooper, 'after the recent experience the women folk were very frightened'.[79] Cooper may have been unwilling to admit that he – and other men – had been frightened too, but it was an indication of his own anxiety that a few weeks later he 'had the cellar altered and an exit made out into the front garden so that in the event of another bombardment we could get down there safely without running so much risk of being buried alive'.[80] Middle-class men's accounts of air-raids thus stressed fears for their families', rather than their own safety. According to Yearsley, he only missed one training session with the Volunteer Training Corps: 'on whitsunday, May 19th, the last air-raid on London occurred. Being right in the midst of it, with a baby son born on May 5th, the dropping of a high-explosive bomb in the street behind my flat, I was so shaken that on whit Monday I remained at home'.[81]

Experience eventually enabled people to recognise periods of heightened air-raid danger: calm, windless and moonless nights. There were also other signs of peril, aside from official sirens or other announcements: by October 1916 the Cossins had learnt that a sudden drop in gas pressure meant an imminent Zeppelin attack.[82] Households in the worst affected areas developed routines that helped them cope. The Yearsleys, for example, found refuge in the corridor of their London flat, sitting with the maids, the cat and eventually their new-born baby, until the sound of the guns had died down. It was Macleod, in his role as the head of the household, who was responsible for checking regularly the progress of raids, leaving the flat to try to find out whether and when it was safe to return to bed.[83] That said, civilians may have developed knowledge and routines that enhanced (or, at least, were supposed to enhance) the chances of surviving unhurt, but air-raids remained sources of fear and uncertainty throughout the war, their deadliness experienced at first hand and in shocking ways by many unfortunate individuals. Yearsley's cousin, for example, was on his way to Folkestone station when he was caught up in a daytime Gotha raid in May 1917: 'he was obliged to pick his way among limbs and heads of men, women and horses. He passed one poor woman who had both arms and legs blown off, and she turned her head and looked at him'.[84]

Only a small proportion of the civilian population was forced to witness such scenes.[85] However, a consequence of air-raids did affect almost all on the home front: the imposition of lighting regulations.[86] In October 1914 the Great Leighs villagers were informed that no lamps were to be shown in shop windows, the streets were to be as darkly lit as possible, no lights were to show from the upper storeys of houses, and no lobby-lights were to be used.[87] At the end of January 1915, in the aftermath of an air-raid on Cromer and Yarmouth on the Norfolk coast, a more comprehensive lighting order was issued: no lights were to be visible from houses between 5p.m. to 7.30a.m. the following day. Special constables were to ensure compliance, visiting 'all places from which lights were shown' and refusing to 'depart till the lights were put out or effectively concealed'.[88] Unsurprisingly, 'several people in Leighs' proved 'most unreasonable about the no lights order … Mrs Louis Wright, e.g., refuses to darken her windows, on the plea that she is "not afraid of Zeppelins"'.[89] Eight months later attitudes had changed considerably. According to Clark, 'it was abundantly evident that the recent Zeppelin raids have done a great deal to obtain observance of orders as to obscuring lights'.[90]

The dangers and inconvenience of the 'unaccustomed darkness and gloom'[91] of streets and public places should not be underestimated. In October 1916 J. H. Tritton, the squire of Lyons Hall, Great Leighs, and a Barclays Bank director, was laid up with a broken knee-cap, caused by tripping over a pavement in a dimly lit London street.[92] A year earlier, Cossins had observed that lighting regulations made walking after sunset 'quite an exciting adventure'. Mabel, the Cossins's maid, went out to post some letters, became confused on the way back and tried to get into the wrong house.[93] A couple of days later, as he cycled home in St Albans, he almost ran over a number of people who preferred to walk on the road, rather than risk bumping into each other on the pavement.[94] In January 1916 Frank Lockwood noted that 'by a further order as to the restriction of lights Huddersfield has become darker than ever. The few lights that are lit tend to confuse, rather than help. It is a miserable place now, and it will be a wonder if accidents do not occur'.[95] By October 1916, according to Gibbs, 'the lights in Camberley have disappeared from the roads altogether ... the shopkeepers are also made to veil their lights more effectually than last year'. As a result, the main roads were 'in inky darkness. One slips off the kerb, bumps into people and collides with lamp-posts'. Ironically, given the 'modern' nature of industrialised warfare, 'it is like living in the time of King Alfred'.[96]

The lighting regulations could also bring inconvenience of a different nature, as middle-class households found themselves coming under unprecedented police scrutiny. In January 1915 the Robinsons received a visit from a police inspector, 'who came to give us orders that no lights in the house were to be visible from outside'.[97] A year later the Cossins were woken up at three in the morning by a policeman, who asked why 'we showed a light in our room contrary to the Defence of the Realm Act. It was a wild and stormy night, and as our stock of nightlights had run out, I pulled up the blinds to let in what light there was out of doors'. However, this had not been enough for his wife, who, 'being unable to sleep, lighted the candle by the bed', which had been visible from the street.[98] Five days later Cossins received 'a summons to appear at the Police Court on Wednesday next'.[99] He added no comment in his diary, but it is difficult to believe that he would have relished the experience. In any event, he 'was agreeably surprised ... to hear the prosecutor ... say that he didn't want to press the case as the light from our window was only a reflection from a candle. However, "as an offence had actually been committed", I had to pay costs, which amounted to 4s'.[100]

The regulatory and financial demands of war

Lighting regulations were only one example of unprecedented state intervention in middle-class men's (and, of course, other civilians') lives: the pressures and demands of the wartime economy meant that activities, services and commodities previously taken for granted were increasingly restricted, or even prohibited entirely.[101] Initially affecting primarily the working class,[102] regulations soon began to have an impact on the rest of society too. When limitations on the sale of alcohol were debated in spring 1915, for example, it was taken for granted that the problem to be addressed was that of working-class drunkenness and the attendant problems of industrial productivity. William Brown told Clark that 'he sincerely wished the government would prohibit sale of alcohol for, say, six months'. He did not believe that working men were especially 'fond of drinking, but that they had not resolution enough to stop. After six months, probably many of them would have formed a temperate habit'.[103] When the king announced that no alcohol would be consumed in any of his houses for the duration of the war, Cossins doubted 'whether the lower classes and workers will see fit to do likewise'.[104] Soon after, he noted that 'the drink question is much to the fore and all sorts of startling proposals are being made, such as the buying out of the breweries by the state'. He considered it unlikely 'that anything so drastic will be attempted and the strictest restrictions will no doubt only be imposed in the neighbourhood of large munitions works'.[105] He was proved right: in May it was announced that 'public houses etc. were to be taken under government control when in vicinity of munitions factories'.[106] By September, he noted, the areas affected by the regulations had seen figures for drunkenness reduced by half.[107]

Middle-class men did not remain unaffected by wartime restrictions for long: a variety of regulations soon began to impinge on their lives too. In October 1918 Cooper complained that 'people take advantage of the slackness of civil control in many ways … going down the yard near my office recently I was surprised to see two fat pigs in an outhouse within a few feet of Denny's workroom (a tailor) and not a hundred feet from the Market Place and I believe there are many similar cases about, imagine the fuss this would have caused in prewar days'.[108] However, most middle-class men were struck not by the slackness, but by the extent and stringency of regulations. As R. D. Blumenfeld put it in December 1915: 'You must not do this and you shall not do that are the edicts which gush from the pens of officialdom in every quarter'.[109] A year later Cossins noted the introduction of new limitations on London restaurant meals: a maximum of two courses were permitted, except between 6 and 8.30p.m., when three were allowed. Cossins, who worked in London, worried that 'perhaps … I shan't be able to have my bun if I have had two courses already'.[110] In May 1916 Clark was irritated by a last-minute circular from the Home Office, asking church incumbents to put church clocks forward on Saturday night or Sunday morning, in line with the new Summer Time Act. He complained that 'the parson is asked to change, without notice, the hour of service on Sunday morning so that he only may attend, and everyone else an hour late'.[111] The middle classes may have been relatively unaffected by the cancellation of cheap holiday train tickets in 1915, but the announcement in December 1916 that 'travelling facilities are to be severely cut down in the New Year', while fares were to increase sharply, was a source of worry, particularly for those men, such as Cossins and Robinson, who commuted to work.[112] Cossins anticipated that 'business trains' would become uncomfortably crowded, and on his first day back at work after the Christmas holidays noted that his train had been 'full to the last seat'.[113] In May 1918 Robinson complained that trains were getting ever more crowded and expensive: 'certainly there is nothing to induce people to travel for pleasure … moreover at most stations one has now to be one's own porter'[114] (Figure 3).

As the price of most consumer goods, including food, began to rise sharply in 1916, with some items becoming difficult or even impossible to obtain, price regulations and (eventually) rationing were gradually introduced. The impact of wartime restrictions on middle-class men's consumer and leisure habits will be considered more fully in Chapter 7, but it is worth noting here that certain regulations were felt to have a disproportionate (and unfair) impact on middle-class lifestyles. Petrol rationing, introduced in June 1916, was a good example. The Robinsons were among the small minority of the British population who owned their own motor-car, and received their petrol card in July. Having applied 'for the modest quantity of 25 gallons per month … about half the quantity we used before the war', they found that they had only been allotted 24 gallons for three months. In view of the need for petrol at the Front, Robinson wrote: 'one must try to be content – even if it *does* mean walking to the railway station occasionally'.[115] Fifteen months later further restrictions were announced on the use of private cars, to be driven only if absolutely necessary. Their use in travelling to and from golf links was prohibited: 'this will involve the doom of many links throughout the country, probably including the one to which the writer is a member'. More annoying was the fact that not everybody was sacrificing their pleasure to save petrol: 'one sees scores of cars on the roads driven by young men in khaki or naval blue out with their "best" girls … It is not surprising people are getting discontented and pessimistic'.[116]

Middle-class civilians did not accept restrictions unquestioningly. In August 1917 the usually measured Clark was exasperated by the prohibition of pictures in cigarette packets, complaining of 'the unspeakable fools who are government officials': 'if open imbecility could win a war' he wrote, 'we are on the sure road to victory'.[117] Of the men who feature in this book, Robinson was the most vocal in expressing his displeasure. In his view, most regulations and restrictions served little purpose, other than to cause hardship to a civilian population whose interests were

3 'How Biddlecombe spent his week's holiday', *The Bystander*, 19 June 1918. Reproduced with permission of the Bodleian Libraries, University of Oxford, Per.2705 d.161, p. 513.

largely disregarded by the authorities. In September 1916 he discovered that the Constitutional and the National Liberal Clubs had been requisitioned by the government, for use as offices. This would cause 'considerable inconvenience' to the members. 'The writer being a member of the former will suffer with the rest, but nothing seems to matter now-a-days'.[118] Three months later he complained that 'scarcely a day goes by, but what some additional burdens or restrictions are imposed. If these sacrifices would win the war, no one would object but we don't seem to get any "forrider"'.[119]

Most importantly, he noted in March 1917, restrictions were not accompanied by 'any abatement in the rates and taxes'.[120] In his opinion, this was at the heart of middle-class discontent: 'at one end the government deducts more and more from one's income, and at the other end it is constantly adding to the cost of living'.[121] Taxation, and particularly income tax, was felt to weigh especially heavily on the middle classes. In November 1914 Cossins noted that income tax had just doubled, while taxation on tea and beer had also increased. He believed that this was to be only 'the first means of collecting something towards the expense of the war which is expected to amount to £328,400,000'.[122] Robinson was unenthusiastic: 'the Income Tax payer is always the milch-cow. One is prepared to make sacrifices, but one is at liberty to doubt whether the course proposed is the best … However, the money has to be found … and those who do not fight must do it'.[123] Just under a year later, Tritton feared that that 'the budget will be no pleasant reading'. Income tax was likely to be increased, 'but this will be to kill the goose that lays the golden eggs, because income-tax payers must protect themselves a. by stopping subscriptions. b. by ceasing to use excisable commodities'.[124]

After a new parliamentary vote of credit in February 1916, Cossins observed that 'it doesn't do to think of what enormous National Debt we shall have. I don't see how we shall be able to do without some sort of Customs tariff; poor income tax payers cannot be squeezed much more'.[125] When, two months later, the Chancellor of the Exchequer announced new increases, he complained: 'I don't think there will be any incomes left soon to tax'.[126] Robinson tried to be philosophical: 'it is after all better for the British government to take one third or one fourth of one's income for a year or two than for the Germans to come and take the lot'.[127] In the course of the following two years, however, his tone became increasingly angry. He stressed the government's wasteful spending: 'millions', he believed, were being 'chucked in the gutter' by the Ministry of Munitions, 'altogether a disgusting state of things from the tax-payer's point of view'.[128] The people who suffered most, he believed, were those on 'fixed incomes': not only were their salaries not rising to match the increasing price inflation, but they were also being asked to pay ever higher taxes.[129] The 'luxury tax' introduced in August 1918 was the last straw: 'of all the egregious folly and nonsense surely this is the limit. Practically everything that makes life worth living is to be subject to the tax collector's rapacious maw'.[130]

Taxation and price inflation, furthermore, were not the only pressures on middle-class purses. For many, the war also brought a noticeable increase in requests for charitable donations, particularly (but by no means exclusively) from war-related charities.[131] Falconer Madan, the Bodleian librarian, preserved many of the seemingly endless stream of appeals that he received during the war. In December 1917, for example, these included requests for donations to Charing Cross Hospital, to the *Weekly Dispatch* Tobacco Fund and Christmas Table Collection (for 'our brave fighting men'), the Local War Museums Association, the Bible Study League (including their 'khaki bibles'), Sir Arthur Pearson's Christmas Appeal for the Children of Blinded Soldiers, Dr Barnardo's Homes and Lord Roberts Memorial Workshops for Disabled Soldiers and Sailors.[132] In September 1914 Joseph 'sent my field-glasses to Lord Roberts and a blanket to [illegible] and pyjamas and socks to the Red Cross',[133] but it was impossible for even the most generous individuals to respond to every request for donations they received.

Complaints soon began to be voiced about the unreasonable frequency of war-related fund-raising appeals, as well as about the way in which these often diverted funds away from local charities.[134] In September 1914 a collector for the League of Mercy called on Clark: 'this is the charity, for which various people, repeating the inconsiderate chatterings of London "society" ladies, have said that the villagers should *double* their subscription, and have shown the way to do so by cutting down to one half their every subscription to their local and county charities – including Chelmsford Hospital'.[135] The following day, the post brought him 'two requests for money collecting! – (i) The Church Army (ii) the bishop of the Diocese. Does it ever dawn on the thoughts of outsiders that country parishes are doing their utmost to help, along their own lines?'[136] A month later he received 'a bulky envelope of circulars' from the Prince of Wales Fund. 'The fussiness[?] of these London official beggar-letter writers has no bounds either of shame or of likelihood of results. The parish has already been "circularised" and "re-circularised"'.[137] Such appeals continued to arrive throughout the war years. In November 1916 he was incensed by a proposal by the Archbishops of Canterbury and York, that the last Sunday in December should be a day of special prayer 'in connection with the war, and the collections given to the Red Cross'. He pointed out that:

> Collections in country parishes, at best of times, have always been barely sufficient for the most urgent needs such as firing, lighting, and cleaning … subscriptions to local hospitals and other charities … unavoidable repairs to Church … For two years they have been reduced … They are now possibly only 1/3rd of what they were before the war. Yet the high and mighty lords spiritual, being obviously without knowledge of conditions in poor agricultural parishes … assume that all … expenditure by the Churchwardens can be met quite easily.[138]

A further source of annoyance was the multiplication of 'flag days', during which (mostly female) volunteers sold small flags to be worn on a coat lapel, the money going towards a particular war charity. 14 July 1915, for example, was French flag day, flags being sold to raise funds for French hospitals and the Red Cross. According to Cossins, there seemed to be practically a flag day a week: 'the amount of money collected must be very great as everyone buys – but it is getting rather a nuisance'.[139] 18 November was 'Russian flag day, the last flag day of the year. A lot of money has no doubt been collected during the day but more people refuse now and I saw many without a flag in their lapel. The idea is getting overdone'.[140] On 8 November 1914 Joseph noted that 'Yesterday was "Belgium Day"'. As he had not left the grounds of the college, 'I missed being asked for a favour', adding that 'it's not a mode of collecting I like'.[141] By April 1917, according to Yearsley, people had become 'a little sick' of the 'innumerable' flag days: 'They appeared rather a waste of energy and a painful misdirection of effort, but they brought in a good deal of money'[142] (Figure 4).

From the summer of 1915, appeals to invest surplus cash in government war loan schemes were added to the continued calls for charitable donations.[143] Such appeals made clear that the purchase of war loans was a sound, long-term investment, offering excellent interest rates. Cossins was impressed by the 4½ per cent offered by the War Loan announced in June 1915: 'the whole thing is a great financial revolution and now that a British government security can be had to yield 4½ per cent everyone will be looking for higher rates on less well-secured stocks'.[144] A year later, he observed that 'investors certainly have some splendid opportunities nowadays – if they have any money to invest; I wish I had'.[145]

4 'Dodging the flag', *Punch*, 12 July 1916. Reproduced with permission of Punch Limited.

At the same time, while making much of their profitable nature, war loan advertisements also stressed that such investments were a patriotic duty. A National War Loan handbill in August 1915, for example, pointed out that 'this is one of the ways of helping our country in the War, and every little counts'.[146] Just under three years later, a leaflet advocating the purchase of War Savings Certificates stressed that 'some people scarcely realise even now that the Winning of the War depends as much upon the efforts of the people at home as it does upon the efforts of the men at the Front'.[147]

Such appeals were not always well received. In June 1915 Robinson noted that advertisements in the papers were 'literally begging people to subscribe to the new War Loan', claiming that 'the youth of the country has responded nobly, the working man is meeting the needs of the hour magnificently. Will you who have money do your share too … Your country needs that investment'. According to Robinson, 'the whole thing is in questionable taste, and can only be justified by necessity'.[148] Such appeals were even less welcome in 1917 and 1918, as the middle class felt under increasing financial pressure.[149] Robinson was relieved when the latest war loan scheme closed in February 1917, 'and with it the newspaper propaganda', adding that 'it was getting on one's nerves! … It is not pleasant to be told if you don't subscribe your last farthing, you are "not only unpatriotic, but a fool"'.[150] Seven months later he complained that the people who concocted war loans advertisements 'don't seem to appreciate that it is as much and more than many can do, to make both ends meet, what with reduced dividends … immensely increased cost of living … coupled with a 5/- income tax'.[151] Five months before the end of the war, he lamented that 'between the Tax Collector and the War Savings Committee the persons who have any money left are having a poor time'.[152]

Conclusion

A year after the outbreak of hostilities, just as many middle-class men were losing the initial, intense interest in the events of the war, the conflict began to impinge on their lives in new and generally unpleasant ways. By the end of 1915 men in the armed forces were no longer an amorphous group of anonymous and often suspect strangers; they were relatives, friends, acquaintances or colleagues. Servicemen were also increasingly ubiquitous, their presence on the home front frequently a source of pleasure and profit, and just as often a destructive, obstreperous nuisance. One's 'own' soldiers were one thing, their well-being a source of interest and concern. As Saunders pointed out in September 1915, attitudes towards soldiers had changed a great deal since the outbreak of war. No longer were they viewed as rough ne'er-do-wells. On the contrary, 'everyone tries to do all they can for them and as the majority of them are from decent homes, camp life was very hard for them, and those who had boys of their own naturally set the example in welcoming other peoples boys'.[153] However, real-life 'Tommies' in need of accommodation, provisions and entertainment, were not always quite so acceptable, particularly when they disrupted, damaged or otherwise impinged on the well-being of middle-class homes.

By 1915, furthermore, the war had also become an increasingly noisy presence on the home front: gun and bomb practice, aircraft flying overhead, as well as the more mundane noises associated with the presence of large troop numbers, all provided audible reminders of war. Quiet, peaceful days were worthy of note. In 1917, for example, Cooper spent a 'quiet and happy Christmas' with his family at Southbourne, away from the frequent air-raid alarms of their east coast home town. Southbourne was crowded and 'most provisions were scarce and very dear, but for that and some perfunctory Lighting Restrictions one would not know there was a war on. I saw a few Air and Sea Patrols … and some kharki [*sic*] … but never heard an alarm all the time, splendid'.[154] The danger and destructiveness of enemy air-raids also served to bring the war ever closer to home. Echoing many servicemen's determination to maintain a facade of stoicism in the face of danger, middle-class civilian men rarely admitted to feeling fear. Rather, they frequently took on the mantle of protectors of frightened 'womenfolk', although feelings of helplessness and vulnerability emerge all too clearly from the accounts of those middle-class men who witnessed aerial bombardments at first hand.

Of course, only a minority of civilians were ever caught up in an air-raid. Most, however, were affected by the growing regulatory and financial demands of the wartime state, including those that were a direct result of Zeppelin and other raids: most notably, lighting regulations. That said, it was the financial burden of the war that was felt to weigh most heavily on middle-class men, bringing them, it was feared, close to ruin. According to Robinson, by July 1915 it was 'very difficult to see how it *is* possible for the war to continue for a further two years – countries and individuals will all be bankrupt before then'.[155] Such burdens brought into sharp relief middle-class civilian men's reservations about the war effort. Faced on the one hand with regulations that – disturbingly – could bring middle-class households to the attention of the police and on the other, with the increasing demands made on their already stretched pockets by tax authorities, charitable organisations and war loan appeals, discontent grew with official 'waste' and inefficiency, as well as with what was seen as the unfair burden being placed on their shoulders.

Unsurprisingly, middle-class civilians' outlook became increasingly gloomy as the war dragged on. Writing in December 1917, Robinson noted that 'each Christmas is less joyous than the previous and the country seems to be settling down into a state approaching despondency. The outlook is not encouraging either as regards the military or the economic side'.[156] Few would have disagreed with this assessment of the situation at the end of 1917. Joseph observed on the last day of the year that 'so ends a sad and cheerless year: but no hopeful prospect for the next'.[157] Morale on the home front probably fell to its lowest point in late 1917 and early 1918. Even then, however, despair and an acknowledgement of the possibility of defeat were not acceptable responses to the deepening gloom. There were, of course, exceptions, such as the ever-pessimistic Gibbs, who on the first day of 1915 noted that 'peering ahead into the gloom I can see nothing but evil omens and portents of coming horrors'.[158] A much more common reaction was Robinson's, who, despite his frequent complaints, continued to stress the nation's determination and unity of purpose in the midst of adversity. In December 1917 he acknowledged the impact of setbacks and bad news, but emphasised that 'there is none who would draw back, everyone realises that this country has got to see the thing through to the end'.[159] It is this unity of purpose – and middle-class civilian men's role in fostering it – that will be the focus of the next chapter.

Notes

1 F. A. Robinson, 'Diary of the Great War', 1 January 1918, vol. 4, P.402, Department of Documents, Imperial War Museum (hereafter IWM Documents), London.

2 A. Marwick, *The Deluge: British Society and the First World War* (Palgrave Macmillan, Basingstoke, second edition, 2006, first published 1965), pp. 180. See also J. Williams, *The Home Fronts: Britain, France and Germany 1914–1918* (Constable, London, 1972), pp. 121–6.

3 All survived the war. Ingleby's and Saunders' relationship with their sons will be explored further in Chapter 8.

4 J. Hollister to 'dad', 19 March 1917, J. Hollister Letter, 1917, 98/10/1, IWM Documents.

5 A. Clark War Diary, 'Echoes of the 1914 War in an Essex Village' (hereafter Clark Diary), 24 September 1914, Ms Eng. Hist. e.89, Special Collections, Bodleian Library, University of Oxford (hereafter Bodleian Special Collections), Oxford.
6 *Ibid.*, 14 October 1914, Ms Eng. Hist. e.90.
7 *Ibid.*, 25 September 1914, Ms Eng. Hist. e.89.
8 *Ibid.*, 14 October 1914, Ms Eng. Hist. e.90.
9 *Ibid.*, 23 January 1915, Ms Eng. Hist. e.96. A third son was reported dead in July 1916. See 26 July 1916, Ms Eng. Hist. e.90. The Great Leighs 'Memorial Tablet' records four Fitches: Arthur, Dick, Archie and George Bennett, as well as fifteen other names. J. Munson (ed.), *Echoes of the Great War: The Diary of the Reverend Andrew Clark 1914–1919* (Oxford University Press, Oxford, 1985), p. 292.
10 Clark Diary, 4 June 1915, Ms Eng. Hist. e.104, Bodleian Special Collections.
11 H. C. Cossins Diary, 1914–18 (hereafter Cossins Diary), 27 December 1915, PP/MCR/371, IWM Documents.
12 *Ibid.*, 28 December 1915.
13 Robinson, 'Diary of the Great War', 2 May 1915, vol. 1, P.401, IWM Documents. See also 5 September 1916, vol. 2, P.401; 29 June 1917, vol. 3, P.402.
14 Diary of R. W. M. Gibbs, 1914–20 (hereafter Gibbs Diary), 26 April 1917, Ms Eng. misc. c.188, Bodleian Special Collections. See also 21 September 1914, 26 September 1914, Ms Eng. misc. c.159; 25 June 1915, Ms Eng. misc. c.168; 23 August 1916, Ms Eng. misc. c.180; 8 September 1916, Ms Eng. misc. c.181. Gibbs's school, Holmdale, prepared students for entry into Sandhurst: it can be assumed that a high proportion, if not all, eventually entered the army.
15 Wartime Diaries of H. W. B. Joseph 1914–18 (hereafter Joseph Diaries), 13 October 1915, Ms. Top. Oxon. e.288, Bodleian Special Collections. See also 15 September 1915. As Adrian Gregory points out, citing Cynthia Asquith's wartime diaries, 'not all losses were equal'. A. Gregory, *The Last Great War: British Society and the First World War* (Cambridge University Press, Cambridge, 2008), p. 124.
16 R. Saunders to son, 28 October 1917, R. Saunders, Letters to Son in Canada, 1914–18 (hereafter Saunders Letters), 79/15/1, IWM Documents. See also 13 September 1916.
17 *Ibid.*, 11 March 1917.
18 *Ibid.*, 17 October 1915.
19 Joseph Diaries, 14 August 1915, Ms. Top. Oxon. e.288, Bodleian Special Collections.
20 J. H. Butlin to B. Burnett Hall, 10 August 1914, Letters of Lieutenant James H. Butlin (hereafter Butlin Letters), 67/52/1, IWM Documents.
21 Clark Diary, 4 November 1914, Ms Eng. Hist. e.91, Bodleian Special Collections.

22 R. Saunders to son, 31 May 1915, Saunders Letters, 79/15/1, IWM Documents.

23 Cossins Diary, 27 March 1915, PP/MCR/371, IWM Documents. See also M. MacDonagh, *In London during the War: The Diary of a Journalist* (Eyre and Spottiswoode, London, 1935), pp. 57–8.

24 Joseph Diaries, 4 October 1917, Ms. Top. Oxon. e.288, Bodleian Special Collections. See also 8 November 1914. As Joanna Bourke points out, the wounded were especially visible in areas such as Brighton, where they were sent to convalesce. J. Bourke, *Dismembering the Male: Men's Bodies, Britain and the Great War* (Reaktion Books, London, 1996), p. 34. The treatment of disabled veterans is explored in D. Cohen, *The War Come Home: Disabled Veterans in Britain and Germany, 1914–1939* (University of California Press, Berkeley, CA, 2001), especially pp. 15–37.

25 A. Carden-Coyne, *Reconstructing the Body: Classicism, Modernism and the First World War* (Oxford University Press, Oxford, 2009), pp. 87–8.

26 G. Hyam interview, 9567, reel 2, Department of Sound, Imperial War Museum (hereafter IWM Sound), London.

27 M. Yearsley ('Eyewitness'), 'The Home Front, 1914–18', pp. 47–8, DS/MISC/17, IWM Documents. See also, for example, Cossins Diary, 16 August 1915, PP/MCR/371, IWM Documents.

28 Clark Diary, 16 October 1914, Ms Eng. Hist. e.90, Bodleian Special Collections. See also 25 August 1915, Ms Eng. Hist. e.109.

29 Cossins Diary, 26 September 1915, PP/MCR/371, IWM Documents. The term 'shell-shock' was coined in an article in *The Lancet* in February 1915. By 1918 Britain had six specialist hospitals for officers and thirteen for other ranks. G. Robb, *British Culture and the First World War* (Palgrave, Basingstoke, 2002), pp. 47, 203.

30 Clark Diary, 24 November 1916, Ms Eng. Hist. e.138, Bodleian Special Collections. Wartime attitudes towards shell shock and its treatment are considered, for example, in F. Reid, *Broken Men: Shell Shock, Treatment and Recovery in Britain, 1914–1930* (Continuum, London, 2010); P. Barham, *Forgotten Lunatics of the Great War* (Yale University Press, New Haven, CT, 2004); Bourke, *Dismembering the Male*, pp. 107–23.

31 D. French, *Military Identities: The Regimental System, the British Army and the British People, c.1870–2000* (Oxford University Press, Oxford, 2005), p. 253.

32 Gregory, *The Last Great War*, p. 135.

33 I. F. W. Beckett, 'The nation in arms, 1914–18', in I. F. W. Beckett and K. Simpson (eds), *A Nation in Arms: A Social History of the British Army in the First World War* (Manchester University Press, Manchester, 1985), pp. 18–19.

34 P. Simkins, 'Soldiers and civilians: billeting in Britain and France', in Beckett and Simpson (eds), *A Nation in Arms*, p. 171.

35 Clark Diary, 24 September 1914, Ms Eng. Hist. e.89, Bodleian Special Collections.
36 *Ibid.*, 1 November 1914, Ms Eng. Hist. e.91.
37 *Ibid.*, 25 February 1916, Ms Eng. Hist. e.121.
38 *Ibid.*, 8 December 1914, Ms Eng. Hist. e.92.
39 Cossins Diary, 17 October 1914, PP/MCR/371, IWM Documents.
40 *Ibid.*, 14 March 1915.
41 Clark Diary, 18 October 1914, Ms Eng. Hist. e.90, Bodleian Special Collections.
42 *Ibid.*, 16 October 1914.
43 *Ibid.*, 28 October 1914.
44 *Ibid.*, 29 December 1914, Ms Eng. Hist. e.95.
45 *Ibid.*, 17 January 1915, Ms Eng. Hist. e.96.
46 *Ibid.*, 10 July 1915, Ms Eng. Hist. e.107.
47 The Diary of Ernest R. Cooper, 'Nineteen Hundred and War Time', 28 July 1914 – 3 December 1918 (hereafter Cooper Diary), 31 October 1914, P.121, IWM Documents.
48 *Ibid.*, 13 March 1915.
49 *Ibid.*, 15 October 1918.
50 *Ibid.*, 25 November 1916.
51 *Ibid.*, 1 July 1915.
52 *Ibid.*, 6 August 1916.
53 R. Saunders to son, 12 May 1918, Saunders Letters, 79/15/1, IWM Documents.
54 Holcombe Ingleby to Clement, 3 June 1916, The First World War Letters of Holcombe Ingleby MP (hereafter Ingleby Letters), P.343, IWM Documents.
55 Clark Diary, 13 September 1916, Ms Eng. Hist. e.134, Bodleian Special Collections. But see also the newly quiet metropolitan streets, considered in E. Cronier, 'The street', in J. Winter and J.-L. Robert (eds), *Capital Cities at War: Paris, London, Berlin 1914–1919 Volume 2: A Cultural History* (Cambridge University Press, Cambridge, 2007), pp. 62–4.
56 Cossins Diary, 26 May 1916, PP/MCR/371, IWM Documents.
57 Cooper Diary, 9 August 1915, P.121, IWM Documents.
58 Cossins Diary, 1 July 1916, PP/MCR/371, IWM Documents.
59 R. Saunders to son, 16 July 1916, Saunders Letters, 79/15/1, IWM Documents. See also 29 July 1917.
60 Clark Diary, 6 September 1917, Ms Eng. Hist. e.153, Bodleian Special Collections.
61 Cossins Diary, 13 October 1915, PP/MCR/371, IWM Documents.
62 Cooper Diary, 13 October 1915, P.121, IWM Documents. The raid, 'the most severe … of the middle period of the war', affected large tracts of south-east England and caused 199 casualties. Marwick, *The Deluge*, p. 177.

63 Robinson, 'Diary of the Great War', 19 May 1918, vol. 4, P.402, IWM Documents.
64 F. Dawkins to P. Liddle, 16 March 1986, DF148, Liddle Collection (1914–18), Special Collections, Brotherton Library, Leeds University (hereafter Liddle Collection), Leeds.
65 Clark Diary, 1 October 1917, Ms Eng. Hist. e.154, Bodleian Special Collections. See also 24 September 1917.
66 'Notices of air-raids and matters arising out of air-raids', in A. Clark, 'Scrapbooks of leaflets, newspaper cuttings etc., illustrating aspects of the Great War', Bodleian Library, University of Oxford, Oxford.
67 Cossins Diary, 22 May 1915, PP/MCR/371, IWM Documents.
68 *Ibid.*, 16 June 1915.
69 R. Saunders to son, 30 September 1917, Saunders Letters, 79/15/1, IWM Documents. Win was one of Saunders's daughters.
70 Robinson, 'Diary of the Great War', 29 September 1917, vol. 3, P.402, IWM Documents. See also 28 May 1917.
71 Gibbs Diary, 3 August 1916, Ms Eng. misc. c.180, Bodleian Special Collections. For personal experiences of naval and aerial bombardments, see also R. Van Emden and S. Humphries, *All Quiet on the Home Front: An Oral History of Life in Britain during the First World War* (Headline, London, 2003), Chapters 2 and 6.
72 Cooper Diary, 15–16 April 1915, P.121, IWM Documents.
73 Ex-servicemen's reflections on the nature of fear and combat are explored in M. Roper, 'Between manliness and masculinity: the "war generation" and the psychology of fear in Britain, 1914–1950', *Journal of British Studies*, vol. 44, no. 2 (2005), pp. 343–62.
74 C. Copeman to T. Copeman, 30 April 1916 [the letter mistakenly gives the date as 1915], Letters to Tom Copeman from Family Members, 1916, MC81/26/405–8, Norfolk Record Office, Norwich. An account of aerial and naval bombardments in Norfolk can be found in F. Meeres, *Norfolk in the First World War* (Phillimore, Chichester, 2004), Chapter 4.
75 Clark Diary, 16 June 1917, Ms Eng. Hist. e.149, Bodleian Special Collections. The raid on 13 June 1917 was the deadliest of the war: 162 were killed and 432 injured. Marwick, *The Deluge*, p. 237.
76 G. D. Wilkinson interview, 9104, reel 2, IWM Sound.
77 R. Saunders to son, 25 March 1917, Saunders Letters, 79/15/1, IWM Documents.
78 Cooper Diary, 25 January 1917, P.121, IWM Documents.
79 *Ibid.*, 16 February 1917.
80 *Ibid.*, 3 May 1917.
81 Yearsley 'The Home Front', p. 95, DS/MISC/17, IWM Documents.
82 Cossins Diary, 2 October 1916, PP/MCR/371, IWM Documents.
83 Yearsley 'The Home Front', pp. 122–3, DS/MISC/17, IWM Documents.

84 *Ibid.*, p. 221. The raid left seventy-one dead, including twenty-five children. Van Emden and Humphries, *All Quiet on the Home Front*, p. 177. See also pp. 174–6.

85 According to Marwick, in the course of the war there were fifty-one Zeppelin and fifty-seven aeroplane raids, resulting in 5,611 civilian casualties, of whom 1,570 were killed. Marwick, *The Deluge*, p. 238. Jay Winter suggests a lower estimate of 1,266 civilians killed by air and sea bombardments. J. M. Winter, *The Great War and the British People* (Palgrave Macmillan, Basingstoke, 2003, first published 1985), p. 71.

86 Lighting restrictions were imposed as part of the Defence of the Realm Act (DORA), emergency legislation first introduced in August 1914 and then constantly updated and added to in the course of the war. Marwick, *The Deluge*, pp. 76–7.

87 Clark Diary, 17 October 1914, Ms Eng. Hist. e.90, Bodleian Special Collections.

88 *Ibid.*, 28 January 1915, Ms Eng. Hist. e.97. See also Cooper Diary, January 1915, P.121, IWM Documents.

89 Clark Diary, 30 January 1915, Ms Eng. Hist. e.97, Bodleian Special Collections. The order was withdrawn two days later. See *ibid.*, 1 February 1915.

90 *Ibid.*, 4 September 1915, Ms Eng. Hist. e.110. Nevertheless, there continued to be complaints about infringements of the lighting regulations. See, for example, 31 January 1916, Ms Eng. Hist. e.119.

91 Yearsley, 'The Home Front', p. 28, DS/MISC/17, IWM Documents. MacDonagh, *In London during the War*, pp. 46–7.

92 Clark Diary, 1 October 1916, Ms Eng. Hist. e.135, Bodleian Special Collections.

93 Cossins Diary, 5 October 1915, PP/MCR/371, IWM Documents.

94 *Ibid.*, 8 October 1915.

95 F. T. Lockwood, 'Notes Written by F. T. Lockwood', 24 January 1916, 96/52/1, IWM Documents.

96 Gibbs Diary, 18 October 1916, Ms Eng. misc. c.182, Bodleian Special Collections.

97 Robinson, 'Diary of the Great War', 26 January 1915, vol. 1, P.401, IWM Documents.

98 Cossins Diary, 4 February 1916, PP/MCR/371, IWM Documents.

99 *Ibid.*, 9 February 1916.

100 *Ibid.*, 16 February 1916

101 Changes to middle-class men's consumer and leisure activities will be considered further in Chapter 7.

102 B. Waites, 'The government of the home front and the "moral economy" of the working class', in P. H. Liddle (ed.), *Home Fires and Foreign Fields: British Social and Military Experience in the First World War* (Brassey's, London, 1985), pp. 175–93.

103 Clark Diary, 5 April 1915, Ms Eng. Hist. e.101, Bodleian Special Collections.
104 Cossins Diary, 6 April 1915, PP/MCR/371, IWM Documents.
105 *Ibid.*, 16 April 1915.
106 *Ibid.*, 7 May 1915.
107 *Ibid.*, 25 September 1915. For a (not entirely dispassionate) account of the introduction of liquor regulations see Marwick, *The Deluge*, pp. 102–8.
108 Cooper Diary, 20 October 1918, P.121, IWM Documents.
109 R. D. Blumenfeld, *All in a Lifetime* (Ernest Benn, London, 1931), p. 43.
110 Cossins Diary, 6 December 1916, 17 December 1916, PP/MCR/371, IWM Documents. See also 20 December 1916.
111 Clark received the circular on 18 May 1916, the Summer Time Act 1916 coming into effect on 21 May: clocks were to be moved forward an hour. Clark Diary, 18 May 1916, Ms Eng. Hist. e.126, Bodleian Special Collections.
112 Cossins Diary, 8 December 1916, PP/MCR/371, IWM Documents. See also Robinson, 'Diary of the Great War', 9 December 1916, 21 December 1916, vol. 2, P.401, IWM Documents.
113 Cossins Diary, 29 December 1916, 1 January 1917, PP/MCR/371, IWM Documents.
114 Robinson, 'Diary of the Great War', 9 May 1918, vol. 4, P.402, IWM Documents.
115 *Ibid.*, 31 July 1916, vol. 2, P.401.
116 *Ibid.*, 15 October 1917, vol. 3, P.402.
117 Clark Diary, 14 August 1917, Ms Eng. Hist. e.152, Bodleian Special Collections.
118 Robinson, 'Diary of the Great War', 7 September 1916, vol. 2, P.401, IWM Documents.
119 *Ibid.*, 21 December 1916, vol. 2, P.401.
120 *Ibid.*, 30 March 1917, vol. 3, P.402.
121 *Ibid.*, 12 July 1918, vol. 4. In 1914 fewer than 1.25 million people paid income tax, less than 7 per cent of the occupied population. The threshold for liability was £160 per annum. Marwick, *The Deluge*, p. 61. Incomes between £160 and £500 were taxed at nine pence in the pound, those over £500 at one shilling and three pence in the pound. J. M. Bourne, *Britain and the Great War 1914–1918* (Edward Arnold, London, 1989), p. 191.
122 Cossins Diary, 18 November 1914, PP/MCR/371, IWM Documents. For a similar estimate see also Robinson, 'Diary of the Great War', 20 October 1914, vol. 1, P.401, IWM Documents. Expenditure turned out to be closer to £8.5 billion. I. F. W. Beckett, *Home Front 1914–1918: How Britain Survived the Great War* (The National Archives, London, 2006), p. 199. On the financing of the war, see also P. Dewey, *War and Progress in Britain 1914–1918* (Longman, Harlow, 1997), pp. 28–31.

123 Robinson, 'Diary of the Great War', 18 November 1914, vol. 1, P.401, IWM Documents. For details of the – modest – tax increases of November 1914, see Marwick, *The Deluge*, p. 80.
124 Clark Diary, 13 September 1915, Ms Eng. Hist. e.110, Bodleian Special Collections. See also Cossins Diary, 15 September 1915, 21 September 1915, 22 September 1915, PP/MCR/371, IWM Documents. Income tax was increased by 40 per cent, 20 per cent in the current year, while abatement was reduced from £160 to £120. See also Marwick, *The Deluge*, p. 169.
125 Cossins Diary, 22 February 1916, PP/MCR/371, IWM Documents. See also Robinson, 'Diary of the Great War', 22 February 1916, vol. 2, P.401, IWM Documents. Over two billion pounds had been voted since the beginning of the war. According to Robinson, 'such a sum is beyond one's powers of comprehension'.
126 Cossins Diary, 5 April 1916, PP/MCR/371, IWM Documents.
127 Robinson, 'Diary of the Great War', 5 April 1916, vol. 2, P.401, IWM Documents. See also Yearsley 'The Home Front', p. 163, DS/MISC/17, IWM Documents.
128 Robinson, 'Diary of the Great War', 10 June 1918, vol. 4, P.402, IWM Documents.
129 *Ibid.*, 23 April 1918.
130 *Ibid.*, 14 August 1918.
131 T. Wilson, *The Myriad Faces of War: Britain and the Great War, 1914–1918* (Polity Press, Cambridge, 1986), pp. 774–6.
132 'Miscellaneous papers relating to the Great War, 13 volumes', vol. 3, Bodleian Library, University of Oxford, Oxford. In August 1918 The *Daily Telegraph* asserted that there were more than 6,700 war charities in the country as a whole. Clark Diary, not dated, *c.* August 1918, Ms Eng. Hist. e.167, Bodleian Special Collections.
133 Joseph Diaries, 25 September 1914, Ms. Top. Oxon. e.288, Bodleian Special Collections.
134 There were also complaints about the ineffectiveness of legislation against 'bogus war charities'. See, for example, C. Sheridan Jones, *London in War-Time* (Grafton, London, 1917), pp. 64–5.
135 Clark Diary, 28 September 1914, Ms Eng. Hist. e.89, Bodleian Special Collections.
136 *Ibid.*, 29 September 1914.
137 *Ibid.*, 18 October 1914, Ms Eng. Hist. e.90.
138 *Ibid.*, 8 November 1916, Ms Eng. Hist. e.138.
139 Cossins Diary, 14 July 1915, PP/MCR/371, IWM Documents.
140 *Ibid.*, 18 November 1915.
141 Joseph Diaries, 8 November 1914, Ms. Top. Oxon. e.288, Bodleian Special Collections.
142 Yearsley 'The Home Front', p. 213, DS/MISC/17, IWM Documents.

143 Gregory examines the 'geography' of responses to the war loan appeals of 1918, and speculates about the existence of a 'crisis in morale' among 'middle England'. Gregory, *The Last Great War*, pp. 220–35. Three war loans were issued in Britain, with over 1 billion pounds, for example, raised between October 1917 and September 1918. I. F. W. Beckett, *The Great War 1914–1918* (Pearson Education, Harlow, 2001), p. 254.
144 Cossins Diary, 22 June 1915, PP/MCR/371, IWM Documents. The loan was redeemable between 1925 and 1945.
145 *Ibid.*, 17 July 1916.
146 Clark Diary, 21 August 1915, Ms Eng. Hist. e.109, Bodleian Special Collections.
147 *Ibid.*, 11 May 1918, Ms Eng. Hist. e.163.
148 Robinson, 'Diary of the Great War', 26 June 1915, vol. 1, P.401, IWM Documents.
149 Gregory, *The Last Great War*, p. 225.
150 Robinson, 'Diary of the Great War', 16 February 1917, vol. 3, P.402, IWM Documents.
151 *Ibid.*, 28 September 1917.
152 *Ibid.*, 1 June 1918, vol. 4, P.402.
153 R. Saunders to son, 2 September 1915, Saunders Letters, 79/15/1, IWM Documents.
154 Cooper Diary, 25 December 1917, P.121, IWM Documents.
155 Robinson, 'Diary of the Great War', 16 July 1915, vol. 1, P.401, IWM Documents.
156 *Ibid.*, 25 December 1917, vol. 3, P.402.
157 Joseph Diaries, 31 December 1917, Ms. Top. Oxon. e.288, Bodleian Special Collections.
158 Gibbs Diary, 1 January 1915, Ms Eng. misc. c.163, Bodleian Special Collections. For the wide-spread 'depression' at the beginning of 1916, and more hopeful outlook at the beginning of 1917, see Robinson, 'Diary of the Great War', 1 January 1917, vol. 3, P.402, IWM Documents.
159 *Ibid.*, 25 December 1917. See also *ibid.*, 31 December 1917.

3

A united home front?

Introduction

Editing his wartime diaries in 1938, Macleod Yearsley was clear in his belief that during the war civilians had belonged to a 'home front' separate from the fighting forces. He stressed that 'the majority of these men and women (not, of course, including those who seized the opportunity to make huge profits thereby)' had 'carried on … ungrudgingly, fighting upon what may appropriately be called "the Home Front", bearing … privations … buoyed up by love of country and without thought of possible reward other than the satisfaction of having done their best'.[1] While the war was in progress, however, most people did not see such a stark separation between 'fronts'. Although well aware of the distance between themselves and the actual fighting, most middle-class civilian men stressed instead the connection between all those involved in the war effort, whether at home or abroad.[2] Even Reginald Gibbs, who condemned the glamorisation of war as 'a rejuvenator of old age, a purifier of morals and I know not what else',[3] regularly wrote of the British forces as a 'we', even as he condemned the futility and waste of the fighting. In July 1916, for example, he wondered 'just what real progress *we* [my emphasis] are making'.[4]

Combatants' attitudes towards those left behind on the home front may often have been ambivalent, but for their part, most civilians stressed the links between themselves and the fighting forces.[5] In January 1917 Harold Cossins noted that '*we* have two million men now at the front'.[6] Six months later, Holcombe Ingleby wrote to his son that '*our* work in France has lately been beyond all praise',[7] while in March 1918 Frederick Robinson lamented that 'we get no information as to *our* casualties, which one dreads to contemplate'[8] [all my emphasis]. It is this sense of a nation united behind the war effort, where battle and home fronts were inextricably linked, which this chapter seeks to explore further. It begins by investigating the rhetoric of national unity that underlay the personal writings of most middle-class civilian men, paying especial attention to the notion of the war effort as something in which 'everybody' was willingly involved, fighting against a well-defined – and hateful – enemy. The chapter then delves further into such attitudes, revealing the exclusions from this picture of national unity, the contemptible 'others' who were suspected of undermining, rather than contributing, to the war effort: not only cowardly pacifists and ungrateful Belgian refugees, but also 'alien' Jews, affluent munitions workers and spendthrift soldiers' wives, as well as young 'shirkers' who, unlike their elders, refused to shoulder their fair share of the burdens of war. Ultimately, this chapter suggests, the patriotic 'us' created and endorsed by middle-class civilian men turned out to be highly selective, as the supposed lack of patriotism of large sections of the population excluded them from middle-class men's conception of a united wartime nation.

A nation united

Writing to his brother Samuel in November 1915, Alfred Bradburn expressed doubts about the nation's fortitude in the face of a more determined enemy. Talking with munitions workers who stated carelessly: 'Oh, let them beat us', he feared 'that the war is useless, so far as we are concerned. Germany is today what England was in Drakes [*sic*] and Raleigh's days … with a national spirit which cannot be broken; I cannot see how we as a Nation are to do it, unless … we alter considerably'.[9] Such doubts about the country's chances of victory were rarely expressed by middle-class civilians. In 1978 William McIvor explained that 'throughout [the war] I cannot recall a time when we were not quite confident that we would win'.[10] He was echoed three years later by A. E. J. Hepworth, who agreed that 'rightly or wrongly, none of us thought we should fail to win'.[11] A rhetoric of national unity, of a nation 'pulling together' against a common enemy, was a central element of most middle-class men's personal wartime writings. According to Ingleby, in December 1915 there was widespread hope that the war might end soon. 'However', he added, 'no one is building on that, but everyone is quietly content to persevere – even unto the end. One never hears a murmur in England – which is really wonderful'.[12] Although the outlook appeared bleak at the end of 1917, Robinson believed that 'there is none who would draw back, everyone realises that this country has got to see the thing through to the end'.[13] According to Yearsley, the Germans may have 'believed us to be a degenerate nation … thinking only of sport and games, but the old British spirit of patriotism, the old dogged pluck, was still uppermost'.[14]

Terms such as 'the nation', 'the country', 'England', 'the English' (rather more frequently than 'the British')[15], as well as more indefinite 'we' or 'us', were all used to indicate a community united against a common enemy. Even innocent-sounding initiatives that might conceivably disrupt this sense of common purpose were viewed with ambivalence. Thus, Robinson was sceptical about the 'repentance' angle of the 'National Mission of Repentance and Hope', launched by the Church of England in October 1916, which he considered inappropriate at a time 'when the country and every individual more or less, is making supreme sacrifices to uphold the right and to put down the wrong … We are now engaged in fighting against barbarism, without any thought of material gain, we have sacrificed the flower of our manhood, and untold wealth in our endeavour'.[16] Doubts about the resilience of the war effort occasionally crept in, but were quickly dismissed. In March 1918 Robinson admitted that people were getting 'sick' of wartime regulations, 'especially as they can see neither the end, nor … any solution of the awful business'. However, he immediately added: 'people … are prepared to make any sacrifice to win the war and although they are occasionally heard to do a little grousing they don't really mean it'.[17]

Reflecting on the war years from the vantage point of the 1980s, Frank Dawkins recalled that 'we lived, thought, and felt, regardless of our ages … that England was right and honourable – that the enemy was downright wicked and MUST be crushed or else the way of life that we knew and trusted would be gone for ever'.[18] Indeed, there was little doubt about the identity of the main enemy: Germany. In November 1915 Walter Goodwin's father's imagination led him to picture 'the bally lot in a cage, the Kaiser, Emperor of Austria, Sultan of Turkey, Ferdinand, Tino, and all their broods and advisors, so that we could all go and torment them'.[19] However, Germany's allies were far less frequently the objects of civilian men's anger and disgust than were the 'Huns' and the 'Boche'. From the early days of the war, the press had reported stories focusing on the atrocities committed by German troops, and their importance in feeding civilian animosity should not be underestimated. As Yearsley commented in 1938, 'I doubt if any of the present generation can realise how continuously our ears were wrung by tales of "Hun Horrors"',[20] while decades later Sidney Bond also emphasised the role of newspaper stories in turning 'the German into an absolute swine'.[21]

As with other rumours and war stories, middle-class civilians struggled with what to believe. According to Gibbs, no sooner had the war started that 'ugly rumours of atrocities' began to circulate. He did not doubt the 'admitted horrors, such as wholesale shootings and destruction of cathedrals and public buildings and private property', but was unsure whether to believe the 'unsubstantiated rumours of atrocities almost too horrible to mention', which filled the papers. 'At the same time', he added, 'I have no sympathy with those superior people who roundly declare that they don't believe a word of it'.[22] At the end of August 1914, following the news that the Germans had 'utterly destroyed Louvain', Horace Joseph wrote that 'I was at times unwilling to believe the stories of their barbarities, or thought they must be only sporadic; but my disbelief is giving way'.[23]

As the war dragged on, it became easier to believe the worst. In April 1915 Thomas Lockwood observed that 'the Germans are indeed a barbaric and brutal enemy. They care nothing about the laws of warfare … The latest rule they have broken, is the use of appliances and shells that give off asphyxiating gasses'.[24] May 1915 saw a spike of anti-German feeling, both because of the sinking of a Cunard liner, the *Lusitania*, with the loss of over one thousand lives, and because of rumours that German troops had 'crucified' Canadian soldiers, using their bayonets. During a trip to London, James Caldwell spoke with a convalescing Canadian officer, who told him that 'the report about the "crucifying" of Canadians was true. He had himself seen one of his men who was nailed by bayonets on to wooden boards'.[25] In October 1916 Robinson recorded 'another example of the diabolical methods of the Germans': during an air-raid on Russia, it was alleged, the Germans had dropped poisoned sweets and garlic infected with cholera. 'This sort of thing', he added, 'would be a disgrace to the most uncivilised savages'.[26] Following the publication of the Bryce Commission report in May 1915, Gibbs came to the conclusion that it was no longer possible to dismiss atrocity stories as 'the product of hysterical imagination'.[27] In April 1917 he was thus horrified by, and all too ready to believe, a story published in the *Evening News*, 'to the effect that the Germans are extracting fat from their dead soldiers, and are using the flesh and the bones for pig-food and artificial manure'.[28] This, he observed, was 'only the last and lowest step into the abyss of degradation to which war is leading mankind'.[29]

Despite sharing the more general anti-German feeling, middle-class civilians for the most part sought to distance themselves from the violent backlash on the home front, including riots and the looting of German-owned shops.[30] In May 1915 Cossins noted that 'Anti-German riots continue to take place all over England and no doubt many innocent people are suffering as well as guilty'.[31] Serious, respectable (and, indeed, kind) men like Cossins did not sympathise, let alone participate in such attacks, much as they shared the general anger against Germany.[32] Interviewed decades after the conflict, Leslie Friswell, who had left school and started work as a junior clerk for the Royal Insurance Company in 1917, dismissed the looting as the product of 'hooliganism',[33] while George Wilkinson believed it to have been the result of 'idiocy'.[34] Percy Attwood, who was a schoolboy in Hackney during the war, condemned it as a 'wicked thing'.[35] However, McIvor's recollections were perhaps more representative of contemporaries' contradictory emotions. Writing in 1978, he recalled witnessing the looting and destruction of a German shop: 'my feelings were mixed. On the one hand I felt that the action was one of just retribution and on the other, a sorrow that ordinary human beings should be treated in this way. But thats [*sic*] how it was'.[36]

In fact, most civilians rarely came into contact with Germans or other 'enemy aliens'. Doing so clearly made them uncomfortable, but they did not necessarily behave (or admit to behaving) in an outwardly hostile way. During a stay at a boarding house in London in August 1915 Cossins noted that among the other guests there was 'an Austrian who is awaiting internment, from which he has been so far free owing to illness. There is also a clergyman who rashly discusses the war with him'.[37] In February 1915 Caldwell told Clark that he had had an apparently amicable conversation 'with a very old German friend, many years resident in this country, a man of wide experience and discretion, and not unfriendly to this country in which he has lived so long', who was 'by no means confident that Germany will win'.[38] Two years later Ernest Cooper attended a parade of Volunteers in Bungay and then spent the night with a Captain Barratt. He was taken aback to find that Barratt had a German wife, 'and I must say a thundering good housefrau'.[39] George Edinger's parents were naturalised Germans, and his family undoubtedly suffered a good deal during the war. His brother was forced to resign his army commission, while his father was asked to stop attending his hunt and his club. He had been up for re-election to the Stock Exchange when he suddenly died from a tumour. This, Edinger felt sure, 'was brought on by the worry that his whole world had collapsed'. However, George's own experiences were rather different. In 1914 he was in his second year at Wellington. There he found that far from displaying hostility, his contemporaries 'went out of their way to be friendly generous and helpful'.[40]

While civilians were undoubtedly angered and horrified by reports of atrocities abroad, it was the deadliness and destruction of air-raids at home that provoked the strongest reactions.[41] By 1916 middle-class men were increasingly willing to countenance the adoption of a policy of reprisals. Thus, in February 1916 Robert Saunders wrote to his son that 'most thinking people are beginning to recognise the fact that Air Raids can not be prevented, and therefore Reprisals' were the only way to bring the 'enemy to reason'.[42] According to Robinson, the idea of reprisals may have been 'hateful',[43] and 'we don't want to gloat over the destruction of women and children but we *do* want to stop their gloating over the murder of our people and this is the only way to do it'.[44] As evidence of German brutality mounted up, there emerged among some (although by no means all) middle-class civilians a tendency to hate and condemn all Germans as a 'race'. Adrian Gregory, for example, suggests that 'the net result' of the events of 1915 'was a growing belief in the "racial" depravity of the German people, a rhetoric of dehumanisation'.[45] In August 1917 Gibbs expressed his disagreement 'with the commonly held opinion that the Germans as a race are blackguards and fiends'. He suspected that in every nation there was 'a small percentage (say 3 per 1000) of the population … possessed of the cruelty mania'.[46]

However, others were not so measured in their reactions. Following a new spate of air-raids in 1917, Robinson wrote that 'it is as though a whole race of devils had been let loose upon the earth in human form'.[47] Yearsley's hostility towards Germany was especially strident. Typing up extracts from his wartime diaries in 1938, he noted the 'steady growth of loathing for the German people' in the last year of war, and wondered: 'how far did we learn to hate our enemy through propaganda, and how far by our own independent reasoning based upon evidence which we could judge to be undoubted? … It is probably a case of 6 of 1 and half-a-dozen of the other'.[48] He harboured few such doubts during the war. He felt little sympathy for the owners of the shops looted in May 1915 ('after ten months of war, [they] ought not to have been there')[49] and was convinced of the need for reprisals: by September 1917 'it seemed that the systematic bombing of the Rhine towns was the only possible means of bringing home to the Hun the appropriate punishment'.[50]

In August 1915 he joined the Anti-German League, paying the annual subscription of one shilling and adding a donation of five shillings.

The League's aim was to challenge Germany's growing industrial power and capture its markets. Its membership form stated that: 'the time for false sentimentality has gone. It is quite useless fighting savages with silk gloves on. Let us get to business and destroy – destroy first of all the fabric of their fast approaching commercial supremacy – ostracise them socially as a pestilent and cankerous growth – and, lastly, make it impossible for them, with all their knavish tricks and subtle devices, to ever enter our markets again in unfair competition'.[51] As an undated poster of the British Empire Union ('with which is incorporated the anti-German Union') put it more succinctly, its aim was to 'Keep Germans and German goods out of the British empire'.[52]

Dividing lines

Many (perhaps most) middle-class civilian men cherished the patriotic belief that they were part of a nation united against a common – and ruthless – foreign enemy. However, such a belief was not always sufficient to bridge the many dividing lines that remained as important in wartime as they had been in pre-war society. This was perhaps clearest where politics were concerned. Individuals such as Cossins, whose political sympathies are difficult to discern, but who seems to have held broadly liberal views, stressed the extent to which the exigencies of war had brought about a new political consensus. Thus, in December 1916, during the power struggle that led to Asquith's resignation and his replacement as Prime Minister by Lloyd George, he observed that 'the country is almost unanimously in favour of the latter, who has shown himself one of the few men of vigour'.[53]

However, the war certainly did not bring an end to political partisanship. Cooper, a Conservative, was contemptuous of Asquith's 'Radical' government. He believed that there had been widespread 'relief that we had at last got rid of old Asquith and his Wait and See Ministry' at the end of 1916. He thought that 'but for his party there would have been no war for some years and certainly if they had been at all competent it might have been over by now and we should not have had the food shortage which is now threatening us. I sincerely trust I shall never live to see another Radical Government and we are lucky to have got rid of them before they lost us the war'.[54] More succinctly, in October 1914 a gloomy Frederick Rust[?], corn-factor and parish church-warden of Little Waltham, Essex, told Clark that 'the country was bound to go to the dogs from the time a "Liberal" government came into power'.[55] It is perhaps unsurprising that Ingleby, the Conservative MP for King's Lynn, should remain resolutely partisan, although his antagonism towards opposing factions within his own party seems to have been almost as fierce as his hostility towards other parties. Thus, in August 1914 he observed that 'the House was great yesterday and would have been greater, had it been shorn of the dirty crowd of [Tory] Little Englanders. But Balfour rapped their knuckles for them at the close and ... stopped their chatter', adding that 'the Liberal government did well – for them! ... the infringement of the neutrality of Belgium will drive them into definite action, and we must then go the whole hog'.[56]

The two main parties were thus certainly not exempt from middle-class criticism. Nevertheless, the greatest amount of political bile was reserved for socialists, trade unions and the Labour Party. In April 1916 Clark was pleased to hear 'that a good many Socialists have been swept into the army ... they are generally known by their filthy ways, but ... the officers are reducing them to decency by punishments, and ... their comrades will devote some pains to making them cleanly'.[57] Three months earlier, Ingleby had welcomed the introduction of conscription, adding that 'only those who have inside knowledge realise the enormous difficulties we are up against with the trade unions. Whether we shall ever be able to put them in their place I do not know'.[58] In September 1915 Yearsley was enraged when a Labour MP was 'allowed to threaten the House with a general strike of Railway men'. He believed that the only 'way of dealing with such a traitor' involved 'a firing squad and a wall, but fear about votes prevented it. Luckily, the railway men were too patriotic to act as pawns for a Labour member and themselves countered the threat'.[59]

The war did not thus bring about a new cross-party political consensus, and civilian men's attachment to notions of a country united against a common enemy was often undermined by many of the same tensions that had marked pre-war society, particularly their dislike and distrust of the labour movement. In addition, just as old antagonisms did not suddenly disappear, new ones also came to the fore, challenging further the idea of the wartime nation as a unified 'we'. As the war dragged on, middle-class civilians increasingly identified certain individuals and groups as undermining, rather than contributing, to the war effort, and as profiting from war, rather than making sacrifices for the greater good. Foremost among these were people who expressed anti-war opinions, pacifists and conscientious objectors, all of whom were viewed with considerable hostility. In May 1915, for example, Clark reported to the military authorities a foreman at a nearby farm, accusing him of 'treasonable talk'. The man, an 'offensive Radical' and non-Conformist, had been making 'very offensive speeches saying that the authorities are sending out our poor lads to certain slaughter'.[60] A few days later Robinson observed in his diary that what lay at the basis of organisations such as the No Conscription Fellowship was not 'conscience', but 'cowardice'.[61]

Decades after the conflict George Cole, who in 1914 was a ten-year-old schoolboy, recalled that during the war his 'headmaster became increasingly senile and after morning prayers we were frequently treated to a political tirade which included a reference to "those scoundrels Ramsay Macdonald and Philip Snowdon [*sic*]" presumably because of their anti-war attitude'.[62] By the end of August 1918, Yearsley believed that victory was in sight, although there were still obstacles to be overcome. These 'included Huns in government offices, pacifists backed by German gold, and the "block vote" in Labour, which enabled a handful of despicable defeatists to control trade unions'.[63] Conscientious objectors attracted little sympathy.[64] Lockwood was in a minority in being concerned about their 'inhuman treatment (even under provocation)'.[65] According to Clark, such men wished 'all the benefits of citizenship without sharing of its burdens'.[66] They were 'a great nuisance'[67] and 'a discredit to the country'.[68] In March 1916 Saunders noted that 'the appeals for exemption [from military service] to the different tribunals have disclosed the existence of a class of men having no trace of patriotism, courage, or self-respect, though the conscientious objector claims both the latter'.[69] Looking back on the war years from the vantage point of 1971, Charles Ward recalled that the 'most opprobrious of all' wartime terms 'was the new nickname "conchie"'.[70]

Although little sympathy was expressed for the motivations and ethical stance of pacifists and conscientious objectors, they were by no means the only group of people on the home front to be vilified for their supposed lack of commitment to the war effort, as the unity and comradeship that were supposed to underlie wartime alliances soon began to show signs of strain. None did so more clearly than in the case of Belgian refugees. In the early months of war Britain saw the influx into the country of approximately 200,000 Belgian refugees, seeking to escape from the German occupation of their country. The initial reaction of the host communities was a sympathetic one.[71] Cooper noted in his diary that 'we hardly realised what war really meant until 15 October', when a fishing smack arrived in Southwold harbour carrying Belgian refugees. Cooper 'boarded her with a Pilot … and found her crowded with men, women and children from seventy years to an infant, who had fled just as they were with pitiful bundles and boxes, leaving everything else to the Germans ... these people were well looked after by the Southwold folks but were ordered to London ... There was great excitement about these poor people and we thought it might be our fate later'.[72] George Wilkinson's parents housed a Belgian family for three months, until the father found work and secured alternative accommodation. The relationship between the two families seems to have been amicable: significantly, the Belgians were thought to be 'very appreciative of English hospitality'.[73] In October 1914 Ingleby wrote to his son that 'our Belgians are rather nice and give no sort of trouble'.[74]

However, discontent at refugees' behaviour soon began to emerge, focusing especially on their supposed lack of gratitude, surliness and unwillingness to help themselves. After the war McIvor recalled that a big old house in Birkenhead had been used to accommodate Belgian refugees. 'I saw them frequently and was not favourably impressed ... [by] their surly and dour countenance. At first they were welcomed in typical British fashion but as time went on their generally ungrateful behaviour dissipated the initial sympathy extended to them and we were finally glad to see them go'.[75] In October 1914 Robinson wrote of his ambivalence about the Belgian refugees 'one meets about the streets': 'many of them look as if they should be in the fighting line and not loafing about in London; on the other hand, some of the women in widows weeds present a sad spectacle'.[76] Jeffrey Axton, who was a young boy at the outbreak of war, was taken by his mother 'to visit some large Victorian houses which had been converted into temporary accommodation for Belgian refugees ... The Belgians who were mostly rough-looking peasants in ugly black or dark clothes did not seem to be grateful. I remember comments that they were "a surly lot"'. Looking back from the vantage point of 1992, he conceded that 'perhaps they thought we were making rather an exhibition of them, like animals in a zoo, but', he emphasised, 'it is certain that it was all well meant'.[77]

As the war ground on, hostility increasingly focused on the refugees' supposed determination to take advantage of British generosity. In August 1916 a Mr Varley mentioned to Gibbs 'the unpopularity of Belgians in this country', adding that 'they are beginning to stink'. According to Varley, 'they trade on their disasters. Well-to-do Belgians are not ashamed to take money and favours which ought to go to their poorer fellow countrymen ... Then too they are sly and treacherous'.[78] In August 1917 an acquaintance told Clark that 'the Belgians are detested in Deal.

The town at one time was inundated with them. People tried to give them work to do, but found them lazy and disobliging'.[79] Alfred Bradburn's letters to his brother reflected the more general change in attitude towards refugees. In January 1916 he was moved when one of the Belgian men with whom he worked received the news that his family was safe nearby, adding that 'I sometimes hope that some of our workmen had a taste of what Belgium have had; they would wake up some and get on with work'.[80] However, by mid-1917 his attitude had changed. He wrote: 'I have no use for Belgians and very little respect for Frenchmen. I have yet to meet a really good class Belgian, and I have met a good few since the war. They are a dirty race, and bad in the main, and to leave them on their own means they will cease to exist as a nation, and they should be under some stronger rule if they are to be any good. They are something like the Egyptians, bad by themselves but alright [sic] under strong rule'.[81]

The experiences of Belgian refugees were not unique. Indeed, the status of all foreign 'aliens' on the British home front was an uneasy one: such people did not fit easily into middle-class civilians' 'imagined community' of a nation united for the war effort.[82] Unsurprisingly, Germans (including naturalised Germans) were viewed with the greatest suspicion, but as suggested in Chapter 1, anybody who looked or sounded 'foreign', irrespective of their actual nationality, could attract hostility and be suspected of being a spy or a saboteur. A small – but vocal – minority of middle-class civilians, furthermore, also identified a particular group of supposedly 'foreign' people as being especially indifferent, and even hostile, to the war effort: Jews.

James Caldwell was one such man. He made no secret of his low opinion of Jews, 'a race he cordially detests, but with whom he does much business'.[83] In May 1915, for example, he told Clark that corruption was 'rampant' among Jewish businessmen, and that 'no real good will be done in supply of munitions until all the Jewish firms are removed from the list of firms allowed to tender for War-office and Admiralty contracts'.[84] In November 1917 he blamed the high price of commodities at Braintree market on 'Whitechapel Jews' who arrived before the market opened and bought up butter, eggs and poultry 'at an old song', leaving few items for local consumers.[85] Nine months later he was of the opinion that there was little point in interning Germans 'so long as Jews are allowed about. Most of the "spying" and "sending information useful to the enemy" has been, and is being, done by Jews'.[86] According to Clark, 'Major Caldwell is no "Jew-baiter" but has no trust in the Jews. They have no country, no touch of patriotism, and … are most willing to send useful information to the

Jewish clique in Germany which has made fortunes out of the war'.[87]

Yearsley shared Caldwell's vitriolic anti-Semitism and perception of Jews as foreign and potentially dangerous outsiders. In the early months of 1918 he and his wife found themselves in a tube train during an air-raid. The train, which was very crowded, 'contained a large proportion of alien Jews. These people, who, I thought, ought not to be allowed to remain in the country, were in the habit of posting sentries at the Police Stations, who gave their compatriots notice whenever the Police were reinforced, so that they could rush for the tube and travel backward and forward in the trains until the raid was over'.[88] Not only were Jews a separate community and a race apart, but – according to Yearsley – they all too often received favoured treatment. He stressed the overlap between Germans and Jews, and condemned 'the curiously loth way the authorities got rid of certain aliens in our midst', adding that 'a German name and accent seemed at times to pass unnoticed when accompanied by a large nose and a difficulty in pronouncing sibilants'.[89] F. Ashe Lincoln, who was a schoolboy in Plymouth during the war, recalled that 'there was a tremendous amount of anti-Semitism. Jews were attacked … all Jews were described as being "Germans"'. He explained that 'the depth of feeling against Germans was … intense during that war, and any Jew was regarded as being good game'. Significantly, he thought that at the basis of the 'anti-Jewish feeling' was the belief 'that Jews were Germans'. The results were predictably unpleasant. Although adults did not participate in the violence, Lincoln and his brother were forced to endure 'many an attack from schoolboys in Plymouth'.[90]

Patriotism, class and gender

In November 1914 Gibbs asserted that 'a considerable section of the English admire … our aristocracy and would unhesitantly … follow their lead whenever they called for war'. He believed the views of 'a draper or commercial traveller of some sort', with whom he had struck up a conversation on a train journey, were 'typical'. The man had stressed 'how *nobly* our aristocracy have stood up and sacrificed themselves as they always have done, when their country is in danger'.[91] In reality, the upper classes were not always above middle-class criticism. In spring 1915, for example, Clark was outraged by the news that the squire in a nearby parish was refusing to billet soldiers either in his own house, or in those of his tenants. This was a landowner who had gone 'all about the county at recruiting meetings, urging enlistment … [putting] ten men's backs up against enlistment for every recruit that was got. The idea of a man with a big house, 7/8ths unoccupied, in which he refused to allow either officers or men to be billeted, advocating enlistment!'[92] Throughout the war, rumours regularly cropped up in the village of Great Leighs about the unpatriotic behaviour of certain local landowners, including a 'big house' where the only 'war economies' were those being made on servants' food.[93] In 1918, for example, there was outrage at the behaviour of a local MP, who – it was said – 'had got his son … exempt from military service by getting him a financial post in the Canadian Government service'.[94]

The wartime behaviour of the upper classes was thus not always considered above reproach. However, criticism of their lack of patriotism was almost negligible by contrast to the hostility directed at the other end of the social spectrum: the working classes.[95] In the first six months of war attitudes were not always unsympathetic. In January 1915 Caldwell told Clark that 'the big shipping firms are coining money'. In some instances, the cost of freight had increased from 12s 3d per ton to 63s per ton. 'The seamen know that their bosses are getting this big money, of which they have no share. There is bound, before long, to be a strike of shipping workers'.[96] Two months later Joseph worried about the possibility of a coal strike 'unless advances in wages asked for are granted. No one seems to know who is getting the benefit of the high price of coal'.[97] It was widely believed that large businesses were making huge profits out of the war, pursuing self-interest at the expense not only of their workers, but of all citizens and consumers.[98] In February 1916 Caldwell returned once again to the subject of shipping firms. He believed that it was they who made 'provisions excessively dear by extravagant profits … A great number of shipping firms, which previously earned modest returns, are now paying fabulous dividends'.[99] Sixteen months later Robinson noted that beef and mutton, for which they were paying 2s per lb and more, were sold in Australia for 5d per lb 'and costs delivered in London about 6½d per lb. How is the enormous difference accounted for? Who makes the profit?'[100] By September 1917 he had become convinced of the need to protect consumers 'against the "profiteers" who had been making huge fortunes out of the misfortunes of other people'.[101] Saunders agreed, complaining that 'prices are simply awful and the Profiteers manage to checkmate every order'.[102]

Middle-class men did not hesitate to voice their disapproval of the conduct of big business and of 'profiteers', but this did not result in a sense of comradeship with the working classes: any early sympathy soon evaporated. In January 1916 Joseph observed in his diary that 'the situation at home seems to me deplorable. The government have allowed thousands to wax fat on the war: and there is a widespread unwillingness to make sacrifices'. There was no doubt in his mind about who had been getting 'fat': 'thousands of semi-skilled men were earning £4, and skilled men in exceptional cases even up to £20. We can't stand the waste'.[103] Gibbs's was one of the few middle-class voices raised in defence of the working class. In February 1915, in reference to a strike of Clydeside workers, he commented that 'the tendency seems to blame the engineers for their selfishness in holding up important work at such a time. Nobody ever blames the masters for their share in it'.[104] Or, as he put it more acerbically five months later, in connection with a strike of Welsh coal-miners: 'The coal-owners are robbing the public with both hands, openly and shamelessly, and the miners want a share in the plunder'.[105] He ridiculed the speeches made by cabinet ministers at a trade union conference in December 1915:

> They tried to persuade working-men to accept smaller wages than they could get. When the sacred laws of supply and demand cause the working-man to suffer, he is told to put up with it … When the same laws operate to his benefit, he is told to be altruistic … As no such appeal is likely to be made to munitions manufacturers, coal merchants, ship-owners and others who are waxing fat out of their country's sufferings, I cannot think the working man will be quite such a fool as to be influenced by these Three Wise Men of Westminster.[106]

There were occasional acknowledgements of the hardships being endured by some sections of the working classes. In September 1916, for example, Cossins considered that the munitions workers of Woolwich and elsewhere deserved the short holiday they had been granted: 'the work hitherto has on the whole been unremitting and many have suffered from the superhuman effort made'.[107] A month earlier, Gibbs had pointed out that 'in these days when it is commonly supposed that all the manual labourers in this country are making fortunes' it was sobering to discover – from a letter published in *The Herald* – that 'some families have to support themselves on 30/- weekly, which is about equivalent to 18/- in purchasing value before the war'.[108]

According to Arthur Marwick, 'from the beginning of 1916 newspaper references to the condition of the working class concentrated on the high cost of living rather than affluence'.[109] However, this shift was not reflected in middle-class men's personal writings:[110] few doubted that the working classes were doing well out of the war.[111] In January 1917 Clark received a letter from his daughter, a medical student at St Andrews. She wrote: 'the wealthiest people of the period are the dockers at Invergordon many of whom are earning £8 a week and never less than £4 … They hire motor cars on Sundays and go for long excursions over the country with their wives resplendent in furs and jewels'.[112] Most critical comments were focused on the supposed new-found wealth of munitions workers, 'a name that', according to Cossins, 'has become proverbial for rich workers'.[113] Thus, in November 1916 he complained that the price of food continued to increase: 'In the Stores today I saw that new laid eggs are 3s 9d per dozen, a prohibitive price except to munitions makers'.[114] Eight months earlier Saunders had noted that 'I don't know a single article that has not gone up in price'. Of course, he added, youngsters of fourteen working in munitions could earn 30s to 40s a week, while 'men earn up to £5 or £6, so the rise in price doesn't affect them as much as the people with fixed incomes who are forced to economise'.[115] In August 1917 he went on a day trip to Brighton with two of his sons, and found it very crowded with 'all sorts and conditions of people … and of course the Munitioners are now-a-days millionaires and can afford to spend freely'.[116]

Working-class women did not escape censure either. There were some grumbles about the scandalous behaviour of girls who came into contact with soldiers. In April 1915 'very evil reports' reached Clark about 'the immorality of young women in Chelmsford, Halsted and Terling, where soldiers have been quartered'. Members of the Mothers' Meeting 'affirmed that the illegitimacy of this year in all these three places will be shocking beyond not only record, but also belief'.[117] That said, it was the behaviour of older, married women, rather than young girls, which attracted most negative middle-class comment.[118] In December 1914 Clark's brother-in-law wrote from Cupar, Fife, that 'one thing is being very much overdone – separation allowances. Lots of women in Dundee are having the time of their lives – drawing their allowances and … money from as many relief funds as they can – It is paying the public-houses splendidly'.[119] There was a widespread perception that separation allowances were bringing unprecedented prosperity to many working-class women. In November 1914 Gibbs sympathised with the plight of many families: 'a young married man who gives his services to his country does so with the … knowledge that if he loses his life his wife will only receive five shillings a week with … some miserable pittance of two-pence a day for each child. The government … not only ask[s] him to fling his body in the firing line, but also to fling his wife and children into the gutter'.[120] However, he too was favourably impressed by the revised separation allowances announced in spring 1915: 'the new scale ... is really very good. The wife of a private with four children living in the London district will get £1 10s 6d a week and in a good many cases this is more than she got before her husband enlisted'.[121]

Talk soon began to circulate of soldiers' wives indulging in unprecedented shopping sprees. In May 1915 the owner of a Birmingham firm told Caldwell that the only section of their business that was doing a good trade was in 'Brummagen jewellery'. Soldiers' wives now had allowances of thirty-five shillings a week, rather than sixteen or seventeen, so they were 'lavishly bedecking themselves' with 'such "trash jewellery"'.[122] According to Clark's brother-in-law, in September 1915 the women of Cupar were 'drinking like fish, thanks to the ridiculous separation allowances'. He had heard that 'two women at Dundee, in D. M. Brown's shop, were talking loudly to each other. One said: "I hope the war will last a long time. I have more money than I ever had when my man was at home, and I haven't him to feed"'.[123] Cossins believed that many 'elderly fathers of families' were being 'urged to enlist by their wives who are ever so much better off in this way than they were before the war'.[124] Even Gibbs was prepared to believe that in November 1916 'the poor women in the villages round here have never been as well off as they are now'. Accordingly, 'the small shops are thriving like pigs on offal. The war is, it seems, a great bit of fun all round'.[125]

Given the widespread perception that working-class people were enjoying a period of unprecedented prosperity, it is perhaps unsurprising that middle-class men should respond to industrial unrest and strikes with a mixture of incredulity and anger. Even before munitions became a byword for 'rich workers', strikes had attracted little middle-class sympathy. Alfred Bradburn was representative of many when he wrote to his brother in January 1916: 'I would shoot some of the South Wales Blighters'.[126] In March 1915 Cossins condemned strikes in the engineering works on the Clyde as 'a disgrace to the country at such a time as this',[127] adding a few days later that 'there is no doubt that a section of Labour is acting very disloyally in this crisis'.[128] Whatever the workers' grievances, stoppages in wartime were condemned as unpatriotic. In July 1915 Cossins stated that although striking miners in South Wales 'seem to have some justification for their acts if it had been in time of peace, it is criminal in times like these to hold up supplies of a commodity that is required by every industry'.[129]

It was rare for middle-class commentators to make even such a lukewarm acknowledgement that workers had some genuine grievances. In March 1916 Robinson described a strike on the Clyde as 'disgraceful', especially as he had read that 'in some of the ship yards on the Clyde some of the men are earning over £500 a year'.[130] A week later, he wrote that 'the only thing to do is to make an example of the ring-leaders by shooting a few or perhaps better still by sending them to the trenches to be shot by the Germans'.[131] Attitudes hardened further in the years that followed. Of striking engineers, Robinson believed in March 1918 that 'shooting is too good for such traitors!'[132] Yearsley was prepared to go further than most: he had little doubt about what would provide the most effective solution to the problem of industrial unrest, or, as he termed it in 1915, 'sedition'.[133] Following a strike of Coventry munitions workers in July 1918, he wrote – apparently quite seriously – that 'many of us' felt that 'a few executions under martial law would produce a most satisfactory effect'.[134]

Age and youth

Middle-class civilian men harboured grave doubts about the patriotic credentials of foreign 'aliens', the working classes and (many) women. In addition, while the post-war belief that a 'lost generation' of young men had been sent to the slaughter by their heartless elders had yet to take root, there was also considerable debate over the respective contributions to the war effort of the young and the old.[135] Some men over military age certainly felt that they were useless to a wartime nation. In September 1914 among the speakers at a recruiting meeting in Great Leighs was Charles Strutt, 'sometime MP for the Maldon division of Essex'. Strutt admitted that 'I myself am an old man, fit only to be put on the shelf. It is for strong arms and stout hearts of Essex men that we now appeal'. He stressed 'how poor Belgium has been suffering … We old people ask you young men to go to the front'.[136] Gibbs, himself of military age, was not impressed by such appeals. In May 1916 he complained that older men like his headmaster and his father 'are determined to "fight to the death" to the last drop of *my* blood. Young men', he added, enlisted because they were 'exhilarated by their illusions, and old men, secure in their immunity, drum them on'.[137]

Gibbs's cynicism was understandable, but at least some older men seem to have found their marginalisation a source of genuine regret. After his beloved eldest son's enlistment, the middle-aged protagonist of H. G. Wells's wartime novel *Mr Britling Sees it Through* found it 'shameful to him that all these fine lads should be going off to death and wounds while the men of forty and over lay snug at home. How stupid it was to fix things like that! Here were the fathers, who had done their work, shot their bolts … unable to be of any service, shamefully safe … while their young innocents … went down into the deadly trenches … he felt himself a cowardly brute, fat, wheezy, out of training'.[138] In October 1914 Ingleby wrote to his son – who at the time was serving as a Lieutenant in the Royal Naval Volunteer Reserve – that 'I feel rather ashamed of myself to be doing so much partridge shooting at this critical time. But really, when you are over sixty, you are apt to be off the active list. Of course I address meetings and discourse[?] eloquently on one's duty to one's country but it doesn't amount to much!'[139] Eight months later he and his wife spent a weekend in Rutlandshire, enjoying 'a quiet time playing croquet and basking in the sun. It seems very absurd that we should be doing this sort of thing while you and others are serving their country but it is the fate of young people to live and old people to exist, and it is no use discussing the matter'.[140] He returned to the same theme in August, observing that 'we are just jig-jogging along in an inanimate kind of fashion. We are the left-behinders'.[141] Indeed, older men attempting to take on military and paramilitary duties better suited to younger men were often not an object of admiration, but of ridicule and contempt. In January 1915 Clark's sister-in-law wrote from Newport, Fifeshire, that 'We have a "citizens corps" here, composed of all the decrepit old men in the place. I am told that to see them drilling is as good as a circus'.[142] Six months later his daughter described the official inspection of the Newport Volunteer Training Corps, adding that 'it was so amusing to see these old men doubling and forming fours and whenever a moments [*sic*] respite was given taking out white handkerchiefs and mopping'.[143] In a later letter she dismissed them as 'a corps of elderly men who drill and fancy themselves capable of home defence'.[144]

Older men's patriotic efforts may often have been dismissed as ridiculous and ineffective, but doubts were also expressed about younger men's willingness and fitness to take on the responsibilities they were expected to shoulder. In May 1916 the Superintendent of the Chelmsford division of the special constables responded to Clark's letter of resignation by writing that: 'I quite agree with you that the younger men should come forward and take their part. There are plenty of men who although past military age', nevertheless could undertake 'this kind of work and I think it is slack and unpatriotic of them not to come forward when they know how greatly their services are needed. I am very much afraid there is a good deal of selfishness and lack of patriotism'.[145] A year earlier Caldwell had lamented that there was 'an abundance of men of experience in this country', who were excluded from military service because they were a few years over enlistment age. On the other hand, commissions were being 'given freely to lads from school who are idle, pleasure-seeking, dissolute and set their men a bad example. In the trenches they are hysterical, observe no precautions and get shot'.[146] He returned to this theme in January 1916, telling Clark that 'nearly all the groaning and grumbling in the camps are due to soft-cakes who have all their lives been coddled ... the absence of manliness and sense of discipline among the younger men of the country is painful and deplorable'.[147]

It was widely – and, it seems, unfairly[148] – believed that there were plenty of young men who, far from behaving heroically, were in fact shirking their patriotic duty and refusing to volunteer for military service. In May 1915 Cossins noted that the recent rise in the military age to forty had aroused a good deal of discontent: 'people feel that it is unfair to call upon men of that age to enlist when so many young "slackers" are about'.[149] As late as the end of 1915 it was generally thought that there were still plenty of such young 'slackers' around on the home front. In September 1915 Joseph spent a few days in Weston, 'where there seem to be many men of military age loafing'.[150] As one informant told Clark in November 1915, in Essex a large number of young men had 'crowded into munitions works to escape being taken into actual army service'.[151] Speaking to Clark in January 1916 on what clearly was a favourite theme, Caldwell complained that 'it is positively disgraceful to see the crowds of men of twenty-five or so who sit all day in cafes in London, sipping coffee, smoking cigarettes and playing dominoes'. A few days earlier he had escaped a rain shower by entering 'The Mecca' in Cheapside, which he had found 'full of such men – and not an armlet to be seen among them, though he slipped about the room looking for them'.[152] According to Yearsley, when the figures relating to attestation under the Derby scheme, which marked a last attempt to avoid compulsory military service, were published in January 1916, they 'struck us all as a disgrace to the youth of this country'[153] (Figure 5).

Even conscription did not entirely silence complaints about youthful 'shirkers', particularly those who were exempted because in reserved occupations or – worse still – in government employ. In March 1917 Gibbs noted that: 'for weeks (or is it months?) past hardly a day passes but *The Evening News* publishes a cartoon depicting "Cuthbert" as a rabbit. Cuthbert is a mythical figure supposed to represent millions of available young men "sheltering in funk holes". These funk holes are supposed to be chiefly government offices, where people of influence are sheltering their young ones'.[154] In April 1917 there was talk of extending the military age to forty-five. And yet, as Yearsley wrote in 1938: 'there were hundreds of young men permitted to evade military service. It was proposed to re-examine and call back men who had already "done their bit" … this seemed an abominable injustice when there were young men protected by Government employ. This preferential manipulation of young-man power', he concluded, bluntly rejecting any generalisation about 'doomed youth', 'will always remain one of the worst injustices of the war'.[155]

Conclusion

In September 1914 Gibbs noted in his diary the incessant talk of '"inevitable wars" and "the national honour demands this" and "the British

5 'The "indispensable" and the grandfather in the trenches', *Punch*, 22 November 1916.

prestige demands that"'.[156] Such a rhetoric of a nation united in support of a righteous cause was important to many middle-class civilians, who made frequent reference to terms such as 'we', 'us', 'the nation' or 'the English' to indicate a patriotic community united against a barbaric enemy. As Michael MacDonagh put it in December 1915, for example: 'the country continues solidly united in its cause and its will to win'.[157] However, as Adam Seipp points out, by the final two years of war the rhetoric of national unity was increasingly challenged by conflicting pressures: 'for many Britons, the war crystallized prewar resentments, added new complaints, and called into question the reciprocal relationship between the state and its … citizenry'.[158]

As far as middle-class civilian men were concerned, their belief in a united home front was constantly undermined by what they saw as the unpatriotic and selfish behaviour of other sections of the population: they were convinced that not everybody was doing their 'bit' and making patriotic sacrifices to help the country to victory . People, according to Caroline Playne, writing in 1933, were not fooled by the 'continual babble about "equality of sacrifice"'.[159] On the contrary, they believed that certain sections of the population were not to be trusted, were not pulling their weight, or were selfishly taking advantage of wartime conditions to enjoy unprecedented wealth and prosperity. Behind middle-class men's use of a rhetoric of national unity there thus lurked a view of society divided on ethnic, gender, generational and (especially) class lines, divisions that – they believed – led to an unfair apportioning of the burdens of war.

Apparently affluent, strike-happy and selfish munitions workers became a particular middle-class *bête noire*. As Robinson observed in October 1917, the war was 'hitting some people very hard', while others 'are far better off than they ever expected to be'.[160] The notion of a working class doing well out of the war, in contrast to an impoverished middle class battered by financial pressures, had by then become a well-established refrain, compounded by a belief that workers were using their new-found wealth and power with little thought for the war effort. As the war went on, the rhetoric of national unity endorsed by middle-class civilian men thus rang increasingly hollow, as the patriotic 'us' revealed itself as a highly select and exclusive group, its membership for the most part limited to other middle-class men.

Notes

1 M. Yearsley ('Eyewitness'), 'The Home Front, 1914–18', p. 1, DS/MISC/17, Department of Documents, Imperial War Museum (hereafter IWM Documents), London.

2 See also the 'avalanche of reportage, propaganda, and patriotic portraits of the war efforts of individuals, military units, and communities' produced by civilian writers during and in the aftermath of war. J. M. Winter, *The Great War and the British People* (Palgrave Macmillan, Basingstoke, 2003, first published 1985), p. 285.

3 Diary of R. W. M. Gibbs, 1914–20 (hereafter Gibbs Diary), 12 February 1915, Ms Eng. misc. c.164, Special Collections, Bodleian Library, University of Oxford (hereafter Bodleian Special Collections), Oxford.

4 *Ibid.*, 21 July 1916, Ms Eng. misc. c.179.

5 Combatants' attitudes towards civilians and civilian life have attracted a good deal of scholarly attention. Alienation and a sense of separateness are stressed, for example, in J. Meyer, *Men of War: Masculinity and the First World War in Britain* (Palgrave Macmillan, Basingstoke, 2009), p. 162; Winter, *The Great War and the British People*, Chapter 9; R. Graves and A. Hodge, *The Long Weekend: A Social History of Great Britain* (Abacus, London, 1995, first published 1940), pp. 14–18; R. M. Bracco, *Merchants of Hope: British Middlebrow Writers of the First World War, 1919–1939* (Berg, Oxford, 1993), pp. 101–8; P. Fussell, *The Great War and Modern Memory* (Oxford University Press, Oxford, 1977, first published 1975), pp. 86–90; A. Marwick, *The Deluge: British Society and the First World War* (Palgrave Macmillan, Basingstoke, second edition, 2006, first published 1965), p. 258. As David Englander points out, however, 'criticism of civilians did not imply a rejection of civilian society'. Quoted in I. F. W. Beckett, *The Great War 1914–1918* (Pearson Education, Harlow, 2001), p. 229. The interconnections between home and front are emphasised, for example, in M. Roper, *The Secret Battle: Emotional Survival in the Great War* (Manchester University Press, Manchester, 2009); H. McCartney, *Citizen Soldiers: The Liverpool Territorials in the First World War* (Cambridge University Press, Cambridge, 2005), Chapter 5; S. R. Grayzel, *Women's Identities at War: Gender, Motherhood, and Politics in Britain and France during the First World War* (University of North Carolina Press, Chapel Hill, NC, 1999), pp. 11–49; S. M. Cullen, 'Gender and the Great War: British Combatants, Masculinity and Perceptions of Women, 1918–1939' (Unpublished DPhil thesis, University of Oxford, 1998).

6 H. C. Cossins Diary, 1914–18 (hereafter Cossins Diary), 7 January 1917, PP/MCR/371, IWM Documents.

7 Holcombe Ingleby to Clement, 15 June 1917, The First World War Letters of Holcombe Ingleby MP (hereafter Ingleby Letters), P.343, IWM Documents.

8 F. A. Robinson, 'Diary of the Great War', 29 March 1918, vol. 4, P.402, IWM Documents.

9 A. Bradburn to S. Bradburn, 13 November 1915, Letters from Alfred Bradburn to his Brother Samuel (hereafter Bradburn Letters), 95/16/1, IWM Documents. See also *ibid.*, 19 September 1917.

10 At the outbreak of war McIvor was a twelve-year-old schoolboy and lived in Birkenhead, Cheshire, where his parents ran 'a small family business engaged on vital war work connected with ship repairing'. W. L. McIvor, Recollections, October 1978, DF148, Liddle Collection (1914–18), Special Collections, Brotherton Library, Leeds University (hereafter Liddle Collection), Leeds.

11 Hepworth worked throughout the war as a 'surveyor of taxes'. A. E. J. Hepworth to P. Liddle, 18 September 1981, DF148, Liddle Collection.

12 Holcombe Ingleby to Clement, 25 December 1915, Ingleby Letters, P.343, IWM Documents.

13 Robinson, 'Diary of the Great War', 25 December 1917, vol. 3, P.402, IWM Documents.

14 Yearsley, 'The Home Front', p. 46, DS/MISC/17, IWM Documents. See also G. S. Street, *At Home in the War* (William Heinemann, London, 1918), pp. 26–33.

15 See also George Robb's analysis of the notion of 'Britishness' promulgated by the authorities during the war, one 'narrowly defined along ethnic and racial lines'. G. Robb, *British Culture and the First World War* (Palgrave, Basingstoke, 2002), p. 31.

16 Robinson, 'Diary of the Great War', 15 October 1916, vol. 2, P.401, IWM Documents. The National Mission is considered further in A. Gregory, *The Last Great War: British Society and the First World War* (Cambridge University Press, Cambridge, 2008), Chapter 5.

17 Robinson, 'Diary of the Great War', 21 March 1918, vol. 4, P.402, IWM Documents.

18 Dawkins worked as assistant and clerk to the works manager of a London firm manufacturing telephones. F. Dawkins to P. Liddle, 26 March 1986, DF148, Liddle Collection.

19 'Dadd' to 'Wallie', 4 November 1915, W.A. Goodwin Collection (hereafter Goodwin Collection), Con Shelf, IWM Documents. In November 1915 Wallie, then serving in the London Regiment, was in hospital in Egypt with an infected hand, which he had contracted at Gallipoli.

20 Yearsley, 'The Home Front', p. 22, DS/MISC/17, IWM Documents. See also the analysis of 'the rape of Belgium and wartime imagination' in N. F. Gullace, *'The Blood of our Sons': Men, Women and the Renegotiation of British Citizenship during the First World War* (Palgrave Macmillan, Basingstoke, 2002), Chapter 1.

21 R. Van Emden and S. Humphries, *All Quiet on the Home Front: An Oral*

History of Life in Britain during the First World War (Headline, London, 2003), p. 59. Bond's father ran a small bakery business in Liverpool.

22 Gibbs Diary, 20 September 1914, Ms Eng. misc. c.159, Bodleian Special Collections.

23 Wartime Diaries of H. W. B. Joseph 1914–18 (hereafter Joseph Diaries), 29 August 1914, Ms. Top. Oxon. e.288, Bodleian Special Collections. See also M. Derez, 'The flames of Louvain: the war experience of an academic community', in H. Cecil and P. H. Liddle (eds), *Facing Armageddon: The First World War Experienced* (Leo Cooper, London, 1996), pp. 617–29.

24 F. T. Lockwood, 'Notes Written by F.T. Lockwood', 19 April 1915, 96/52/1, IWM Documents.

25 A. Clark War Diary, 'Echoes of the 1914 War in an Essex Village' (hereafter Clark Diary), 12 May 1915, Ms Eng. Hist. e.103, Bodleian Special Collections.

26 Robinson, 'Diary of the Great War', 13 October 1916, vol. 2, P.401, IWM Documents.

27 Gibbs Diary, 16 May 1915, Ms Eng. misc. c.167, Bodleian Special Collections. In December 1914 the Bryce Commission, headed by Lord Bryce, a highly respected former ambassador to Washington, was charged with investigating stories of German atrocities in Belgium. Its report, based on what has subsequently been condemned as flimsy and uncorroborated evidence, asserted that 'murder, lust and pillage prevailed over many parts of Belgium on a scale unparalleled in any war between civilised nations during the last three centuries'. Quoted in Marwick, *The Deluge*, p. 172. Most of the more lurid stories were later discredited, but this does not mean that atrocities, including the killing of Belgian civilians in the early weeks of the war, did not take place. Gregory, *The Last Great War*, pp. 44–7. See also A. Kramer, *Dynamics of Destruction: Culture and Mass Killing in the First World War* (Oxford University Press, Oxford, 2008, first published 2007), especially Chapter 1; T. Wilson, *The Myriad Faces of War: Britain and the Great War, 1914–1918* (Polity Press, Cambridge, 1986), chapter 17.

28 Gibbs Diary, 16 April 1917, Ms Eng. misc. c.188, Bodleian Special Collections.

29 *Ibid.*, 19 April 1917. The following day doubt began to be cast on the story, when it was pointed out that in this context the term 'kadaver' referred to horse flesh.

30 'Anti-German manifestations' are examined in P. Panayi, *The Enemy in our Midst: Germans in Britain during the First World War* (Berg, Oxford, 1991), Chapter 7. For the anti-German riots, see also pp. 252–3.

31 Cossins Diary, 13 May 1915, PP/MCR/371, IWM Documents.

32 Adrian Gregory notes that most of the 1915 riots were confined to working-class districts. Gregory, *The Last Great War*, p. 237. See also A. R. Seipp, *The Ordeal of Peace: Demobilization and the Urban Experience in Britain and*

Germany, 1917–1921 (Ashgate, Farnham, 2009), p. 55.

33 L. F. Friswell interview, 8774, reel 1, Department of Sound, Imperial War Museum (hereafter IWM Sound), London.

34 G. D. Wilkinson interview, 9104, reel 2, IWM Sound.

35 P. Attwood interview, 9559, reel 1, IWM Sound.

36 McIvor, Recollections, October 1978, DF148, Liddle Collection.

37 Cossins Diary, 6 August 1915, PP/MCR/371, IWM Documents.

38 Clark Diary, 11 February 1915, Ms Eng. Hist. e.97, Bodleian Special Collections.

39 The Diary of Ernest R. Cooper, 'Nineteen Hundred and War Time', 28 July 1914 – 3 December 1918 (hereafter Cooper Diary), 31 October 1914, P.121, IWM Documents.

40 G. Edinger, Memoirs, not dated, DF148, Liddle Collection. See also G. Pember, 'Some Memories of the Great War', not dated, DF148, Liddle Collection. In May 1915 the Stock Exchange asked members of German or Austrian birth 'not to attend the House until further notice'. Panayi, *The Enemy in Our Midst*, p. 200. For similar moves by commercial and professional organisations see pp. 199–201.

41 Gregory, *The Last Great War*, pp. 55–7.

42 R. Saunders to son, 24 February 1916, R. Saunders, Letters to Son in Canada, 1914–18 (hereafter Saunders Letters), 79/15/1, IWM Documents. See also the anger over the treatment of British prisoners of war. Robinson, 'Diary of the Great War', 21 May 1918, vol. 4, P.402, IWM Documents.

43 *Ibid.*, 9 July 1917, vol. 3, P.402.

44 *Ibid.*, 4 October 1917.

45 Gregory, *The Last Great War*, p. 62.

46 Gibbs Diary, 2 August 1917, Ms Eng. misc. c.192, Bodleian Special Collections. See also *ibid.*, 14 May 1915, Ms Eng. misc. c.167.

47 Robinson, 'Diary of the Great War', 17 June 1917, vol. 3, P.402, IWM Documents.

48 Yearsley, 'The Home Front', p. 279, DS/MISC/17, IWM Documents. The role of propaganda and of the state in fostering anti-German sentiment on the home front remains a matter of debate. See Robb, *British Culture*, Chapter 4.

49 Yearsley, 'The Home Front', p. 64, DS/MISC/17, IWM Documents.

50 *Ibid.*, p. 122.

51 The Anti-German League, P. M. Yearsley membership form, 24 August 1915, Letters to P. M. Yearsley, P. M. Yearsley Collection, 71/11/1, IWM Documents.

52 Poster of British Empire Union, 'Miscellaneous war posters', in 'Miscellaneous papers relating to the Great War, 13 volumes', Bodleian Library, University of Oxford, Oxford. See also Panayi, *The Enemy in Our Midst*, pp. 202–10.

53 Cossins Diary, 5 December 1916, PP/MCR/371, IWM Documents.
54 Cooper Diary, 25 March 1917, P.121, IWM Documents. See also *ibid.*, 18 February 1916.
55 Clark Diary, 24 October 1914, Ms Eng. Hist. e.90, Bodleian Special Collections.
56 Holcombe Ingleby to Clement, 4 August 1914, Ingleby Letters, P.343, IWM Documents. Conservative Party politics at the outbreak of war are considered in N. Keohane, *The Party of Patriotism: The Conservative Party and the First World War* (Ashgate, Farnham, 2010), especially pp. 11–24. Ingleby's reference was to Arthur Balfour, ex-Prime Minister and until 1911 Tory leader.
57 Clark Diary, 30 April 1916, Ms Eng. Hist. e.125, Bodleian Special Collections.
58 Holcombe Ingleby to Clement, 7 January 1916, Ingleby Letters, P.343, IWM Documents.
59 Yearsley, 'The Home Front', pp. 144–5, DS/MISC/17, IWM Documents.
60 Clark Diary, 6 May 1915, 8 May 1915, Ms Eng. Hist. e.103, Bodleian Special Collections.
61 Robinson, 'Diary of the Great War', 29 May 1915, vol. 1, P.401, IWM Documents.
62 Cole began to attend grammar school in September 1915. G. W. Cole, 'Some Recollections of the 1914–18 War', January 1990, DF148, Liddle Collection.
63 Yearsley, 'The Home Front', p. 308, DS/MISC/17, IWM Documents.
64 This tallies with the findings in L. S. Bibbings, *Telling Tales about Men: Conceptions of Conscientious Objectors to Military Service during the First World War* (Manchester University Press, Manchester, 2009). Attitudes towards conscientious objection shifted considerably after the war. See Bracco, *Merchants of Hope*, pp. 108–10.
65 Lockwood, 'Notes', 30 October 1916, 96/52/1, IWM Documents.
66 Clark Diary, 10 June 1916, Ms Eng. Hist. e.127, Bodleian Special Collections.
67 Cossins Diary, 23 August 1916, PP/MCR/371, IWM Documents.
68 E. R. Cooper, 'The 3rd Volunteer Battalion Suffolk Regiment', June 1920, p. 6, P.121, IWM Documents.
69 R. Saunders to son, 21 March 1916, Saunders Letters, 79/15/1, IWM Documents. The 16,500 appeals for exemption on the basis of conscience represented a tiny minority of the total claims made to tribunals in the course of the war. Beckett, *The Great War*, p. 214.
70 C. H. Ward, 'Recollections of the First World War', 1971, DF148, Liddle Collection. Ward was nine years old when the war broke out. In later years he became a bank clerk in his native Sunderland.

71 At the beginning of 1916 there existed at least sixty-nine Belgian relief charities. Wilson, *The Myriad Faces of War*, p. 775.
72 Cooper Diary, 31 October 1914, P.121, IWM Documents.
73 Wilkinson interview, 9104, reel 3, IWM Sound. Wilkinson's father was a colliery under-manager in County Durham. Wilkinson had left school in 1912 and found work as a chemist for a colliery firm.
74 Holcombe Ingleby to Clement, 15 October 1914, Ingleby Letters, P.343, IWM Documents. No further mention was made of 'our' Belgians.
75 McIvor, Recollections, October 1978, DF148, Liddle Collection.
76 Robinson, 'Diary of the Great War', 19 October 1914, vol. 1, P.401, IWM Documents.
77 J. Axton to P. Liddle, 12 January 1992, DF148, Liddle Collection.
78 Gibbs Diary, 6 August 1916, Ms Eng. misc. c.180, Bodleian Special Collections.
79 Clark Diary, 27 August 1917, Ms Eng. Hist. e.152, Bodleian Special Collections.
80 A. Bradburn to S. Bradburn, 16 January 1916, Bradburn Letters, 95/16/1, IWM Documents.
81 *Ibid.*, 6 July 1917.
82 The terms are drawn from B. Anderson, *Imagined Communities: Reflections on the Origin and Spread of Nationalism* (Verso, London, 1983).
83 Clark Diary, 21 July 1917, Ms Eng. Hist. e.151, Bodleian Special Collections.
84 *Ibid.*, 1 May 1915, Ms Eng. Hist. e.102.
85 *Ibid.*, 2 November 1917, Ms Eng. Hist. e.155.
86 *Ibid.*, 13 July 1918, Ms Eng. Hist. e.165.
87 *Ibid.* Clark did not endorse Caldwell's views, but neither did he condemn them or seem to find them objectionable.
88 Yearsley, 'The Home Front', p. 134, DS/MISC/17, IWM Documents. There is little evidence that Caldwell's and Yearsley's extreme anti-Semitic views were shared by the other middle-class men who feature in this book (with the possible exception of Clark). As Gregory suggests, 'a fully-fledged popular anti-Semitism' may not have 'become pervasive among the middle classes' by 1918, but it was certainly present as part of 'a bundle of wartime fears and hatreds'. Gregory, *The Last Great War*, p. 241. See also A. Pendlebury, *Portraying 'the Jew' in First World War Britain* (Vallentine Mitchell, London, 2006), especially pp. 61–9; Robb, *British Culture*, pp. 10–11; J. Bush, *Behind the Lines: East End Labour 1914–1919* (Merlin Press, London, 1984), Chapter 6.
89 Yearsley, 'The Home Front', p. 39, DS/MISC/17, IWM Documents. Jewish financiers of German origin, including Edgar Speyer and Ernest Cassell, were vilified in some sections of the press. P. Panayi, *Immigration, Ethnicity*

and Racism in Britain, 1815–1945 (Manchester University Press, Manchester, 1994), p. 117.

90 F. Ashe Lincoln, Interview, 1993, DF148, Liddle Collection.

91 Gibbs Diary, 7 November 1914, Ms Eng. misc. c.161, Bodleian Special Collections.

92 Clark Diary, 1 May 1915, Ms Eng. Hist. e.102, Bodleian Special Collections.

93 *Ibid.*, 16 February 1917, Ms Eng. Hist. e.144.

94 *Ibid.*, 30 June 1918, Ms Eng. Hist. e.164.

95 See also Gregory, *The Last Great War*, pp. 208–12.

96 Clark Diary, 16 January 1915, Ms Eng. Hist. e.96, Bodleian Special Collections.

97 Joseph Diaries, 5 March 1915, Ms. Top. Oxon. e.288, Bodleian Special Collections.

98 For the wartime subversion of an idea central to political economy, 'that the common good was served by the pursuit of self-interest', see A. Gregory, 'Lost generations: the impact of military casualties on Paris, London, and Berlin', in J. Winter and J.-L. Robert (eds), *Capital Cities at War: Paris, London, Berlin 1914–1919* (Cambridge University Press, Cambridge, 1999, first published 1997), p. 57. See also J.-L. Robert, 'The image of the profiteer', in Winter and Robert (eds), *Capital Cities at War*, pp. 104–32.

99 Clark Diary, 7 February 1916, Ms Eng. Hist. e.120, Bodleian Special Collections. On shipping see also Cossins Diary, 18 January 1915, PP/MCR/371, IWM Documents.

100 Robinson, 'Diary of the Great War', 26 June 1917, vol. 3, P.402, IWM Documents.

101 *Ibid.*, 3 September 1917.

102 R. Saunders to son, 1 September 1917, Saunders Letters, 79/15/1, IWM Documents. For a discussion of 'profiteers', see also Gregory, *The Last Great War*, pp. 136–42. Wartime profit-making is considered further in Chapter 6 of this book.

103 Joseph Diaries, 5 January 1916, Ms. Top. Oxon. e.288, Bodleian Special Collections. Debates over the role of the wartime state in regulating labour are considered in A. J. McIvor, *A History of Work in Britain, 1880–1950* (Palgrave Macmillan, Basingstoke, 2008, first published 2001), pp. 158–61.

104 Gibbs Diary, 27 February 1915, Ms Eng. misc. c.164, Bodleian Special Collections.

105 *Ibid.*, 15 July 1915, Ms Eng. misc. c.169.

106 *Ibid.*, 2 December 1915, Ms Eng. misc. c.173.

107 Cossins Diary, 28 September 1916, PP/MCR/371, IWM Documents. Wartime occupational health is considered in McIvor, *A History of Work*, pp. 130–2.

108 Gibbs Diary, 8 August 1916, Ms Eng. misc. c.180, Bodleian Special Collections.

109 Marwick, *The Deluge*, p. 165.

110 The praise heaped on women munitions workers by the press from 1916 was also not reflected in middle-class men's writings. Gullace, *'The Blood of our Sons'*, pp. 160–6.

111 The issue of working-class standards of living during the conflict has long been a matter of debate. The work of Jay Winter has been enormously influential, especially his book *The Great War and the British People*, where he argues that 'through the workings of the labour market, through shifts in patterns of working-class expenditure and consumption, and through elements of social policy, standards of living were at least maintained for the majority and improved for the worst off sections of British society'. Winter, *The Great War and the British People*, p. 2. Also Chapters 4 and 7. See also, for example, Gregory, *The Last Great War*, chapter 6; Robb, *British Culture*, pp. 67–95; J. Manning, 'Wages and purchasing power', in Winter and Robert (eds), *Capital Cities at War*, pp. 255–85; T. Bonzon, 'Transfer payments and social policy', in Winter and Robert (eds), *Capital Cities at War*, pp. 286–302; Marwick, *The Deluge*, especially chapters 2 and 6; P. Dewey, *War and Progress in Britain 1914–1918* (Longman, Harlow, 1997), especially pp. 37–42; L. Bryder, 'The First World War: healthy or hungry?', *History Workshop Journal*, no. 24 (1987), pp. 141–57.

112 Clark Diary, 21 January 1917, Ms Eng. Hist. e.142, Bodleian Special Collections.

113 Cossins Diary, 22 April 1916, PP/MCR/371, IWM Documents.

114 *Ibid.*, 2 November 1916.

115 R. Saunders to son, 21 March 1916, Saunders Letters, 79/15/1, IWM Documents.

116 *Ibid.*, 12 August 1917. It is worth noting that far from revelling in their supposed affluence and well-being, there developed among workers too 'a growing sense that the burdens of war fell unequally'. As Adam Seipp points out, 'perceptions of inequality and the absence of fair play were particularly evident in the labour movement'. Seipp, *The Ordeal of Peace*, p. 70. For 'the mood of labour' in 1917 see also Wilson, *The Myriad Faces of War*, Chapter 47.

117 Clark Diary, 20 April 1915, Ms Eng. Hist. e.102, Bodleian Special Collections. Tellingly, these stories were circulating at a time when 'the problem of "War Babies"' was attracting much press attention. Cossins Diary, 17 April 1915, PP/MCR/371, IWM Documents. See also Marwick, *The Deluge*, p. 147; A. Woollacott, 'Khaki fever and its control: gender, class, age and sexual morality on the British homefront in the First World War', in *Journal of Contemporary History*, vol. 29, no. 2 (1994), pp. 325–47.

118 See also R. Wall, 'English and German families in the First World War', in R. Wall and J. Winter (eds), *The Upheaval of War: Family, Work and Welfare in Europe, 1914–1918* (Cambridge University Press, Cambridge, 1988), pp. 95–6.
119 Clark Diary, 1 December 1914, Ms Eng. Hist. e.92, Bodleian Special Collections.
120 Gibbs Diary, 8 November 1914, Ms Eng. misc. c.161, Bodleian Special Collections.
121 *Ibid.*, 14 March 1915, Ms Eng. misc. c.165.
122 Clark Diary, 15 May 1915, Ms Eng. Hist. e.103, Bodleian Special Collections.
123 *Ibid.*, 3 September 1915, Ms Eng. Hist. e.110.
124 Cossins Diary, 9 August 1915, PP/MCR/371, IWM Documents.
125 Gibbs Diary, 1 November 1916, Ms Eng. misc. c.183, Bodleian Special Collections.
126 A. Bradburn to S. Bradburn, 16 January 1916, Bradburn Letters, 95/16/1, IWM Documents. On industrial unrest on the South Wales coalfields see Gregory, *The Last Great War*, pp. 187–8; Marwick, *The Deluge*, pp. 115–16.
127 Cossins Diary, 10 March 1915, PP/MCR/371, IWM Documents.
128 *Ibid.*, 18 March 1915.
129 *Ibid.*, 19 July 1915.
130 Robinson, 'Diary of the Great War', 31 March 1916, vol. 2, P.401, IWM Documents.
131 *Ibid.*, 7 April 1916. On 'red Clydeside', see Gregory, *The Last Great War*, pp. 188–90; Marwick, *The Deluge*, pp. 111–12.
132 Robinson, 'Diary of the Great War', 24 March 1918, vol. 4, P.402, IWM Documents.
133 Yearsley, 'The Home Front', p. 68, DS/MISC/17, IWM Documents.
134 *Ibid.*, p. 289. The war years actually saw a marked reduction in days lost to strikes compared to the 1910–14 period, but this was certainly not reflected or acknowledged in middle-class men's writings. McIvor, *A History of Work*, p. 160; G. J. DeGroot, *Blighty: British Society in the Era of the Great War* (Longman, Harlow, 1998, first published 1996), p. 110.
135 R. Wohl, *The Generation of 1914* (Weidenfeld and Nicolson, London, 1980), Chapter 3. See also Winter, *The Great War and the British People*, p. 98.
136 Clark Diary, 6 September 1914, Ms Eng. Hist. e.88, Bodleian Special Collections.
137 Gibbs Diary, 26 May 1916, Ms Eng. misc. c.177, Bodleian Special Collections.
138 H. G. Wells, *Mr Britling Sees it Through* (The Hogarth Press, London, 1985, first published 1916), p. 317.
139 Holcombe Ingleby to Clement, 15 October 1914, Ingleby Letters, P.343, IWM Documents.

140 *Ibid.*, 22 June 1915.
141 *Ibid.*, 21 August 1915.
142 Clark Diary, 26 January 1915, Ms Eng. Hist. e.97, Bodleian Special Collections.
143 *Ibid.*, 3 July 1915, Ms Eng. Hist. e.106.
144 *Ibid.*, 27 December 1915, Ms Eng. Hist. e.117. Middle-class men's volunteer activities on the home front, including Clark's own experiences of drill, will be considered further in Chapter 5.
145 *Ibid.*, 9 May 1916, Ms Eng. Hist. e.125.
146 *Ibid.*, 24 April 1915, Ms Eng. Hist. e.102.
147 *Ibid.*, 22 January 1916, Ms Eng. Hist. e.119.
148 Approximately 70 per cent of men who saw active service during the war were under thirty, while about 40 per cent were under twenty-four. Roper, *The Secret Battle*, p. 5. 74 per cent of the men who died were under thirty. Winter, *The Great War and the British People*, p. 83. Jay Winter also suggests that 'the survival chances of older men [over the forty to forty-five range] were actually greater than they would have been had the war never occurred'. J. Winter, 'Some paradoxes of the First World War', in Wall and Winter (eds), *The Upheaval of War*, pp. 12, 15. See also Winter, *The Great War and the British People*, pp. 76–83.
149 Cossins Diary, 20 May 1915, PP/MCR/371, IWM Documents.
150 Joseph Diaries, 28 September 1915, Ms. Top. Oxon. e.288, Bodleian Special Collections.
151 Clark Diary, 3 November 1915, Ms Eng. Hist. e.114, Bodleian Special Collections.
152 *Ibid.*, 1 January 1916, Ms Eng. Hist. e.118. The 'armlet' referred to the brassard that was handed out to men who 'attested' their willingness to enlist under the Derby scheme. Recruiting will be considered further in the next chapter.
153 Yearsley, 'The Home Front', p. 155, DS/MISC/17, IWM Documents. On attestation and the Derby scheme, see also the next chapter of this book.
154 Gibbs Diary, 3 March 1917, Ms Eng. misc. c.187, Bodleian Special Collections.
155 Yearsley, 'The Home Front', p. 211, DS/MISC/17, IWM Documents.
156 Gibbs Diary, 23 September 1914, Ms Eng. misc. c.159, Bodleian Special Collections.
157 M. MacDonagh, *In London during the War: The Diary of a Journalist* (Eyre and Spottiswoode, London, 1935), p. 89.
158 Seipp, *The Ordeal of Peace*, p. 48.
159 C. E. Playne, *Britain Holds on 1917, 1918* (George Allen & Unwin, London, 1933), p. 63. On the use of the 'immensely malleable' language of sacrifice, see Gregory, *The Last Great War*, pp. 142–51. As Gregory points out, 'sacrifice is insatiably demanding'. See p. 149.

160 Robinson, 'Diary of the Great War', 16 October 1917, vol. 3, P.402, IWM Documents.

4

Civilians and military service

Introduction

In October 1914 Holcombe Ingleby and his wife received the news that their son Clement, a Lieutenant in the Royal Naval Volunteer Reserve, was on his way to the Front. As Ingleby explained to Clement, they hoped 'that you will bear yourself like a man', but could not help worrying 'that anything may happen to you'. However, such fears were cancelled out by larger considerations: 'the business has to be faced, and any man who doesn't offer himself at this moment to his country is a cur'.[1] Many – perhaps most – of his middle-class contemporaries would have agreed with the sentiment.[2] And, indeed, thousands of men did just that. By 22 August 1914 more than 100,000 had enlisted.[3] The publication of the Mons Despatch in *The Times* on 25 August, presenting the battle as a 'heroic defeat' and ending 'with an appeal for more men to join up', provided a new fillip to recruitment: almost 175,000 men enlisted between 30 August and 5 September.[4] 'Sport-mad' upper- and middle-class men, often – it has been suggested – deeply influenced by a public school ethos of 'chivalric, militaristic manhood' that called on men to apply the courage and determination developed on the playing field to 'imperial battlefields', provided a disproportionate number of these early recruits.[5]

However, the enthusiasm of August and September 1914 should not obscure the fact that the great majority of adult men, including the majority of middle-class men, did *not* volunteer their services to the armed forces: if almost a quarter of English and Welsh men aged between fifteen and forty-nine volunteered before December 1915,[6] it must follow that three-quarters did not. Thus, it is the aim of this chapter to explore further the reasons behind the decision *not* to enlist, or at least not to enlist *immediately*, even in the face of overwhelming pressure to do so.

Did those middle-class men who did not volunteer see themselves, or were seen by others, as 'curs'? The chapter begins by considering the pressures placed on middle-class men to enlist at the outbreak of war, before turning to the often overlooked pressure exerted *by* middle-class men on others, particularly those individuals who depended on them for their employment. The qualifications to the notion that all men should enlist immediately are explored next: not only the more obvious limitations imposed by age or physical unfitness, but also the widespread belief that there were responsibilities that kept many middle-class men tied to the home front. The chapter thus considers the impact of 'business' and family responsibilities, before turning to the debates over the fairness of including married men in the conscription laws introduced in 1916. It then concludes by assessing the relative strength of conflicting notions of middle-class manliness in wartime, which on the one hand required men to serve their country in its hour of need, but on the other still expected them to achieve successful careers and, most importantly, to protect and provide for their dependants.

Middle-class manliness and military service

In April 1915 Andrew Clark noted that 'on the front of the Mansion-House' in London 'are two enormous posters – yellow with white letterpress. The top one reads: "Fellow citizens! I rely on you to do your share". The lower one "We are fighting for nothing less than our life as a nation". There are similar posters at the Nelson column'. In addition, all motor-buses and taxicabs carried recruiting bills, which asked: 'why are you here when men are wanted there?' The banks also had 'a very effective poster showing the Houses of Parliament with the legend underneath: "Men of London, will you do your duty" or "If it is impossible for you to serve will you try to get a recruit"'.[7] Such recruiting bills and posters became a common sight soon after the outbreak of war, and remained so until the introduction of conscription in 1916. They left little room for doubt about the behaviour that was expected of manly, patriotic men. A poster issued as part of the Earl of Lonsdale's recruiting campaign put it rather more bluntly than most:

> Are you a man
> or
> Are you a mouse?
> Are you a man who will forever be handed down to Posterity as a Gallant Patriot?

or
Are you to be handed down to posterity as a rotter and a coward?[8]

Prominently displayed posters were only one of the methods used to pressure men into enlisting in the armed forces. In October 1914 Clark, who had a keen eye for advertisements and ephemera, received a circular from a coal merchant, with a 'superlatively silly recruiting-slip' stuck on it, 'said to be official'. It stated: 'Recruit for your country. Use your influence with the unmarried men you know between the ages of 19 and 35 to join the Army to-day. Your country needs them all'.[9] A month later he was surprised to find 'war-advertisements' (of correspondingly small size) in a book of stamps, including one stating: 'A Call to Arms. Join the Army until the war is over'.[10] At around the same time, Frank Lockwood noted that 'the illuminated [tram] car made another journey up our valley tonight' in order to 'stimulate recruitment'. The effect was 'most picturesque … The Band of the 7th Battalion occupied the upper deck and played patriotic airs. The car bore the messages "Your existence is at stake" and "Your country needs you"'.[11]

In December 1914 Horace Joseph spent a few days in London, where he was struck by the 'slightness of the difference that war has made', with the exception of darkened streets and 'the appeals everywhere for recruits'. He considered that these were 'so much reiterated that I think one would learn to ignore them'.[12] No doubt more difficult to ignore were the personal pressure and shaming tactics used on men of military age who seemed to be 'shirking' their duty. According to Clark, in September 1914 there was 'a great … outcry' in the village of Great Leighs 'against lads who are of age and physique to enlist, and who have not done so, James Searles[?], [?]Hales, Herbert Milton'.[13] Writing in January 1916, Reginald Gibbs rejected the idea that since the outbreak of war all recruits had 'volunteered from inclination or patriotism'. Rather, some had been 'discharged from their employment', while others had 'found the jeers and contempt of their sisters, sweethearts and even of their mothers' impossible to bear. He knew of at least 'one case in which a mother decided her son's course of action by telling him openly that he was only holding back because he was a coward at heart'.[14]

In December 1914 James Butlin, fresh out of public school, wrote to his friend Basil Burnett Hall that he planned to join up in the next few days: 'I hope to start wearing uniform as soon as possible … in Weymouth all females glower at a man in ordinary clothes'.[15] Hard looks were only one of the ways in which the community – women, it seems, often prominent among them – sought to shame young men into enlisting. On his return to London after his summer holiday in September 1914, Macleod Yearsley found that 'the feeling against slackers, dodgers, and shirkers was awakening … Soon young girls of all ages and styles of beauty … were parading the streets offering white-feathers to young men in mufti, with a fine disregard for discrimination'.[16] Yearsley himself, despite being over forty, was berated at least once for not being in uniform,[17] while sixteen-year-old Harry Kitchener 'received a few white feathers … probably because I was … six feet tall and fairly well-built'.[18]

In 1914 William Ostler was employed as a railway booking clerk at Crouch Hill, North London. He had been working there for quite a few years and was 'quite happy'. Interviewed in 1973, he recalled that soon after the outbreak of war 'patriotism built up very intense around London and on alternate weeks I used to meet my fiancée at Finsbury Park'. Getting on the tram, 'being so tall and fairly conspicuous … I was soon made to feel that my place would be in the forces in fact on one or two occasions I was given white feathers'. He remembered one incident particularly clearly, when a lady had marched up to him in a crowded tram and put a white feather in his button-hole, much to his 'embarrassment and discomfiture and I began to think about service in one or the other of the forces', despite being in a reserved occupation.[19] In November 1914 Frederick Robinson, whose own son was employed by the Board of Trade and had been refused permission to enlist, wrote angrily that 'a sort of persecution' was taking place: 'young men (who may have excellent reasons for not enlisting) are subject to reproaches and insults. Girls go about offering young men *white* feathers, and they write letters to their young men friends urging them to enlist and wanting to know the reasons for *not* doing so'.[20]

At the outbreak of war George Wilkinson was working as a chemist for a colliery firm in County Durham, an occupation that exempted him from military service. Decades after the end of the conflict he still remembered only too vividly the treatment meted out to young men not in uniform. By the time the Conscription Act was passed in 1916 he had reached military age: 'you were insulted everywhere you went by people who didn't know any better, ignorant people' who would make 'rude remark[s]' like 'you ought to be in khaki'. He explained that the insults had been 'very hurtful', especially since he had wanted to enlist, but had not been allowed to, as he was in a reserved, or 'starred', occupation. The situation was 'very distressing' and 'sometimes you'd stay in the house rather than go out'. Most of the people in his village and workplace, he added, knew and understood his situation; it was 'strangers' who would make the most hurtful remarks, although he also found people jokingly asking 'you not in khaki?', or making similar comments, irritating.[21]

Women were often identified as being the prime movers behind attempts to bully or shame men into enlisting, the irony of non-combatants trying to convince others to join the armed forces not being lost on contemporaries. However, plenty of men also played their part in this 'informal' recruitment drive, including middle-class men who were too old or otherwise ineligible for military service. In December 1915, for example, Rory Macleod recorded in his diary that he had 'routed out two slackers, who promised to go to recruiting office today'.[22] In reality, middle-class men were not often found handing out white feathers or publicly berating strangers not in uniform, but this may have been because, unlike most women, they were accorded a role and a voice in the 'official' recruiting machine.[23]

In October 1914 Holcombe Ingleby was busy addressing meetings and giving speeches 'on one's duty to one's country', although he lamented that 'it doesn't amount to much!'[24] A few weeks earlier he had written: 'how I wish I were thirty years younger! It is curious that, though a modern battle is a perfect inferno, one asks for nothing better than to be in it!'[25] In September 1914 Ernest Cooper was appointed joint honorary secretary of the 'Suffolk War Relief Fund and we raised over £600 in Southwold and district'. In addition, 'in connection with this I organised a recruiting "meeting" in the Market Place which resulted in over 60 recruits joining including 2 of my own clerks'. Editing his diaries after the war, and clearly aware of the swing in public opinion against the 'old men' who had sent young recruits to their deaths, he wrote that he was 'glad to add both [his clerks] … returned safely in 1919 after 4 years' service abroad'.[26]

In the village of Great Leighs both J. H. Tritton and his family were actively involved in recruiting. At the end of August 1914 Tritton wrote to Clark, informing him that 'now that the harvest is over I am arranging … a meeting of the men and women of Great and Little Leighs … in order to make clear to them the causes and the justice of the war, and the nation's need for soldiers; and further to make an appeal to the young men to offer themselves'.[27] Rectors of nearby parishes made reference to the need for recruits in their Sunday services. In August 1914 Clark's daughter heard one clergyman preach 'a harrowing sermon, on the horrible scenes of the battlefield, and exhorted all the young men to join the army. He had a big union-jack hung in front of the pulpit'.[28] Such appeals were not restricted to the early weeks of war. In July 1915 the vicar of Little Leighs 'drew a harrowing picture of the imminence of invasion, and horrors in Essex worse than in Belgium, and urged all unmarried men to enlist at once'.[29] Clark does not seem to have followed his fellow clergymen's example, but neither did he keep entirely aloof from the recruitment drive. In May 1915 his assistance was requested in publicising a forthcoming recruiting march, and he 'spent a long time writing postcards to schools, shops, public-houses, post office and individuals'.[30]

For his part, Tritton was willing to go a step further than simply exhort young men to join the armed forces. In September 1914 'pressure' was put on his household's two footmen to 'compel' them to enlist, much to the village's disapproval.[31] A year later a Tritton groom and a chauffeur were given the choice of enlistment or one month's notice.[32] Not long after, Clark heard that Tritton had sacked the estate carpenter as 'fit for munitions work', adding that 'it will be an unhappy parish when all the good men are driven out of it'.[33] Tritton's actions were by no means unique. In November 1915 Clark noted that an acquaintance, 'a married man with children', had been dismissed by the Prudential Assurance Company, 'for which he has been traveller for some years. The firm will employ no man of military age'.[34] A few weeks later he received a letter from a friend, saying that he had lost his job as a butler because his employer thought men were needed 'so badly for other things'.[35]

Not all employers were willing to exert such pressure. In September 1914 Joseph received a letter from a Mrs Haldane, saying that unmarried college employees 'should be told to enlist on pain of dismissal', a request that he turned down, replying that his 'authority is not so absolute'.[36] Four months later Gibbs reported a newspaper story, according to which the 'squire' of Finchingfield in Essex, 'where he owns most of the land', had written to the surveyor 'asking him to dismiss two roadmen who would not enlist'. The Braintree Rural District Council had responded by agreeing unanimously that 'as a public body they were not prepared to put pressure on their employees to enlist in the army'.[37]

After the introduction of conscription in 1916, furthermore, many employers proved very willing to apply for exemption from military service on their workers' behalf.[38] In June 1916 Joseph applied for his clerk,[39] while the Alberta Land Company supported Cossins's application for exemption.[40] Despite their frequent arguments on the subject of the war, in May 1916 Gibbs's headmaster, William Tinniswood, applied for exemption on his behalf.[41] In July 1917 he appeared in front of the Guildford tribunal to support Gibbs's application for an extension to his exemption. Gibbs had no doubt that the success of his application was largely down to Tinniswood: he 'made a fine defence … He looked pale and ill … His manner of speaking, in crisp telling sentences, and his general appearance of clear-cut intellectuality, and his aristocratic bearing, made a good impression'.[42] Some employers went a step further, and sought to stop their workers from enlisting or exerted pressure on reluctant workers to apply for exemption. When war broke out E. K. Quick had recently become a deacon, having been ordained eight months earlier: 'I wanted to join up as all my friends and contemporaries were doing. But the Bishop said "no", so thoroughly dissatisfied I carried on at St Leonards' until 1915'.[43] By May 1916 the Tritton estate was suffering from severe labour shortages and in a significant reversal of earlier practice, Thomas Stoddart, the land steward, asked 'C. Collins to appeal against call to go on military service on 23rd May. C. C. is unwilling to do so; would rather go now when lads he knows are going, than later when he might have to go alone'.[44]

Employers who attempted to 'keep men back' risked being accused of selfishness and lack of patriotism. For example, Clark's unsuccessful application for exemption for his gardener and general factotum, Charlie Ward, was ridiculed in the local press as frivolous and unreasonable.[45] However, despite the opprobrium it received, the practice of trying to deter one's workers from enlisting was thought to be widespread. Patriotic employers who promised to keep jobs open or provided financial assistance to employees who enlisted were – it was believed – in a minority.[46] In July 1915 James Caldwell 'had occasion to be in many places of business'. He noticed 'that in most offices there were quite as many men of military age as before the war'. Only 'in a very few instances boys have replaced men; a few banks are employing girls'. He complained that 'the great majority of employers are unpatriotic and, rather than lose a brass farthing by having less accustomed people on their staff, are willing to let the whole burden fall on the patriotic tenth of their class'.[47] The use of personal influence to secure exempted employment for favoured individuals was seen as especially objectionable. According to Clark, in June 1918 'much feeling … [was] expressed in the Malden division of Essex that their MP … had got his son … exempt from military service by getting him a financial post in the Canadian Government service'. The young man now intended to join up. Unless he did so, it was widely thought that his father would lose his seat at the next election.[48]

One way or another, many middle-class employers seem to have wielded considerable power over their workers' fates. In December 1915 Clark noted that a local farmer 'did not know what to do with his men under

Lord Derby's scheme. So he bundled them all, married and unmarried, into a wagon, and sent them to Chelmsford to be "attested"'.[49] Unsurprisingly, the consequences of employers' actions were often felt long after the end of hostilities. In October 1916, for example, Cooper heard that 'our waterworks man Dedman is to go out to France quite shortly'. After the war, he added to this diary entry that 'I appealed for this man but he enlisted before the hearing and when he was killed later his widow said we forced him to go'.[50]

Loafers and shirkers?

Most middle-class men seem to have shared the general belief that all physically fit men of military age should offer their services to the armed forces, and continued to hold this belief well beyond the first few weeks and months of war. In May 1916 Harold Cossins noted that the Compulsion Act had just passed its third parliamentary reading and would soon become law. He observed that 'everyone seems to have accepted it quite as a matter of course', adding that: 'it is strange how insensibly one's outlook changes. It seems quite wrong for young men to be in civilian clothes now, whereas before the war it seemed inconceivable that people would soon be demanding that all able bodied men should be taken away from their employments and put into the Army'.[51]

Terms such as 'shirker', 'slacker' and 'loafer' were thus used to describe those men who sought – or so it seemed – to avoid doing their patriotic duty. According to Charles Ward, the term '"shirker" gained the added opprobrium of meaning to continue in the enjoyment of income from less essential pursuits instead of "doing one's bit" by volunteering for the services or munitions factory'.[52] During a stay in Weston in September 1915 Joseph (who at the time was in his late forties) observed that 'there seem to be many men of military age loafing'.[53] Three months earlier Robert Saunders, who had three sons serving in the armed forces, had noted approvingly that 'on Saturday a big motor with an important official and a Recruiting Sergeant came round to the houses where men of military age had not joined so they are beginning to look up the slackers'.[54] Anger towards 'shirkers' did not entirely dissipate with the introduction of conscription: according to Saunders, writing in April 1917, 'it does make your blood boil to know that fellows who have done their bit and been wounded should have to go back again to be wounded while so many shirkers get off scot free'.[55]

The pressure on men of military age – or indeed on men who *appeared* to be of military age – to enlist should thus not be underestimated, and neither should the widespread consensus that it was the duty of manly, patriotic men to join the armed forces. However, this consensus also hid contradictory impulses and beliefs, which acknowledged that it was not always possible, or indeed even desirable, for men – even men of military age – to enlist, or at least, to enlist immediately. Perhaps most obviously, it was recognised that some men were too old or not physically fit for military service. Jeffrey Axton's father, the manager of the London agents of a Bradford woollen manufacturing firm, had caught tuberculosis just before the war. Nevertheless, he tried to enlist several times, but was always rejected.[56] According to Clark, 'Humphrey Watney, who kindly helped us in a Great Leighs concert by rag time songs which took the village by storm, has several times offered himself for service … but has always been refused, on account of chest-weakness'.[57] Edwin Yates's appeal for men who were under regulation army height to form a Special Auxiliary Army Service Corps revealed the existence of a group of men who were excluded from military service by their physical limitations, much against their wishes. Eli Chambers, for example, a thirty-four year-old clerk and storekeeper in a cotton mill, wrote to Yates in September 1914 that he was 5ft 4in tall: 'I am willing to go abroad and do whatever required. I wear glasses but I can see as well as anyone. No disease in eyes, and am strong physically'.[58]

Physical fitness thresholds were altered in the course of the war, with the pressure to provide the army with new recruits leading to 'a dramatic decline in rejection rates from 29 per cent in 1916 to only 3 per cent at the beginning of 1917'.[59] For example, in December 1915 Burnett Hall was diagnosed with a weak heart,[60] but subsequent re-examination led to a change in his categorisation. Writing to his friend from Craiglockhart War Hospital in May 1917, Butlin 'was vastly entertained by your experiences or rather the narrative of those experiences by which you were raised from a C3 to a C1. Though no prophet, I would wager that by the end of the war you will be an A1 and a very fine specimen of that'.[61] Despite such lowering of standards, rejection rates remained significant. In September 1918 the Prime Minister, Lloyd George, asserted that in the course of the war around one million men had been turned down as physically unfit for military service.[62]

It is worth noting that physical unfitness did not necessarily ensure sympathetic treatment. As healthy, strong bodies gained a new centrality to late Victorian and Edwardian notions of good citizenship, with 'the fit male body of the worker and soldier' held up as 'emblematic of national vigour', bodies that belonged to a 'C3', rather than an 'A1' nation were frequently made the object of scathing comment.[63] On a more speculative note, as contemporary 'quack' literature and advertisements listed weakness, debilitation and lack of vigour – caused, it was implied, by excessive masturbation – among the ills they could cure,[64] it is possible that such associations also had some (unspoken) influence on attitudes towards physical unfitness. Furthermore, David Silbey points out that although rejection rates were not broken down by class, it was generally assumed that these were far lower among middle- than working-class recruits (between 5 and 10 per cent compared to between 30 and 50 per cent).[65] Presumably, this made rejection all the worse for middle-class examinees. Frank Dawkins, the clerk to the Works Manager of a London firm manufacturing telephones, experienced such humiliation at first hand. Writing over seventy years after the event, he recalled that 'by the time I was 18½, my pals were all joining up. So I did likewise – only to be rejected. The M.O. [medical officer] took one look at the specimen of humanity in front of him – did a few taps on the chest – and rudely said "My God what is it" – meaning what a specimen of manhood. C3 (N. B. G.) [no bloody good]'.[66]

Although perhaps the most obvious, age and physical unfitness were only two of the qualifications to the widely held view that all patriotic men should respond to the emergency by volunteering their services to the armed forces. Some men, it was acknowledged, had other responsibilities that precluded them from volunteering, or at least from doing so immediately, work and family being the two most important. Giving a talk to prospective special constables in the village of Great Leigh in August 1914, for example, Sir Richard Pennefather, 'a distinguished member for many years of the Metropolitan Police Force', told his audience that 'young men who are eligible for army-service should enlist'. This appeal, however, was a qualified one: 'the call is for all men of 19 to 35 to join the colours unless they hold such positions that they cannot really be spared from it', or were married men with dependent young children.[67]

Some conscientious individuals worried a great deal about their proper priorities in wartime. Ernest Tancock worked as a schoolmaster in Yorkshire. In December 1914 'several of the masters wanted to enlist, but were deterred by the thought that it would be next to impossible … to find substitutes to do their work in training the coming generation of the country's manhood'. At their request, the headmaster wrote to Lord

Kitchener, who replied 'that they ought to stick to their work, but, in spare time, to undergo drill and training' in case they were needed in the future.[68] Reserved or 'starred' occupations, exempt from military service, tended to cluster in working-class trades such as engineering or mining.[69] However, some middle-class occupations were included too. A. E. J. Hepworth was an inspector of taxes: 'we were reserves because Kitchener said he did not want us, we could do more for the war effort by carrying on raising money than we could do by fighting'.[70] Robinson's son was told by the Board of Trade that 'he could not be spared'[71] and in December 1915 received a letter informing him that 'you are, in performing your duties in this department, giving the country the service which is the most valuable you can render during the war'.[72] Once conscription was introduced, he was given a formal exemption certificate.[73]

Despite the widely shared belief in the equation between patriotic manliness and military service, middle-class men felt a good deal of sympathy for those individuals who were not exempt from enlistment, but whose businesses would be 'utterly ruined by their absence'.[74] In November 1914 Clark mentioned – without any hint of disapproval – the case of a local man, 'a very clever saddler. The army authorities are very anxious to secure his services, but he has, with great struggle, built up a promising saddlery business, and cannot quit it, until he can find some sort of caretaker for it'.[75] After the introduction of conscription in 1916 Gibbs warned that 'when father returns (if ever he does)' from war service, 'his position in the business or professional world is gone and he has to start all over again'.[76] Only a few days before complaining to Clark about young shirkers who spent all their time sitting in cafes drinking coffee and smoking cigarettes, Caldwell advised his twenty-seven year-old nephew 'against seeking a commission, because he thought his duties in civilian life were too important to be left'. He was a 'traveller for Carvan(?) the big Edinburgh paper makers … He had built up a big business … the man he leaves his work to was by no means a success formerly'. Caldwell 'was very urgent that he should stick to his commercial duties'.[77]

It was considered reasonable, especially at times when the demand for soldiers did not seem too pressing, for individuals to think of the impact of military service on their own career and 'prospects'. In September 1914 Joseph noted that 'recruiting is going much better … so that being contacted by [illegible]', who asked his advice about whether he should continue his studies or apply for a commission, taking into account the fact that the young man's 'prospects would be much jeopardised by interrupting his work, and considering him not really much fitted for being an officer, I advised him to come up next term'.[78] Four years later Caldwell told Clark that 'there are now so many new recruits in camps that the authorities do not know what to do with them; but they keep carting off more and more men'. He considered that this was 'very hard on men who have, with great pains, built up a business, only to have it destroyed by their enforced absence. He is very sorry for Herbert Henry Cass, cycle shop, 69 High Street Chelmsford, who suffers in this way'.[79]

The acceptability of putting career before military duty should not be exaggerated. In the play 'The Man Who Wouldn't', performed at the Kilburn Empire in April 1915, the middle-aged solicitor who tried to stop his daughter's fiancé from enlisting, pointing out that 'there are plenty of men who haven't much to give up … who haven't got a house or a profession and good prospects. Let them go and fight', revealed himself as arrogant and selfish and his views as reprehensible.[80] And yet there was a good deal of sympathy for those men for whom enlistment would entail completely oversetting their working lives. Although never stated explicitly, it is clear that such sympathy applied to middle-class businesses and careers, rather than to working-class trades or job prospects. In contrast to the latter, the work of the former was often thought irreplaceable. Thus, in November 1915 Clark noted the case of a local farmer who was 'mad to go out to the war; thinks it his duty'. However, he also had other responsibilities, particularly to his children and to his farm, 'which needs his personal care. His "horseman", and his other men are, as usual, mere machines, and can do nothing except what they are told by their master each morning'.[81]

Family responsibilities

'Business' responsibilities – middle-class opinion acknowledged – were an important consideration when a man had to decide whether to delay joining the armed forces or, after the introduction of conscription, whether to seek exemption. Another, and perhaps more important consideration, was the pull of family responsibilities. Few contemporaries would have disagreed with the view that married men had a duty not only to their country, but also to their wives and children.[82] Edwardian notions of manliness were deeply enmeshed with the ability to support and look after one's family, and entering the armed forces risked undermining this ability, causing unacceptable hardship to men's vulnerable dependants.[83] The definition of 'dependants' was elastic. In February 1916 Humphrey Gleave appealed for exemption from military service and asked his brother Edward – then serving in France as an ASC officer – to write letters of support, confirming his ill-health as well as the fact that he was the only one left at home to look after their mother, who was ill with bowel cancer. This was to be 'the second string so to speak, in case the doctors accept me for light duties'. Edward seems to have been happy to oblige.[84]

Despite the wide definition of 'dependants', it was married men and fathers of families who attracted the most sympathy. In January 1915 Gibbs observed that at a time when the authorities were calling on men to enlist in order to fulfil their roles as 'protectors' of women, the reality was that if a married man of about thirty with two children, 'in receipt of £2 to £3 a week', enlisted, he would see his income reduced dramatically to around 7s a week for himself and roughly the same for his wife. 'This means that she and her children have either to live on the charity of friends or go to the poor-house'. He had spoken to a man in this position the previous day, who said that 'so far as I am concerned, I would just as soon the Germans did get here as face that possibility. My first duty is to my wife and children and patriotism be hanged'.[85] It was implied here that it was middle-class families whose standard of living would suffer from the paterfamilias' enlistment. The working classes, Gibbs pointed out, were well looked after by separation allowances, especially after rates were increased in 1915. In March that year he observed that 'the new scale of allowances to the dependants of soldiers is really very good', with many wives now receiving more money than they had at their disposal before their husbands enlisted.[86]

By spring 1915 complaints were being voiced about the crassness of recruiting appeals, which sought to increase the pressure on those men who had not yet enlisted, but did not take into account their domestic responsibilities. For example, a widely published Parliamentary Recruiting Committee advertisement focused on 'The man to be pitied'. This was the man who refused to volunteer: 'no crowds will cheer him through the streets. He will hear the praise of other men's courage and patriotism, but he will have no share in it. His lot is hard. He is to be pitied'. In March 1915 the *Pall Mall Gazette* called on the government to stop such 'importunate appeals, which have ceased to be effective … those who are left are most of them perplexed by their private responsibilities'. To such men, the authorities simply offered 'a series of vague and humiliating appeals which are becoming the mockery of our neighbours, of neutral peoples, and of the enemy'.[87] In May the same year a leader column in the *Evening News* condemned a 'scandalous advertisement', in which Kitchener had appealed for a further 300,000 men and raised the military age to forty. The columnist stated that there were still around four million unmarried men aged between eighteen and thirty-eight left in the country, 'but, instead of demanding compulsion for those who ought to go … Lord Kitchener appeals to the patriotism of a new class, the men of between thirty-eight and forty … who are mostly married men with families … while the young slackers who crowd our streets are to be left behind'.[88]

The notion of a dividing line between young single 'shirkers' and older married men on whom unreasonable demands were being made was firmly established by September 1915, when Robinson noted that *The Daily Mail* had refused to publish a recruiting advertisement for men 'of whom over 80 per cent are married'. The paper regarded 'the enlistment of married men … when there are in London alone three quarter of a million of possible unmarried recruits as injurious to the Army and to the nation'. It added that it was 'a gross injustice that married men should be taken while single eligibles remain at home stealing their jobs and businesses'.[89] The publication of attestation rates under the Derby scheme, introduced in autumn 1915, whereby individuals were asked to 'attest' their willingness to enlist in the armed forces and to be called up when needed, seemed to confirm widely held suspicions about single men's lack of patriotism.[90] According to Yearsley, 'the figures struck us all as a disgrace to the youth of this country'.[91]

Whether such condemnation of single men was justified or not,[92] there is no doubt that family responsibilities forced many men to make difficult decisions. In August 1914 Saunders noticed that his son Ron was 'awfully restless and keeps on about Bob and Wally [his brothers] doing something and he nothing for England'. Saunders had 'reasoned with him quietly about the need of one boy being left to help in case of necessity at home', although 'I shouldn't be surprised to find he had enlisted when he gets back to London'. He soon did, the pull of family responsibilities proving weaker than the desire to do something 'for England'.[93] Indeed, patriotism and the desire to 'do one's bit' should not be underestimated. In May 1917, for example, Captain E. W. Hewish assumed that it would not be long before he was posted to France: life at home with his wife 'is very sweet but I do want to take a man's part in this show'.[94] Seven months later and still in Britain, he acknowledged that he had been 'fortunate to be spared the horrors of the trenches, but when I go I shall be happier in a different way … I shall feel the parting from Wendy, but on the other hand I shall be going to do a man's work'.[95]

Some men, of course, may have welcomed the opportunity to leave family responsibilities behind: such men were perhaps less likely to acknowledge their motives and leave documentary evidence than those who fully embraced their roles as family men[96] (Figure 6).

There were plenty of men, however, particularly those with children, who were deeply worried about their families' well-being in the event of their being called up. In May 1915 Clark received a visit from F. J. Lowden, a shop assistant with a firm of wine merchants in Braintree: 'he is much troubled in mind over recruiting meetings. He is of military age but has just settled nine months ago in Braintree. His wife has been ill since Christmas. She was away six months for an operation and is still ill in bed … In case of conscription would he be required to serve?'[97]

The experiences of Harold Cossins illustrate the dilemmas faced by men with family responsibilities.[98] At the outbreak of war he was thirty-six years old and was married with one small child. The necessity of supporting them made it impossible for him to enlist: in November 1914

6 'Leaving family responsibilities behind', *Punch*, 8 March 1916. Reproduced with permission of Punch Limited.

he noted that 'I am under the age limit of Army recruits but I could not possibly give up my position to enlist as Marjorie and John would be left practically unprovided for … It is no easy matter to decide but it is hard that one cannot serve one's country without risking so much trouble for one's family'.[99] By autumn 1915, furthermore, his wife was suffering from poor health. In October her doctor recommended that she should spend the winter months by the seaside. Cossins wrote in his diary: 'four or five months … at sea, free from worries and anxieties, will I hope make Marjorie stronger than she has ever been since I knew her'.[100] When, a fortnight later, he was canvassed in connection with the Derby scheme, 'the canvasser's chief difficulty was to find room for a recital of my circumstances on his card, rendering it impossible for me to do more than I am doing at present by joining the Volunteers. These reasons include physical, financial and business circumstances'.[101]

His conflicting responsibilities continued to trouble him after the introduction of conscription. In January 1916 he condemned Welsh miners, who were threatening to strike unless the Conscription Bill was dropped. He complained that 'there are a great many slackers in Wales whom it would do one's heart good to see compelled to do something for their country'. Self-consciously, he added that 'perhaps I am a "slacker" myself, however much I might be otherwise in other circumstances'.[102] In April 1916, as conscription for both single and married men seemed inevitable, he worried that mortgage and rent relief for married recruits 'is not to exceed £104 per annum each. This would not be enough for me as there would still be another £30 or so per annum to be found before there would be anything for Marjorie and John to live upon. But I think I should be exempted if compulsion came'.[103] A week later, as 'compulsion for all at once' was announced, he observed that 'if I were free I would go like a shot but I have others besides myself to consider'.[104] He returned to this theme two months later, writing that 'I should think it rather jolly and exciting to join up, if I were free'.[105]

However, he was not 'free' and in June 1916 he submitted a claim for exemption. His employers, the Alberta Land Company, 'are putting in one for me and I am attaching a memorandum myself'.[106] In August he heard that he had been granted 'three months exemption, with leave to appeal at the end of that time … I shall not have to appear at any tribunal until then'.[107] A month later he received his exemption certificate, 'exempting me till the 6th January on the grounds of national expediency'.[108] In January, with the renewal of his exemption pending, he wrote that 'I don't like to think of what Marjorie would do if I had to go', although her health had by then improved, and they were now back at home in St Albans.[109] At the end of the month, having been interviewed in connection with his exemption application, he was 'told I would probably have to appear before the Tribunal', but was reassured that 'I was almost certain to get three or more months extension with leave to apply at the end of that time'.[110]

Early in February, however, a set-back occurred that threatened to throw all of Cossins' plans into disarray. On the first of the month he noted that 'the War Loan continues to attract huge sums of money for investment', thus diverting money away from industry and commerce. His own company felt 'its effect by the continued demands for repayment by those from whom we have had loans. One lender of £6,000 is most insistent and has gone as far as to issue a writ against us. We are doing our best to get the money over from Canada but the situation is certainly a serious one'.[111] The following day was a 'day of great commotion both political and personal, and I hardly know what is going to happen'. In the afternoon there was to be a board meeting of the Alberta Land Company, to discuss the issue of debt repayment. Some directors favoured immediate liquidation. This would have meant an end both to Cossins' salary and to his reason for exemption. As a consequence, 'I should be better in the Army than out of it, no one being willing now to engage anyone of military age. So far as I am myself concerned this would be all right but it would be all wrong for Marjorie and John. Altogether I am passing through a very anxious time, and Marjorie, whom I had to tell last night, will be feeling it still more and will await my return tonight with dreadful anxiety'.[112] Eventually it was decided against liquidation, although it was clear that the company was facing difficult times: 'but the sense of relief tonight is very great, and one contemplates a reduction in salary almost with equanimity'.[113]

A fortnight later he appeared before the Guildhall Tribunal, where, despite his hopes for an extension to his exemption, he was told: 'claim disallowed! So here begins a new era'. He immediately thought of his wife: 'I … must get back to Marjorie. Poor girl, I suppose it means another upheaval for her just as she was getting stronger'.[114] The following day he was 'much worried about financial matters', as he tried to work out how his wife could support herself and their child in his absence. He would 'try to get something from the Alberta Company but this will be driven almost to liquidation by my removal'. He thought (erroneously) that Marjorie would get twenty-five shillings a week separation allowance for herself and their son, 'and I shall try to get £2 a week from the Civil Liabilities

Committee. But this alone won't be enough to meet all my fixed obligations. Everything feels very blank but I suppose one will soon settle down.'[115] Eventually, they decided that Marjorie and John should move to Minehead with relatives, leaving the St Albans house to be rented out. Early in March Cossins took John to Paddington station and put him on a train to Minehead. He reflected: 'the first step towards the break-up of the home has been taken and we both feel rather dreary'.[116] Four days later he was in the army, drafted to the Northamptonshire Regiment.[117]

The Derby scheme, conscription and the 'problem' of married men

In October 1915 it was announced that one final attempt was to be made to satisfy the needs of the armed forces for manpower without having recourse to conscription. Accordingly, the Derby scheme, named after the new Director of Recruiting for the Army, was put in place: all men between the ages of nineteen and forty, including those in 'starred' occupations, were called upon to 'attest' their willingness to volunteer.[118] They would then be placed in 'groups' based on age and marital status, and only called up when needed. In the meantime, they would be free to return to their civilian lives, having been provided with an armlet to signify their status as 'attested' men, although in fact, 'the government … lost no time' in calling up attested men, beginning in December 1915 with classes two to five: single men aged between nineteen and twenty-two.[119]

Although intended to be as inclusive as possible – *all* men of military age were invited to attest – in fact, the group system was felt to lay bare the contradictory pressures on married men such as Cossins, as well as the supposed lack of patriotism of the single men who had not yet enlisted. According to Caldwell, it was widely agreed that by December 1915 'more married men than single men have come forward. In town it is said that the proportion is one single man to eight married men'. He thought that 'an exaggeration, but there can be no disguising this fact that single men have held back'.[120] In an attempt to conform to the generally held view that single men should 'go' before those with family responsibilities, in November 1915 the Prime Minister Herbert Asquith – without consulting the Cabinet, it seems – issued a reassurance to married men that under the group system, 'you will not be called upon to serve until the Young Unmarried Men have been summoned to the Colours', a pledge that was subsequently reiterated in recruiting propaganda and returned to haunt the government in the following months.[121]

By the end of December 1915 it had become clear that the Derby scheme had failed to attract the recruits needed, and that the introduction of some form of conscription was inevitable, although the idea that single men should 'go' first had not yet been abandoned. Thus, the first Conscription Bill, introduced in Parliament in January 1916, only applied to single men or widowers with no dependent children.[122] However, what had been intended as a nod to the dominant opinion about the respective responsibilities of married and single men,[123] proved a serious miscalculation. Despite Asquith's pledge, in March 1916 the first groups of married men who had attested under the Derby scheme were called up – before all single men had been conscripted. If this were not bad enough, it seemed as if married men who had *not* attested might avoid military service entirely. The result, Ingleby wrote in a letter to his son, was a 'rumpus … over the question of the single men shirkers and the married men who have attested. The latter consider that the government has not kept its pledge. The government are sitting uncomfortably between two stools, having endeavoured, as usual, to conciliate all parties'.[124]

By mid-March, 'indignant meetings' of attested married men were being held throughout the country.[125] According to Cossins, they complained that they had been misled, and 'that there are still great numbers of single men sheltering in munitions works and protected trades'. Cossins was not entirely unsympathetic, but believed 'that married men who, like myself have heavy obligations … should not have attested. They were praised for doing so and now that they are asked to fulfil their engagement they ask to be let off. It is a very difficult position'.[126] According to Robinson, 'some take the view that married men are endeavouring to get out of the obligations which they voluntarily took upon themselves'.[127] Ten days later he added that 'the married men are not behaving well. It would seem that all our patriots are already used up and the men who are left are doing their utmost to avoid serving the country, although attested'.[128] Lockwood, a single man of military age who had not attested because he was 'not strong enough for a soldier's life',[129] had little sympathy for attested married men: now that they were being called up 'they are whining and squealing and finding fault with everything and everybody'. They seemed to think that the 'Single Men First' pledge meant that 'every single man (whether a munitions worker, indispensable or not) should be called up before a married man was touched'.[130]

Gibbs was among the half million married men who attested under the Derby scheme, just a few days short of his thirty-seventh birthday.[131] In March 1916 he shared the anger of many, wondering whether the 'craftiness' of those married men who had refrained from attesting was 'going to be rewarded with immunity from all military obligations? If so, it is a glaring shame'. He discussed the matter with his grocer, who replied 'with a crafty grin creeping round the side of his face "they knew what they were doing, when they attested, didn't, they? They did it of their own free will"'. He had not attested, as '"I knew better"'. So it seems', Gibbs added, 'that the attested married men are not only going to be victimised, they are also going to be sneered at into the bargain, as being fools'.[132] He returned to this theme a few weeks later, stressing that married men had been 'given to understand that they would only be asked to serve as a last resort'. He believed that 'it is one thing to offer to fight ... when the country is in danger of being overrun by foreign armies and quite another to be called up ... when the available single men have not been used'.[133]

However, this seemingly straightforward statement of the relative obligations of single and married men in wartime hid the more complex reality of Gibbs' own – and no doubt, many other middle-class men's – motivations for attesting. At the end of October 1915 Gibbs had received 'the recruiting appeal issued to everybody by Lord Derby' and responded by setting out the reasons why 'I certainly do not intend to offer myself as a recruit'. First of all, he openly acknowledged that 'I fear intensely death and mutilation such as is likely to befall soldiers on the firing line'. Furthermore, 'if my country were in danger of sharing such as fate as Belgium I should offer to fight as the lesser of two evils'. However, the present call was not to defend England, but 'to defend the Empire in other words to keep our heel on the necks of conquered peoples'. Finally, 'I have six children, whom I wish to keep in bread and margarine and boots'. He then added that 'even if I conceived it my duty to sacrifice myself for a ramshackle Empire ... I should hesitate ... before placing myself in the position of a pawn in the hands of the incompetent military autocrats who are ... mismanaging the war'. Being all too aware of the high casualties of recent campaigns, including Gallipoli, he concluded by stating that 'I prefer to be a live coward to a dead hero'.[134]

Two weeks later he received a visit from an acquaintance, General Christopher, who asked him to join up. In his reply Gibbs did not mention his fear of death and mutilation, but rather stressed his perhaps more acceptable scruples: his family 'circumstances and ... my objections to fighting to hold Egypt and India'. He added that 'I am not going while others in a similar position cry off', but would be 'willing to recruit if the Government compelled other men in like circumstances to go also'.[135]

However, early in December, as the Derby scheme was about to close, he was thrown into confusion when Tinniswood told him 'from information he has acquired at his club', that the men who did not attest 'are going to be denied the right to appeal to the local tribunals for exemption'.[136] He noted that 'I am very worried about the recruiting business. There is only a few hours left now to decide what to do'.[137] By the following day he had made his mind up: 'I am trying to find out whether … I have done a foolish thing. The fact is I have just *recruited!* If anyone had told me a year ago that I should do this, I should not have believed him'.[138] His opinion of the war had not changed. He still believed that 'we are not asked to fight against a German invasion … but to enlist for a new land-snatching adventure'.[139] He had attested because he was afraid that otherwise he would be 'denied all right of appeal to be exempted' and 'be badgered to death with "moral suasion"'.[140] On meeting General Christopher in the new year, he 'pointed proudly to my armlet (I thought it would please the old man). I did not tell him that it is my sincerest wish that it will never be anything more than an ornament'.[141]

As attested married men began to be called up in spring 1916 while unattested married men seemed on the verge of escaping military service entirely, Gibbs came to regret his decision, feeling that like many others, he had been 'fooled'. He worried about what would become of his family if he was called up, 'and then comes the sudden spasm of mortification that if I had *not* attested all this anxiety would have been avoided … I have been caught in a booby trap, while men younger and with fewer responsibilities put their fingers to their nose and laugh'.[142] By then, he had apparently forgotten that his decision to attest had been precipitated by the (as it transpired, unfounded) fear that he might otherwise have been unable to claim exemption, and expressed his discontent by adopting the arguments widely used by attested married men and their supporters: that they had been misled into thinking that they would be called up only as 'a last resort', after all the single men had 'gone'.[143]

Various compromise solutions were proposed to the problem of married men's enlistment, including the suggestion that those who could 'prove' that they had been misled into attesting should be released from their obligations, that the military age should be lowered, or that the call-up should be suspended while a 'comb-out' of eligible single men was carried out. However, by the end of March 1916 it had become clear to most people that the distinction between married and single men could no longer be sustained in the face of the armed forces' continued demand for manpower, particularly in view of a widely anticipated Western Front 'offensive' in summer 1916. A clear solution to the 'married men's muddle' thus emerged: 'compulsion for all able-bodied men'.[144]

Conclusion

Contrary to what one might expect, the introduction of universal conscription did not bring an end to complaints of unfairness. The local tribunals set up to assess claims for exemption, for example, attracted a good deal of adverse comment, generally focusing on their lack of consistency and perceived harshness. According to Clark, in March 1916 there was much discussion in the locality about 'the inequality between tribunal and tribunal Chelmsford refusing any postponement of service; Braintree granting exemption whole-sale'.[145] A month earlier, Robinson had noted that 'in most cases the applicants appear to receive little consideration ... which is probably very different from what they expected ... judged from the promises held out on the posters and hand-bills'. For the most part, they were 'peremptorily told that "national needs must come before personal considerations"'[146] (Figure 7).

That said, most claimants attracted little sympathy outside tribunals too. In February 1916 Cossins acknowledged that 'there seems to be many hard cases ... but there naturally are very few men left who have not got family or financial obligations'.[147] Others were not so understanding. In February 1916 Saunders wrote to his son that 'the papers are full of the applications for exemption that are coming before the tribunals and the miserable excuses put forward make one's blood boil to think Englishmen are so degenerate'.[148] By 1916, what had once been considered perfectly valid reasons for not enlisting were being dismissed as 'miserable excuses', the demand of the armed forces for middle-class men's services proving more powerful than the pull of business, family or other responsibilities.

The supremacy of the military's claims, firmly established by 1916, had not always been a foregone conclusion. In December 1914, for example, Clark had pasted a recruiting handbill on the pages of his diary. It called on men to 'join the army yourself *at once*', before somewhat diluting its appeal by adding: 'unless for any sufficient reason you cannot do so'.[149] This telling phrase revealed that alongside the belief that all manly and patriotic men should enlist, there was an acceptance that there could be 'sufficient reasons' why this course of action was not always possible. Most obviously, some men were too old (or too young) for military service, while others were not sufficiently fit for the rigours of army life.

“That Tribunal Feeling”

A SENSATION THAT HAS BEEN THE DAILY EXPERIENCE OF MANY THOUSANDS OF CITIZENS

7 ‘That tribunal feeling’, *The Bystander*, 15 November 1916. Reproduced with permission of the Bodleian Libraries, University of Oxford, Per.2705 d.161, p. 343.

Such men, it must be said, were not always treated with much sympathy. In a context where notions of good citizenship were increasingly linked to a healthy physique, and individuals and organisations stressed that a strong, healthy body could be achieved by everyone, provided they were willing to put in the effort, those middle-class (and other) men who did not reach a minimum physical standard risked being dismissed contemptuously as 'n. b. g.'

Perhaps more fundamentally, debates over enlistment revealed two different and ultimately incompatible notions of middle-class manliness: on the one hand, one that stressed the importance of patriotism and willingness to serve one's country, even to the extent of making the 'ultimate sacrifice'. On the other hand, a notion of manliness linked to hard work, entrepreneurship, business success and especially the ability to support and protect family and dependants. Asquith's pledge that married men would not be called up until all single men had been 'summoned to the Colours', their exclusion from the first conscription bill and the protests as attested married men began to be called up while plenty of young 'shirkers' were supposedly still at large, all show the continued potency of a notion of middle-class manliness linked to domestic and family responsibilities, although the ridicule heaped on many of the claimants for exemption in 1916 suggests that this understanding of manliness had by then lost a great deal of ground in the face of overwhelming military need. However, it is surely significant that it required an event of the magnitude of the First World War to undermine the link between middle-class masculinity, the workplace and the domestic hearth.

Notes

1 Holcombe Ingleby to Clement, 4 October 1914, The First World War Letters of Holcombe Ingleby MP (hereafter Ingleby Letters), P.343, Department of Documents, Imperial War Museum (hereafter IWM Documents), London.

2 G. Robb, *British Culture and the First World War* (Palgrave, Basingstoke, 2002), Chapter 2. N. F. Gullace, *'The Blood of our Sons': Men, Women and the Renegotiation of British Citizenship during the First World War* (Palgrave Macmillan, Basingstoke, 2002), Chapters 2 and 5.

3 A. Gregory, *The Last Great War: British Society and the First World War* (Cambridge University Press, Cambridge, 2008), p. 31.

4 *Ibid.*, p. 32; I. F. W. Beckett, *The Great War 1914–1918* (Pearson Education, Harlow, 2001), p. 211.

5 J. A. Mangan, '"Muscular, militaristic and manly": the British middle-class hero as moral messenger', *The International Journal of the History of Sport*, vol. 13, no. 1 (1996), p. 44. See also Gregory, *The Last Great War*, pp. 317, 244, 130–1; A. Woollacott, *Gender and Empire* (Palgrave Macmillan, Basingstoke, 2006), pp. 75–8.
6 I. F. W. Beckett, 'The nation in arms, 1914–18', in I. F. W. Beckett and K. Simpson (eds), *A Nation in Arms: A Social History of the British Army in the First World War* (Manchester University Press, Manchester, 1985), p. 11. See also Gregory, *The Last Great War*, pp. 89–95; J. M. Winter, *The Great War and the British People* (Palgrave Macmillan, Basingstoke, 2003, first published 1985), p. 27. See also the introduction to this book.
7 A. Clark War Diary, 'Echoes of the 1914 War in an Essex Village' (hereafter Clark Diary), 7 April 1915, Ms Eng. Hist. e.101, Special Collections, Bodleian Library, University of Oxford (hereafter Bodleian Special Collections), Oxford.
8 Quoted in D. Birley, 'Sportsmen and the deadly game', in J. A. Mangan (ed.), *A Sport-Loving Society: Victorian and Edwardian Middle-Class England at Play* (Routledge, Abingdon, 2006, article first published 1986), p. 277.
9 Clark Diary, 2 October 1914, Ms Eng. Hist. e.89, Bodleian Special Collections.
10 *Ibid.*, 19 November 1914, Ms Eng. Hist. e.92.
11 F. T. Lockwood, 'Notes Written by F. T. Lockwood', 4 November 1914, 96/52/1, IWM Documents. See also Robb, *British Culture*, pp. 103–8; M. L. Sanders and P. M. Taylor, *British Propaganda during the First World War, 1914–18* (Macmillan, Basingstoke, 1982), especially pp. 16–17.
12 Wartime Diaries of H. W. B. Joseph 1914–18 (hereafter Joseph Diaries), 23 December 1914, Ms. Top. Oxon. e.288, Bodleian Special Collections.
13 Clark Diary, 15 September 1914, Ms Eng. Hist. e.89, Bodleian Special Collections.
14 Diary of R. W. M. Gibbs, 1914–20 (hereafter Gibbs Diary), 8 January 1916, Ms Eng. misc. c.174, Bodleian Special Collections. The impact on recruiting of economic distress in the early weeks of war is considered, for example, in Gregory, *The Last Great War*, p. 31.
15 J. H. Butlin to B. Burnett Hall, 2 December 1914, Letters of Lieutenant James H. Butlin (hereafter Butlin Letters), 67/52/1, IWM Documents.
16 M. Yearsley ('Eyewitness'), 'The Home Front, 1914–18', p. 19, DS/MISC/17, IWM Documents. On the white feather campaign, see Gullace, '*The Blood of our Sons*', chapter 4; N. F. Gullace, 'White feathers and wounded men: female patriotism and the memory of the Great War', *Journal of British Studies*, vol. 36, no. 2 (1997), pp. 178–206.
17 Yearsley, 'The Home Front', p. 20, DS/MISC/17, IWM Documents.
18 H. J. Kitchener to P. Liddle, not dated, DF148, Liddle Collection (1914–18), Special Collections, Brotherton Library, Leeds University (hereafter Liddle Collection), Leeds.

19 W. G. Ostler interview, 21 March 1973, 39, Department of Sound, Imperial War Museum (hereafter IWM Sound), London.
20 F. A. Robinson, 'Diary of the Great War', 10 November 1914, vol. 1, P.401, IWM Documents. See also Gullace, *'The Blood of our Sons'*, Chapter 2.
21 G. D. Wilkinson interview, 9104, reels 3 and 4, IWM Sound. Feeling that he was not doing 'his bit' and not doing 'enough', Wilkinson joined up in January 1918.
22 R. H. Macleod Diary, 10 December 1915, R. H. Macleod Papers, DF087, Liddle Collection.
23 For the importance of 'local leadership' in recruiting, see Gregory, *The Last Great War*, pp. 88–9.
24 Holcombe Ingleby to Clement, 15 October 1914, Ingleby Letters, P.343, IWM Documents.
25 *Ibid.*, 27 September 1914.
26 The Diary of Ernest R. Cooper, 'Nineteen Hundred and War Time', 28 July 1914 – 3 December 1918 (hereafter Cooper Diary), 3 September 1914, P.121, IWM Documents. It is not clear exactly when Cooper edited his diary.
27 Clark Diary, 29 August 1914, Ms Eng. Hist. e.88, Bodleian Special Collections. The family's activities, especially those of Tritton's daughters and granddaughters, caused a good deal of resentment, both among their workforce and in the village in general. See, for example, *ibid.*, 1 May 1915, Ms Eng. Hist. e.102, Bodleian Special Collections.
28 *Ibid.*, 30 August 1914, Ms Eng. Hist. e.88.
29 *Ibid.*, 12 July 1915, Ms Eng. Hist. e.107. According to George Robb, 'the Church [of England] helped transform a campaign to safeguard national interests into a veritable holy war'. Robb, *British Culture*, p. 114. See also Gregory, *The Last Great War*, Chapter 5; A. Wilkinson, *The Church of England and the First World War* (SCM Press, London, 1996, first published 1978); A. J. Hoover, *God, Germany and Britain in the Great War: A Study of Clerical Nationalism* (Praeger, New York, 1989); A. Marrin, *The Last Crusade: The Church of England in the First World War* (Duke University Press, Durham, NC, 1974).
30 Clark Diary, 13 May 1915, Ms Eng. Hist. e.103, Bodleian Special Collections. The march turned out to be a 'very poor show' and the speeches 'rotten'. *Ibid.*, 15 May 1915, 16 May 1915, Ms Eng. Hist. e.103, Bodleian Special Collections.
31 *Ibid.*, 1 September 1914, Ms Eng. Hist. e.88.
32 The former chose enlistment, the latter 'cheerfully chose the month's notice'. *Ibid.*, 14 September 1915, Ms Eng. Hist. e.110.
33 *Ibid.*, 9 October 1915, Ms Eng. Hist. e.112. Relations between the Trittons and Clark were cordial, although the latter was aware of (and, it seems, sometimes shared) the village's dislike of the squire's family.

34 *Ibid.*, 13 November 1915, Ms Eng. Hist. e.114.
35 *Ibid.*, 30 November 1915, Ms Eng. Hist. e.115.
36 Joseph Diaries, 1 September 1914, Ms. Top. Oxon. e.288, Bodleian Special Collections.
37 Gibbs Diary, 1 January 1915, Ms Eng. misc. c.163, Bodleian Special Collections.
38 Following the introduction of conscription, local tribunals were given the responsibility of assessing exemption applications. The grounds on which applications could be made are considered further in Chapter 6.
39 Joseph Diaries, 19 June 1916, Ms. Top. Oxon. e.288, Bodleian Special Collections.
40 H. C. Cossins Diary, 1914–18 (hereafter Cossins Diary), 21 June 1916, PP/MCR/371, IWM Documents.
41 Gibbs Diary, 18 May 1916, Ms Eng. misc. c.177, Bodleian Special Collections.
42 *Ibid.*, 14 July 1917, Ms Eng. misc. c.191.
43 After a spell as army chaplain, in 1917 he resigned and joined the Rifle Brigade. E. K. Quick, '1914–1918', not dated, DF148, Liddle Collection.
44 Clark Diary, 17 May 1916, Ms Eng. Hist. e.126, Bodleian Special Collections.
45 *Ibid.*, 27 February 1916, Ms Eng. Hist. e.121; 9 March 1916, Ms Eng. Hist. e.121. See also J. Munson (ed.), *Echoes of the Great War: The Diary of the Reverend Andrew Clark 1914–1919* (Oxford University Press, Oxford, 1985), p. 116. Clark received the news of Ward's death in December 1917. Clark Diary, 11 December 1917, Ms Eng. Hist. e.157, Bodleian Special Collections.
46 However, they did exist. See, for example, A. W. Savage to K. A. Scott-Moncrieff, 1 November 1915, K. A. Scott-Moncrieff, General Manager, Electrical Supply Company, DF115, Liddle Collection. Savage thanked Scott-Moncrieff, the general manager of the Electrical Supply Company, having heard 'from home that the company is sending my mother £2 monthly'.
47 Clark Diary, 3 July 1915, Ms Eng. Hist. e.106, Bodleian Special Collections.
48 *Ibid.*, 30 June 1918, Ms Eng. Hist. e.164.
49 *Ibid.*, 18 December 1915, Ms Eng. Hist. e.116.
50 Cooper Diary, 8 October 1916, P.121, IWM Documents.
51 Cossins Diary, 17 May 1916, PP/MCR/371, IWM Documents.
52 C. H. Ward, 'Recollections of the First World War', 1971, DF148, Liddle Collection. See also Gregory, *The Last Great War*, p. 90.
53 Joseph Diaries, 28 September 1915, Ms. Top. Oxon. e.288, Bodleian Special Collections.
54 R. Saunders to son, 14 June 1915, R. Saunders, Letters to Son in Canada, 1914–18 (hereafter Saunders Letters), 79/15/1, IWM Documents.

55 *Ibid.*, 1 April 1917.
56 J. Axton to P. Liddle, 12 January 1992, DF148, Liddle Collection.
57 Clark Diary, 5 January 1915, Ms Eng. Hist. e.96, Bodleian Special Collections.
58 E. Chambers to E. Yates, 9 September 1914, E. Yates, Correspondence, 1914, DF146, Liddle Collection. 5ft 4in corresponds to approximately 1.62m. At the outset of war the minimum height required was 5ft 3in (1.6m), briefly raised between September and November 1914 to 5ft 6in (1.68m). In November 1914 the requirement was lowered again and 'bantam' units were formed. G. J. DeGroot, *Blighty: British Society in the Era of the Great War* (Longman, Harlow, 1998, first published 1996), p. 46.
59 I. Zweiniger-Bargielowska, *Managing the Body: Beauty, Health and Fitness in Britain, 1880–1939* (Oxford University Press, Oxford, 2010), p. 194. See also Winter, *The Great War and the British People*, p. 52. The passing of so many men as physically fit proved counter-productive, and in November 1917 a new system of four 'grades' was introduced. It is worth noting that in 1917–18 only 36 per cent of the 2.5 million men examined were graded as 'fit for full military service'. Robb, *British Culture*, p. 80. See also Winter, *The Great War and the British People*, pp. 50–64.
60 J. H. Butlin to B. Burnett Hall, 15 December 1915, Butlin Letters, 67/52/1, IWM Documents.
61 *Ibid.*, 24 May 1917.
62 Zweiniger-Bargielowska, *Managing the Body*, p. 151. The medical examination statistics for 1917–18 can be found in Winter, *The Great War and the British People*, pp. 57–8.
63 Zweiniger-Bargielowska, *Managing the Body*, p. 13. See also A. Carden-Coyne, *Reconstructing the Body: Classicism, Modernism and the First World War* (Oxford University Press, Oxford, 2009), pp. 160–6. Although note, for example, the sympathetic treatment of a civilian man 'who because of heart-trouble had been unable to join the army', in Wyndham Lewis's short story 'The French poodle', published in 1916. T. Tate (ed.), *Women, Men and the Great War: An Anthology of Stories* (Manchester University Press, Manchester, 1995), p. 168.
64 L. A. Hall, *Hidden Anxieties: Male Sexuality, 1900–1950* (Polity Press, Cambridge, 1991), pp. 60–2.
65 D. Silbey, 'Bodies and cultures collide: enlistment, the medical exam, and the British working class, 1914–1916', in *Social History of Medicine*, vol. 17, no. 1 (2004), p. 71. Self-employed men were thought to be the least fit among middle-class recruits, a healthy physique not being quite so necessary to enable them to keep their positions. See also Zweiniger-Bargielowska, *Managing the Body*, p. 218; Winter, *The Great War and the British People*, pp. 62–4.
66 F. Dawkins to P. Liddle, 16 March 1986, DF148, Liddle Collection. In the 1919 satirical novel *The Old Indispensables*, the protagonist is told by the

doctor to 'get dressed and get away before you slip down one of the cracks in the floor'. E. Shanks, *The Old Indispensables: A Romance of Whitehall* (Martin Secker, London, 1919), p. 102. Although see also the (real-life) case of Arthur Burge, who felt vindicated by his medical examination, despite his rejection as medically unfit: 'at least no one can call me a coward now I have a certificate'. R. Van Emden and S. Humphries, *All Quiet on the Home Front: An Oral History of Life in Britain during the First World War* (Headline, London, 2003), p. 25.

67 Clark Diary, 31 August 1914, Ms Eng. Hist. e.88, Bodleian Special Collections. Another qualification was 'men with bad teeth'.

68 *Ibid.*, 24 December 1914, Ms Eng. Hist. e.94.

69 In October 1918 there were approximately 2.5 million men in reserved occupations. Beckett, *The Great War*, p. 214.

70 A. E. J. Hepworth to P. Liddle, 18 September 1981, DF148, Liddle Collection.

71 Robinson, 'Diary of the Great War', 26 October 1915, vol. 1, P.401, IWM Documents.

72 *Ibid.*, 9 December 1915.

73 *Ibid.*, 2 March 1916, vol. 2, P.401.

74 *Ibid.*, 24 July 1916.

75 Clark Diary, 11 November 1914, Ms Eng. Hist. e.91, Bodleian Special Collections.

76 Gibbs Diary, 14 May 1916, Ms Eng. misc. c.177, Bodleian Special Collections.

77 Clark Diary, 25 December 1915, Ms Eng. Hist. e.116, Bodleian Special Collections.

78 Joseph Diaries, 4 September 1914, Ms. Top. Oxon. e.288, Bodleian Special Collections.

79 Clark Diary, 31 August 1918, Ms Eng. Hist. e.168, Bodleian Special Collections. See also servicemen's worry that their time in the military would leave them 'without a defined career path at an age when such a situation could only be an embarrassment to both themselves and their parents', in J. Meyer, *Men of War: Masculinity and the First World War in Britain* (Palgrave Macmillan, Basingstoke, 2009), p. 39.

80 Quoted in L. J. Collins, *Theatre at War, 1914–18* (Macmillan Press, Basingstoke, 1998), p. 180. For a condemnation of men who put career before duty, see also R. H. Mottram, *Sixty-four, Ninety-four!* (Chatto & Windus, London, 1925), p. 83.

81 Clark Diary, 4 November 1915, Ms Eng. Hist. e.114, Bodleian Special Collections. Tenant farmers' apparently poor military record is considered in Gregory, *The Last Great War*, pp. 117–22. There was bitterness at tenant farmers' apparent 'want of patriotism in keeping their sons back and sending their labourers to get killed'. Quoted in P. Horn, *Rural Life in England*

in the First World War (Gill and Macmillan, St Martin's Press, New York, 1984), p. 190. For the relatively low enlistment rates among employers of labour in general, see Winter, *The Great War and the British People*, p. 37.

82 Meyer, *Men of War*, p. 15.

83 J. Tosh, *A Man's Place: Masculinity and the Middle-Class Home in Victorian England* (Yale University Press, New Haven, CT, 1999), p. 85. Not all middle-class men, of course, lived up to the ideal. See, for example, J. Benson, 'Domination, subordination and struggle: middle-class marriage in early twentieth-century Wolverhampton, England', *Women's History Review*, vol. 19, no. 3 (2010), pp. 421–33.

84 H. Gleave to E. T. Gleave, 12 February 1916, E.T. Gleave Letters, 78/31/1, IWM Documents.

85 Gibbs Diary, 3 January 1915, Ms Eng. misc. c.163, Bodleian Special Collections. For servicemen as 'protectors' of women, see Gullace, *'The Blood of our Sons'*, Chapter 2.

86 Gibbs Diary, 14 March 1915, Ms Eng. misc. c.165, Bodleian Special Collections.

87 'The man to be pitied', *c.*1915, cutting; *Pall Mall Gazette*, 29 March 1915, cutting, both in A. Clark, 'Scrapbooks of leaflets, newspaper cuttings, etc., illustrating aspects of the Great War', Bodleian Library, University of Oxford, Oxford.

88 *Evening News*, 20 May 1915, cutting, in Clark, 'Scrapbooks of leaflets, newspaper cuttings, etc.'.

89 Robinson, 'Diary of the Great War', 17 September 1915, vol. 1, P.401, IWM Documents. For representations of the 'shirker' as an unmarried man see also Silbey, 'Bodies and cultures collide', p. 72.

90 According to Jay Winter, 'the most damning result' was the fact that only 37 per cent of 'unstarred' men not in reserved occupations had attested. Moreover, while 'over forty per cent of married "unstarred" men had done so ... only thirty-one per cent of single "unstarred" men had signed up under the Derby scheme'. Winter, *The Great War and the British People*, p. 39. See also R. J. Q. Adams, 'Asquith's choice: the May coalition and the coming of conscription', *Journal of British Studies*, vol. 25, no. 3 (1986), p. 257.

91 Yearsley, 'The Home Front', p. 155, DS/MISC/17, IWM Documents. See also Gibbs Diary, 5 January 1916, Ms Eng. misc. c.174, Bodleian Special Collections, who noted that 43.5 per cent of the total number of men of military age 'failed to attest'.

92 Gregory suggests that contrary to contemporary perceptions, married men 'were much more reluctant to volunteer' than bachelors. Gregory, *The Last Great War*, p. 94. The youth of most recruits, discussed in Chapter 3, would also suggest the likelihood of a preponderance of single men.

93 R. Saunders to son, 15 August 1914, Saunders Letters, 79/15/1, IWM Documents.

94 E. W. Hewish, 1917 Diary and Accounts (hereafter Hewish Diary), 6 May 1917, 02/43/1, IWM Documents.

95 *Ibid.*, 31 December 1917.

96 Tosh suggests that the late Victorian period saw a 'flight from domesticity' among young middle-class men. See Tosh, *A Man's Place*, Chapter 8.

97 Clark Diary, 31 May 1915, Ms Eng. Hist. e.104, Bodleian Special Collections. Peter Barham notes that 'worries about their families … figured prominently in the defences' of soldiers who suffered a mental breakdown and were court martialled as a result of their failings. P. Barham, *Forgotten Lunatics of the Great War* (Yale University Press, New Haven, 2004), p. 74. See also pp. 130–1, for post-war lobbying 'on behalf of the "home man", whose spirits were easily broken if he was forcibly separated from the domestic hearth'.

98 See also the rather different account of these experiences in Gregory, *The Last Great War*, pp. 92–4.

99 Cossins Diary, 30 November 1914, PP/MCR/371, IWM Documents.

100 *Ibid.*, 31 October 1915. The nature of her illness was never explicitly stated, but seems to have been partly a nervous breakdown. In November they moved to Brighton, where she spent some weeks in a nursing home. See *ibid.*, 20 November 1915, 10 December 1915, 1 January 1916.

101 *Ibid.*, 13 November 1915.

102 *Ibid.*, 13 January 1916.

103 *Ibid.*, 26 April 1916.

104 *Ibid.*, 2 May 1916.

105 *Ibid.*, 11 July 1916.

106 *Ibid.*, 21 June 1916.

107 *Ibid.*, 9 August 1916.

108 *Ibid.*, 15 September 1916. His exemption was conditional on his drilling with the Volunteer Training Corps. The Corps and other volunteer bodies will be considered further in Chapter 5.

109 *Ibid.*, 22 January 1917.

110 *Ibid.*, 31 January 1917.

111 *Ibid.*, 1 February 1917.

112 *Ibid.*, 2 February 1917.

113 *Ibid.*

114 *Ibid.*, 14 February 1917.

115 *Ibid.*, 15 February 1917. The weekly separation allowance was 19s. See *ibid.*, 17 February 1917.

116 *Ibid.*, 10 March 1917.

117 Cossins survived the conflict. The diary continues into 1919, detailing his war service in France, mostly with the Army Service Corps.

118 'Starred' occupations were those exempt from military service.

119 Robinson, 'Diary of the Great War', 20 December 1915, vol. 1, P.401, IWM Documents.

120 Clark Diary, 18 December 1915, Ms Eng. Hist. e.116, Bodleian Special Collections.
121 Parliamentary Recruiting Committee leaflet no. 56, not dated; Parliamentary Recruiting Committee poster no. 134 and no. 135, not dated, 'Miscellaneous war posters', all in 'Miscellaneous papers relating to the Great War, 13 volumes', Bodleian Library, University of Oxford, Oxford. See also Adams, 'Asquith's choice', p. 257.
122 'An outline of the Military Service Act', 1916, leaflet, in Clark, 'Scrapbooks of leaflets, newspaper cuttings, etc.'
123 In February 1916 Great Leighs 'village opinion' believed that there would be 'civil war' in England if married men were called up before 'the young ones'. Clark Diary, 20 February 1916, Ms Eng. Hist. e.121, Bodleian Special Collections.
124 Holcombe Ingleby to Clement, 19 March 1916, Ingleby Letters, P.343, IWM Documents.
125 Robinson, 'Diary of the Great War', 15 March 1916, vol. 2, P.401, IWM Documents.
126 Cossins Diary, 11 March 1916, PP/MCR/371, IWM Documents.
127 Robinson, 'Diary of the Great War', 20 March 1916, vol. 2, P.401, IWM Documents.
128 *Ibid.*, 30 March 1916.
129 Lockwood, 'Notes', 6 December 1915, 96/52/1, IWM Documents.
130 *Ibid.*, 6 March 1916.
131 Gibbs Diary, 11 December 1915, Ms Eng. misc. c.173, Bodleian Special Collections. He was thirty-seven on 22 December 1915.
132 *Ibid.*, 7 March 1916, Ms Eng. misc. c.175.
133 *Ibid.*, 31 March 1916.
134 *Ibid.*, 31 October 1915, Ms Eng. misc. c.171. See also *ibid.*, 29 November 1916, Ms Eng. misc. c.183.
135 *Ibid.*, 13 November 1915, Ms Eng. misc. c.172.
136 *Ibid.*, 9 December 1915, Ms Eng. misc. c.173.
137 *Ibid.*, 10 December 1915.
138 *Ibid.*, 11 December 1915.
139 *Ibid.*, 5 December 1915.
140 *Ibid.*, 18 December 1915.
141 *Ibid.*, 10 January 1916, Ms Eng. misc. c.174.
142 *Ibid.*, 10 March 1916, Ms Eng. misc. c.175.
143 *Ibid.*, 31 March 1916. Having been placed in class A, Gibbs was granted a six-month exemption in January 1917. See 10 January 1917, Ms Eng. misc. c.185. Having failed to find work in an exempted occupation, he was called up in November 1917. See 21 November 1917, Ms Eng. misc. c.195.
144 *Ibid.*, 19 March 1916, Ms Eng. misc. c.175. According to Gibbs, this solution was being pushed by the powerful newspaper proprietor 'Lord Almighty Northcliffe'.

145 Clark Diary, 22 March 1916, Ms Eng. Hist. e.122, Bodleian Special Collections.

146 Robinson, 'Diary of the Great War', 21 February 1916, vol. 2, P.401, IWM Documents. This impression is confirmed by Cooper, who was appointed Clerk to the Southwold tribunal. See Cooper Diary, 18 February 1916, P.121, IWM Documents. The work of the Preston tribunal is described in H. Cartmell, *For Remembrance: An Account of some Fateful Years* (George Toulmin & sons, Preston, 1919), Chapters 5 and 6. For an even-handed assessment of the record of tribunals in Northamptonshire, see J. McDermott, 'The Work of the Military Service Tribunals in Northamptonshire, 1916–1918' (Unpublished PhD thesis, University of Northampton, 2009).

147 Cossins Diary, 24 February 1916, PP/MCR/371, IWM Documents.

148 R. Saunders to son, 24 February 1916, Saunders Letters, 79/15/1, IWM Documents. For debates over tribunals' 'fairness' see also L. S. Bibbings, *Telling Tales about Men: Conceptions of Conscientious Objectors to Military Service during the First World War* (Manchester University Press, Manchester, 2009), pp. 29–31 and McDermott, 'The Work of the Military Service Tribunals in Northamptonshire'.

149 Clark Diary, 22 December 1914, Ms Eng. Hist. e.94, Bodleian Special Collections. The appeal continued: 'in that case help to make it easy for others to respond to the mother country's call to arms'.

5

Home front volunteers

Introduction

Writing a 'Prefatory note' to his wartime diaries in November 1918, Frederick Robinson observed that his contribution to the war effort 'might perhaps have been greater'. This was not, he stressed, from want of trying: he had been 'denied the opportunity. Personal service without payment was offered several times and declined. It was not possible to get within the ring fence. One had not the physical strength to dig potatoes, nor the inclination to make crutches'. Nevertheless, his 'conscience … [was] clear. Members of the family have done their "bit" in various ways, in the Civil service, VAD nursing, bandage-making, etc. All as the opportunity came – time and labour given ungrudgingly, without expectation of reward'.[1] As Robinson implicitly acknowledged, and as discussed in Chapter 4, many men may have had good reasons for not enlisting in the armed forces. However, this did not mean that they could simply get on with their peacetime lives as though nothing had changed. On the contrary, all on the home front were expected – and indeed, many wanted – to contribute to the war effort by doing their 'bit'.

Attempting to persevere with peacetime activities, thus demonstrating an 'inappropriately passive behaviour in wartime' could be an uncomfortable experience.[2] Towards the end of August 1914 Harold Cossins met up with his friend Fred and joined him for a game of tennis. 'We both felt as if we were doing something to be ashamed of, and that we ought to have been drilling'.[3] A couple of weeks later they had another game of tennis, finding themselves the only players on the club's seventeen courts, despite the lovely weather. Fred had by then joined a civilian 'Veterans' Corps, restricted to 'Public School Men'. They were to drill three times a week and do some 'camping' at weekends. Cossins was sceptical: 'I daresay that members think they are doing their duty'.[4] By mid-November his attitude had clearly changed, and he attended a meeting in St Albans to inaugurate a Drill Association. It was very well attended and he estimated an initial membership of around five hundred. 'I signed an application form and shall probably begin drilling next week'.[5] According to Macleod Yearsley, by the beginning of 1915 more and more people were 'longing to be more actively engaged in "doing something" … the war obtruded itself into everything and we were fired by all we saw, read, or heard'. As a result, 'everyone who was normal (… the great majority, abnormality [being] … the peace-cranks, profiteers and the like) made every effort to do his or her best in whatever sphere to which he or she was called, were it special constable, first-aid man, or land-worker. All', he concluded, 'were doing their utmost in "war work"'.[6]

It is middle-class men's involvement in this home front 'war work' that is the focus of this chapter. After a brief survey of the options open to middle-class male volunteers and an examination of individuals' motives for selecting the particular activities and organisations with which to become involved, the chapter considers more in detail two of the most common volunteering choices made by middle-class men: enlistment in the Volunteer Training Corps and the special constables. After assessing the extent to which participation in these two bodies allowed middle-class men to gain a sense that they were making a manly contribution to the war effort, the chapter considers a rather different, more private and individualistic, although publicly endorsed, form of 'war work': allotment keeping and vegetable growing. The chapter concludes by arguing that it was such experiences of home front volunteering, from drilling in the public gaze to digging a vegetable patch in the privacy of one's garden, which help explain middle-class men's reactions to the 'farce'[7] and 'browbeating'[8] of the National Service scheme of 1917.

Civilian war work

While on holiday near Wells in August 1914, Horace Joseph went to a meeting in the town hall 'about organising work'. However, 'it turned out to be needle-work, and a meeting really for women, so I slipped away'.[9] Despite some overlaps, there was a marked gender division of labour in voluntary war work on the home front. Activities such as sewing and knitting for the troops, auxiliary nursing, serving at YMCA and other canteens or selling small flags on 'flag days' to raise money for war charities, were all seen as primarily the province of women,[10] while men were expected to engage in a different range of war work. Thus, although in October 1914 it appeared that 'everyone' in Minehead was 'working for the Red Cross or similar objects', it is likely that most men and women would have worked separately, on different tasks and for different objectives.[11]

There were a variety of ways in which middle-class men could contribute to the war effort. Having just left school and before joining up in December 1914, James Butlin spent a few months doing voluntary work at the National Reserve Offices in Weymouth. In August 1914 he wrote to Basil Burnett Hall: 'Last Tuesday Col. Lymes met Beck and myself in the town and asked us if we would do a little work for him at the National Reserve Offices. We said yes, not knowing what we were going to be let in for. The work is *honorary* worst luck … we write letters, make lists of 1st class etc. men, compile registers, address envelopes, and every other conceivable work under the sun'.[12] Early in 1915 Yearsley volunteered his services in response to a call by the Royal Society of Medicine for a 'voluntary first-aid body for air-raids among its Fellows',[13] while Derrick Martin's father joined the City of London detachment of the British Red Cross. 'With three other London businessmen' he regularly met 'trains at the London termini and … [moved] wounded soldiers by stretchers from the trains to ambulances for transfer to hospitals'.[14] In June 1915 wide publicity was given to the 'great numbers of Stock Exchange and similar men [who] now work regularly on war munitions at the Arsenal'.[15] According to Robinson, 'City men are being organised to work on the manufacture of shells at Woolwich Arsenal on Saturdays and Sundays'. Almost a thousand men had 'volunteered from the Stock Exchange, Baltic, Lloyds, etc., in fact, everybody is most anxious to do anything they can to help'.[16]

The image of 'city men' spending their spare time manufacturing munitions made good journalistic copy, but was hardly typical of middle-class men's volunteer activities on the home front. In fact, it was much more common for them to become involved in a range of 'committee' work, to offer their services to organisations such as special constables or Volunteer corps, or, in the latter part of the war, to respond to the call to tend allotments and grow more food, none of which required their straying into the working-class environments of munitions and other factories. In fact, there were considerable continuities with pre-war activities. In the village of Great Leighs, for example, the men who were already active as members of the church vestry or of the parish council also provided the membership of special constables, as well as of bodies such as the 'Invasion' committee, set up in spring 1916,[17] or the local branch of the National War Savings Committee, which confounded Clark's and others' initial scepticism by raising over £700 in the twelve months following its establishment in July 1917.[18]

Some men took on more than one role, both in connection with charitable organisations and with the many bodies set up to administer wartime regulations, including tribunals and food control committees, although few held as many positions as E. G. Bratchell, an Essex JP who took on no less than thirty-one.[19] William McIvor recalled in 1978 that during the war his father had 'engaged in many activities, including joining the 2nd (Birkenhead) Battalion of the Cheshire Volunteer Regiment (nicknamed the Old Crocks), being a volunteer with the Fire Brigade, a member of the Food Control Committee, and of an organisation which developed the growth of vegetables in the district. All this in addition to running the small family business engaged on vital war work connected with ship repairing'.[20] In Great Leighs William Brown, a local farmer, told Clark in September 1916 that in addition to his position as Sergeant of the local corps of special constables, he had 'much official duty in connection with the district Invasion and other war committees'.[21] George With, the headmaster of the local Council School, was a parish churchwarden, a member of the Invasion committee and (briefly) a special constable. In 1917 he also took on the role of Treasurer to the Great and Little Leighs National War Savings Committee.[22] James Caldwell's wartime activities stood out as especially energetic. As well as taking on roles as special constable and Boy Scout instructor, he was also active in the Church Lads Brigade and – far less enthusiastically – in the Volunteer Training Corps.[23]

Individuals' reasons for joining a particular organisation or committee often reflected their existing civic responsibilities and professional standing in their community, rather than personal preference. In March 1917, for example, Clark had to be coaxed into becoming a member of the local War Savings Committee, which he feared would involve the type of '"fussing" over "business" [that] … I despise and loathe'.[24] At the outbreak of war, in addition to his role as Town Clerk, Ernest Cooper also held the posts of captain of the fire brigade, manager of the harbour and member of the lifeboat crew. He was soon appointed joint honorary secretary of the Suffolk War Relief Fund and in spring 1915 became involved in the Volunteer movement.[25] He thus seems to have been the 'obvious' choice to act as clerk to a variety of wartime committees: in February 1916 he was 'appointed Clerk of the Tribunal under Lord Derby's scheme' and when, soon after, a Canadian Relief Fund was established 'to help lodging house keepers to carry on', 'as usual' he was appointed clerk of the local committee. 'During the next three years and over I had to administer and distribute this Fund, this meant many meetings and much work as well as some unpleasantness with unsuccessful candidates, this was however the salvation of many homes'.[26] He emphasised the burden involved in such work. In May 1915, after his resignation from the position of joint honorary secretary of the Suffolk War Relief Fund, he felt 'much relieved to be free of such a thankless troublesome office'.[27] In January 1918 he retired from the fire brigade: 'I intended to see the war out but it is lasting too long [and] … I do not wish for another three years of war conditions and air raid watches … I am greatly relieved to be clear of the responsibility of the night work' and hoped 'to get rid of other honorary jobs by degrees'.[28]

In some cases, individuals were guided in their choice of volunteer activities by earlier experiences. Caldwell, for example, had a long record of voluntary military service. At seventeen he had joined the Queen's Edinburgh Volunteers and upon moving to Glasgow some years later had obtained 'a commission in the Glasgow Highlanders Volunteers, a kilted battalion of the Lanarkshire Volunteers'.[29] Similarly, between 1894 and 1902 Yearsley had 'held a commission in a well-known Volunteer Corps, and when I left I became a Captain of the National Reserve and was on the Marylebone committee of that body'.[30] He had also been a member of the National Service League, which campaigned for compulsory military training for all young men: it is unsurprising that he should become an active member of the Volunteer Training Corps.[31] Others joined by more circuitous routes. George Wilkinson, who as a chemist for a colliery firm was in an exempted occupation, nevertheless wished to enlist, despite his employer's opposition: he was made a special constable in an (unsuccessful) attempt to satisfy his wish to do his 'bit', short of allowing him to volunteer for the army.[32] However, many – perhaps most – individuals simply volunteered for those organisations available in their locality, which did not require their straying too far from their middle-class milieu, and whose membership was made up of friends, acquaintances and other men of a similar social background.

Volunteer Training Corps

Soon after the outbreak of war, a rash of local defence forces sprang up across the country, often based on existing social, sports and rifle clubs.

The aim of these largely middle-class organisations, which included bodies such as the Surrey Athletes' Volunteer Force, the Holloway Drill and Rifle Club and the Oldham Rifle Volunteer League,[33] was to provide a fully trained civilian defence force, ready to spring into action in case of invasion 'or other grave national emergency'.[34] In August 1914 Sir George Pragnell, presiding over a meeting of the newly formed National Patriotic Association, 'composed of business men in London', described 'the new force as a fifth line of defence', made up of those men who, 'on account of age, business duties or home ties, did not feel able at this time' to enlist, but 'would gladly do so if occasion arose, and who desired at once to get some drill and some lessons in arms'.[35]

Unsurprisingly, probably mindful of pre-war events in Ireland, the government's reaction to the establishment of paramilitary forces outside its control was unenthusiastic. Within a few days of the outbreak of war, it issued a notice in the press 'vetoing all forms of voluntary military effort'.[36] This stance was subsequently softened, and in September 1914 H. J. Tennant, the Under Secretary of State for War, wrote that the government had no objection to an organisation that provided 'such lessons in drilling and musketry … to those men not of age for service … or other disqualification for active service'.[37] A Central Association of Volunteer Training Corps was thus quickly established as a coordinating body for those local associations that had already sprung into existence.[38] By the end of 1914 'hundreds of corps had affiliated to the Central Association',[39] its membership 'held to be approaching one million'.[40] Numbers declined fairly quickly after the initial spurt of enthusiasm, but remained significant: in May 1917 the total numbers were just under 300,000.[41] Among the men who joined the movement were Ernest Cooper, Harold Cossins, Horace Joseph and Macleod Yearsley.

Despite their initial success in attracting recruits, there remained significant contradictions at the heart of the volunteer movement. While its proponents continued to see the role of the Corps in a more ambitious light, as a 'home defence body in case of invasion',[42] the authorities were reluctant to countenance more than training organisations for those individuals who were unable to join up, or to join up immediately.[43] Thus, Volunteer Training Corps (VTC) drilled, went on route marches, paraded, practiced shooting at miniature ranges and were regularly inspected, including by important military figures such as Lord French.[44] They occasionally received more advanced training, such as in sentry duty or in 'attack drill',[45] while specialist corps like the 1st London Engineers Volunteers undertook not only the routine activities of drill, parades, route marches, trench digging and shooting instruction, but also offered courses on topics such as the management of searchlights and the internal combustion engine. Indeed, 'any man of education who was keen to train himself in the technical work with a military bearing was made welcome'.[46]

Nevertheless, despite the 'tax' on individuals' time imposed by these activities,[47] Volunteers were rarely given the opportunity to make a more active contribution to the war effort. More than a year after joining the Oxford VTC, Joseph noted in October 1915 that they had finally 'begun to be of use': they had spent two days at Didcot Arsenal, shifting army stores.[48] A year later his Volunteer Battalion was 'asked to provide guards for Leefield[?], should the War Office require it, two nights a week for the next six months … It will be highly inconvenient, but one can only say yes'.[49] However, this came to nothing, as did many other proposals to make more use of Volunteers' services. In October 1915 Cossins was told that the VTC 'are taking part in guarding the St Albans anti-aircraft guns. I think I shall volunteer for one night', but then found out a few days later that the 'gun has been moved from Hatfield and our expected outpost and sentry duties cancelled'.[50]

Hopes were raised that the Volunteers would be allowed greater scope when the government granted the movement official recognition in 1916.[51] In June 1916 Robinson noted that 'the National Training Corps came into its own, and was recognised by the War Office. A review of these patriotic veterans was held in Hyde Park by General French, when they were officially raised to the standard of Volunteers … Up to the present the War Office has not recognised them and in fact, has rather snubbed them'. Volunteers had been required to pay for their own uniforms and accoutrements, the government making no contribution to the running and equipping of the corps beyond the provision of bright red brassards with GR printed in large letters.[52] They were now to be allowed khaki uniforms and some arms, subsidised by the authorities.

Such renewed hopes were eventually disappointed too. In April 1917 Yearsley inserted a notice in *The London County Council Gazette*, explaining that the 1st London Engineering Volunteers, of which No. 2 company was formed of London County Council staff, 'has now received official recognition by the War Office … the general idea being that, in case of actual service, the Corps will be used to the utmost of its technical and expert capabilities'.[53] However, by August 1917 there was still no sign that their services were required. During parliamentary questions, the MP Annan Bryce asked the under-secretary of state for war if he knew that although the corps had been recognised in March 1917, it had been met with official disinterest and had not yet received any information about 'the work it should undertake'. The unhelpful reply was that demand for their services would depend on 'military considerations'.[54]

Eventually, the VTC played its most important wartime role in the spring and early summer of 1918, 'when the Allies ... were in full retreat before the advancing German hordes'. Volunteers took over coastal defences, allowing regular troops to be 'hustled overseas'.[55] In June 1918 Cooper was among the 13,000 Volunteers who undertook 'active service on the [East] coast'. At the end of the month he was called upon 'to take command of a Special Service Company', and 'started training at once with the 2/8 Essex, Cyclists', with whom they took their 'share in the ordinary routine of the Coast Defences'. Nevertheless, the whole experience turned out to be more in the nature of a holiday than an active deployment: towards the end of July, he 'hired a furnished cottage ... and fetched my people there'. He finished his stint at the end of August, and as it was obvious that they were no longer serving a useful purpose, he decided to return home.[56]

It is perhaps unsurprising that a sense of futility should eventually have crept in. In August 1918 Joseph was in charge of a Volunteer Company in the absence of their regular commander: 'there is a very great deal of office work, which takes a great amount of time, and also, I think, to very little purpose'.[57] Cooper, who was appointed adjutant and later Battalion Commander of his local volunteer corps, noted after the war that 'the work of organisation was difficult and tedious owing' at least in part 'to the government discouraging the movement as much as possible, their only contribution' being the brassard with GR on it.[58] H. G. Wells observed in his 1916 novel *Mr Britling Sees it Through* that 'after a stout resistance to any volunteer movement at all', the War Office had finally recognised it 'in such a manner as to make it ridiculous'. He added that 'there was a very general persuasion that to become a volunteer when one ought to be just modestly doing nothing at all, was in some obscure way a form of disloyalty'.[59]

Official disinterest and snubs were key to many volunteers' sense of dissatisfaction. However, this was not the only problem at the heart of the volunteer movement. From the outset, both organisers and participants also struggled with the question of who should be allowed – and indeed encouraged – to join the movement. In a letter to the *Times* in October 1914, for example, H. G. Wells emphasised that there were plenty of 'surplus people' in the country 'who while not being of an age or physique suitable for full military services were anxious to undertake defence work of a quasi-military character'.[60] A 1914 circular to London County Council staff pointed out that the mobilisation of 'the greatest part of the manhood of the nation' was being organised by the military authorities, adding that 'with this we have nothing to do except to induce as many eligible men to join as we can'. However, there remained 'a large residue' who could not enlist 'on account of age, or for other reasons. At present this residue, which in a greater national emergency could supply many men who would make useful soldiers for internal defence, or for defence of their own hearths and homes, has no Military Training'.[61]

It was this 'large residue,' or in Wells's terms, 'surplus people', who were to form the membership of volunteer corps. However, this emphasis on attracting men ineligible for military service created problems for the corps. Most obviously, their age profile made them vulnerable to ridicule and contempt. As noted in Chapter 3, in January 1915 Clark's sister-in-law dismissed her local 'citizens corps' as 'composed of all the decrepit old men in the place'.[62] According to Yearsley, his corps consisted of around two hundred men who may have been middle-aged, but were also fit and willing. In spring 1915 they were issued with 'the red flannel brassard with a black GR'. During route marches, it 'caused much amusement … and comment by the crowd. The general opinion of the spectators was that it meant either "Genuine Relics" or "Grandpapa's Regiment", the balance being in favour of the latter'.[63]

While the proponents of the volunteer movement sought to emphasise that many of its members might be 'over the enlistable age', but 'were still hale and vigorous',[64] outsiders saw them very differently. According to Cooper, the authorities' insistence that men of military age should not be enrolled meant that the ranks of volunteers were 'filled with greybeards or septuagenarians and the force earned the sobriquet of grandfathers scouts, England's last hope, and when the Red Brassard came out, Georges Wrecks and various other derogatory titles'.[65] In reality, Cossins' experiences suggest that the exclusion of men of military age was not always strictly enforced,[66] while tribunals' practice from mid-1916 of demanding membership of a VTC as a condition for temporary exemption eventually changed the nature of the organisation's membership, with older volunteers increasingly replaced by younger men of military age.[67]

Nevertheless, the image of volunteers as frail, elderly and ineffectual men proved a resilient one. Caldwell soon lost any enthusiasm for the movement, coming to the conclusion that it was driven mainly by 'the desire to peacock it in uniform'.[68] In June 1917 he told Clark that the only men left on the home front were either too busy working 'in some occupation of national importance' to train with the volunteers or were 'men rejected as physically unfit on grounds of bad health or physical infirmity, and what use would these "rejects" be if called out' in case of invasion? 'What was the use', he asked, 'of men of over 60 who had never done a march in their life and did not know one end of a rifle from the other training as volunteers?'[69] Thus, when J. F. Crowder's father – fifty-four in 1914 – carried 'the sword borne by his grandfather Major John Crowder in the peninsula' during the Napoleonic wars while parading with the Local Defence Volunteers, he no doubt saw himself as carrying on a family tradition of patriotic volunteering. However, he may also have contributed to an image of volunteers and of the volunteer force as 'relics' of the past and as figures of fun, irrelevant to the present conflict.[70]

The Volunteer movement never entirely resolved the contradictions at its heart: as a home defence force, should it try to attract young, physically fit men who, the authorities stressed, should more properly enlist in the armed forces? Or should it focus on men over military age, running the risk of attracting ridicule and contempt as a 'grandpapa's regiment'? Even after tribunals were allowed to demand membership of a VTC as a condition for exemption, the authorities never viewed the movement with any great enthusiasm, suspecting it of providing 'shirkers' with a way of avoiding military service. There were plenty who thought like Lord French, who put it bluntly: 'if the men were fit, they ought not to be kept back'.[71] This left VTC members, especially those such as Cooper and Yearsley, who devoted a good deal of time and energy to the movement, feeling undervalued and unappreciated, despite the fact that, as Yearsley put it, there was not 'one single officer or man in the Volunteer Force who was not actuated by a strong sense of duty and a patriotic determination to do his utmost for his country and the honour of his Corps'.[72] Both Cooper and Yearsley felt bitter about the lack of recognition for Volunteers' efforts at the end of the war.[73] According to Cooper, 'they were the only Branch of the Services unrepresented in the Victory Parades', adding that 'even the Special Service men who threw up everything and proceeded voluntarily on active service in the dark days of 1918 remain without any adequate acknowledgement of their patriotism'.[74]

Special constables

Unlike the spontaneous setting up of Volunteer groups, the enrolment of special constables, acting as auxiliaries to the police, was sanctioned and controlled by the authorities. This was partly a response to the increased wartime duties required of the police, and partly to its depletion: a year into the war, provincial forces had lost approximately one man in every five to the military, while over a quarter of the Metropolitan Police had enlisted or been called up as reservists.[75] The response to the call for special constables was generally (albeit not universally) positive: more than 20,000 men had been enrolled in London by mid-August 1914, while by the end of the year 10,000 men had joined the ranks in Manchester, 6,000 in Essex and 2,000 in Birmingham.[76] The swearing in of special constables was not limited to the larger towns and cities. At the end of August 1914, for example, a meeting was held in Great Leighs to explain the duties of special constables, attended by around forty 'persons'. J. H. Tritton was in the chair. He 'stated briefly that in the present great crisis, there was great need of the services of Special Constables throughout the country'. He then introduced Sir Richard Pennefather of Little Waltham Hall, who had been 'a distinguished member for many years of the Metropolitan Police Force'.[77]

Pennefather explained that at the 'general meeting of the county authorities in Chelmsford' there had been a 'universal feeling that Special Constables were urgently needed under the critical circumstances of the present time'. The 'authorities felt that they knew not what fresh dangers any day might bring forth'. The war, he added, had brought extra duties for the police, with more than twenty Emergency Acts already passed by parliament. Particularly important was the Defence of the Realm Act, which required especial care of roads, railways and reservoirs, as well as the 'Act about aliens'. Essex only had 'five hundred regular Police Constables', so it was especially important 'that the citizens themselves should come forward to relieve the County Police of some of their ordinary duties, as well as of much of the new work occasioned by the 25 Emergency Acts'. The special constables' main duties, he concluded, would be to organise patrols 'to protect all roads, and especially the abutments of bridges, telegraph points and the like', where 'the hired agents of the enemy may try to do damage'.[78] A week later twenty-five Great Leighs men enrolled, including Clark and Caldwell.[79]

Given their official status, it would be reasonable to suppose that special constables did not experience the same sense of futility and were not subjected to the same scornful treatment as Volunteers. In fact, their status was not quite as straightforward as might seem at first glance. From the start, there was the same uncertainty among special constables as among Volunteers about who should join the movement.[80] The notice calling the meeting in Great Leighs to explain the role of special constables in August 1914 stated that 'no one who is of an age to serve in the Army or Navy is eligible as a Special Constable'.[81] Indeed, Pennefather confirmed that 'young men who are eligible for army-service should enlist'. However, he acknowledged that there were men who 'hold such positions that they cannot really be spared from it' or married men with dependent young children who could not join the armed forces: such men, of military age but 'unable to enlist for any such real reasons, may and ought to, join with the older men of the county in undertaking the duties of the special constable'.[82]

Special constables do not seem to have been the butt of jokes about elderly men taking up arms as Volunteers were – perhaps because they did not seek the same quasi-military status – but it is clear that issues of age and physical frailty were problematic for them too. Press cartoons made much of their limited physical presence, unthreatening looks and small stature compared with the individuals they were meant to police (Figure 8), but for most special constables it was not imaginary confrontations with burly men that proved the most challenging, but other physical demands linked to their duties.

In the village of Great Leighs the newly enrolled special constables practiced drill once a week for six weeks during September and October 1914, Caldwell acting as drill instructor. Their first attempts were light-hearted. According to Clark, the drill was 'carried out vigorously, till light failed'. There were 'various unusual difficulties: (a) the surface of the field … was very uneven … (b) the wind was blowing a gale, and the drill-instructor's voice was mostly inaudible (c) the instructor is not a tall man and he stood beyond much taller men … so that his demonstrations … were invisible to three quarters of the company'. As a consequence, 'the right about movement produced, time after time, the most ludicrous clumps, or dispersed confusion of individuals, which produced shouts of mirth on the part of the company when they took breath to see the tangle they had got into'.[83] Two weeks later Clark noted that 'the drill was not altogether successful. I think the fault was not altogether with us, but because the instructor is not content with making sure, to begin with, of the simpler movements, but tries prematurely to begin complicated movements'.[84] During their final drill Caldwell 'was complimentary enough to say that for the limited number (five practices) at which on no occasion the whole number had been able to be present, the results were very creditable'.[85]

EXTRY SPESHUL!

THE SPECIAL (*compelled to make an embarrassing arrest*): Look here, old chap. If you'll come quietly I'll give you half-a-crown.

8 ‘Extry speshul!’, *The Sketch*, 10 November 1915. Reproduced with permission of the Bodleian Libraries, University of Oxford, N.17078 c.32, p. 125.

In reality, despite Caldwell's encouraging words, drill was felt to highlight the lack of aptitude for such exercises and the physical weaknesses of many middle-class men, both among special constables and among Volunteers. Drill, whether military exercises or the modified form taught in schools, was overwhelmingly associated with youth, perhaps contributing to a lack of confidence among middle-aged or older recruits about their ability to keep up.[86] When drill was reinstated among Great Leighs special constables in April 1915, Caldwell convinced sixty-seven year-old Thomas Stoddart, the Lyons Hall land steward, not to attend. According to Clark, Stoddart was 'elderly and finds it difficult to make out the commands. Being deeply conscious that, from physical failings, I myself hinder the drill, I made the same request. I am at times very deaf and do not hear the commands distinctly … Being crippled with rheumatism, I cannot step out as the men thirty years younger than myself do'.[87]

As a much younger man in his thirties, Cossins did not find drilling with the VTC so challenging, but admitted that during their first attempt in December 1914 'everyone seemed very keen but a good many found it hard to remember the difference between right and left. After an hour and a half one felt as if one had had quite enough exercise'.[88] Route marches could also be difficult. In December 1916 he went out with the Volunteers, patrolling the Midland railway line: 'the five mile march over the ballast found out the weak points of one's feet, so we were not sorry to get home'.[89] Eighteen months earlier Robert Saunders had found it impossible to keep up with the VTC drill: 'I was sorry to come to the conclusion I was physically unfit owing to my right arm being practically useless at times'.[90]

Like members of Volunteer corps, furthermore, many special constables came to feel that their services were both undervalued and underused. In Great Leighs and surrounding parishes the main duty of special constables resolved itself in the night-time patrolling of local roads and lanes, ensuring that the lighting regulations were observed and stopping motors and motor-cycles. At a meeting in October 1914 they were told that 'the roads in Great Leighs are to be patrolled nightly from 9pm to 5am, 4 constables on duty each night, 2 from 9pm to 1am, 2 from 1am to 5am'. According to Clark, the county's Chief Special Constable, Captain Finch, justified this command 'by the most inconsequential remarks about soldiers in the front serving in the trenches, and by foolish drivel about an army of German mechanics who were shortly to be launched against Essex and Suffolk to destroy waterworks'. The audience may have been sceptical, but a 'roster of turns for patrol duty' was drawn up[91] and early in November Clark began his patrol duty, accompanied by Edwin Luckock, a 'retired missionary'. He thought the patrols 'absolutely unneeded. There is nothing in Great Leighs that it would benefit an enemy to destroy – no reservoir, no railway, no wireless station, no barracks'.[92] Nevertheless, in the course of the following eighteen months he spent approximately one night a week patrolling the roads of Great and Little Leighs, until his resignation from special constable duty in May 1916.

The patrols proved almost entirely uneventful. In mid-November 1914, for example, Clark and Luckock heard some dogs barking, but 'not a creature appeared the whole time on patrol'.[93] A month later he went out with William Brown, both of them getting 'soaking wet. Not a living creature seen or heard of the whole patrol'.[94] In January 1915, 'as showing the senseless futility of the nightly patrols asked of Special Constables in this out-of-the-way corner … we met saw or heard no living creature (neither human, beast, nor fowl)'.[95] Despite persistent reports in spring 1915 of 'a motor-car which is supposed to pass along the main road here, with powerful headlights' in order to guide Zeppelins on air-raid missions, Clark 'never … encountered a car on my special constable patrol at night; nor has any of the parishioners who take turns on such patrols'.[96] There was a brief flurry of excitement in May 1915, when Clark heard that Caldwell had discovered a Belgian man wandering around the parish at night: 'it has yet to be discovered whether he is a man gone somewhat silly from what he has come through, or a man simulating silliness to escape serving in the Belgian army'.[97] However, the rumour turned out to be untrue: the following day Caldwell told Clark that 'the night prowler had been mentioned to him several times', but no trace had been found of him.[98]

The night patrols were not without their pleasures. In November 1915 Clark noted 'stars, large and small, superbly bright. Orion and the Plough both very distinct. Other groups so resplendent that I bitterly regret having been so long indoors that I forgot my boy's knowledge of their names'.[99] However, these did not make up for the discomfort of being out on 'most disagreeable' nights, whatever the weather,[100] only to find 'no sight or sound of man, beast, or bird'.[101] Special constables soon began to voice their discontent. In December 1914 Clark received a note from Luckock, stating that 'I find patrolling our lanes, as it is arranged, too much for my strength, and as it appears to me of very little practical utility I have sent in my resignation as Constable'.[102] In January 1915 the Essex Chief Special Constable 'and his adviser (Sir Richard Pennefather) have had it well rubbed into them that they have made most unreasonable demands on their volunteers, and that without any apparent purpose, or advantage however remote'.[103] At a meeting of Great Leighs special constables a few days later, Caldwell 'pointed out the absurdity' of the patrols. Every Monday night he and Stoddart walked around the parish for three hours. They had not yet 'passed, nor been passed by any vehicle. They had not passed anybody on the road. It is possible that intending evildoers were kept away by the knowledge that the roads were being patrolled, but there was not the slightest ... evidence to show that there were any such people ... in this district'.[104]

Many special constables, furthermore, felt that they were being asked to bear an unfair share of the burden of wartime patriotism, while other, often younger, men did very little. In November 1914 George With, the headmaster of the Council School, told Clark that night-time special constable patrols 'had given him a chilblain on his nose. He was going to resign. There were plenty of lazy young fellows in the district who ought to take their turn'.[105] In May 1916 Clark received a letter from the Superintendent of the Chelmsford division of the special constables in response to his resignation, which clearly echoed his own feelings: 'I quite agree with you that the younger men should come forward and take their part. There are plenty of men who although past military age have [illegible] to do this kind of work and I think it is slack and unpatriotic of them not to come forward when they know how greatly their services are needed. I am very much afraid there is a good deal of selfishness and lack of patriotism'.[106]

Allotment-keeping and vegetable growing

By 1917 the authorities were becoming increasingly vocal in encouraging civilians to counter the shortage of various foodstuffs by tending allotments and growing their own vegetables.[107] As well as posters and conventional print publications, new propaganda media were also put to use: films such as *Fighting U-Boats in a London Back Garden* showed how even suburban families could feed themselves by growing their own produce. As an activity undertaken away from an often scathing public gaze, without the need for membership of an official body, and where the benefits were tangible (indeed, edible), food-growing promised to provide a fulfilling wartime role for middle-class civilians. As 'the food situation worsened' Frank Dawkins was among those who 'took an allotment and grew vegetables – mostly potatoes', adding that 'it was surprising how some "superiors" found time to be friendly if a few spuds were likely to be forthcoming'.[108] Saunders, an experienced gardener, found himself spending more and more time tending his vegetable crop. In March 1917 he lamented that the wet and cold weather was making gardening 'impossible … and yet there is such urgent need for it this year'. Food prices continued to increase, 'so unless we all grow something we shall have to eat less and less'.[109] Being able to count not only on his own experience, but also on the help and advice of other gardeners, his efforts paid off.[110] In May he was able to give a 'good bag' of sprouting broccoli to his daughter Em to take back to London: 'we have had abundance'.[111] In July 1918 he noted that 'the garden has been a boon as I have been able to supply unlimited new potatoes, broad beans, peas, carrots, lettuce, radishes, onions, gooseberries, currants and raspberries'.[112]

However, vegetable growing did not always prove such a positive experience. Gardening had been a popular middle-class leisure pursuit since at least the mid-nineteenth century,[113] but expertise in tending ornamental plants did not necessarily guarantee success in vegetable-growing, with many individuals underestimating the labour and difficulties involved. The results could be disappointing. According to Clark, Tritton's 'endeavour after winter garden cultivation, in preparation for spring-scarcity, has no success. The … cabbage and kale that were planted have been eaten by rabbits. His own men, knowing that potatoes don't grow in winter, have (purposely) "forgotten" the order to set them'.[114] In March 1917 Joe Hollister wrote to his father that he had tried 'vegetables instead of flowers in the garden last year, not that I expected much, more from patriotic motives, beans, savoys, sprouts, lettuce, onions, carrots'. However, it had turned out to be a 'waste of money and time and so disheartening, and so I think I shall just keep it tidy this year and no more'.[115] The labour involved in growing vegetables from scratch soon became clear. Writing some time after the events, Cooper recalled that in February 1917 he had 'joined with Meadows in cultivating the kitchen garden at Blackwater Covert[?]'. They 'started digging it in March, this was a very rough month with bitter frosts snow and gales, our inside water pipes were frozen for the first time for several years'.[116] In April he and his wife 'spent this Easter Monday at Blackwater Garden putting in potatoes it was very cold with snow squalls but Sissie and I worked hard all day and got a good piece planted'.[117]

The Coopers were soon forced to realise the amount of labour demanded by allotment-keeping. By June, whenever they 'had an hour or two to spare we used to rush up to Blackwater and slave in that hungry old garden which seemed a weeds paradise'. When he came back 'from ten days' [VTC] duty at Felixstowe the weeds were almost up to my waist'. However, he added, the garden 'was a great help with the housework'.[118] In November, as many goods became scarcer, he congratulated himself on the fact that 'I expect to have at least 5 cwt of potatoes as my share from the garden so that I should avoid starvation whatever happens if they don't go bad'.[119] Seven months later he had to admit that neither he nor his wife had the time or the energy needed for successful allotment-keeping: 'we find it more and more difficult to cultivate Blackwater Garden but we have managed to get in potatoes and green stuff and hope for the best'.[120]

Victorian and Edwardian gardening enthusiasts had made much of the health-giving properties of gardening, particularly for those men who spent most of their lives sitting behind desks. As one writer put it in 1911: 'as an antidote to lassitude, the martyrdom of indigestion and the worries of everyday work, gardening cannot be excelled'.[121] However, the reality was that like other volunteer activities on the home front, work on vegetable patches often revealed the physical frailties of many middle-aged and elderly men. Even Saunders, a capable and experienced gardener, sometimes found the work too much for him. In June 1916 he was not able to do much in the garden because of a recurrent problem with his right arm.[122] In March 1918, missing his youngest son's help while he was away, he (half jokingly) put in an application to get one of his other sons a few days' leave to help with the garden 'as his Father was getting on and wanted help, etc.'[123] In August 1917 Holcombe Ingleby wrote to his son that 'a portion of our day is devoted to potato-digging. Its [*sic*] a much more serious matter this year than last. Not only is the area three or four times as large as that of last year, but the crop is more bountiful'.[124] A month later, he was forced to admit that his body had not proved up to the task: 'I've had a dose of lumbago and I am not quite free of the thing yet. It all comes of a man trying to do his bit by going potato-digging!'[125] (Figure 9).

National Service

In the light of earlier experiences of volunteering on the home front, which left many middle-class men feeling that far from being appreciated, their efforts were either treated with contempt or ignored, it is perhaps not surprising that they responded with little enthusiasm to the National Service scheme, launched in February 1917 by Neville Chamberlain, the recently appointed Director-General of National Service. The aim of the

WE MUST TILL THE LAND!

THE FASHIONABLE COMPLAINT: GROWING PAINS!

DRAWN BY H. HARRIS

9 'The food question: growing pains', *The Sketch*, 28 February 1917. Reproduced with permission of the Bodleian Libraries, University of Oxford, N.17078 c.32, p. 190.

scheme was to 'supply man power where it is most needed'.[126] A pamphlet setting out 'the scheme in brief' explained that 'the chief work for which labour is required is ship-building, food production, engineering, coal and ore mining, building construction, the felling and sawing of timber, munition making, and the construction of airplanes'.[127] According to a newspaper report, 'every man between the ages of 18 and 61 is invited to become a national volunteer. Those in non-essential trades will be transferred to essential trades. The wage will be the current rate for the new work, with a minimum of 25s a week. Men to whom the new rate means a sacrifice may claim a subsistence allowance of 17s 6d a week in addition … The call to women will come later'.[128]

Men ineligible for military service, as well as 'the idle rich – if any such remain'[129] were the prime targets: 'If you cannot fight for your country', a National Service poster stated, 'work for it. Enrol to-day'.[130] Volunteering, it was stressed, was a patriotic duty and a way to 'Back up the boys in the trenches'.[131] As one anonymous pamphleteer put it: 'every man who enrols will be able, with a clear conscience, to reflect that in the hour of our Nation's peril, he offered "to do his bit" by placing himself at the service of his country'.[132] One appeal, playing on civilians' awareness of the sacrifices being demanded of servicemen, asked in February 1917: 'Have you enrolled for National Service? … Are you helping to grow food – or are you merely eating the bread which has been bought with British lives?'[133]

Most middle-class civilians seem to have been unimpressed by these appeals, such rhetoric having perhaps lost some of its power after three years of war. According to Cossins, the fact that the scheme was a voluntary one was 'found fault with, as likely to cause delay and penalise the willing as against the shirkers'.[134] Discussing the scheme with Clark in February 1917, Caldwell argued that 'any man who volunteers … would be acting very foolishly'. He pointed out that 'there was absolutely no security that a man, so volunteering, would be put on to work he was cognisant of' or 'that he would not needlessly be sent out of his own district, that he would receive more than the 25s a week'. After all, he concluded, little trust could be placed in official assurances: in the past, 'many government promises have been most misleading'.[135]

Caldwell returned to the theme a month later, telling Clark that 'business people in London have the worst opinion of the National Service Office'. They believed that it had been set up solely so that 'a number of highly salaried and altogether incompetent clerks, of military age, may have exemption from the service on the lying pretext of doing work of actual service'. They had been given 'the big lounge and corridors of a large hotel in which to slope about and smoke in their long hours of leisure'. He added that 'many good business men, earning as much as £500 before the war, offered to work at National Service at the first call, for very small wages, at the duties they were well fitted for, but not one has had his application even acknowledged'.[136] The incompetence of those responsible for running the National Service scheme, often suspected of being young men trying to avoid enlistment, was a constant refrain of middle-class observers: by June 1917 Clark had become convinced that the scheme was futile, its failure due to 'the imbecility of the highly-paid government officials in charge of it'.[137] In August, following the announcement of Chamberlain's resignation, he wrote that that 'the ruinously expensive and utterly useless "National Service" Department has long been a subject of general scoffing'. He had not heard of anybody in the locality finding 'it of any use in providing farm labourers'.[138]

Appeals to volunteer in order to enable other men to join the armed forces were not well received.[139] In April 1917 Frank Lockwood noted that the last week of March had been 'officially recognised as "National Service Week" – but the general public have been very indifferent'. He believed that the scheme 'is doomed to failure … All men, whether engaged on work of national importance or not … are invited to volunteer and "relieve a fit man for the front"'. However, 'no sane man *wants* to go to the front and if he has any man about him at all, he should not want to send anybody where he is unwilling to go himself'.[140] Issues of age and physical fitness, furthermore, posed the same problems as with other volunteering activities on the home front. Lockwood wondered: 'When they enrol the Mayor of Huddersfield who is 76 … does it not look ludicrous? And he is not the only old man who has enrolled. What good can he do? Will they send him to work in the congenial atmosphere of British Dyes? I think not'.[141]

Robinson greeted the initial announcement of the national service scheme with scepticism, uncertain how 'this is going to affect the individual'. He had 'over and over again offered his gratuitous services to the War Office and Munitions Department to do work he is fully qualified and fitted to do'. His offers had been turned down and he wondered: was he 'now to be regarded as a "slacker" and put on the land to dig potatoes'?[142] Implicit in his reaction to the scheme was a sense of the ludicrousness of asking educated middle-class professional and business men to undertake hard, menial work for a working-class wage.[143] Despite official reassurances that 'every effort' would be made to find 'professional

… and business men … work of a suitable kind at a rate of remuneration that would enable them to live as they and their dependants have been accustomed to live',[144] Robinson was among the majority who refused to volunteer. 'If later I am compelled to dig potatoes or tend pigs, all right I must – but what about my other … duties by which the government derives large sums by way of taxation?'[145] In subsequent weeks his tone became increasingly angry. He noted in March 1917 that men such as he were being 'told with jibes, offensive suggestions, and even insults … that he is practically a traitor to his country' if he did not volunteer for what the *Sunday Pictorial* described as 'casual employment in jobs for which they are not fitted'.[146] (Figure 10) In August 1917 he was not alone in greeting the news of Chamberlain's resignation with relief, adding that the department of National Service was generally viewed as a 'farce' and as 'one of the conspicuous failures of the war'.[147]

Conclusion

After the first few weeks of war, the eponymous hero of H. G. Wells's novel *Mr Britling Sees it Through* became convinced that 'every man ought to be in training … everyone ought to be participating … in some way … At an rate we ought not to be taking our ease … any more … '.[148] Middle-class men's volunteering activities on the home front were intended to prove those qualities of manly patriotism and willingness to contribute to the war effort embodied by Mr Britling's enthusiasm, but ultimately fell far short of this objective. There were uncertainties and difficulties about both who should 'volunteer' and what should they do. In the early months of war it was the men who wished to demonstrate their patriotic credentials but were over age or were 'unable or unwilling to enlist for service overseas',[149] who seemed the obvious candidates for service as special constables or as Volunteers. In August 1914 an anonymous 'London lady' observed in her diary that 'Mr Fox has joined the Special Constables Force, and Mr Combe[?] is joining. They think it is the best way men over thirty, married, and with business can help'.[150] According to G. S. Street, for 'over-aged buffers like myself, who were out of the main business',[151] service as special constables or as volunteers 'took a little from the shame of being alive at all. For that is the sting [of war] to us older men … that it reverses the rule of nature by which the old go first'.[152]

However, these men's position proved ambiguous and contradictory. VTC members and special constables who were ineligible for military

10 'National Service', *The Bystander*, 28 March 1917.
Reproduced with permission of the Bodleian Libraries, University of Oxford, Per.2705 d.161, p. 629.

service because of unfitness or because over military age were often dismissed as useless or subjected to ridicule, contributing to their own awareness of their bodies' physical limitations and unsuitability for strenuous effort. Later in the war, middle-class efforts at vegetable growing and other forms of self-provisioning were by no means always a failure. The pleasure and pride men like Saunders gained from being able to provide extras for their families in a context of growing shortages should not be underestimated. Indeed, habits such as Cooper's in February 1918 of 'shooting for the pot regularly twice a week' fed directly into notions of middle-class manliness that stressed the importance of providing for dependants: 'I am able to send regularly to the missis, as her meat ration at Southbourne is only 6 to 8oz per week and she has to stand in a queue to get it'.[153] Just as often, however, failed crops, gardening injuries and allotments that seemed to require endless labour, all contributed to many middle-class men's heightened awareness of their own physical inadequacies and lack of expertise.

Fit men of military age, of course, could provide special constables or VTC with a more impressive body of volunteers than those popularly dismissed as 'George wrecks' or 'grandpapa's regiment'. However, such men aroused suspicions that, far from being animated by patriotic feelings, they were simply trying to evade military service. Furthermore, there was a widespread feeling among volunteers that their contribution to the war effort was being ignored and that their sacrifices remained unacknowledged: members of the VTC felt constantly snubbed by the authorities, while even members of the special constabulary, an officially sanctioned body, often felt that a good deal was asked of them, but with little 'apparent purpose, or advantage however remote'.[154] The patriotic desire of middle-class men, including those over military age, to do their 'bit' were felt to be unappreciated. 'G. J.', the protagonist of Arnold Bennett's 1918 novel *The Pretty Lady*, for example, 'had tried several times to get into a government department which would utilise his brains, but without success'. His experiences were not unique. The description of G. J.'s club as humming 'with the unimaginable stories related by disappointed and dignified middle-aged men whose too eager patriotism had been rendered ridiculous by the vicious foolery of government departments',[155] reflected the real experiences of many middle-class men.

It is unsurprising, then, that middle-class civilians should have responded to National Service appeals with scepticism and outright hostility. Contempt for the officials in charge of the scheme, together with a reluctance to undertake what were seen as menial, low-paid occupations unsuited to educated middle-class men, both played their part in influencing responses. By the time the National Service scheme was announced, volunteering activities that were supposed to prove the manly patriotism of those middle-class men who were unable or unwilling to enlist in the armed forces, had all too often revealed instead their physical frailties, subjected them to ridicule and contempt, demanded sacrifices that went unrecognised and unappreciated and, of course, could not bear comparison with the suffering of servicemen overseas.

Notes

1 F. A. Robinson, 'Diary of the Great War', 15 November 1918, vol. 1, P.401, Department of Documents, Imperial War Museum (hereafter IWM Documents), London.
2 A. Gregory, *The Last Great War: British Society and the First World War* (Cambridge University Press, Cambridge, 2008), p. 72. See also pp. 70–3.
3 H. C. Cossins Diary, 1914–18 (hereafter Cossins Diary), 27 August 1914, PP/MCR/371, IWM Documents.
4 *Ibid.*, 4 September 1914.
5 *Ibid.*, 16 November 1914.
6 M. Yearsley ('Eyewitness'), 'The Home Front, 1914–18', pp. 60–1, DS/MISC/17, IWM Documents. On the 'volunteer ethic', see also Gregory, *The Last Great War*, pp. 95–100.
7 Robinson, 'Diary of the Great War', 10 August 1917, vol. 3, P.402, IWM Documents.
8 *Ibid.*, 6 October 1917.
9 Wartime Diaries of H. W. B. Joseph 1914–18 (hereafter Joseph Diaries), 17 August 1914, Ms. Top. Oxon. e.288, Special Collections, Bodleian Library, University of Oxford (hereafter Bodleian Special Collections), Oxford. On knitting as a 'socially approved, if sometimes gently mocked' wartime activity suitable for women, see also J. S. K. Watson, *Fighting Different Wars: Experience, Memory and the First World War in Britain* (Cambridge University Press, Cambridge, 2004), p. 109.
10 And, to some extent, children. See, for example, A. Clark War Diary, 'Echoes of the 1914 War in an Essex Village' (hereafter Clark Diary), 28 September 1915, Ms Eng. Hist. e.111; 3 June 1917, Ms Eng. Hist. e.148, Bodleian Special Collections.
11 Cossins Diary, 9 October 1914, PP/MCR/371, IWM Documents.
12 J. H. Butlin to B. Burnett Hall, 10 August 1914, Letters of Lieutenant James H. Butlin (hereafter Butlin Letters), 67/52/1, IWM Documents.
13 Yearsley, 'The Home Front', pp. 104–5, DS/MISC/17, IWM Documents.
14 D. J. Martin, Reminiscences, not dated, DF148, Liddle Collection (1914–

18), Special Collections, Brotherton Library, Leeds University (hereafter Liddle Collection), Leeds.

15 Cossins Diary, 15 June 1915, PP/MCR/371, IWM Documents.

16 Robinson, 'Diary of the Great War', 12 June 1915, vol. 1, P.401, IWM Documents.

17 Clark Diary, 24 April 1916, 27 April 1916, Ms Eng. Hist. e.124; 3 May 1916, Ms Eng. Hist. e.125, Bodleian Special Collections. The purpose of the committee was to make preparations for the evacuation of the local population in case of invasion.

18 *Ibid.*, 23 June 1917, Ms Eng. Hist. e.149; 19 July 1917, Ms Eng. Hist. e.151; 6 June 1918, Ms Eng. Hist. e.164; 5 July 1918, Ms Eng. Hist. e.165; 2 August 1918, Ms Eng. Hist. e.166. Unlike the 'Invasion' committee, the Great and Little Leighs War Savings Committee included both men and women. In Southwold, it was 'the Mayoress and ladies' who 'ran a campaign in aid of the War Loan with very good results': £47,000 was subscribed. The Diary of Ernest R. Cooper, 'Nineteen Hundred and War Time', 28 July 1914–3 December 1918 (hereafter Cooper Diary), 16 February 1917, P.121, IWM Documents.

19 Gregory, *The Last Great War*, p. 95. James McDermott observes that Northamptonshire tribunals were overwhelmingly made up of male local worthies, whose 'status was intended to imbue the process with a necessary degree of gravitas and reassure the applicant that his concerns had been given an appropriate measure of the Establishment's attention'. J. McDermott, 'The Work of the Military Service Tribunals in Northamptonshire, 1916–1918' (Unpublished PhD thesis, University of Northampton, 2009), p. 176.

20 W. L. McIvor, Recollections, October 1978, DF148, Liddle Collection.

21 Clark Diary, 12 September 1916, Ms Eng. Hist. e.134, Bodleian Special Collections.

22 *Ibid.*, 19 July 1917, Ms Eng. Hist. e.151.

23 *Ibid.*, 5 April 1915, Ms Eng. Hist. e.101; 21 October 1916, Ms Eng. Hist. e.137; 6 July 1917, Ms Eng. Hist. e.150.

24 *Ibid.*, 22 March 1917, Ms Eng. Hist. e.146.

25 Cooper Diary, 3 September 1914, May 1915, P.121, IWM Documents.

26 *Ibid.*, 18 February 1916.

27 *Ibid.*, May 1915.

28 *Ibid.*, 21 January 1918.

29 Clark Diary, 1 January 1916, Ms Eng. Hist. e.118, Bodleian Special Collections.

30 Yearsley, 'The Home Front', p. 13, DS/MISC/17, IWM Documents.

31 *Ibid.*, p. 40. Established in 1902, by 1911 the National Service League claimed a membership of approximately 100,000. J. Lowerson, *Sport and the English Middle Classes 1870–1914* (Manchester University Press, Manchester,

1993), p. 289; A. Summers, 'Militarism in Britain before the Great War', *History Workshop Journal*, vol. 2 (1976), pp. 112–17.

32 G. D. Wilkinson interview, 9104, reel 2, Department of Sound, Imperial War Museum (hereafter IWM Sound), London.

33 J. Morton Osborne, 'Defining their own patriotism: British Volunteer Training Corps in the First World War', *Journal of Contemporary History*, vol. 23, no. 1 (1988), p. 60. In 1914 the National Rifle Association clubs had a membership of approximately 30,000. Lowerson, *Sport and the English Middle Classes*, pp. 290–1.

34 Yearsley, 'The Home Front', pp. 73–4, DS/MISC/17, IWM Documents.

35 'Patriotic Association Defence Force', *The Daily Telegraph*, 11 August 1914, 'The Great War scraps, 1914–March 1915', in 'Miscellaneous papers relating to the Great War, 13 volumes', Bodleian Library, University of Oxford, Oxford.

36 Anon., *The Volunteer Force and the Volunteer Training Corps during the Great War: Official Record of the Central Association of Volunteer Regiments* (P. S. King and Son, London, 1920), p. 3.

37 *Ibid.*, p. 3.

38 *Ibid.*, p. 4.

39 *Ibid.*, p. 7.

40 Morton Osborne, 'Defining their own patriotism', p. 67.

41 J. D. Sainsbury, *Herts Volunteer Regiment* (Hart Books, Welwyn, 2005), p. 14.

42 Anon., *The Volunteer Force*, p. 6. See also H. Cartmell, *For Remembrance: An Account of some Fateful Years* (George Toulmin & sons, Preston, 1919), p. 109.

43 Morton Osborne, 'Defining their own patriotism', pp. 64–7.

44 See, for example, Joseph Diaries, 25 September 1914, 1 October 1914, Ms. Top. Oxon. e.288, Bodleian Special Collections; Cooper Diary, May 1915, P.121, IWM Documents; Cossins Diary, 2 December 1914, 10 January 1915, 26 September 1915, 10 October 1915, 22 October 1916, 12 January 1917, 10 February 1917, PP/MCR/371, IWM Documents. The Suffolk and the Hertfordshire Volunteers were inspected by Lord French in October 1916. See Cooper Diary, 22 October 1916, P.121, IWM Documents; Cossins Diary, 29 October 1916, PP/MCR/371, IWM Documents. See also Yearsley, 'The Home Front', Chapter 3, pp. 73–101, DS/MISC/17, IWM Documents.

45 Cossins Diary, 25 March 1915, 2 May 1915, PP/MCR/371, IWM Documents.

46 Anon., 'The 1st London engineering volunteers', in *Electrical Industries and Investment*, 6 December 1916, pp. 1350–2, especially p. 1351, in P. M. Yearsley, '1st London Engineers Volunteers May 1916 to December 1917' folder, P. M. Yearsley Collection, 71/11/1, IWM Documents.

47 Joseph Diaries, 23 November 1915, Ms. Top. Oxon. e.288, Bodleian Special Collections.

48 *Ibid.*, 17 October 1915.
49 *Ibid.*, 26 September 1916.
50 Cossins Diary, 20 October 1915, 23 October 1915, PP/MCR/371, IWM Documents.
51 In February 1916 it was announced that volunteers would come under the terms of the 1863 Volunteer Act, while a supplementary act was passed later on in the year. For the details, see Morton Osborne, 'Defining their own patriotism', p. 71; Sainsbury, *Herts Volunteer Regiment*, especially Chapter 1; Anon., *The Volunteer Force*, especially pp. 18–23.
52 Robinson, 'Diary of the Great War', 18 June 1916, vol. 2, P.401, IWM Documents. See also Cossins Diary, 7 March 1916, 3 November 1916, PP/MCR/371, IWM Documents. The 'GR' presumably stood for George Rex.
53 'Notices' in *The London County Council Gazette*, 2 April 1917, p. 81, in Yearsley, '1st London Engineers Volunteers May 1916 to December 1917' folder, P. M. Yearsley Collection, 71/11/1, IWM Documents.
54 Cutting, 20 August 1917, in Yearsley, '1st London Engineers Volunteers May 1916 to December 1917' folder, P. M. Yearsley Collection, 71/11/1, IWM Documents.
55 Anon., *The Volunteer Force*, p. 25.
56 Cooper Diary, 4 June 1918, 9 June 1918, 27 June 1918, 29 June 1918, P.121, IWM Documents. See also I. F. W. Beckett, 'The nation in arms, 1914–18', in I. F. W. Beckett and K. Simpson (eds), *A Nation in Arms: A Social History of the British Army in the First World War* (Manchester University Press, Manchester, 1985), p. 16.
57 Joseph Diaries, 25 August 1918, Ms. Top. Oxon. e.288, Bodleian Special Collections.
58 Cooper Diary, May 1915, P.121, IWM Documents.
59 H. G. Wells, *Mr Britling Sees it Through* (The Hogarth Press, London, 1985, first published 1916), p. 247.
60 Quoted in diary of R. W. M. Gibbs, 1914–20 (hereafter Gibbs Diary), 31 October 1914, Ms Eng. misc. c.160, Bodleian Special Collections.
61 London County Council Staff Volunteer Training Corps circular, n.d., *c.* 1914, in Yearsley, 'London County Council Staff Volunteer Training Corps' folder, P. M. Yearsley Collection, 71/11/1, IWM Documents.
62 Clark Diary, 26 January 1915, Ms Eng. Hist. e.97, Bodleian Special Collections. See also Clark's daughter's jeering references to the 'corps of elderly men' in chapter 3 of this book.
63 Yearsley, 'The Home Front', p. 77, DS/MISC/17, IWM Documents.
64 Platoon Commander, 'Is the Volunteer movement a success? War Office slights and snubs for 1,500,000 loyal, willing men', press cutting no. 104, not dated, *c.* 1915, in 'Miscellaneous papers relating to the Great War, 13 volumes', Bodleian Library.

65 E. R. Cooper, 'The 3rd Volunteer Battalion Suffolk Regiment', June 1920, p. 2, P.121, IWM Documents.

66 Cossins was thirty-six at the outbreak of war, perhaps close enough to being over military age to allow the rules to be bent. In any case, he was not the only one: on at least one occasion a recruiting officer spoke to all the St Albans volunteers of military age and questioned their reasons for not enlisting. Cossins Diary, 20 April 1915, PP/MCR/371, IWM Documents.

67 Cooper Diary, June 1916, 10 February 1918, P.121, IWM Documents. See also McDermott, 'The Work of the Military Service Tribunals in Northamptonshire', Chapter 9; Morton Osborne, 'Defining their own patriotism', pp. 70–5; Anon., *The Volunteer Force*, pp. 12–13. On 11 November 1918 'there were 137,800 ordinary Volunteers; 97,000 men sent into the Force by the Tribunals'. Anon., *The Volunteer Force*, p. 26.

68 Clark Diary, 24 April 1915, Ms Eng. Hist. e.102, Bodleian Special Collections.

69 *Ibid.*, 23 June 1917, Ms Eng. Hist. e.149.

70 J. F. Crowder, Reminiscences, August 1991, DF148, Liddle Collection.

71 Clark Diary, 28 January 1918, Ms Eng. Hist. e.159, Bodleian Special Collections. See also Beckett, 'The nation in arms', pp. 15–16.

72 Yearsley, 'The Home Front', pp. 100–1, DS/MISC/17, IWM Documents.

73 *Ibid.*

74 Cooper, 'The 3rd Volunteer Battalion Suffolk Regiment', June 1920, p. 16, P.121, IWM Documents.

75 In 1914 the police force in England and Wales numbered just over 53,000 men, mostly of military age. C. Emsley, *The English Police: A Political and Social History* (Longman, Harlow, 1996, first published 1991), pp. 121–7; D. Englander, 'Police and public order in Britain 1914–1918', in C. Emsley and B. Weinberg (eds), *Policing Western Europe: Politics, Professionalism and Public Order 1850–1940* (Greenwood Press, New York, 1991), pp. 90–138.

76 C. Leon, 'Special constables in the First and Second World Wars', *Police History Society Journal*, vol. 7 (1992), p. 4. A Special Constables Act was passed on 26 August 1914, providing the legal framework for their enrolment.

77 Clark Diary, 31 August 1914, Ms Eng. Hist. e.88, Bodleian Special Collections.

78 *Ibid.*, For special constables' responsibilities see also Leon, 'Special constables', especially pp. 5–8.

79 Clark Diary, 7 September 1914, Ms Eng. Hist. e.89, Bodleian Special Collections.

80 It is worth noting that there does not seem to have been any question that women might join. But see also the experiences of Emily Galbraith, who at the outbreak of war was training to become a teacher. She wrote to Kitchener, pointing out that she and her fellow students 'were able-bodied young

women and I didn't see why we shouldn't be a Home Guard and fight at home so as to let the boys go and do the job of fighting the Germans'. Predictably, Kitchener responded that 'he didn't approve of women fighting; it was the men's job to look after the women, but he thanked me very much'. R. Van Emden and S. Humphries, *All Quiet on the Home Front: An Oral History of Life in Britain during the First World War* (Headline, London, 2003), p. 19.

81 Clark Diary, 29 August 1914, Ms Eng. Hist. e.88, Bodleian Special Collections.

82 *Ibid.*, 31 August 1914. Like the VTC, the special constabulary was also suspected of harbouring conscientious objectors and 'shirkers'. Leon, 'Special constables', pp. 10–12.

83 Clark Diary, 14 September 1914, Ms Eng. Hist. e.89, Bodleian Special Collections.

84 *Ibid.*, 28 September 1914.

85 *Ibid.*, 19 October 1914, Ms Eng. Hist. e.90.

86 J. Bourke, *Dismembering the Male: Men's Bodies, Britain and the Great War* (Reaktion Books, London, 1996), pp. 180–92.

87 Clark Diary, 18 April 1915, Ms Eng. Hist. e.101, Bodleian Special Collections. It was the decision to resume drilling that eventually led Clark to tender his resignation in May 1916. See 4 May 1916, Ms Eng. Hist. e.125.

88 Cossins Diary, 2 December 1914, PP/MCR/371, IWM Documents.

89 *Ibid.*, 31 December 1916.

90 R. Saunders to son, 14 June 1915, R. Saunders, Letters to Son in Canada, 1914–18 (hereafter Saunders Letters), 79/15/1, IWM Documents. See also the difficulties faced by seventy-year-old Mr Smith in the novel by K. Howard, *The Smiths in Wartime* (John Lane The Bodley Head, London, 1917), pp. 57–76.

91 Clark Diary, 30 October 1914, Ms Eng. Hist. e.90, Bodleian Special Collections. The initial rota included twenty-two names. See also 9 November 1914, Ms Eng. Hist. e.91.

92 *Ibid.*, 2 November 1914.

93 *Ibid.*, 17 November 1914

94 *Ibid.*, 15 December 1914, Ms Eng. Hist. e.94.

95 *Ibid.*, 20 January 1915, Ms Eng. Hist. e.96.

96 *Ibid.*, 8 May 1915, Ms Eng. Hist. e.103.

97 *Ibid.*, 22 May 1915, Ms Eng. Hist. e.104.

98 *Ibid.*, 23 May 1915.

99 *Ibid.*, 2 November 1915, Ms Eng. Hist. e.114.

100 *Ibid.*, 15 November 1915.

101 *Ibid.*, 21 February 1916, Ms Eng. Hist. e.121.

102 *Ibid.*, 8 December 1914, Ms Eng. Hist. e.92.

103 *Ibid.*, 12 January 1915, Ms Eng. Hist. e.96.

104 *Ibid.*, 18 January 1915.
105 *Ibid.*, 22 November 1914, Ms Eng. Hist. e.92. Although see also the case of Isaac Hicks, who, 'after some months service' with the Bourne End special constables, 'was, to his disgust, retired on account of his age'. See *ibid.*, 26 December 1915, Ms Eng. Hist. e.116.
106 *Ibid.*, 9 May 1916, Ms Eng. Hist. e.125, Bodleian Special Collections. Clark went on his last patrol on 15 May 1916.
107 Appeals had begun as early as 1915. R. D. Blumenfeld, *All in a Lifetime* (Ernest Benn, London, 1931), p. 26. During the war the number of allotments in England and Wales increased from 570,000 to more than 1,400,000. P. E. Dewey, 'Nutrition and living standards in wartime Britain', in R. Wall and J. Winter (eds), *The Upheaval of War: Family, Work and Welfare in Europe, 1914–1918* (Cambridge University Press, Cambridge, 1988), p. 218, note 34.
108 F. Dawkins to P. Liddle, 16 March 1986, DF148, Liddle Collection.
109 R. Saunders to son, 25 March 1917, Saunders Letters, 79/15/1, IWM Documents.
110 *Ibid.*, 8 July 1917.
111 *Ibid.*, 20 May 1917.
112 *Ibid.*, 14 July 1918.
113 S. Constantine, 'Amateur gardening and popular recreation in the 19th and 20th centuries', *Journal of Social History*, vol. 14, no. 3 (1981), pp. 388–9.
114 Clark Diary, 11 February 1915, Ms Eng. Hist. e.97, Bodleian Special Collections.
115 J. Hollister to 'dad', 19 March 1917, J. Hollister Letter, 1917, 98/10/1, IWM Documents.
116 Cooper Diary, 17 February 1917, P.121, IWM Documents.
117 *Ibid.*, 9 April 1917.
118 *Ibid.*, 9 June 1917.
119 *Ibid.*, 12 November 1917.
120 *Ibid.*, 9 June 1918.
121 F. Hadfield Farthing, *Saturday in my Garden* (London, 1911), quoted in Constantine, 'Amateur gardening', p. 389.
122 R. Saunders to son, 4 June 1916, Saunders Letters, 79/15/1, IWM Documents.
123 *Ibid.*, 24 March 1918. The application seems to have been unsuccessful.
124 Holcombe Ingleby to Clement, 19 August 1917, The First World War Letters of Holcombe Ingleby MP (hereafter Ingleby Letters), P.343, IWM Documents.
125 *Ibid.*, 17 September 1917.
126 Anon., 'Twelve good reasons why every able-bodied man should enrol for national service', pamphlet, not dated, in 'Miscellaneous papers relating to the Great War, 13 volumes', Bodleian Library. See also K. Grieves, *The*

Politics of Manpower, 1914–18 (Manchester University Press, Manchester, 1988), Chapters 5 and 6.

127 'National Service: the scheme in brief', not dated, in R.H. Macleod Papers, DF087, Liddle Collection.

128 Clark Diary, 7 February 1917, Ms Eng. Hist. e.144, Bodleian Special Collections.

129 Cossins Diary, 20 December 1916, PP/MCR/371, IWM Documents.

130 National Service poster, not dated, *c.*1917, 'Miscellaneous war posters', in 'Miscellaneous papers relating to the Great War, 13 volumes', Bodleian Library.

131 *Ibid.*

132 Anon., 'Twelve good reasons'.

133 Robinson, 'Diary of the Great War', 23 February 1917, vol. 3, P.402, IWM Documents.

134 Cossins added that 'another fault found is the statement that only men will be registered at first, it being felt that a serious mistake is being made in leaving the women out'. Cossins Diary, 29 January 1917, PP/MCR/371, IWM Documents.

135 Clark Diary, 7 February 1917, Ms Eng. Hist. e.144, Bodleian Special Collections.

136 *Ibid.*, 21 March 1917, Ms Eng. Hist. e.146.

137 *Ibid.*, 26 June 1917, Ms Eng. Hist. e.149. The waste and inefficiency of government departments was the focus of satirical novels such as E. Shanks, *The Old Indispensables: A Romance of Whitehall* (Martin Secker, London, 1919) and F. O. Mann, *Grope Carries On: Being the Further Adventures of Albert Grope during the War* (Faber and Faber, London, 1932). The former was set in the 'Circumvention Branch of the Circumlocution Office', the latter in the 'Department of Minor Equipment'.

138 Clark Diary, 14 August 1917, Ms Eng. Hist. e.152, Bodleian Special Collections.

139 This is in contrast to the early years of war, when appeals to 'free up' men so that they could join the army do not seem to have attracted adverse comment.

140 F. T. Lockwood, 'Notes Written by F.T. Lockwood', 5 April 1917, 96/52/1, IWM Documents.

141 *Ibid.*

142 Robinson, 'Diary of the Great War', 20 December 1916, vol. 2, P.401, IWM Documents.

143 A useful comparison is with the army experiences of Henry Fowler, who was unhappy with the 'menial' duties allotted to him at base camp. As Adrian Gregory points out, 'it says a great deal about the relationship between class and patriotism … that a man might be willing to die for his country, but not to wash dishes for it'. Gregory, *The Last Great War*, p. 79.

144 'National Service: the scheme in brief', p. 1.
145 Robinson, 'Diary of the Great War', 27 January 1917, vol. 3, P.402, IWM Documents.
146 *Ibid.*, 31 March 1917.
147 *Ibid.*, 10 August 1917. In October he noted that 351,383 men and 41,984 women had enrolled in the National Service scheme, and that only 19,951 men had been found employment. The scrapping of the scheme had been announced earlier in the month. See *ibid.*, 6 October 1917, 27 October 1917. A different (and even worse) set of figures is given in G. J. DeGroot, *Blighty: British Society in the Era of the Great War* (Longman, Harlow, 1998, first published 1996), p. 101. In any case, it is clear that the target of enrolling 500,000 men by the end of March 1917 was missed by a large margin. DeGroot, *Blighty*, p. 101.
148 Wells, *Mr Britling Sees it Through*, p. 224.
149 Cooper, 'The 3rd Volunteer Battalion Suffolk Regiment', June 1920, p. 2, P.121, IWM Documents.
150 Anon., Diary of a London Lady, 7 August 1914, Misc. 29, Item 522, IWM Documents.
151 G. S. Street, *At Home in the War* (William Heinemann, London, 1918), p. 16.
152 *Ibid.*, p. 17.
153 Cooper Diary, 20 February 1918, P.121, IWM Documents.
154 Clark Diary, 12 January 1915, Ms Eng. Hist. e.96, Bodleian Special Collections.
155 A. Bennett, *The Pretty Lady: A Novel* (Cassell, London, not dated, *c.* 1918), p. 194–5.

6

Working lives

Introduction

In September 1914 Thomas Stoddart, the Great Leighs churchwarden, told Andrew Clark that 'although it is a time of stress and sorrow of war, it is the wish of the parish that the Harvest Festival shall be held ... as usual in thankfulness for the extraordinary bounty of this year's harvest'.[1] Like many others across the country in the early days of war, the inhabitants of Great Leighs had to make decisions about the extent to which they should modify their working practices in light of the conflict. While they chose to maintain pre-war practices, at least as far as the harvest festival was concerned, others opted for change. Horace Joseph, the bursar of New College, Oxford, for example, reacted to Britain's entry into the war by ordering 'some economies' in college dinners. He also 'wrote to the London branch of the B[?] Metal works, where I was about to order goods of about £18 value, saying that the order must stand over, and I told the gardener we must do without a bulb order. These are small things', he acknowledged, 'but if you cannot do bigger you must do smaller'.[2]

Middle-class men, particularly those involved in commerce or manufacturing, were not immune to the economic dislocation of the early days of the war. In mid-August 1914, for example, Frank Lockwood noted that 'owing to the war, firms (manufacturers, etc.) all over the country are working short time and the Colne Valley is no exception'.[3] That said, decisions to change working practices were motivated not only by economic circumstances, but also by the widespread belief that it was inappropriate to continue with peacetime habits as though nothing had occurred. The outcome was thus often unpredictable. In September 1914 Clark noted that at Joseph Smith's harvest supper, Mrs Smith defied calls to economise by making 'lavish preparations. Two joints of beef were on the table of 40 to 50lb weight, whereas joints of 15lb would have been ample'.[4] A week later, on the other hand, it was 'intimated that, because of the economy required by the war, Lyons Hall estate will give no harvest supper to its employees this year'.[5]

The Trittons and the Smiths may have responded differently to the pressure of farming and gathering the harvest as war broke out, but it is clear that neither household could ignore the conflict as they sought to continue with their day-to-day work in the months and years that followed: the aim here is to explore further the impact of war on middle-class men's working lives. The chapter opens by arguing that the pressures of war led many to reassess the 'value' of their work in a wartime society, with the slippery concept of work of 'national importance' providing a new benchmark against which men sought to measure themselves. The chapter considers next the impact on working lives of wartime regulations, as well as of the vicissitudes and added responsibilities linked to war on the home front more in general, before turning to the increasingly serious problem of labour shortages, as well as the solutions that were intended to remedy it. The chapter then concludes by examining the problems and opportunities that were particularly associated with the world of business. In a sense, the wheel turns full circle here. The chapter opens with the ideal of work that contributed to the war effort and closes with its polar opposite: work that – it was thought – allowed certain individuals to 'profiteer' from the calamity of war.

The value of work

In January 1915 Clark noted that Humphrey Watney had tried to enlist several times since the outbreak of war, but had always been turned down, 'on account of chest-weakness'. In any case, 'as all his Gilbey and Gold uncles and cousins are at the front, his services in the business at home are greatly needed to carry on their work'.[6] As discussed in Chapter 4, middle-class men's responsibilities towards their business, profession or career were a significant consideration – and were widely recognised as such – when deciding whether to enlist, or, after the introduction of conscription, whether to seek exemption. In July 1918, for example, Arthur Tritton, one of J. H. Tritton's sons, was 'passed Grade 1, but is appealing. There is now no one in the Stock Exchange business with him'.[7] The prospect of a successful business folding was not viewed lightly, and wherever possible, compromises were reached between the claims of work and war. Thus, the elder brother of one of Clark's acquaintances 'is in a gas engineering firm near Bridlington, Yorkshire. It was a toss-up between his partner and him as to who should enlist and who should carry on. His partner obtained the lot for enlisting'.[8] In July 1916 Frederick Robinson sympathised with the plight of 'tradesmen whose businesses are utterly ruined by their absence'. He wondered: 'could not men who have retired from active business, too old also to fight, undertake to run such businesses for their proprietors during their absence? One would gladly do this'.[9]

Such an option was clearly unrealistic in more than a small number of cases.[10] Indeed, despite the widespread sympathy for interrupted careers or faltering businesses, it is unsurprising that the war should provide a powerful competing claim on the services of fit men of military age. A letter (allegedly) from a 'man at the Front', read in Parliament in March 1916, expressed the anger felt by those who 'went without fuss at the beginning of the show', unselfishly giving up 'our work, our businesses, our little shops, our jobs', while those left at home 'have been filling jobs we vacated … making money and drawing wages higher than their wildest dreams imagined'.[11] In such a charged atmosphere many, perhaps most, middle-class men were thus moved to re-evaluate the 'value' of their work, a development whose significance should not be underestimated, given the importance of occupational identities, values and associational life to many Victorian and Edwardian middle-class men.[12]

A. D. Gardner was among those who found it necessary to take into account the demands of war when making decisions about his career, although – it should be noted – he did not go to the length of abandoning his work entirely in order to enlist. At the outbreak of war he was a thirty-year-old assistant pathologist at St Thomas's Hospital, London, having chosen a laboratory career, rather than surgical work. He quickly volunteered for the RAMC but, as he explained in his memoir, it was made clear to him that the army had no need for pathologists. He was offered a job training stretcher-bearers, which, 'somewhat deflated', he turned down. He later volunteered as a Red Cross surgeon and went out to France. He was then offered the post of first assistant brain surgeon to the army, which would have been a 'gorgeous' offer to any young surgeon, except that he had already come to the conclusion that surgery was not for him. 'But after much anxious thought I came to the conclusion that I had better do it, particularly as my beloved pathology and research seemed right outside the national war-effort'. He was thankful, then, when 'red tape' meant that he could not take up the job after all. In 1915 he was offered a post in a new bacteriological laboratory in Oxford 'that would greatly help the fighting services in their endless struggle with typhoid fever … and similar infections'. At last, that 'was, to me, the ideal work – medical science and research right within the national "war effort", and miraculously in my beloved Oxford'.[13]

As discussed in Chapter 4, it was widely agreed that some individuals could make a more valuable contribution to the war effort through their work than they would by enlisting. These included not only working-class 'skilled artisans whose labour is necessary for the manufacture of war material',[14] but also certain middle-class and lower-middle-class, white-collar occupations. In January 1915 Clark's sister-in-law wrote from Wolverhampton that her eldest son Noel 'went up to the recruiting station for examination, but they would not take him, as he is engaged in a business [corn-milling] providing food for the country'.[15] William Ostler, a railway booking clerk, did not join up at the outset of war because 'the railway exemp[ted] me. I was in what they called a key job … the railway thought they just couldn't carry on without booking clerks'.[16] Cyril Winchcombe's father 'was not required to join up partly because he had two young children to support, and partly because his job was necessary to keep electricity supplies in operation'.[17]

After the introduction of conscription in 1916, applications for exemption could be made on various grounds, including that of conscience.[18] However, the most significant ground for exemption was the man's occupation, and whether 'it is expedient in the national interests that the man should, instead of being employed in military service, be engaged in other work in which he is habitually engaged', or 'in other work in which he wishes to be engaged'.[19] The definition of work that was 'in the national interest' was open to interpretation. After receiving six months' exemption, Reginald Gibbs observed that 'it is lucky for me that coaching up your aristocrats in Mathematics, Science and Engineering is considered very important War Work'.[20] However, there were men – lower-middle-class white-collar workers such as clerks and shop assistants prominent among them – whose occupation, far from appearing vital to the 'national interest', seemed quite irrelevant to it.[21] Added to the existing mixture of patriotic and social pressures, this ensured that 'by July 1917, fifty-eight per cent of all men employed in commerce' and 'fifty-seven per cent of those in the entertainment trades … were in uniform'.[22] In the four years following the outbreak of war the number of men employed in 'commerce' declined from approximately 1,225,000 to 746,000.[23]

It was often the claims for exemption of men in white-collar occupations that were singled out for mockery in the press.[24] When Frank

Lockwood, a trainee lithographic artist with Netherwood, Dalton & Co., a Huddersfield printing firm, applied in April 1916 for exemption from military service so that he could finish his apprenticeship, he found himself the butt of sarcasm and jokes. His case was mentioned in the local paper, where he was described as a 'map-drawer's apprentice'. The article quipped: 'the apprentice might be wanted before long to alter the map of the world'. According to Lockwood, 'I shall be getting quite hardened to these sarcastic remarks before long'.[25] When he was finally called up in April 1917 he stressed that 'I have had a good stay at home and far from being idle, as many people seem to have supposed I have worked fairly hard. I have been taking postal lessons with the Press Art School … and … I have been making good progress with my work'.[26] This may well have been the case, but such work was simply not thought to count for much in wartime (Figure 11).

That said, even work that was seemingly far removed from the war effort did not always meet with an entirely straightforward condemnation.

Hairdresser. "LOOK AT THE LOTS OF FIT YOUNG MEN WE SEE ABOUT WHO OUGHT TO BE IN THE ARMY. SLACKERS, I CALL 'EM. IT FAIRLY MAKES MY DANDRUFF RISE!"

11 'Slackers, I call 'em', *Punch*, 1 November 1916.

In February 1917 Clark found only one man, instead of the usual three, working at Gage's barber's shop in Braintree, and had a long wait to get his hair cut. The barber told him that 'his master has been compelled to go on munition work' by the Braintree tribunal, as they 'did not think Mr Gage's barber's work in his shop of the slightest military use'.[27] This seemingly reasonable assessment found little favour with his customers. One local farmer was 'very sarcastic about the folly of the Braintree Enlistment Tribunal. They compelled ... Gage ... to go to work in the munitions factory. He is an unskilled workman, and his work there could have been just as well done by a boy or a woman'. Meanwhile, farmers had to wait for hours to get their hair cut.[28] Gage's work may not have been essential to the war effort, but that of his customers, forced to wait idly for hours, was.

As Gage's case shows, the authorities had to make choices not only between the demands of the military for manpower and the need for men's work on the home front, but also between forms of home front work considered most useful to the war effort. The Braintree tribunal seems to have been especially keen to push men whose occupations it did not consider useful to the war effort into munitions work. In April 1917 Clark noted that 'there is great pressure put on men in this district to go munitions-making. George Stokes, blacksmith, has to go this week. H. W. Thorogood, landlord of "the Dog and Partridge", has also had to go'.[29] Although perhaps more willing than most similar bodies to force individuals to change jobs, the Braintree tribunal did reflect a wider belief that some occupations were more useful to the war effort than others. Holcombe Ingleby was among those who felt sidelined. In August 1915 he received his National Registration form, which required respondents to state their 'capabilities'. He found it 'surprising how few we possess when it comes to being ticketed', or perhaps more accurately, that few of his 'capabilities' were useful in wartime. He joked that:

> I incline to say that my specialisms are Poetry and Vocalism, but these seem hardly the sort of accomplishments that would be useful in wartime. I might label myself 'a bit of an organiser', but if they took me at my word they might uproot me and plant me in Glasgow or some other dram-drinking place that smelt of anything but fresh air. I might try 'politician' but that might label me as absolutely useless ... Happy thought! I might describe myself as 'head of a firm engaged on Munitions of War'. That would cover a vast multitude of ineptitudes.[30]

The National Service appeals of 1917 were also based on the belief that not all work had equal value in wartime. One pamphlet, listing 'Twelve good reasons why every able-bodied man should enlist for National Service', made the point explicitly: 'Certain occupations are essential, while others are non-essential, and at any cost to ourselves and our comfort, the former should not want for a moment for labour which can be supplied by those engaged in the latter, or by those who are not engaged in either'.[31] An appeal published in February 1917 made clear what type of work was the most valuable: 'Have you freed a man to fight ... ? Are you helping to grow food ... ? Are you helping to make the shells to smash the German machine-guns and save ourselves?'[32] Ultimately, according to Cossins, the 'revolutionary' purpose of National Service was to ensure that 'everyone ... give his or her services to the state and be employed on work of national importance', presumably giving up occupations that were not.[33]

Although few responded to National Service appeals, some middle-class men voluntarily sought to engage in the most 'useful' – and perhaps at the same time, remunerative – occupation they could find. F. W. M. Drew's father, for example, was 'too old for active service', but 'found his niche in the war effort as one of the food commissioners for England, mustering agricultural production and distribution'.[34] By the winter of 1915 Alfred Bradburn's business had come to a 'complete standstill'.[35] His only income derived from his work in a Bristol munitions factory, manufacturing shells: a 'skilled class of work'. As he explained to his brother, 'I have an insurance and out of work card etc. in the proper working man line'.[36] The pay was 'not much as we have not got into proper full working order as yet'. Despite the loss of income, 'I am A1 and as tough as nails. The hard work agrees with me ... it has completely spoiled my hands, they are hard and rough now, but it's some satisfaction to know I am helping to blow the Blight off Europe'.[37] In September 1916 Lieutenant Archie Steavenson received a letter from his friend Dudley, a schoolmaster and 'still a civilian having been deferred till January 25th next'. He was spending the summer working on a farm: the work 'is a fine brain rest but becomes monotonous in the extreme as you may imagine – however it is work that needs doing which is something'.[38]

The sense of making a contribution to the war effort was an important spur. By 1917 Hallie Eustace Miles and her husband's expertise in 'Food-Values and 'Meat-Substitutes' was much in demand: 'it is such a joy to us to find that our knowledge about Foods is of use to our Country'.[39] Between 1914 and 1916 Mr Wilson was the chemist in charge of the TNT department at Millbridge Chemical Works, Huddersfield, one of only three such works in existence at the outbreak of war. Interviewed in 1963, he explained that in the course of the conflict 'we had a crowd coming to see us from Woolwich research department, research chemists from other places'. When such visitors were due, 'the head of the f[irm] … used to impress upon me regularly "Mr Wilson give everything you know to these people it's our patriotic duty as Britishers"'. Wilson had been 'very much impressed with that', adding that 'everybody on the job pulled their weight because of the sense of urgency. We knew that TNT was … an urgently required munition of war just as the men in the forces were required and the guns which they fired the explosives with'.[40]

James Butlin followed with amusement his friend Basil Burnett Hall's (clearly rather vague) plans to find some form of useful work while still an undergraduate at Oxford. In June 1915 Butlin wrote from France that 'I am glad you are thinking of a munitions job: really joking aside you ought to do something, even if it is only keeping me supplied with delicacies'.[41] He returned to the topic a month later, writing that 'I am awfully delighted to hear that you are making some effort to serve your King and Country. Knowing all these knuts in the War Office you ought to get pushed into some soft job'.[42] In October 1915 he was still teasing Burnett Hall: 'I am sorry you persist shirking work in a munition factory: of course you'll have to work hard and why not? At present you are doing nothing except eat, sleep, and run after Oxford flappers'.[43] In October the following year, once Burnett Hall had graduated, Butlin tackled once again the question of work: 'Your prospects of joining a sanitary squad appear particularly rosy especially in view of the fact that no fit man will be allowed to remain in this country any length of time'.[44] In January 1917 he was interested 'to hear that the Foreign Office has at last recognised your undoubted genius for organisation. I suppose you will wear some sort of uniform and draw a large salary: you may even be able to get me a staff job'.[45]

As Burnett Hall's less than half-hearted plans to undertake munitions work show, there were limits to middle-class men's willingness to give up their occupations (or, indeed, studies) and engage in more 'useful' work. In June 1915, for example, Joseph received a wire asking if he 'would take a commission and do munitions work at once'. He acknowledged that 'the prospects for next term as to numbers are very alarming, from a financial point of view … so I think it possible more of us should go and make ourselves useful elsewhere'. However, he clearly was not keen on the idea of munitions work, wiring back that he would not be able to leave the college before the end of the month and asking 'if it would be for the period of the war, which I should find difficult'. He received no answer 'so I suppose that is at an end', adding that in any case 'I am not sure it is what I am suited for'.[46]

At the same time as Joseph was receiving a wire inviting him to undertake munitions work, Robinson noted that 'everybody is most anxious to do anything they can to help'.[47] In reality, as suggested in Chapter 5, there were limits to the work he and many others in his position were prepared to undertake. In December 1916, following the announcement of the National Service scheme, he complained that 'over and over again' he had 'offered his gratuitous services to the War Office and Munitions Department to do work' he was 'fully qualified and fitted to do'.[48] These offers had always been turned down, and he now faced the – clearly appalling – possibility that he might be 'compelled to dig potatoes or tend pigs' instead.[49] Men in his position, he stressed, were doing their 'bit' in 'probably lots of ways', including by paying taxes and rates, but were being pushed into undertaking what – it was implied – was at best unsuitable and at worst menial, demeaning work.[50] Unsurprisingly, they were not keen.

Working lives

Most middle-class civilian men did not change their occupations as a result of the war. This does not mean, however, that their working lives were unaffected by the conflict. Wartime regulations, for example, soon began to have an impact on working practices. Early in 1915 the 'no-lights order' threatened the Sunday evening service at Great Leighs church. Clark worried about the effect of putting the service back to the afternoon: 'The younger people are much attached to the music of the evening service', but choir members, 'owing to distance, could not attend at that hour and the service would have to be read'.[51] In September 1917, as nights began to draw in, evening services had to be abandoned once again. Clark acknowledged that 'this was inconvenient for us all, but we must obey orders, especially when we know that they are given with good reasons for them'.[52]

The effects of regulations on working practices were not always unwelcome. In December 1915 James Caldwell considered that the new restrictions on restaurant meals 'undoubtedly [caused] much hardship to many worthy people', but were 'really needed in a great many cases. In all branches of business, heads of departments had got into the habit of sitting long over their wine with their intimates, chatting about whatever form of sport, or music-hall, or theatre was their special hobby'. They did not return to their office until early afternoon, and were 'very disinclined to settle to work again. In the meantime, if an especial direction was required … the responsible person could not be found'.[53] Most regulations, however, were thought to add to the difficulties of wartime work. In May 1915 the Great Leighs farmers 'who brew their own beer and have harvest-work in prospect, are much put about by Lloyd George's beer proposals. They think that the MPs who voted for them should be sent here for a month's harvesting, without beer'.[54] Food regulations added to the perplexities of many civilians' working, as well as private lives. In March 1918, for example, Joseph complained that in his role as college bursar 'I have been a great deal occupied with difficulties over rationing. It affects the kitchen staff, and those in the Buttery who are fed'. They had been exceeding their voluntary rations and 'the Chef thinks it will be very difficult to satisfy them with substitutes, except at great expense, and wants to commute for a money payment'.[55]

Other changes to working practices were not directly tied to wartime regulations, but were linked rather more loosely to the evolving circumstances of war on the home front. Lockwood found himself working long stretches of overtime in early October 1914. He explained that 'the reason we have been so busy during the past week is that the price of sweets has gone up and we have had practically all T and Ws small cards to litho'.[56] In July 1915 Mr Follows, a county council auditor from Oxford who had to travel a great deal around Oxfordshire, complained that he could not 'get rooms, hardly anywhere. People from London are all leaving their houses, for fear of Zeppelins, and are taking all available places in the country'.[57] In Great Leighs Clark gave extra Sunday services for the soldiers under canvas in Lyons Hall park during the spring and summer of 1916 and 1917.[58] His relationship with the camp chaplain was not without friction. In October 1917 he complained that he had lent him over a hundred and fifty hymn books for 'his camp-service' and now that the camp was being dismantled, there seemed to be no prospect of getting these back.[59]

Joseph's diary is particularly revealing of the extent to which his working days were increasingly made up of the normal routine of his lecturing job and college bursarship, as well as additional responsibilities tied to the war.[60] In August 1914 New College was asked to provide accommodation for a number of cadet officers, and Joseph briefly returned to Oxford from his holiday in Somerset to make the necessary arrangements.[61]

Officers then remained billeted in college throughout the war, occasionally proving a troublesome presence. In January 1915 there were complaints about the mess arrangements, with college servants accused of behaving as if the soldiers were a nuisance and the meals at times 'too slight'. An obviously resentful Joseph thought that the commanding officer 'ignored the position of the Mess as guests for whom the College had done a good deal at a very moderate charge, in the way he spoke, but I could do nothing but express my great regret, and say that I did not think his impression justified'. He later 'gave the scouts a good dressing down'.[62]

On returning to college for the new term in September 1914 he joined a Volunteer corps, of which he remained an active member throughout the war. He described a typical working day towards the end of September. He 'turned out to drill at 7.0 and again 2.0 to 3.30 on our ground ... Spent all the morning on Bursary work, and part of the afternoon on matricul[?] papers. Viva voce at 6.00. Found myself quite tired by dinner time'.[63] A week later, he noted that the college had lost a large number of servants, who had either joined up or re-joined their various regiments. But by far the greatest worry was the loss of revenue from the fall in student numbers. He expected that 'the Tuition Fund will be some £1,500 down on/over the year' and feared that the college would also lose heavily on 'internal revenue'.[64] A week later he noted that only thirty out of the expected sixty-five freshmen had arrived.[65]

In a sense, then, the first eighteen months of war brought Joseph both more and less work. Despite the burden of volunteering, billeting arrangements and bursary work, the smaller student numbers lightened his academic load, in a way that he did not really welcome. In March 1915 he observed that 'term is over, but with none of the sense of relief which the end of this term generally brings: and instead of heavy Collection, I had to read the papers of one man'.[66] Three months later he worried that they would struggle to attract as many as twenty-five students in the new academic year,[67] although by October the college's prospects had improved. The Warden told him that reports had become more 'encouraging' and they were likely to have thirty-three undergraduates in the new term,[68] although the following spring only six candidates took the entrance exam. 'None would come up during the war, except for one who wants to reside this term and work for Sandhurst'.[69] By October 1916 Joseph's workload seems to have increased once more: 'It bids fair to be a strenuous term, what with teaching (five lectures a week), Volunteering, Bursary, finding a new cook, opening a discussion at the Political Sciences Club October 28, and examining at Winchester'.[70]

In June 1916 he gave an account of his activities over a not 'untypical' day, revealing the mixture of 'normal' and war-related activities that made up his working day. He began by working on a lecture between 7 and 8, 'when I went across to breakfast with Davies. After seeing him off, I read through *Gazette* and casualty lists till 8.55'. He continued on his lecture, 'with interruption from a boy applying for SCA messenger's post'. He then gave a lecture and saw a pupil from Lady Margaret's college, followed by letter-writing, 'a call from a member of my [VTC] platoon and a visit to the Registry about the [college] Roll of Service'. After lunch he wrote various letters and notes in connection with VTC and examinations, 'then on my bicycle, delivering notes, with calls in connection with some, and getting a reference for the boy who called this morning'. At 4.35 pm he had tea with a William Waller, before setting off for a Board of Faculty Committee meeting 'and then to the Appeal Tribunal to ask exemption for my Bursary clerk, Gibbs (aged 40.9). Then to see Warden and letters; and about twenty minutes reading before Hall'. Just before 9p.m. he went to a meeting of the College Servants Society, 'about its closing down and storing its belongings'. At 9.30p.m. he 'did a little reading, till I finished my book (Webb, *Group Theories of Religion and the Individual*)'. Then, just after 10p.m. he 'took up this diary'.[71]

While the war brought Joseph a mixture of added war-related duties and (at least during the first half of the conflict) lighter academic workload, Holcombe Ingleby's experiences were more straightforward, as he increasingly found his work counting for less and less in a wartime society. In October 1914 he wrote to his son Clement that 'everything is rather dull just now to those not actively engaged in some sort of service connected with the war. Parliament meets on the 11th November', but even this did not have great importance: 'I imagine the only business will be voting supplies'.[72] By this time Ingleby no longer seems to have been practicing as a solicitor, while his work as a backbench MP did not appear to fulfil a worthwhile purpose. In September 1915 he wrote to Clement from London that 'Parliament is to sit three days a week, which doesn't suit me at all – it means four days of idleness and the other three days are purposeless also'. He had decided to return home to Norfolk 'and whether I shall come back next week is uncertain. It depends on how the parliamentary cat is jumping'.[73] The following month there was a brief flurry of excitement, as Ingleby's time was 'much taken up with what is called "Finance (No 3) bill" … I am here to try to stop it. The Bill hits industries hard by way of a sop to the trades unionists. Lord! What fools we be!'[74] A few days later he 'had to get on my legs in the House to try and prevent some of the iniquities in the new Finance Bill'.[75] By Christmas, however, he was once again despondent. As he explained to Clement, 'the life of the House is to be prolonged for 8[?] months, and I was so seedy the latter part of the time that I doubt if I shall care for another spell of that dreary state of existence'. His 'present inclination', he added, 'is to chuck it'.[76] That said, Ingleby's continued poor health and lack of enthusiasm for his parliamentary duties certainly did not mean that he welcomed losing his seat in 1918, following a constituency reorganisation. Writing once again to Clement, he lamented that 'having been uprooted, time will hang rather heavily on my hands. The man most to be pitied in the world is the man who is out of work'.[77]

While the war marked the end to Ingleby's career, at least as an MP, it saw the beginning of Philip Ashton Murray's. Born in 1900, in 1914 he became a trainee reporter for a weekly Macclesfield paper, where he continued to work until his call-up in June 1918. Interviewed about his wartime experiences in 1985, he stressed the extent to which work had dominated his life. Asked about his impressions at the outbreak of war, he replied that he had been 'immersed in my work – it made no impact'. The war had also had 'no' impact on his work, except that the staff at the newspaper had been 'depleted' and he had been required to work 'very very hard'. News items had remained 'purely local': town council meetings, inquests, funerals, weddings, court cases, church sales and so on. Murray had 'noticed no difference' to life in Macclesfield in the early days of the war. That said, his working life had not been entirely isolated from the events of the war: he had been responsible, for example, for calling on the homes of the relatives of casualties and collecting photographs and information for the 'roll of honour' they published in the newspaper.[78]

Murray sounded surprised when the interviewer asked him whether he had considered enlisting once he turned seventeen. He explained that he had been too 'immersed' in his work and his first loyalty had been to the newspaper, adding that 'all journalists are like that'. Staff shortages had not only meant longer working hours, but also more assignments than a trainee reporter would normally have been expected to cover. He was thrown in at the deep end, 'pushed into assignments for which he was not qualified. Sent to report things which were beyond me. I was too young'. He had to attend political meetings, court cases and council meetings where he was too young 'to comprehend the proceedings'. He had to 'muddle through', despite often being 'out of my depth', especially in county or police courts, where he began reporting well before he turned sixteen.[79]

Murray was not unique in his – not always pleasurable – absorption with work. Reginald Gibbs, for example, spent a good deal of his spare time working on a book of mathematical exercises. In June 1916 he noted that he had 'been working very hard indeed' on his book: 'if I have written some of the sheets once I have written and rewritten them twenty times, before I was satisfied. Even now I can see faults'. He did not 'suppose the book will ever be published, for the scholastic public does not require anything good or scholarly but something easy to use and well within their own capacities'.[80] Five months later he wrote that 'tonight I bound up the last chapter of my book. I have only to complete a number of drawings and then the thing is finished. It has been hanging over me like a nightmare for two years'. He added that 'after it is finished I shan't mind quite so much if I have to go and get killed … It has been a race against time. As it is, a lot of the structure of the book is rather slipshod'. He had, however, identified what he thought was an original proof of an equation. 'I cannot find any flaw in it … It is nothing of course, anything I ever do is always nothing, but anyway, I am pleased with it'.[81]

More commonly, however, middle-class men noted the difficulties of concentrating on their daily working routines when much more exciting events were taking place outside the confines of their workplaces. In February 1918 Ernest Cooper was sitting in his office in Southwold when he heard the lifeboat signal. He joined the lifeboat crew to assist a seaplane in trouble, although it turned out that their help was not needed. On his return to the office he found that 'after this it was rather tedious work taking down evidence as Magistrates Clerk the whole afternoon'.[82] In November 1916 Robert Saunders, a National School headmaster, wrote to his son that 'life with school on is very much treadmill'. It kept him occupied until 3.30p.m., 'after which it is getting in wood, emptying ashes in the garden, emptying the pail of leaves, parings, etc. or a little gardening till tea is ready. After tea I smoke a pipe and read the paper then set to work at my correspondence'.[83] Almost two years later little had changed: 'my day seems to be a routine of school and garden … I go nowhere and shall lose the desire and power to walk'.[84] Editing his wartime diaries in 1938 Macleod Yearsley was 'not ashamed to say' that by the beginning of 1915, as 'the war obtruded itself into everything and we were fired by all we saw, read, or heard', he too had been affected by 'a growing blood-lust on the Home Front … With it', he explained, 'came a loss of interest in our ordinary work, which we carried on perfunctorily and listlessly, longing to be more actively engaged in "doing something"'.[85]

Labour shortages

In August 1915 Cossins noted that the price of wheat had almost returned to its 'old' level, although the cost of bread remained high. According to bakers, the reason for the continued high price lay in the increased cost of labour.[86] Whatever the truth of this particular claim, there is little doubt that middle-class working lives were deeply affected by wartime shortages of labour. Over two million men had enlisted by the end of July 1915 and according to Kieth Grieves, 'very little thought had been given to the impact of such a large withdrawal of labour on the economy'.[87] If anything, in fact, labour shortages became more acute after the introduction of conscription, despite the setting up of bodies such as the Man-Power Distribution Board, created in 1916 to advise the government on issues of manpower.[88] In May 1916 Cossins observed that 'tradesmen and others employing labour are all bemoaning the loss of their hands, and this will become worse when the remaining men are called up'.[89] These shortages affected widely different sections of the economy. Thus, in June 1915 Clark was told that 'peapicking is beset with shortage of labour this year'.[90] A year later, customers who took a watch to be repaired at 'the chief Chelmsford shop' were told that they were very short of labour and waiting time would be approximately a month.[91]

Shortages occurred not only among working-class 'hands', but also white-collar and middle-class occupations. In November 1915 Cossins noted that his firm had been unable to get a replacement for their accountant, who had enlisted: 'we are thinking of getting a girl if one can be found'.[92] The following month he observed that London banks were to close at 3p.m. rather than 4p.m., both because of the difficulties of 'getting about in the darkened streets' and because of staff shortages.[93] In December 1916 a letter from a French friend to Clark's daughter showed 'that the best professional families in French towns are as hard put to it to carry on their duties as similar people in England, their ordinary assistants, dispensers, etc. having been called out for military service'.[94] Saunders too had problems with staff shortages at his school: 'it is useless trying to get teachers as the War has absorbed so many girls'.[95]

Shortages of male teachers were especially acute: like many others who were at school during the war, Derrick Martin recalled that as younger members of staff were called up, older men were recalled from retirement to take their place. According to Martin, 'they were rudely spoken of as "dug-outs" but for all that in nearly every instance managed very well'.[96] A. E. J. Hepworth spent the war working as an inspector of taxes. Writing in 1981, he recalled that 'since all my male staff were taken into the army I had to spend practically all my waking hours at work because the only staff I could get had to be taught their duties whilst I was doing my own work'. The situation worsened once he was transferred from Ireland to Blackpool, where munitions workers could earn up to £7 per week. As he was only allowed to engage temporary clerks and pay them 25s per week, 'I had to struggle on with the dregs of the labour market'.[97]

Alternative sources of labour thus had to be found. During the 1914 Christmas period Boy Scouts were used in Chelmsford 'to do special post office work. So many men have enlisted that the post office cannot obtain the extra hands it generally finds at this time'.[98] The old as well as the young were sought out. In January 1915 F. J. Cooper, the Felsted pension officer, told Clark that 'so many young men had gone from farm and other work that the men of pension age were going on with their ordinary employment, instead of giving up and asking the pension'.[99] According to R. Briggs, writing in 1919, 'old men of 65 or 70 were eagerly employed … upon any work they were capable of doing'.[100] That said, it was women who seemed to provide the most promising pool of labour to replace the men lost to the armed forces.[101] As early as May 1915 the Great Leighs squire, J. H. Tritton, had begun to employ women in some agricultural tasks. Clark was told that 'Mrs Phillips (wife of the cowman) and Constance Stoddart, the dairymaid (daughter of Thomas Stoddart, the land steward of Lyons Hall and Great Leighs churchwarden) had been … hoeing turnips'. Even such limited deployment of women proved controversial: 'Phillips I heard, was very indignant, and vowed that if his wife was to work in the fields, he would stay at home, other workmen have asserted the same'.[102]

Hostility towards women's employment in the fields was not limited to the workers. In Great Leighs at least, most farmers took on women workers only reluctantly, as a last resort, never entirely shaking the belief that the work was beyond their capabilities. In February 1916 Thomas Sargeant, the Lyons Hall head gardener, told Clark that 'when the groups are called up at the end of this month, garden work will have to stop. He does not believe that women, if brought in, will be able for the work'.[103] Stoddart agreed, explaining in May 1916 that 'the women on the land had been hoeing beans, but they made little progress. Four women did not do as much work as one man'. Tritton believed 'that a woman would do a man's work and earn a man's wage', but, according to Stoddart, 'they have not the strength required even for hoeing'.[104] Despite such lack of enthusiasm, women's work on the land was increasingly recognised as a necessity[105] and during the final summer of the war Clark noted that 'much work in the district is being done by women-labourers'.[106] However, attitudes had not changed much. In November 1918 Clark wrote to the Bodleian librarian that the 'parish is absolutely empty of young men. Farmers who had vowed that they never would have women land-workers have been compelled to employ them. They do not think much of their work, but they cannot get on without it'.[107]

Such negative attitudes seem to have been fairly typical of other sectors of the economy too: women's employment in male occupations was seen as a necessary, but temporary expedient only. In June 1918 Saunders received a visit from the manager of Hannington's, a Brighton firm: 'he told me he had twenty-five girls in his office and they did the work better and gave less trouble than his former staff of men. If this is generally the opinion it rather looks as if the days of the male clerks are numbered'.[108] However, this was not representative of middle-class attitudes generally. According to George Wilkinson, the war saw women entering occupations that would have been unthinkable before 1914, including his colliery's office. Tellingly, he believed that their presence was accepted in the same way as 'rationing': few expected it to continue after the war.[109]

In March 1916 Robinson observed that 'we are getting accustomed to seeing women in many occupations previously occupied by men', not only in manufacturing, but also banks and transport. He wondered: 'how is all this going to be adjusted after the war. Will women be content to go back to their domestic duties, their sewing, their cooking and what not?'[110] In fact, the possibility that women's war work could lead to a permanent disruption of established gender divisions of labour was rarely taken seriously. In March 1917 Joe Hollister wrote to his father that 'the amount of female labour employed in the City' was 'extraordinary'. The Bank of England employed over four hundred women, and 'there was a flutter of excitement in Gracechurch street the other day at two girls with trouser overalls cleaning the windows of shops'. In addition, 'the Railway Companies have employed them of course for a long while, tramcars, omnibuses, mail-vans, motor-cars, Carter Paterson vans, all the caterers, newsvendors, bootblacks, lamplighters, latherers in barbers shops, in fact almost every sphere of activity'. He concluded by suggesting – in a way that was clearly not meant to be taken seriously – that 'when "Tommy" comes home he will be keeping the house and minding the kids while the missus earns the pieces'[111] (Figure 12).

Whatever the strategies adopted by individual employers to cope with wartime conditions, whether they tried to obtain exemption for their 'essential' men, or sought to employ children, older men or women, there was a near-universal perception among middle-class men that labour shortages were allowing the working classes to earn unprecedentedly high wages. According to Cossins, in May 1915 men working in factories had 'more money than they know what to do with so they either spend it on extra drink or work short hours to earn what they've been accustomed to'.[112] High wages, middle-class civilians believed, were one of the results of labour shortages; increased assertiveness among workers was another.[113] Clark, for example, observed with interest the shifting power relations between employers and labour in Great Leighs and nearby parishes. In November 1914 Stoddart told him that farm work at Lyons Hall 'was getting on well. There was no lack of labour. He had as many men as he could employ, and had constant applications from horsemen, stockmen, and other farm-hands asking him to find them a job'.[114] By the following spring, however, the situation had changed. Amid rumours that labourers were about to ask for a wage rise, Stoddart complained that 'another of the … farm-men is leaving. He is going to get, at Little Waltham, 20/- a week and to be allowed to leave off work at 5 pm'.[115] Rising demand for labour put employers at a disadvantage. Richard Arnold, 'tenant of the Glebe', complained in July 1915 that 'it is very difficult work farming this year. Even the old hands will do only what they like … If you find fault, he will tell you he is master now, and you cant [*sic*] do without him'.[116]

A year later, according to Caldwell, conscription served to swing the balance of power back in favour of employers. In December 1916 he told Clark that the men working on Long's farm were 'very discontented'. The continuous flooding meant that they had to work in the wet, but 'they dare not leave', for fear that 'they will be snapped up for military service. Farmers are taking advantage of this fact to tyrannise over the men'.[117] Farmers would have disagreed with this assessment, stressing instead the extent to which they were forced to bow to their workers' demands. In June 1917 Arnold was once again 'much troubled about labour on his farm. He has not enough men, and labour is very costly. You have just to pay the men what they ask. They know that there are not enough men about, and off they go unless they get what they ask in wages'.[118] The

12 'When the boys come home', *Punch*, 10 May 1916.

following summer John Cousins, of Gate-house farm, complained that 'this year the labourers have been "awful"'. They arrived 'when they liked' and 'left off work when they liked'.[119] And, it was implied, there was nothing Cousins and other employers like him could do about it.

In Great Leighs – and no doubt elsewhere too – labour shortages were thus thought to be undermining many employers' authority over their workers. They also had, it was felt, a wider impact on the quality of life of middle-class men in the locality. In April 1916, for example, Clark's 'lad' of all work, Charles Wood, was called up for military service: 'I have no one to take his place, and shall have to undertake personally most of the outside work'.[120] In addition to work in the grounds, garden and house, this also included pumping by hand the rectory's water supply, which 'is weary, heavy, disheartening work'.[121] In January 1917 he attributed his greatly increased smoking to having to do the outdoor work 'of the Rectory, some of it disagreeable, much of it trialsome for a sedentary student' who was no longer a young man.[122]

Clark was not the only middle-class (and indeed, middle-aged or elderly) man forced to undertake unaccustomed hard and monotonous physical labour. In June 1916 William Brown told him that he had been farming for many years but 'this year, owing to his men being taken away, he had to work harder than he has ever done'.[123] In September he was 'busy on top of his harvest-waggon all day, receiving sheaves as tossed up to him, arranging them on waggon, and pitching them on to the stack in his yard'. He told Clark that 'before the war broke out, he had said to himself that he was now come to the age when he could reasonably claim to be free from heavy outdoor work', but 'since the war began he has had to work harder than he has ever done since he was a lad. His young strong men being taken away for military service he has had to do most of the heavier farm tasks'.[124] Even men who were not involved in farming found that the labour involved in maintaining the physical fabric of middle-class homes, including grounds, outbuildings and gardens, increasingly fell on their shoulders. In July 1916 Clark received a letter from a Dr Runwell, now retired, who owned a 'large house and garden and garage'. All his men had been 'called out for service (his chauffeur included), and all his maids have given notice to go into munitions-works, leaving the house without servant, outdoor or indoor'.[125] Five months later he heard that Colonel Ralph Egerton, of Chatham Hall, Great Waltham 'is left with only a boy of thirteen … in place of his former staff of two gardeners and his chauffeur (who also did odd jobs in the grounds) … he has himself to pump water into the cisterns'.[126]

Many middle-class men may have baulked at the idea of undertaking menial tasks for National Service, but some at least found themselves in the position of doing exactly such work around their own homes. In March 1916 Clark wrote to the Bodleian librarian, Falconer Madan, complaining that 'the War Office is taking my lad, so that I shall have to take myself from studies of all sorts to black boots, flush drains, and groom a pony'.[127] He wrote again a few weeks after the end of the war, apologising for the delay in sending the most recent volumes of his diary. He explained that 'the work of the garden and the grounds has kept me busy all year, every minute of daylight that I could spare from my ordinary duties. In addition, the Coal Controller has assigned me a coal allowance insufficient to keep even the kitchen fire going'. As a result, in order 'to have a fire at all, I have to spend some hours before daylight and some after nightfall sawing wood by candlelight in the wood-house'. His difficulties were not unique. His 'neighbours – persons with gardens and grounds – have to fare like myself, or let their places become like jungles'. Some had attempted to 'get an old man – seventy or over – to sweep up leaves and do such odd jobs – but even old men are hard to find. The haler sort of them are pottering about, doing jobs on the farms'.[128] In Great Leighs at least, it seems that middle-aged, middle-class men had become the only source of labour left available to service and maintain middle-class households.

Business, profits and standards of living

Problems such as staff shortages hit all sections of the wartime economy, but other issues affected the business sector more specifically. The upheaval of the early months of war led to a good deal of economic dislocation, with many businesses left at a standstill. By the end of September 1914 the Colne Valley mills were once again 'very busy' after the disruption of the early weeks of war,[129] but other businesses did not recover so easily. Towards the end of October 1914 two Braintree tradesmen called on the Clark household. The first 'came to set the hall-clock going, after cleaning. He said that the clock and watch-making business is one of those which are soonest and most severely prejudiced by the war'. The second was a traveller for a wine merchant, who said that 'owing to the war, their trade was particularly bad'.[130] In December 1915 Bradburn's business was still 'at a complete standstill'.[131] The slogan 'Business as Usual', first coined by H. E. Morgan of W. H. Smith in a letter to *The Daily*

Chronicle on 11 August 1914, was based on a clear awareness that a long-term disruption to trade would be ruinous.[132]

The advertising material produced by many firms in the early months of the war reflected their difficulties: in October 1914 Clark received a circular from The Positive Organ Company, 'the firm from whom we purchased our little organ 2 years ago'. The printed leaflet, headed 'All British', stated that 'they desire to provide work for the married members of their staff of skilled workmen as far as may be possible during the present crisis'.[133] Firms with German-sounding names faced particular difficulties in the face of widespread hostility towards what became known in the latter part of the war as '"The Hun in our midst" and "The Hidden Hand"'.[134] In October 1914 the London wine merchants Ehrmann Brothers added a note to their price list, stressing that 'ours is an English firm … The whole of our large staff is British. While we own vineyard property *in France* … we own no property and have no interests in Germany or Austria'.[135] A month later the directors of the London furniture and furnishings firm Oetzmann and Co. 'beg to announce that the Business was *founded in 1848* by the late *John R. Oetzmann* a British-Born subject and that the Directors, Shareholders and staff are all British subjects'. The price list further emphasised the link between patriotism and business as usual: 'The year 1914 will be ever historic as the year of the Great European War … Economic endurance will be the determining factor of success, and it is all-essential that TRADE SHOULD BE KEPT GOING'.[136]

It was the boom in government demand that provided a vital boost to those businesses that could supply goods to the armed forces.[137] In November 1914 Edwin Luckock, a retired missionary and for a brief period special constable, told Clark that one of his sons worked for a very large motor-machinery factory. 'When the war broke out,' he explained, 'the purchase of cars by private persons suddenly ceased, and this firm saw ruin in the face. Two things warded off calamity: the government brought up a number of the motor-vans they had in stock [and] commandeered for government service a considerable number of their workmen'. Soon 'afterwards, they received an order for 250 big motor vans for the Russian government: had to get all the extra hands they could; and work day and night'.[138] Caldwell was struck by how many businesses were dependent on government orders. In January 1915 he told Clark 'that business in London is at a standstill except for firms engaged in serving the military forces'.[139] He returned to the topic two months later, explaining that 'business men's minds are much exercised as to what will happen when the government has ceased giving large orders – will things brisken up then or will there be great slackness'. He added that 'hundreds of people who had never done anything for the government are now working, night and day, on government orders'.[140]

Even among those businesses that were able to attract government contracts, high prices and shortages of raw materials, high freight costs, 'red tape', excessive regulation and taxation, difficulties in obtaining credit, as well as labour shortages, were all matters of frequent complaint.[141] In June 1915 Caldwell told Clark – no doubt with his own business in mind – that in London few firms were able to make any money. As a result, 'no one with capital will initiate anything fresh. Owners of works can get no contract that will yield any margin. They have to be content with orders which will barely pay enough to keep their hands working'.[142] Indeed, if there was one sentiment that united all the middle-class men who feature in this book, it was the feeling that profits were certainly being made out of the war, but only by 'others'. According to Robinson, by May 1918 the world seemed 'to be divided into two classes, those who want to turn their household gods into money – no doubt to pay the heavy taxation – and those who want to turn their money – no doubt recently acquired – into household gods'. It is not difficult to guess which 'class' Robinson felt he belonged.[143]

It remained for the protagonist of Arnold Bennett's 1918 novel *The Pretty Lady*, to attempt to justify profit-making in wartime. 'G. J.' was a man of about fifty, who having sold his prosperous solicitor's practice, lived comfortably on his investments. At the outbreak of war he had 'given himself up for lost', particularly his investments in the Reveille Motor Horn Co. Ltd: 'No one would want to buy expensive motor horns in the midst of the greatest war the world etc. etc.' But the company 'had somehow continued to do a pretty good business', particularly thanks to the War Office, which had 'given it grand orders at vast prices for all sorts of things that it had never made before'. By 1915, it looked as if profits 'would be doubled, if not trebled – perhaps quadrupled'. Far from risking ruin, G. J. 'was actually going to make money' out of the conflict. 'And why not? Somebody had to make money, and somebody had to pay for the war in income tax'.[144] Perhaps only a fictional character could express himself so bluntly without attracting opprobrium, and even he by 1916 had 'long since … decided I must give away all my extra profits'. He strongly denied being a profiteer.[145]

In any case, rather than profiting from it, large sections of the middle class complained that they were being impoverished by the war. Not only were taxation and charitable appeals making increasingly heavy demands on middle-class pockets,[146] but incomes, particularly among salaried employees and among those dependent on rent or other fixed incomes, struggled to keep pace with price inflation.[147] According to Sheridan Jones, clerks were especially hard hit. Even before the war the typical clerk had led 'a drab life', the work being 'hard, monotonous, exacting. His pay is such that he never ceases to feel its chronic inadequacy'.[148] Since the outbreak of war, furthermore, 'his lot is harder than ever. His work has doubled or trebled', while the increased cost of living had not been matched by increases in salary, leaving him 'worse off than ever; a prey to chronic anxiety, a slave to care'.[149] Jon Lawrence suggests that 'for the middle classes, the lottery of the wartime economy offered the prospects of great riches for some alongside crippling losses for many others'.[150] Few acknowledged being among the former, while suspecting others of doing well out of the opportunities provided by the war.

In November 1917 Cooper noted that his brother 'writes that he has lost £1,000 owing to the maximum price fixed for beef and pork, but I think it probable he has made more out of the rising market before prices were fixed'.[151] Writing in 1992, Jeffrey Axton recalled that his great uncle and aunt 'made over £1,000 profit from selling eggs to local friends. They had a miniature chicken farm in their back garden at Willesden Green'.[152] However, real anger was directed not at entrepreneurial relatives, friends or acquaintance, but at those faceless big businesses whose 'swollen dividends, huge profits' and 'mammoth fortunes'[153] were felt to have crossed the line between profit-making and profiteering. This was a cultural and emotional, as well as an economic boundary, based on norms that stressed the importance of equality of sacrifice in wartime. Profiteers, it was believed, were not simply making excessive profits, but were actually amassing their 'huge fortunes out of the misfortunes of other people'.[154] In October 1916, for example, Lockwood complained that 'the Army Contracts are a hotbed of bribery and get rich quick no matter who suffers method'.[155] The greatest resentment, however, was reserved not for firms that supplied goods to the armed forces, but those that were involved in provisioning the home front.[156] Thus, it was shipping companies that charged excessive freightage, causing prices to rise, as well as food producers, retailers and 'speculators',[157] who were most frequently accused of profiteering.[158]

In January 1915, amidst general concern about the rise in the price of foodstuffs, Gibbs observed that 'the shipowners are profiting by national misfortunes and are amassing fortunes at the expense of the public'.[159] A year later, Caldwell told Clark that 'the government trade-regulations are imbecile'. They set 'maximum prices for coal, interfering with people here needlessly', but left 'shipping-firms to ruin industry and make provisions excessively dear by extravagant profits'. The reason for the increase in the freight rate, he believed, could be found in companies' balance sheets: 'a great number of shipping firms, which previously earned modest returns, are now paying fabulous dividends'.[160] In November 1916 Cossins noted that 'some people are making huge fortunes owing to the high prices, the latest being the potato growers who are netting over £50 per acre profit'.[161] Three months later, according to Caldwell, 'people in town are chuckling over the way in which farmers are hit by the new Board of Agriculture regulations as to future prices of wheat and minimum wages for labour'. The same farmers who were now 'pulling very long faces … have had "a royal time" of it for the last two years'.[162]

However, profiteering businesses were thought to be adept at evading regulations and using the wartime state apparatus to their advantage. According to Yearsley, a 'disgraceful scandal' came to light in August 1917: the Control Boards set up by the Food Control Department were 'packed with tradesmen to whose interest it was to keep up prices whereby the Food Profiteers brought before them were acquitted'.[163] He complained that profiteers were always able to evade regulations and avoid punishment. 'In fact', he asserted after the war, 'the Profiteer could do exactly as he pleased and nothing was done against him'.[164] Robinson would have agreed. In September 1917 he noted that new food regulations were about to be introduced, but he worried that 'the suppliers will probably find a way of turning these … to their benefit'. He had no doubt about who the main victims were likely to be: 'the ordinary middle-class consumer will probably be as badly off as ever'.[165]

Conclusion

In May 1915 Robinson noted that in a recent issue of *The Times*, devoted to the question of 'National Service', a Lionel Holland had suggested that every man between the ages of seventeen and fifty-five 'without distinction of rank and means (and every woman who volunteers) shall be employed in the manner that will increase our national efficiency and contribute towards a triumphal issue to the war'. Robinson was not convinced: 'some of these people when they … write so glibly, overlook the fact that a large number of such persons occupy positions involving great financial and other responsibilities which cannot be neglected without great damage to the community, or a large section of it'. Not only did 'most have financial engagements to keep, rent, rates and taxes to pay', but it could be argued that such men would be most helpful to 'the country by continuing in … [their] employment and contributing … [their] share of what Mr Lloyd George called "silver bullets"'.[166]

Two months earlier R. D. Blumenfeld had observed that it was considered 'a disgrace for an able-bodied man to be out of employment of some sort or other at the present moment'. For the better-off sections of the population, furthermore, 'this employment must be voluntary and patriotic'.[167] In the increasingly charged atmosphere of the wartime home front, it became ever more important for middle-class (and no doubt other) civilian men to be able to justify their work by making reference to its contribution to the war effort. However, as Robinson recognised, definitions of work that would contribute to 'a triumphal issue to the war' were ambiguous and open to negotiation. Men in lower-middle-class and white-collar occupations, for example, were frequently targeted by the authorities and the press as making little contribution to the war effort, often being portrayed as 'Cuthberts' finding shelter in civilian 'funk-holes'.[168] However, as local displeasure at the Braintree barber's removal to a munitions factory shows, definitions of 'useful' work were far from straightforward.

Furthermore, the notion that some work, however patriotic, was simply not suitable for professional, highly educated middle-class men, certainly did not disappear. In a moment of exasperation, Saunders wrote to his son in March 1916 that 'the Government should bring in a Bill for general conscription and organise the whole population for whatever service is necessary for the country's good'.[169] However, he would surely have been horrified if any such measure had really been implemented, truly reorganising the workforce without distinctions 'of rank and means'.[170] Bradburn was of course not unique in moving to work in a munitions factory, while men such as Joseph and Burnett Hall at least considered this option, but the great majority of middle-class men remained in their pre-war occupations or sought work of similar status, for example within the wartime state apparatus.

That said, few working lives were unaffected by the vicissitudes of war. Labour shortages had perhaps the greatest impact: not only did they increase the difficulties of work in wartime, but also created a perceived shift of power in favour of the working class. Workers thus appeared increasingly independent, assertive and prosperous, just at a time when middle-class men were feeling the squeeze on their incomes caused by static salaries, frozen rents, higher taxation and price inflation. Fortunes, it was widely held by middle-class opinion, were certainly there to be made out of the war, but it was always 'others' who were ruthlessly making use of such opportunities: not only 'millionaire' munitions workers, enjoying the high life, but big businesses that were 'profiteering' from the sacrifices and suffering of others, particularly those of the 'the ordinary middle-class consumer'.[171] Perhaps worst of all, many middle-class men were eventually also forced by circumstances to undertake those very menial and often hard labouring tasks that they considered unsuited to their status and physiques. Significantly, much of this labour was undertaken not for a wage in the workplace or in response to patriotic appeals, but in and around their own homes, in order to maintain their fabric and ensure their continued functioning. Indeed, such pressures could also affect men higher up in the social scale, disrupting established practices in ways that were both deeply mundane and unexpectedly significant: in November 1917 Sir George Young wrote to his son, Edward Hilton Young, then serving with the Royal Navy Volunteer Reserve, that with only two servants left, 'home work gets done anyhow … Yesterday I made my bed myself'.[172]

Notes

1 A. Clark War Diary, 'Echoes of the 1914 War in an Essex Village' (hereafter Clark Diary), 6 September 1914, Ms Eng. Hist. e.88, Special Collections, Bodleian Library, University of Oxford (hereafter Bodleian Special Collections), Oxford.

2 Wartime Diaries of H. W. B. Joseph 1914–18 (hereafter Joseph Diaries), 4 August 1914, Ms. Top. Oxon. e.288, Bodleian Special Collections. It is interesting to note that the memorial address given after Joseph's death in 1943 mentioned that 'many might be angered by what seemed to be – and perhaps was – niggardliness and obstinacy in his handling of College funds'. *H. W. B. Joseph 1867–1943: An Address Delivered in Chapel by the Sub-warden of New College (A. H. Smith) 23 November 1943* (University Press, Oxford, not dated), p. 6.

3 F. T. Lockwood, 'Notes Written by F. T. Lockwood', 15 August 1914, 96/52/1, Department of Documents, Imperial War Museum (hereafter IWM Documents), London.

4 Clark Diary, 8 September 1914, Ms Eng. Hist. e.89, Bodleian Special Collections.

5 *Ibid.*, 12 September 1914.

6 *Ibid.*, 5 January 1915, Ms Eng. Hist. e.96.

7 *Ibid.*, 11 July 1918, Ms Eng. Hist. e.165.
8 *Ibid.*, 31 March 1915, Ms Eng. Hist. e.99.
9 F. A. Robinson, 'Diary of the Great War', 24 July 1916, vol. 2, P.401, IWM Documents.
10 Where possible, informal arrangements were made, generally with family members taking over the business for the duration of the war. See, for example, Clark Diary, 7 July 1916, Ms Eng. Hist. e.124, Bodleian Special Collections.
11 Robinson, 'Diary of the Great War', 30 March 1916, vol. 2, P.401, IWM Documents.
12 J. Tosh, *A Man's Place: Masculinity and the Middle-Class Home in Victorian England* (Yale University Press, New Haven, CT, 1999), pp. 24, 33–4; J. Garrard and V. Parrott, 'Craft, professional and middle-class identities: solicitors and gas engineers, c. 1850–1914', in A. Kidd and D. Nicholls (eds), *The Making of the British Middle Class? Studies of Regional and Cultural Diversity since the Eighteenth Century* (Sutton Publishing, Stroud, 1998), pp. 148–68.
13 A. D. Gardner, Reminiscences, not dated, DF148, Liddle Collection (1914–18), Special Collections, Brotherton Library, Leeds University (hereafter Liddle Collection), Leeds.
14 Diary of R. W. M. Gibbs, 1914–20 (hereafter Gibbs Diary), 29 May 1915, Ms Eng. misc. c.167, Bodleian Special Collections. But see also the condemnation of working-class men who were thought to be 'sheltering' in protected and 'starred' trades: calls for the 'comb-out' of such men became a regular feature of the later war years. See, for example, H. C. Cossins Diary, 1914–18 (hereafter Cossins Diary), 3 March 1916, 15 March 1916, 19 March 1916, 21 September 1916, PP/MCR/371, IWM Documents. It was suspected that many young men entered munitions factories purely to escape military service. See, for example, Clark Diary, 21 October 1915, 25 October 1915, Ms Eng. Hist. e.113; 6 December 1915, Ms Eng. Hist. e.115, Bodleian Special Collections. According to Lockwood, 'the patriotism of a large number of munitions workers is false, theirs, is patriotism to save their own skins and enrich their pockets'. Lockwood, 'Notes', 26 March 1916, 96/52/1, IWM Documents.
15 Clark Diary, 15 January 1915, Ms Eng. Hist. e.96, Bodleian Special Collections.
16 W. G. Ostler interview, 21 March 1973, 39, Department of Sound, Imperial War Museum (hereafter IWM Sound), London. In August 1915 Ostler joined the Royal Flying Corps.
17 C. D. Winchcombe, 'The Great War of 1914–1918: Memories of an Octogenarian', not dated, DF148, Liddle Collection.
18 L. S. Bibbings, *Telling Tales about Men: Conceptions of Conscientious Objectors to Military Service during the First World War* (Manchester University Press, Manchester, 2009), p. 30. Only a tiny minority of appeals were

made on the grounds of conscientious objection, perhaps as few as 1 or 2 per cent of the total. A. Gregory, *The Last Great War: British Society and the First World War* (Cambridge University Press, Cambridge, 2008), pp. 101–8. Adrian Gregory notes that most tribunal records were destroyed in the 1920s.

19 Clark Diary, 27 February 1916, Ms Eng. Hist. e.121, Bodleian Special Collections. Exemption could also be sought on the ground that 'he should continue to be ... educated or trained', 'that the principal or usual occupation of the man is one of those included in the list of occupations certified by Government Departments for exemption', or 'that serious hardship would ensue, if the man were called up for Army service, owing to his exceptional financial or business obligations or domestic position'. The assumption was that the application would be made by the man himself, his employer, or 'the military representative'. Both the men who had attested under the Derby scheme and those who had not could apply. Clark Diary, 27 February 1916, Ms Eng. Hist. e.121, Bodleian Special Collections. See also J. McDermott, 'The Work of the Military Service Tribunals in Northamptonshire, 1916–1918' (Unpublished PhD thesis, University of Northampton, 2009), pp. 70–174.

20 Gibbs Diary, 10 January 1917, Ms Eng. misc. c.185, Bodleian Special Collections.

21 Such attitudes can be found reflected in a number of the recruiting advertisements that appeared in the early months of 1915. See, for example, 'Five questions to patriotic shopkeepers', *Daily Express*, 17 February 1915, 'Pictorial advertisements in war time 1914 and 1915', in A. Clark, 'Scrapbooks of leaflets, newspaper cuttings etc., illustrating aspects of the Great War', Bodleian Library, University of Oxford, Oxford.

22 J. M. Winter, *The Great War and the British People* (Palgrave Macmillan, Basingstoke, 2003, first published 1985), p. 37.

23 P. Dewey, *War and Progress in Britain 1914–1918* (Longman, Harlow, 1997), p. 26. The number of women employed in commerce increased from 496,000 to 880,000.

24 Gregory, *The Last Great War*, pp. 105–6.

25 Lockwood, 'Notes', 3 April 1916, 96/52/1, IWM Documents. Lockwood's first application, to the Linthwaite Tribunal, was rejected on the grounds that his trade was not of 'national importance'. However, his appeal was subsequently upheld by the East-Central Appeal Tribunal, which granted him exemption from military service until the completion of his apprenticeship, two months later.

26 *Ibid.*, 23 April 1917.

27 Clark Diary, 8 February 1917, Ms Eng. Hist. e.144, Bodleian Special Collections.

28 *Ibid.*, 13 June1917, Ms Eng. Hist. e.149.

29 *Ibid.*, 25 April 1917, Ms Eng. Hist. e.147. See also 4 March 1917, Ms Eng. Hist. e.145.

30 Holcombe Ingleby to Clement, 10 August 1915, The First World War Letters of Holcombe Ingleby MP (hereafter Ingleby Letters), P.343, IWM Documents. Cossins noted that the National Register, compiled in August 1915, was 'said to be merely for the purposes of ascertaining who are and who are not engaged on government work but it will also come in very useful if compulsory military service is decided upon'. Cossins Diary, 30 June 1915, PP/MCR/371, IWM Documents.

31 'Twelve good reasons why every able-bodied man should enlist for National Service', pamphlet, not dated, in 'Miscellaneous papers relating to the Great War, 13 volumes', Bodleian Library, University of Oxford, Oxford.

32 Robinson, 'Diary of the Great War', 23 February 1917, vol. 3, P.402, IWM Documents. Robinson does not provide an attribution to this appeal.

33 Cossins Diary, 20 December 1916, PP/MCR/371, IWM Documents. For the National Service scheme see also Chapter 5. The distinction between 'essential' and 'non-essential' industries was also central to the policy of the Ministry of National Service, established in 1917 after the collapse of the National Service scheme. The Ministry, under the direction of Auckland Geddes, also took over responsibility for army recruitment. G. J. DeGroot, *Blighty: British Society in the Era of the Great War* (Longman, Harlow, 1998, first published 1996), p. 102.

34 F. W. M. Drew, Recollections, not dated, DF148, Liddle Collection. In 1914 Drew was a ten-year-old boy living in Exeter.

35 A. Bradburn to S. Bradburn, 14 December 1915, Letters from Alfred Bradburn to his Brother Samuel (hereafter Bradburn Letters), 95/16/1, IWM Documents. Bradburn was by then in his forties. The letters do not provide information about the nature of the business.

36 *Ibid.*, 13 November 1915.

37 *Ibid.*, 14 December 1915. In January 1916 he was earning an average weekly wage of £2 15s. See *ibid.*, 16 January 1916.

38 Dudley to A. G. Steavenson ('Dear Old Bottom'), 10 September 1916, A.G. Steavenson Letters, 86/77/1, IWM Documents.

39 H. E. Miles, *Untold Tales of War-Time London: A Personal Diary* (Cecil Palmer, London, 1930), pp. 112–13.

40 Mr Wilson interview, 1963 BBC recording, 4261, IWM Sound. For a similar (and probably unusual) instance of an individual putting patriotism before business interests, see M. Dintenfass, 'Service, loyalty and leadership: the life tales of British coal masters and the culture of the middle class, c. 1890–1950', in Kidd and Nicholls (eds), *The Making of the British Middle Class?*, p. 219.

41 J. H. Butlin to B. Burnett Hall, 23 June 1915, Letters of Lieutenant James H. Butlin (hereafter Butlin Letters), 67/52/1, IWM Documents.

42 *Ibid.*, 19 July 1915.
43 *Ibid.*, 23 October 1915.
44 *Ibid.*, 15 October 1916.
45 *Ibid.*, 3 January 1917. In a telling reversal, after a special 'neurasthenic board' in March 1918 had declared Butlin permanently unfit for further service, he asked Burnett Hall: 'now what the hell am I to do for a living?' See *ibid.*, 29 March 1918.
46 Joseph Diaries, 11 June 1915, Ms. Top. Oxon. e.288, Bodleian Special Collections.
47 Robinson, 'Diary of the Great War', 12 June 1915, vol. 1, P.401, IWM Documents.
48 *Ibid.*, 20 December 1916, vol. 2, P.401.
49 *Ibid.*, 27 January 1917, vol. 3, P.402.
50 *Ibid.*, 31 March 1917.
51 Clark Diary, 29 January 1915, Ms Eng. Hist. e.97, Bodleian Special Collections.
52 *Ibid.*, 30 September 1917, Ms Eng. Hist. e.154.
53 *Ibid.*, 4 December 1915, Ms Eng. Hist. e.115.
54 *Ibid.*, 1 May 1915, Ms Eng. Hist. e.102.
55 Joseph Diaries, 26 March 1918, Ms. Top. Oxon. e.288, Bodleian Special Collections.
56 Lockwood, 'Notes', 9 October 1914, 96/52/1, IWM Documents.
57 Clark Diary, 8 July 1915, Ms Eng. Hist. e.107, Bodleian Special Collections.
58 *Ibid.*, 22 October 1916, Ms Eng. Hist. e.137.
59 *Ibid.*, 10 October 1917, Ms Eng. Hist. e.155. Eventually eighty-four books were returned. See 17 October 1917.
60 The impact of war on (metropolitan) universities is explored in E. Fordham, 'Universities', in J. Winter and J.-L. Robert (eds), *Capital Cities at War: Paris, London, Berlin 1914–1919 Volume 2: A Cultural History* (Cambridge University Press, Cambridge, 2007), pp. 235–79.
61 Joseph Diaries, 18 August 1914, Ms. Top. Oxon. e.288, Bodleian Special Collections.
62 *Ibid.*, 19 January 1915.
63 *Ibid.*, 25 September 1914.
64 *Ibid.*, 1 October 1914.
65 *Ibid.*, 8 October 1914.
66 *Ibid.*, 18 March 1915.
67 *Ibid.*, 11 June 1915.
68 *Ibid.*, 7 October 1915.
69 *Ibid.*, 27 April 1916.
70 *Ibid.*, 7 October 1916.
71 *Ibid.*, 19 June 1916.

72 Holcombe Ingleby to Clement, 27 October 1914, Ingleby Letters, P.343, IWM Documents.
73 *Ibid.*, 15 September 1915.
74 *Ibid.*, 26 October 1915.
75 *Ibid.*, 6 November 1915.
76 *Ibid.*, 25 December 1915.
77 *Ibid.*, 4 November 1918.
78 P. Ashton Murray interview, 14 October 1985, 9114, reel 1, IWM Sound. It was only in his read 'statement' that Murray mentioned the issues the interviewer clearly expected, such as rationing, allotment keeping, tribunals and 'comforts' for the troops.
79 *Ibid.*
80 Gibbs Diary, 24 June 1916, Ms Eng. misc. c.178, Bodleian Special Collections.
81 *Ibid.*, 18 November 1916, Ms Eng. misc. c.183. He later realised, 'after lying awake a long time … that there was a flaw in my wonderful proof after all. I dare say all my ideas have got flaws in them. At any rate I try to find them out'. See *ibid.*, 19 November 1916. A search of the Bodleian Library's catalogue reveals that between 1922 and 1941 Gibbs published at least twelve books on mathematics and geometry.
82 The Diary of Ernest R. Cooper, 'Nineteen Hundred and War Time', 28 July 1914 – 3 December 1918 (hereafter Cooper Diary), 27 February 1918, P.121, IWM Documents.
83 R. Saunders to son, 18 November 1916, R. Saunders, Letters to Son in Canada, 1914–18 (hereafter Saunders Letters), 79/15/1, IWM Documents.
84 *Ibid.*, 4 August 1918.
85 M. Yearsley ('Eyewitness'), 'The Home Front, 1914–18', pp. 60–1, DS/MISC/17, IWM Documents.
86 Cossins Diary, 30 August 1915, PP/MCR/371, IWM Documents.
87 K. Grieves, *The Politics of Manpower, 1914–18* (Manchester University Press, Manchester, 1988), p. 16.
88 *Ibid.*, pp. 40–62.
89 Cossins Diary, 14 May 1916, PP/MCR/371, IWM Documents.
90 Clark Diary, 29 June 1915, Ms Eng. Hist. e.106, Bodleian Special Collections.
91 *Ibid.*, 20 April 1916, Ms Eng. Hist. e.124.
92 Cossins Diary, 12 November 1915, PP/MCR/371, IWM Documents. See also 19 December 1916 and 21 December 1916.
93 *Ibid.*, 1 December 1915.
94 Clark Diary, 27 December 1916, Ms Eng. Hist. e.141, Bodleian Special Collections.
95 R. Saunders to son, 16 July 1916, Saunders Letters, 79/15/1, IWM Documents.

96 D. J. Martin, Reminiscences, not dated, DF148, Liddle Collection.
97 A. E. J. Hepworth to P. Liddle, 18 September 1981, DF148, Liddle Collection.
98 Clark Diary, 23 December 1914, Ms Eng. Hist. e.94, Bodleian Special Collections.
99 *Ibid.*, 21 January 1915, Ms Eng. Hist. e.96.
100 R. Briggs, Memoir, 1919, 01/59/1, IWM Documents.
101 Women's wartime employment has attracted a good deal of scholarly attention. See, for example, D. Thom, *Nice Girls and Rude Girls: Women Workers in World War I* (I. B. Tauris, London, 1998); A. Woollacott, *On Her Their Lives Depend: Munitions Workers in the Great War* (University of California Press, Berkeley, CA, 1994); D. Beddoe, *Back to Home and Duty* (Pandora, London, 1989); G. Braybon, *Women Workers in the First World War* (Routledge, London, 1989); A. Marwick, *Women at War* (Fontana, London, 1977).
102 Clark Diary, 2 May 1915, Ms Eng. Hist. e.102, Bodleian Special Collections.
103 *Ibid.*, 4 February 1916, Ms Eng. Hist. e.119.
104 *Ibid.*, 21 May 1916, Ms Eng. Hist. e.126.
105 See, for example, *ibid.*, 4 December 1916, Ms Eng. Hist. e.140; 8 January 1917, Ms Eng. Hist. e.142; 31 August 1917, Ms Eng. Hist. e.152.
106 *Ibid.*, 15 July 1918, Ms Eng. Hist. e.165.
107 A. Clark to F. Madan, Clark Diary, 25 November 1918, Ms Eng. Hist. e.171, Bodleian Special Collections.
108 R. Saunders to son, 1 June 1918, Saunders Letters, 79/15/1, IWM Documents. For the praise heaped on women war workers by the press, particularly from 1916, see N. F. Gullace, *'The Blood of our Sons': Men, Women and the Renegotiation of British Citizenship during the First World War* (Palgrave Macmillan, Basingstoke, 2002), pp. 160–1.
109 G. D. Wilkinson interview, 9104, reel 3, IWM Sound.
110 Robinson, 'Diary of the Great War', 21 March 1916, vol. 2, P.401, IWM Documents.
111 J. Hollister to 'dad', 19 March 1917, J. Hollister Letter, 1917, 98/10/1, IWM Documents.
112 Cossins Diary, 3 May 1915, PP/MCR/371, IWM Documents. For perceptions that workers were doing well out of the war, see also Chapter 3.
113 The issue of labour's wartime assertiveness is also explored in B. Waites, *A Class Society at War: England 1914–1918* (Berg, Leamington Spa, 1987), pp. 243–50.
114 Clark Diary, 29 November 1914, Ms Eng. Hist. e.92, Bodleian Special Collections.
115 *Ibid.*, 5 May 1915, Ms Eng. Hist. e.103. In August 1916 there was a strike of harvest workers at Lyons Hall. See *ibid.*, 14 August 1916, 16 August 1916,

18 August 1916, Ms Eng. Hist. e.131.
116 *Ibid.*, 6 July 1915, Ms Eng. Hist. e.107.
117 *Ibid.*, 31 December 1916, Ms Eng. Hist. e.141.
118 *Ibid.*, 12 June 1917, Ms Eng. Hist. e.149.
119 *Ibid.*, 5 September 1918, Ms Eng. Hist. e.168. See also R. D. Blumenfeld's complaints about tyrannical boy labour and about the newly assertive 'Master Clerk and Master Employé'. R. D. Blumenfeld, *All in a Lifetime* (Ernest Benn, London, 1931), pp. 59–60 and 60–1.
120 Clark Diary, 8 April 1916, Ms Eng. Hist. e.123, Bodleian Special Collections.
121 *Ibid.*, 13 May 1916, Ms Eng. Hist. e.125.
122 *Ibid.*, 16 January 1917, Ms Eng. Hist. e.143.
123 *Ibid.*, 9 June 1916, Ms Eng. Hist. e.127.
124 *Ibid.*, 12 September 1916, Ms Eng. Hist. e.134.
125 *Ibid.*, 19 July 1916, Ms Eng. Hist. e.129. In 1911 approximately 120,000 gardeners were employed as domestic staff. S. Constantine, 'Amateur gardening and popular recreation in the 19th and 20th centuries', *Journal of Social History*, vol. 14, no. 3 (1981), p. 389.
126 Clark Diary, 28 December 1916, Ms Eng. Hist. e.141, Bodleian Special Collections.
127 A. Clark to 'my dear librarian', 3 March 1916, 'Specimen Advertisements, 1915', in Clark, 'Scrapbooks of leaflets, newspaper cuttings etc.'.
128 A. Clark to F. Madan, Clark Diary, 25 November 1918, Ms Eng. Hist. e.171, Bodleian Special Collections.
129 Lockwood, 'Notes', 29 September 1914, 96/52/1, IWM Documents.
130 Clark Diary, 26 October 1914, Ms Eng. Hist. e.90, Bodleian Special Collections.
131 A. Bradburn to S. Bradburn, 14 December 1915, Bradburn Letters, 95/16/1, IWM Documents.
132 A. Marwick, *The Deluge: British Society and the First World War* (Palgrave Macmillan, Basingstoke, second edition, 2006, first published 1965), p. 79.
133 Clark Diary, 1 October 1914, Ms Eng. Hist. e.89, Bodleian Special Collections.
134 Yearsley, 'The Home Front', p. 204, DS/MISC/17, IWM Documents. For anti-German hostility, see also Chapter 3 of this book.
135 Clark Diary, 10 October 1914, Ms Eng. Hist. e.89, Bodleian Special Collections.
136 *Ibid.*, 10 November 1914, Ms Eng. Hist. e.91. Similar examples can be found in DeGroot, *Blighty*, pp. 192–3.
137 See also the entry of a number of businessmen, 'men of push and go', into government. I. F. W. Beckett, *The Great War 1914–1918* (Pearson Education, Harlow, 2001), pp. 250–1.
138 Clark Diary, 10 November 1914, Ms Eng. Hist. e.91, Bodleian Special Collections.

139 *Ibid.*, 16 January 1915, Ms Eng. Hist. e.96.

140 *Ibid.*, 6 March 1915, Ms Eng. Hist. e.99. See also, for example, *ibid.*, 1 July 1916, Ms Eng. Hist. e.128. Not all companies scrambled to turn to government work or munitions production. See, for example, the case of Burrell's of Thetford, which specialised in the manufacture of agricultural machinery: in 1915 the government had to step in and compel 'the company to undertake the manufacture of munitions'. Quoted in F. Meeres, *Norfolk in the First World War* (Phillimore, Chichester, 2004), p. 111.

141 See also J. McDermott, '"A needless sacrifice": British businessmen and business as usual in the First World War', *Albion*, vol. 21, no. 2 (1989), pp. 263–82.

142 Clark Diary, 26 June 1915, Ms Eng. Hist. e.106, Bodleian Special Collections.

143 Robinson, 'Diary of the Great War', 11 May 1918, vol. 4, P.402, IWM Documents.

144 A. Bennett, *The Pretty Lady: A Novel* (Cassell, London, not dated, *c.*1918), pp. 28–9.

145 *Ibid.*, p. 183. See also, for example, the 1920 novel *How they Did It*, which 'records the ease with which the ambitious and cunning schemer could, in those breathless days, rise to eminence and power'. G. O'Donovan, *How they Did It* (Methuen & Co., London, 1920), front cover.

146 See Chapter 2.

147 J. Lawrence, 'Material pressures on the middle classes', in J. Winter and J.-L. Robert (eds), *Capital Cities at War: Paris, London, Berlin 1914–1919* (Cambridge University Press, Cambridge, 1999, first published 1997), pp. 234–42. This seems to have been the case both with public and with private sector employees. Lawrence also considers the varied impact of the war on investments and income from property. *Ibid.*, pp. 248–52. See also Winter, *The Great War and the British People*, p. 281; G. Robb, *British Culture and the First World War* (Palgrave, Basingstoke, 2002), pp. 68, 89–90; DeGroot, *Blighty*, p. 293; Waites, *A Class Society at War*, especially pp. 113–14.

148 C. Sheridan Jones, *London in War-Time* (Grafton, London, 1917), p. 82. Most Edwardian clerks had yearly incomes of £150 or less. A. A. Jackson, *The Middle Classes 1900–1950* (David St John Thomas Publisher, Nairn, 1991), p. 25.

149 Sheridan Jones, *London in War-Time*, p. 83. Although see also the rather different perspective on the wartime fortunes of the 'little' clerk living in 'Balham or Tooting or Tufnell Park' in Blumenfeld, *All in a Lifetime*, pp. 60–1.

150 Lawrence, 'Material pressures', p. 229.

151 Cooper Diary, 12 November 1917, P.121, IWM Documents.

152 J. Axton to P. Liddle, 12 January 1992, DF148, Liddle Collection.

153 Sheridan Jones, *London in War-Time*, p. 84.

154 Robinson, 'Diary of the Great War', 3 September 1917, vol. 3, P.402, IWM Documents.

155 Lockwood, 'Notes', 30 October 1916, 96/52/1, IWM Documents. Predictably, Caldwell singled out 'Jewish' firms as being especially prone to corruption and profiteering. Clark Diary, 1 May 1915, Ms Eng. Hist. e.102, Bodleian Special Collections.

156 See also J.-L. Robert, 'The image of the profiteer', in Winter and Robert (eds), *Capital Cities at War*, especially pp. 120–6. For working-class hostility towards profiteers, see also J. N. Horne, *Labour at War: France and Britain 1914–1918* (Clarendon Press, Oxford, 1991), pp. 222–3; B. Waites, 'The government of the home front and the "moral economy" of the working class', in P. H. Liddle (ed.), *Home Fires and Foreign Fields: British Social and Military Experience in the First World War* (Brassey's, London, 1985), pp. 175–93.

157 Cossins Diary, 12 October 1916, PP/MCR/371, IWM Documents.

158 Whether accusations of profiteering were deserved or not, many businesses were highly profitable. In 1916, for example, average profits in coal, shipbuilding, iron and engineering industries had risen by 32 per cent compared to pre-war levels. DeGroot, *Blighty*, p. 71. See also J. S. Boswell and B. R. Johns, 'Patriots or profiteers? British businessmen and the First World War', *The Journal of European Economic History*, vol. 11, no. 2 (1982), pp. 423–45; Gregory, *The Last Great War*, pp. 136–42; T. Wilson, *The Myriad Faces of War: Britain and the Great War, 1914–1918* (Polity Press, Cambridge, 1986), p. 73; Marwick, *The Deluge*, pp. 163–4. In one of the post-war studies of the economic impact of war commissioned by the Carnegie Endowment for International Peace, Simon Litman came to the conclusion that 'if profiteering is equivalent to taking advantage of market conditions to make money without any illegitimate manoeuvring, then no doubt there has been a great deal of so-called profiteering, for a great deal of money has been made'. S. Litman, *Prices and Price Control in Great Britain and the United States during the World War* (Oxford University Press, New York, 1920), p. 70.

159 Gibbs Diary, 19 January 1915, Ms Eng. misc. c.163, Bodleian Special Collections.

160 Clark Diary, 7 February 1916, Ms Eng. Hist. e.120, Bodleian Special Collections.

161 Cossins Diary, 14 November 1916, PP/MCR/371, IWM Documents.

162 Clark Diary, 24 February 1917, Ms Eng. Hist. e.145, Bodleian Special Collections. According to John Bourne, farmers did well out of the war, with profits increasing five-fold between 1914 and 1917. J. M. Bourne, *Britain and the Great War 1914–1918* (Edward Arnold, London, 1989), p. 194. See also P. E. Dewey, 'British farming profits and government policy during the First World War', *Economic History Review*, second series, vol. 37, no. 3

(1984), pp. 373–90. Dewey concludes that 'it would have been an unfortunate farmer indeed who did not make high profits during the First World War'. See p. 387.

163 Yearsley, 'The Home Front', p. 229, DS/MISC/17, IWM Documents.

164 *Ibid.*, p. 309.

165 Robinson, 'Diary of the Great War', 3 September 1917, vol. 3, P.402, IWM Documents.

166 *Ibid.*, 29 May 1915, vol. 1, P.401.

167 Blumenfeld, *All in a Lifetime*, pp. 21–2.

168 Gibbs Diary, 3 March 1917, Ms Eng. misc. c.187, Bodleian Special Collections. See also chapter 3 of this book.

169 R. Saunders to son, 21 March 1916, Saunders Letters, 79/15/1, IWM Documents.

170 Robinson, 'Diary of the Great War', 29 May 1915, vol. 1, P.401, IWM Documents.

171 *Ibid.*, 3 September 1917, vol. 3, P.402.

172 G. Young to E. Hilton Young, 7 November 1917, Kennet Papers, Part 1. Papers of Rt. Hon. Edward Hilton Young (1879–1960), first Lord Kennet of Dene, 66/119, Manuscripts Reading Room, Cambridge University Library, Cambridge.

7

Consumption and leisure

Introduction

According to Harold Cossins, immediately after the declaration of war the 'prices of foodstuffs, especially sugar, began to rise' and his wife Marjorie 'laid in a small stock before they went higher'. Later they heard that the government was prepared to 'regulate the price of food if necessary'.[1] Others also noted the disruption to the supply of consumer goods in the early weeks of war. Later in August Andrew Clark reported that 'Mrs Egerton, Chatham Hall, Great Waltham', had recently sent a smaller order than usual to the Army and Navy Stores', only to find that 'the Stores could not supply all her orders' and that 'the price of the whole order was 9s over the usual amount'.[2] A fortnight earlier Horace Joseph had tried, in his role as college bursar, to buy sugar for the forthcoming term, but the city's main grocer 'would not take an order'.[3]

In August 1914 neither consumers nor retailers could be certain of how long the disruption to supplies would last, or what action the government might be prepared to take to tackle the problems. By late September, however, the situation seems to have eased somewhat. Reginald Gibbs noted that during the first week of war 'many people began to hoard food'. One woman in Camberley had even 'walked into the Home and Colonial Stores and bought up the whole contents of the shop for £70 cash'. However, he added, 'this sort of thing soon ceased chiefly owing to the action of the government issuing notices regulating the price of food and to the reassuring tones of the newspapers'.[4] This respite notwithstanding, consumers' problems were not over. This is hardly surprising: in the context of a war that made such heavy demands on people and material, and led to such widespread disruption to international trade, consumer practices were hardly likely to remain unaffected.

The aim of this chapter is thus to examine middle-class men's wartime consumer and leisure practices. Recent research has shown that far from being disinterested in consumption, preferring to leave it to their womenfolk, Edwardian middle-class men were keen purchasers and users of the whole range of commodities and leisure opportunities on offer to those with some money to spend. Indeed, consumption contributed a central element to the assertion of middle-class masculinities: maintaining a well-groomed appearance, wearing a well-cut, clean and well-fitting bespoke suit, purchasing commodities for personal consumption including smoking materials, wine and spirits, buying restaurant, theatre or concert tickets, travelling first class, as well as, of course, ensuring the comfort of family and dependants, were all marks of the successful, self-respecting middle-class man.[5]

This chapter, then, explores middle-class men's consumer practices and identities as a (relative) pre-war abundance of supply turned into a market characterised by prohibitively priced goods and limited availability. It begins by considering the extent to which middle-class consumers were affected by rising prices and shortages, particularly of food, turning next to examine changes to consumer practices: both those adopted voluntarily, as a patriotic gesture, particularly in the early months of war, and those imposed by circumstances outside individuals' control. The chapter then focuses on the impact of the conflict on leisure activities and shopping practices, questioning the extent to which either could justifiably be pursued in wartime, before concluding by exploring responses to 'economy' appeals, shedding light on what these reveal about 'appropriate' consumer behaviour at a time of crisis.

Prices and availability

From the outset of war middle-class civilians followed closely the fluctuations in prices of various commodities, noting any shortage or lack of availability. They did so with an eye to the past, many being well aware of the historic link between war and price inflation.[6] In October 1916, for example, Cossins observed that at Norwich market wheat prices had reached 77 shillings per quarter. 'This', he added, was 'higher than the "famine prices" of the Crimean war which touched 74/ in 1855 … the average pre-war price was 28/. The highest ever recorded was in 1818', in the aftermath of the Napoleonic wars, 'when English wheat sold for 86/3'.[7] Cossins and others paid particular attention to the price of bread, not only because of its importance to the diet of the nation as a whole, but also because of the symbolic significance of the cheap loaf, the product of British free trade: in February 1915 Cossins noted that 'we are paying 8d per quartern loaf'.[8] In January 1916 Frederick Robinson observed that 'bread has risen to 9½d per quartern loaf. The price was 5½d when the war started'.[9] In November 1916 the cost of a loaf of bread in Great Leighs reached 10d,[10] while in London the price was 10½d,[11] increasing to 11d in February 1917[12] and to a shilling a month or so later.[13]

Significantly, in the early months of war most middle-class observers assumed (no doubt correctly) that the rising cost of bread and other commodities would entail hardship for poor working-class consumers, rather than themselves. In April 1915 Clark noted that 'Mrs Thomas Ketley called … to have a certificate of her age, in the hope of inducing the Guardians to grant her some relief. The price of bread being very hard on poor women like her … who is near sixty'.[14] In February the same year Macleod Yearsley stated – almost regretfully – that there had yet 'been no hardships undergone, no eye-witness stories of events' for him to record in his diary. 'True', he added, 'food prices have gone up, yet Asquith told us last week that never in history has the average citizen been so well-fed as he is today, in the middle of a wasteful and destructive war'.[15] However, by spring 1916 such complacency had largely disappeared, as shortages and inflation became a more 'personal' issue for many middle-class civilians. Diaries and letters were thus increasingly punctuated with references to the ever higher prices and the difficulties of obtaining certain goods. In September 1916 Clark ordered 'a ton of coal from Braintree – not good household coal, but very ordinary … kitchen-coal. War conditions are seen in the wrong initial given me by a new clerk, and by the enormous price of this poor quality of coal'.[16] Three months later he bought a ton of low-grade kitchen coal: 'the price is £2 per ton, an extraordinary price for coal of the quality'.[17]

Food posed especial problems.[18] In May 1916 the Cossins rented a set of rooms in the village of Crowborough, Sussex, after a long period in lodgings. Cossins observed that 'it is nice to have control of one's food supply again, though prices are about forty per cent higher than they were when we last had to buy any provisions'.[19] Some items became increasingly difficult to find. According to Clark, in September 1916 the Home and Colonial shop in Braintree had no margarine. The shopkeeper explained that they could not get any because the ships carrying consignments had been sunk. 'They expected a tremendous rush for butter, the price of which would be increased, and the supply quite unequal to requirements'.[20] Three months later Robert Saunders wrote to his son that 'prices keep rising on every article, not a single thing going down, sugar is strictly limited, whiskey will soon be unobtainable except to the rich. The War has been brought home to all of us very clearly during the last year'.[21] Gibbs's outlook was similarly gloomy. He stated that 'the problem of food is beginning to loom in front of us'. He believed that 'it is a case of the biter bit', after they had 'been yelling ourselves hoarse with delight over the impending starvation of the Germans for the last two years'.[22]

At the beginning of 1917, as unrestricted German submarine warfare hit imports further, the situation seemed set to become even worse.[23] In February, having just bought an expensive leg of mutton, Cossins reflected: 'how cheap we should think things at their old prices. I wonder if they will ever return'.[24] He was not hopeful, and his pessimism seemed justified by the growing problems with supply. In March Joe Hollister wrote to his father that 'things in London in this respect are beginning to be serious, no potatoes to be had, sugar almost unobtainable, meat and cheese 1/6, butter 2/4 bread 11',[25] while according to E. W. Hewish 'the submarine piracy of the enemy continues unabated … Prices continue to rise … Potatoes are fast becoming scarcer and soon will be hard to get'.[26] In June he worried that 'our shipping losses last week were much higher again – higher than the average throughout May, and still a source of great anxiety to us'.[27]

In September 1917 Saunders reported that Brighton was 'simply packed with Jews from the East End. By the end of last week there was actually a dearth of food, some of the shops having no tea, sugar or provisions and the Butchers were asking and getting exorbitant prices for the meat'.[28] A month later it was reported that 'Great Leighs people could not buy tea in Braintree yesterday'. The village shopkeeper 'says he has no tea and no butter for sale, and only 11lb. of very fat bacon'.[29] At the same time in Yorktown, near Aldershot, Gibbs found that 'several times lately all the shops … have been without sugar, tea and butter'.[30] In December 1917 Joseph noted that 'food queues are beginning, and already causing discontent'.[31] While spending a few days in London with his family during Easter 1917 Saunders saw 'the first Potato Queue, and it has seemed odd to notice now supplies are short how indispensable an article of food the potato is'.[32]

The scarcity of 'necessities'[33] other than food was also a matter of concern. According to Yearsley in spring 1917 there 'were … uneasy rumours of a coal famine in the winter but as usual, the government appeared to be taking no steps to prevent it'.[34] In August 1917 Robinson noted that 'medicinal drugs' were 'a striking example' of goods that had increased in price since the outbreak of war.[35] In April the following year Richard Arnold told Clark that he had paid '£2 7s 6d for a pair of boots for himself which he used to have at 28s'.[36] In August Saunders wrote to his son that they were 'getting better supplies of meat and bacon, and occasionally of cheese, but clothing, boots, carpet, furniture are outrageous prices'.[37] The quality of the goods available also declined. In September 1918 Clark noted that Freeman Hardy & Willis's shoe shop in Chelmsford 'have got only a quarter of their usual supply. Many of these shoes are "wartime" and not the old leather sort'.[38]

Despite the imposition of price controls on commodities such as milk (in November 1916), bread and meat (both in September 1917), and the piecemeal introduction of rationing of meat, butter, margarine, tea and sugar from December 1917,[39] in the opening weeks of 1918 Joseph was not alone in worrying that 'the food outlook grows more and more threatening. Meanwhile meat, butter and margarine, tea, milk are all getting scarce'.[40] According to Gibbs, 'people are having to line up in queues of hundreds to obtain a few ounces of margarine. In many cases they have to wait for hours to obtain even that little bit'.[41] At about the same time, James Caldwell told Clark that 'for several days in succession, last week, [he had] … tried to get cheese in London unsuccessfully'.[42] Two months later, while at work in London, he walked through Leadenhall market, where he saw that 'Bacon (the inferior sort, fit only for boiling, which used to be sold for 4d or 5d a lb) was 2s 4d and 2s 6d a lb. Everywhere tickets were up "No butter. No cheese"'.[43]

Writing in December 1917, Hewish asserted that although food prices were 'very high, and there is a scarcity of butter and margarine, tea and sugar', there was 'no real shortage. In a sense we have not even yet, in the fourth year of war felt any privations'.[44] Peter Dewey's analysis of the wartime food supply suggests that Hewish was right: ' … the overall energy supply was adequate … the supply of the major foods was not seriously impaired (except for sugar) … the national diet remained sufficiently varied to avoid particular nutritional and vitamin deficiencies'.[45] However, many civilians, including middle-class men, would have disagreed with this assessment, stressing instead the difficulties of obtaining supplies, their high cost and the unwelcome dietary changes they were being forced to endure. According to Robinson, by the end of 1917 middle-class concern over the cost and availability of food had become – and remained to the end of the conflict and beyond – an 'absorbing subject … which is present in everyone's minds'.[46] It was by then an almost inescapable topic of conversation: 'lots of people one meets have not had meat for several days, others have been without butter, cheese or some other article of food'.[47]

Consumer practices

The vicissitudes of war led many middle-class consumers to change their habits. Indeed, there was a widespread feeling in the early months of war that it was only right that they should do so and that inessential consumption should be cut down as much as possible, even when there was no real economic pressure to do so – and traders were begging their customers to shop as usual. Ernest Cooper, for example, vowed not to buy new clothes until the end of the war.[48] In October 1914 Joseph's college decided, on his motion, 'to have the same dinners at High Table as at the Lower Table during the war, and to reduce the table allowance to 2/-'. Pleas that such a reduction would damage trade and that more elaborate meals should be retained for guests were disregarded. Indeed, according to Joseph, 'a guest would be offended by elaborate meals right now'.[49] A month later Cossins planted some bulbs in his garden. He felt uneasy about this, noting that 'times are so strenuous just now that one does not spend more than absolutely necessary'. However, 'a few bulbs make such a difference in the garden in spring that I could not do without them altogether'.[50] A few weeks later he spent a day in London with his wife, observing that the crowds of Christmas shoppers seemed as big as ever: 'we ourselves are not giving any presents this year and many other families are doing the same. This must make a difference to trade but it cannot be helped'.[51]

As the war dragged on, however, middle-class civilians were increasingly forced to change their consumer practices not (or not only) as a patriotic choice, but out of necessity. Food provides a good example. While middle-class observers had noted the rise in the price of bread of the first two years of war with (relative) equanimity, attitudes changed as meals began to lose many of the ingredients central to Edwardian middle-class diets, especially meat, butter and sugar.[52] According to Cossins, in November 1916 'food prices continue to rise and we are gradually learning to do without many things'.[53] In October 1917 Gibbs noted that 'we experience increasing difficulty in getting supplies. Several times lately all the shops in Yorktown have been without sugar, tea and butter. Today we all dine off boiled pudding with precious little jam in it, vegetable soup and boiled chestnuts (which are very plentiful here). We have meat once or twice a week'.[54]

Middle-class civilians were increasingly confronted not only with a narrower range of food, but also with lower quality items than they were used to. Perhaps predictably, their reaction was one of revulsion. Robinson noted in November 1916 that 'good food is already difficult to get – in fact, impossible … the meat is bad and now we are to be reduced to so-called "standard" bread. Gradually, what war really means, is being brought home to us'.[55] A month later Clark saw for the first time a loaf of 'war bread' and could 'perceive very little difference between it and our former bread'.[56] The following summer, however, his reaction to the '"Government cheese" … supplied officially' to the village shop was rather different. He described it as 'vile "American" stuff, with the sour whey not washed out of the curd, smelling filthily and with a horrible taste'.[57] The shop also sold Canadian cheese, which was 'badly made, rank-tasted and over-salted'.[58] In January 1917 Frank Lockwood noted that for over a week they had been without sugar 'and we have been drinking tea without it and cocoa and coffee with treacle in its place. We have also tested a rice pudding with the same sticky substance. The results were quite passable but there is nothing like the right stuff in the right place'.[59]

The Coopers and the Robinsons were among the middle-class households forced to switch from butter to margarine.[60] In 1992 Jeffrey Axton could still 'remember the introduction of margarine in, I think, 1916 … It was disgusting – my father called it "blocks of axle grease"'.[61] Charles Ward, who was nine at the outbreak of war, thought the margarine 'nauseating even to a ravenous but never underfed boy'.[62] According to Robinson, writing in February 1917, 'pleasant meals are becoming a thing of the past'.[63] He was vociferous in his dislike of wartime food. In July 1917 he referred to 'that disgusting and indigestible compound called "bread"'.[64] He thought it 'so beastly, it is not worth eating, and no wonder the consumption has gone down *one third*'.[65] In October he complained that 'the food situation generally gets worse … our meals get poorer and less interesting every day'.[66] In February 1918 he thought that the situation had 'suddenly [become] worse'. The family Sunday 'joint' consisted of '3 lbs of indifferent mutton, which is supplied by the butcher as a favour … This is short commons for a household of six grown-up people'.[67] A few days later he added that 'lots of people one meets have not had meat for several days, others have been without butter, cheese or some other article of food. What has produced this sudden shortage is not known'.[68]

Eating out came to pose particular problems, especially for those middle-class men who commuted to work and ate their midday meal at a café, restaurant or club. Despite the introduction of restrictions on restaurant meals from December 1916,[69] one of Clark's acquaintances found, as he lunched in London in May 1917, that 'people ate as much as they ever did. He himself, just to see what would happen, asked for a second slice of bread. The waiter said "Well, Sir, you are not supposed to have it", but immediately brought it'.[70] However, such laxity was by no means the universal experience. In January 1917 Robinson had 'a most unsatisfactory and unpleasant meal, both in choice and quantity' at his club. He had been 'worried the whole time by first one attendant and then another to see that he did not have more courses than the law allowed'.[71] Three months later, 'dining at the Constitutional Club … I struck a meatless day and had an altogether wretched meal, very indigestible and expensive'.[72] In February 1918 he complained that food at the club was 'very different to what it used to be. Besides being very expensive the quantity … is scarcely enough to feed a fly'[73] (Figure 13). By spring 1918, far from being a pleasant treat, eating out was becoming 'a difficult problem'. Not only did diners have to 'live on fish and eggs, which are becoming nauseating', but 'the food, such as it is, is badly cooked and badly served – as a rule no butter is supplied and of course no sugar.[74] Entertaining guests at home, a practice central to middle-class sociability, became equally difficult. Having invited friends to dine, in January 1918 the Yearsleys found that 'the only decent food we could obtain was a rather forlorn duck, for which we had to pay the preposterous sum of 13 and 4 pence'.[75]

It should be noted that neither price increases nor the difficulties of obtaining supplies always guaranteed an immediate reduction in consumption. In May 1917 Saunders observed that 'we are gradually being weaned off Beer and Bacca. Ale 7d a pint and Bacca 8d an oz, instead of 3d and 4½d as before the war'.[76] However, in January 1917 Clark asserted that 'one indirect result of the war has been an enormous increase in cigarette smoking, both among ladies and lads'. He too smoked far more than he used to: 'in these months I have smoked in each week more cigarettes than I used to do in any whole year before the war', which he attributed to having to do all the outdoor work at the Rectory.[77]

Overall, however, particularly from the second half of 1916, middle-class men were much more likely to stress shortages, difficulties of obtaining supplies, and consequent erosion in their standard of living, rather than any increase in consumption. Statistics seem to support such perceptions: it has been calculated that between 1914 and 1918 UK consumer expenditure fell by approximately 14 per cent.[78] Food aroused the greatest concern, but was by no means the only commodity in short supply. In October 1917 Robinson noted that the coal merchant had brought

Peas and Plenty

A MAGNIFICENT SUGGESTION FOR THE FUTURE

13 ‘Peas and plenty’, *The Bystander*, 17 May 1916. Reproduced with permission of the Bodleian Libraries, University of Oxford, Per.2705 d.161, p. 315.

details of the new coal regulations. Their weekly allowance equated to about a quarter of their normal consumption, and was less than the amount that was consumed in the kitchen only. He wondered: 'are we to sit shivering in the cold, or are we to sit and have our meals in the kitchen with the servants?'[79] A month later, he was scathing about proposals to introduce 'standard' suits, to be sold at fixed prices: 'one can hardly imagine oneself in "slops" of a standard pattern. We should all look like the occupants of a charitable institution'. He believed that 'most people would rather wear their old clothes until they are threadbare'.[80] Standard suits seemed emblematic of the unpleasantly straitened circumstances increasingly being endured by the middle classes. After the war Yearsley recalled hearing in 1917 that 'we were to wear "Standard Clothes" of one universal "Civilian Grey". If these were to be as nasty to wear and as dirty to look at as the Standard Bread had become, we were in for a bad time both sartorially as well as dietetically'.[81]

Leisure

Writing more than sixty years after the end of the conflict, J. W. E. Cory could still 'well remember that on August Bank Holiday Monday 1914, we had a tennis tournament'. In 'between sets the folks went to the post office to read the latest news'. This, he added, 'was the last time we played tennis and my father did not survive to play again'.[82] Many other civilian observers were struck by the disorientating combination of war and holiday atmosphere. Yearsley, for example, noted that on August 1914 Bank Holiday Monday 'one could play nine holes on a by no means deserted golf course, and Bank Holiday crowds filled the char-à-bancs'.[83] Perhaps most importantly, looking back on the war in later years, Cory and many others seemed to suggest that in middle-class milieux at least, holidays and leisure ceased at – or soon after – that fateful August bank holiday.

Evidence of disruption to leisure is certainly not difficult to find. At the end of July 1914 Cooper and his wife had gone 'on board our yacht ... having let our house for a month'. Their intention had been to spend the month sailing around the east coast, but this proved too dangerous. As a result, 'we never let go our moorings and directly our house was vacant we moved in and laid the yacht up'.[84] Two weeks after the outbreak of war James Butlin wrote to his friend Basil Burnett Hall, asking: 'did I tell you that Kingston Park [tennis] Tournament which I entered for was scratched owing to the war?'[85] Two months later Clark saw the East Essex hunt riding by. He thought it a 'depressing show – about half a pack of hounds, three huntsmen in scarlet, the master in mufti, and some two other followers (also in mufti)'.[86] In August 1915 Cossins and his wife spent an afternoon at the British Museum. Several galleries were 'shut up and the exhibits taken away, but we were able to look into two which were curtained off. One was full of sandbags and the walls were protected with some sort of white stuff'. Cossins found that 'the sight of these precautions against air raids brought the war very strongly to one's notice'.[87]

Safety precautions, regulations and the need for 'economy' all had an impact on middle-class leisure. In January 1916 Cossins observed that only a few race meetings were being allowed to take place, and only on condition 'that patrons are not to use the railways to get to them. Any that are discovered doing so are fined and warned off'.[88] A few weeks later it was announced that 'on the plea of economy, the British Museum and Wallace and other collections are to be closed to the public'.[89] The following October Robinson was exasperated by the prohibition of travel by car to and from golf links: 'this will involve the doom of many links throughout the country, probably including the one of which the writer is a member'.[90] Even when not actually prohibited, wartime conditions reduced the pleasure to be gained from leisure pursuits. Travel, it seems, became especially taxing. In May 1918 Robinson complained that trains, reduced in number and with large numbers of servicemen travelling to and from their units, were getting ever more crowded and expensive. 'Certainly', he asserted, 'there is nothing to induce people to travel for pleasure … moreover at most stations one has now to be one's own porter'.[91]

In October 1914 Cossins suggested that while middle-class leisure was being adversely affected by the war, working-class activities continued unchanged: 'racing goes on much as usual, Association Football with its Leagues and Cup Ties has attracted the same great crowds … But Rugby football is practically non-existent owing to the clubs having lost nearly all their members … there is no boat racing or cup tie football and the Inter Varsity events will not take place'.[92] In a similar vein, in November 1914 Yearsley condemned 'the scandal of the continuation of the League Football Matches … in defiance of public opinion', which grew 'daily more indignant at the loafers who flocked in their thousands to see them rather than enlisting for King and Country'. He emphasised the 'strong contrast' with 'the notice which I saw displayed outside a cricket club at Acton: "All future matches cancelled. Every eligible member has enlisted. God save the king"'.[93]

Unsurprisingly, the reality was more complicated. Many sporting activities were indeed curtailed. R. D. Blumenfeld, for example, lamented in August 1915: 'there was no Derby at Epsom, no Gold Cup at Ascot and no week at the Duke of Richmond's Goodwood. There was no University Boat Race for the first time for generations'.[94] However, most middle-class men did not simply abandon all their normal leisure activities at the outbreak of war. In September 1914 Butlin wrote to Burnett Hall that 'I went to see The Girl in the Taxi the other night. It was awfully good and the two leading girls were very pretty'.[95] Yearsley saw nothing contradictory in condemning professional football, while stressing that London 'theatres and music-halls carried on wonderfully, older performers taking the place of those who had gone to the front … We sang patriotic songs and attended special performances and concerts for patriotic funds. I went to many of these'.[96] Not all leisure activities, furthermore, could claim any patriotic aims. While his wife still enjoyed good health, Cossins and she regularly spent Saturdays together in London shopping, sightseeing or going to the theatre. In February 1915, for example, they 'went to see Louis Parker's dramatization of David Copperfield at His Majesty's. The house was packed and the play most enjoyable'.[97] Their trips to town provided a moment of respite from the realities of war. In December 1914 they 'went to the theatre … and forgot the war'.[98] Similarly, in February 1916 Lockwood and his father spent an evening at their local music-hall 'to get a little diversion from the heated Compulsion arguments of the past week'.[99]

Most often, however, middle-class men did not seem so much to seek escape from the realities of war, as to continue with activities that were integral parts of their daily lives. Once term was over in June 1915, Joseph's diary became peppered with references to cycling trips and socialising over tea or meals with (mostly male) friends and colleagues.[100] Towards the end of August he went on a walking holiday in Wales with a friend: all these were clearly well-established vacation practices.[101] Holcombe Ingleby's preferred leisure activity seems to have been shooting, which he indulged in whenever he spent time at his country house in Norfolk. In September 1915, for example, he wrote to his son that he had 'managed to put in five days with the partridges'.[102] Two months later he wrote that 'I hope to be able to return to Sedgeford tomorrow and put in a couple of days shooting. If every partridge were a German and every pheasant a Turk I fancy I should make excellent practice'.[103]

Ingleby's concluding words hint at an underlying discomfort at persisting with peacetime leisure activities in the midst of war. In October

1914, for example, he confided that he felt 'rather ashamed of myself to be doing so much partridge shooting at this critical time'.[104] If a man over sixty, often in poor health and thus 'off the active list'[105] could find his leisure activities troubling, it is not surprising that leisure could be even more problematic in the case of fit men of military age. As press and propaganda strove to associate 'shirking' with the figure of the nattily (if not necessarily expensively) dressed young man-about-town with plenty of time on his hands (a 'nut', or 'knut' in contemporary slang),[106] those men who seemed to conform to this image could be made to feel deeply uncomfortable.[107] As a *Punch* cartoon put it in June 1915: 'It is daily requiring more and more courage for the man of military age not in uniform to be seen enjoying outdoor pleasures' (Figure 14).

The experiences of Frank Lockwood are thus illuminating. At the outbreak of war the diary of the nineteen-year-old apprentice was filled with references to trips to the cinema, the theatre, football matches, as well as walks, visits to relatives, sketching and – it seems – anything interesting happening in the locality, from concerts to cricket matches. Such activities did not end abruptly in August 1914. Towards the end of September 1914, for example, he recorded that 'last Saturday Linthwaite Hall C[ricket] C[lub] lost by one run at Kirkheaton … there is a deciding match today'. In the evening 'A. Wood and I went as far as Leymoor Picture Palace where we saw a splendid programme of pictures. "Proteo II" was a very exciting picture while "A Cinema Johnnie" was very laughable'.[108]

A year later he spent a week's holiday mostly outdoors, going for long walks with friends and family. Although he clearly missed his best friend, who had enlisted in November 1915, he still made regular trips to the cinema and continued to follow local sporting events with interest.[109] However, after he finished his apprenticeship in May 1916, having endured a bruising encounter with his local tribunal two months earlier, Lockwood's life seems to have become increasingly bleak.[110] No longer employed and not yet in the armed forces, he spent a good deal of time in the following months sketching, although 'the new restrictions as to photography and sketching make it a serious offense to do either without a permit'. Obtaining one involved so many formalities that he decided not to bother, and eventually stopped sketching too.[111] Diary references to leisure activities became fewer and fewer, a sense that these were becoming increasingly difficult to enjoy emerging clearly as the weeks passed. In August 1916 he went for a walk with his father and uncle. They 'spent our time enjoying the breezes and view on top of Pike Stee. How

14 'Cover for shirkers', *Punch*, 16 June 1915. Reproduced with permission of the Bodleian Libraries, University of Oxford, N.2706 d.10, p. 477.

nice it would be if only there was Peace. Then we *could really enjoy* the glorious weather, the beauties of nature and other things which now only exist as secondary matters in our thoughts'.[112]

A month later, he was shocked to discover that the police had 'been conducting systematic round-ups of the shirkers, laggards and slackers, as the papers call them. Theatres, music halls, parks, football matches etc. have come in for their share'. The men who visited such places were asked to produce documents demonstrating that they had been exempted from military service. Those who could not were 'taken to the police station pending enquiries. Such a position is not nice for any man to be in'.[113] Lockwood, unable to produce any such document, did not visit a music hall, cinema or other place of amusement that might be targeted by the police until he received his call-up papers in April 1917. That same evening he and his father went to 'the Palace', where they enjoyed 'a fairly good programme', which included a comedian, a magician, singers and a troupe of Japanese acrobats.[114]

In November 1915 Gibbs noticed that there had been 'hardly any fireworks tonight. I fancy this war will be the death-blow to fireworks, County cricket and golf', adding: 'a damned good job too'.[115] Not everyone was such a kill-joy, but there is little doubt that leisure activities considered normal in peacetime could arouse considerable unease during the war, even when they could hardly do any harm to the war effort.[116] Towards the end of August 1914 Cossins spent an evening playing tennis with a friend, but 'we both felt as if we were doing something to be ashamed of, and that we ought to have been drilling'.[117] Two years later Robinson noted that the Duke of Buccleuch was lending his collection of miniatures to 'the South Kensington Museum' for an exhibition. He thought it 'astonishing that anyone can take an interest in such things at a time like this'.[118] In May 1918 Joseph attended a college dinner held in honour of the Halley lecturer. Eighteen people were present and 'it was pleasant enough, but seemed ill-timed', given the worrying situation on the Western Front.[119] Such activities may have caused unease, but – it is worth noting – were not called off. In February 1917, as temperatures plunged and water froze, Cossins observed: 'what skating there would be in peace times, but now people have no time to think much of such things', apparently forgetting that he had himself gone out ice-skating the previous Sunday, and would do so again in the following days.[120]

Holidays provide a good example of the conflicting pull of leisure activities that still played a central role in middle-class life, and of a war that seemed to condemn all such activities as at best frivolous and at worst, unpatriotically wasteful. Despite calls on consumers to reduce 'week-ends', holidays and travel for pleasure to a minimum,[121] many middle-class civilians still found themselves travelling away from home and going on holiday, particularly during the summer months. Blumenfeld's assertion that at the end of August 1914 'pleasure seekers are not to be found, and all are bound hand and foot to the terrible ogre which has swept over Europe with its breath of fire … We have even given up the week-end habit',[122] proved inaccurate. In August 1915 Cossins and his family spent a fortnight in St Leonards, enjoying a spell of lovely weather and 'a holiday which I for one did not expect to have while the war lasted'.[123] In August 1914 the Saunders family gave 'up the idea of going away as prices have gone up for everything and everybody must economise', but contrary to their expectations, they still managed to take a holiday almost every summer during the war.[124] Writing years after the end of the conflict, Geoffrey Wood-Walker recalled that his family spent their holidays as usual 'at our seaside holiday house at Whitstable on the North coast of Kent. Except for registering the boats there were no restrictions to using the house and beach, except black-out of windows'.[125]

That said, such holidays were not always unproblematic. In September 1917 Joseph took his longest holiday since the summer of 1915. This was hardly a luxurious affair, as he mostly travelled by bicycle, visiting friends and relatives, but 'even so, I felt at times as if it was out of place'.[126] Quite apart from the increasing difficulties and expense of train and road travel, as well as the lack of reasonably priced holiday accommodation, leisure sites could be uncomfortable places for civilian men in other ways too. In August 1916, while on holiday in Folkestone, Gibbs went out to the pier one evening, but found that 'out of several hundred men I was the only civilian – so I came away'.[127] Middle-class observers also emphasised the disturbing presence among wartime holidaymakers of newly affluent munitions workers. In Easter 1916 Cossins sought to explain the apparently vast crowds of holidaymakers in Brighton by stressing the presence of working-class visitors: 'no doubt there are many munition workers, a name that has become proverbial for rich workers, among them'.[128] Saunders found their presence uncomfortable. In August 1917 he spent a day in Brighton with two of his sons, and found the beach too crowded with 'all sorts and conditions of people … for one to enjoy a rest … all the South Coast places are crowded and of course the Munitioners are now-a-days millionaires and can afford to spend freely'.[129] Despite the disruption caused by the war, then, middle-class civilians did not entirely relinquish their attachment to those leisure pursuits that formed such an important part of their peacetime social and recreational lives, including activities that could claim no 'serious', patriotic purpose.[130] However, such pleasurable activities were all too often undermined not only by feelings of guilt, but also by the wartime upheaval to transport and supplies and by the unwelcome intrusion into middle-class leisure sites of apparently carefree 'millionaire' munitions workers.

Shopping

Paralleling the ways in which official and semi-official appeals on citizens to limit their consumption – as well as advertisements for food and other household commodities[131] – were often directed at women, many middle-class men assumed that shortages were of especial concern to 'the housewife'. According to Lockwood, by the end of 1916 sugar had become 'very difficult to get hold of and the housewife must spend 5s before she is entitled to 1lb of sugar'.[132] Two months later Robinson noted that 'the food restrictions are beginning to be very onerous. Housewives are taking the matter seriously'.[133] There is also a good deal of evidence of middle-class households where budgeting and shopping for the family, particularly where food was concerned, were a feminine responsibility.[134] In March 1916 Clark heard that the Little Waltham grocer had been unable to supply the rectory '(where three officers are billeted) with all the sugar that they require'. It had been the Canon's eldest daughter who, 'failing to get supplies there, tried a smaller grocer's shop in the village, but could get no more than 1lb of sugar and ½d worth of salt'.[135] A year later Hewish observed that his wife Wendy managed to feed him 'within the food regulations … [she] is always improvising tasty but economical dishes. She is a treasure'.[136] According to D. B. Skinner, writing in 1979, it was because his mother suffered poor health that 'it was my job to queue for food',[137] while in the Saunders household, food shopping was the responsibility of Mrs Saunders, who clearly found the whole thing rather a trial. In August 1914, for example, Saunders observed that 'Ma is very indignant, every time she goes to the grocers or the butchers. Beef is 11d upwards, bacon 1/4 to 1/6, sugar just double, etc.'[138]

That said, there is also plenty of evidence that middle-class men were involved both in budgeting decisions and in the actual shopping. Indeed, many middle-class men responded to the worsening supply situation by seeking to assert their expertise and discrimination, and thus steer their families through the difficulties of the wartime market. Given the nature of most of the sources on which this book is based, which generally start at the outbreak of war, it is difficult to assess the extent to which this represented a new involvement in family consumer matters. However, there is little indication that wartime practices represented a break with the pre-war past. There certainly was little deference to women as the established authorities in consumer matters. In January 1916, for example, Clark noted that 'the great increase in the price of butter owing to war conditions gave an impulse to the sale of margarine'. He believed that 'nothing could be better' than the Maypole Company's margarine, sold at 6d per lb: 'it is perfect in flavour, colour, cleanliness, and infinitely better than most butter at 1s 4d or more a lb'. However, 'our thrifty householders do not value anything cheap' and tended to buy brands such as 'Blue Brand', which was 'chiefly recommended by the fact that it is 1/- a lb'.[139]

As far as middle-class men were concerned, what seems to have been new was not their involvement in family consumption, but its problematic nature, as relative plenty turned into shortages. In this new context, far from entirely delegating responsibility to 'the housewife', many men became involved in attempts to provide their families with food and other commodities. In December 1916 W. Herbert Lee, the church clerk, told Clark that 'he has his groceries from the Stores in Braintree. Three of his children live at home. For his household of five, they could get at the Stores only 1lb of sugar for the whole of last week'.[140] Mrs Saunders ('ma') may have been responsible for shopping for the very large Saunders household, but her husband did not hesitate to offer his advice. In January 1917 he noted that 'prices still keep rising and we get some lively times when Ma goes to shop, and I rather fancy the shopkeepers do too … I used to try to get Ma to see that if the price of an article was unreasonable, instead of making a fuss do without it, but the main idea with her is she WILL have it if she thinks fit'.[141] He returned to the same theme the following month: 'I keep telling Ma when she grumbles about the rise in price of different articles, to do without and persuade other people to follow her example, so as not to let the shopkeepers have their own way so much'. He knew from 'studying the markets' that many prices 'are put up unnecessarily, and people by combining to do without could make the sellers lower the prices'.[142]

Despite Saunders' advocacy of a boycott, there is little evidence of wider middle-class support for collective consumer action: middle-class men do not seem to have been part of the 'unprecedented mobilisation of consumers as an active, organised social movement across Europe'.[143] In October 1916, for example, Gibbs suspected that the campaign to force traders to sell milk at a reduced price was being orchestrated by the press in order to 'distract attention from the sacrifices of the war'.[144] Indeed, despite the importance of associational life to middle-class male culture, their ways of dealing with shortages were essentially individualistic. Decades after the conflict, Geoffrey Pember thus recalled that one day his father 'got up extra early to go on his bicycle to Sweets, the grocers at Crayford, when it was known that some jam would be on sale there'.[145] Despite their attachment to notions of a common wartime endeavour, furthermore, middle-class men were not always above practices that they would probably have condemned as unethical in others. In November 1917 Cooper confided in his diary – carefully avoiding the term 'hoarding' – that 'I bought about ten tons of coal during the summer and filled the cellar at the office at about 35/6. Before the end of November the Fuel Committee fixed the prices at Southwold at 41/- best and 39/- kitchen so I did right'.[146]

While by no means unique, Cossins stood out as especially active in seeking out bargains to supplement his family's supplies, making use of the opportunities provided by his daily commute to London. In August 1916 he noted that 'the price of food continues to rise … Still … I bring back from London many small supplies in which the Crowborough prices exceed the London ones'.[147] Four months later he 'bought some cheese at 9½d per pound as an experiment, on Farringdon Road. We are paying 1s/2d and I daresay there is very little difference in quality. We shall see after we have tried it this evening'.[148] The 'experiment' was unsuccessful, the cheap cheese proving unsuitable for a middle-class palate: it 'will probably find its way to the charwoman'.[149] This set-back did not deter him for long. Two days later he went 'foraging in town this morning for sugar and was lucky enough to get 1 pound of castor at the Haymarket Stores and 1 pound of lump at the Bedford St stores. We hadn't been able to get any from our grocer's all this week'.[150] In February the following year he 'bought twelve Canary bananas to-day for threepence … and six Jamaican bananas for the same sum. I wish I had bought more for they are excellent food and very welcome in these days of restricted supplies'.[151] Hunting for food bargains had by then become part of his daily routine: a few days after buying the bananas, he noted that 'incidentally … I have been buying some excellent potatoes … [at ½d per lb] off the stalls in Leather Lane'.[152]

Cossins was only one among the many middle-class men who sought to assert their discrimination and expertise in consumer matters, often taking advantage of the access to wider markets provided by their daily commute to work. However, wartime circumstances meant that such authority and expertise were constantly challenged, as civilian men experienced first-hand what they condemned as declining standards of service. To some extent, they blamed government regulations. In September 1916 Clark was exasperated by 'another piece of intolerable faddist tyranny'. He had just received a letter from his wine merchant, stating that 'our representative will be unable to call upon you as usual, owing to the new order of the Central Control Board (Liquor Traffic) which stipulates that travellers must not canvass for orders or collect money'.[153] Three months later Cossins was sceptical about the viability of the latest raft of food regulations. He noted that 'there is also to be one meatless day each week, which will add still further to housekeeping perplexities and cause a great run on cheese and flour preparations'.[154] In January 1917 Robinson was horrified by the news that the government 'was looking into the possibility of suspending the credit system in retail shops as a means of enforcing economy'. This would mean that 'when you want a lb of cheese or butter or a tin of sardines, or even a loaf of bread, you will have to send for it or … you will be obliged to fetch it yourself, besides paying for it over the counter. No longer will the butcher be allowed to call for orders, if you want a mutton chop or a joint you may have to trudge miles through snow or rain to get it … it is too stupid for words'. He thought it 'bad enough to have to pay for one's drinkables in advance but one's food and clothes – anathema!'[155]

It was retailers, however, who were blamed the most for middle-class consumers' difficulties: they – it was thought – were making the most of the demand for scarce goods, caring little either for their customers or for the war effort. According to Cooper, writing in November 1917, 'all the tradesmen seem to be on the make'.[156] There appeared to be plenty of ways for shopkeepers to get round regulations. Following the announcement in September 1917 of new rules relating to the sale of meat, butter, cheese and other items, Saunders complained that despite government assurances, 'prices are simply awful and the Profiteers manage to checkmate every order. I tried to get a bottle of beer at every shop and couldn't and tried for a week to get Ma a bottle of whiskey but didn't manage till yesterday'.[157] A month later he explained how the system worked: 'The Food Controller fixes the maximum price … then the shopkeeper tells you he has no controlled tea (for instance) at 2/4 per lb but has only been able to buy a small chest of China tea at 4/- per lb'. It was only 'as a great favour' that he would 'let his regular customers have 2oz'[158] (Figure 15).

Retailers' sharp practices and newfound confidence meant that middle-class men were made to feel a loss of power and prestige, bringing

15 'How the "nation of shopkeepers" justifies its nickname', *The Bystander*, 13 December 1916. Reproduced with permission of the Bodleian Libraries, University of Oxford, Per.2705 d.161, p. 617.

about a significant change in their relationship with a section of the population from whom they had been used to expect a respectful, if not subservient attitude.[159] Saunders observed in September 1918 that 'the shopkeepers have quite the whip hand … No matter how exorbitant the price … there are plenty of buyers, who have to mind their ps and qs in asking for things'.[160] He was echoed by Robinson, who complained in July 1918 that 'shopkeepers – or the flapper assistants – seem rather to pride themselves upon being "out" of things'. You had 'to take what you can get, and any complaint is met by impertinence and possibly by your being asked "do you know there is a war on?"'.[161] He returned to this theme a month later, stressing that shopkeepers seemed 'as prosperous as ever, but are a thousand times more independent – they are often rude and even impertinent'. The customer had to approach them 'with his cap in his hand',[162] dramatically reversing what should have been the 'proper' relationship between retailer and middle-class customer.

Economy

In July 1915 Cossins noted that '"Economy" is the great watch word now'. A variety of appeals were exhorting people not to '"use imported goods if you can help it and don't waste anything"'. In fact, he added guiltily, 'I ought not to be burning gas to write this'.[163] Ten days later Robinson observed that 'the Parliamentary Savings Committee is urging people to sign a pledge to abstain from luxuries', including a commitment to 'ignore the fashions and go on wearing their old clothes until they wear out'.[164] Such appeals were destined to multiply in the following years, as official and unofficial organisations arranged meetings and lectures, produced posters, leaflets, press advertisements, articles and a range of other publications calling on civilians to consume less, in order that commodities might be re-directed to the war effort.[165]

In August 1916, for example, a leaflet 'Issued by order of the Royal Commission on the Sugar Supply' called on all civilians to 'use less sugar … All sugar is imported. Whenever you eat sugar or goods containing sugar, you are using the steamers and the credits that the nation needs to end and to win the war'.[166] Three months earlier a National War Savings Committee poster had put the matter more bluntly. Aiming squarely at a middle-class audience, it stressed that 'you are helping the Germans: when you use a motor car for pleasure. When you buy extravagant clothes. When you employ more servants than you need. When you waste coal, electric light, or gas. When you eat or drink more than is necessary to your health and efficiency'.[167] Appeals carried constant reminders of the loss of lives taking place on the battle fronts. In June 1917 a Ministry of Food circular directed at 'the head of the household' stressed that 'we must all eat less food; especially we must all eat less bread … The enemy is trying to take away our daily bread. He is sinking our wheat ships. If he succeeds in starving us our soldiers will have died in vain'.[168] The self-denial required of civilians was compared to the much greater sacrifices being made by the armed forces. Thus, in September 1918 an appeal to save coal stressed that 'it does not mean hardship. It may mean inconvenience' and a change in habits: 'it may mean having breakfast in the kitchen. It may mean having to live together more than usual. But compare these little things with life in the trenches or life on the seas … and you will see it is no real hardship'.[169]

Few middle-class men disputed the need to economise. However, the organisations producing such appeals were often held in poor esteem, while the rhetoric they adopted frequently provoked irritation, rather than patriotic fervour. Government calls to exercise thrift, furthermore, were set against examples of 'official waste'.[170] According to Cossins, writing in December 1915, 'people are calling for … Parliament and the government to set an example of thrift … to the nation. Mr Asquith's declaration that he won't reduce his own salary has created an unfavourable impression in the country'.[171] In June 1917 Clark described a circular from the Ministry of Food as a 'waste of paper; useless expenditure of clerks' time and of postman's time as though everyone had not heard the whole story over and over again or had any trust in a government office'.[172] The constantly repeated refrains aroused frustration. In March 1916 Robinson reported unenthusiastically that a 'great meeting' had been held at the Guildhall 'to enforce the necessity of economy upon the people', adding that 'they repeated much the same things we have heard and read so often'.[173] Writing up his diaries twenty years after the end of the war, Yearsley reflected that 'the truism, seen in gigantic letters on the hoardings, that "Extravagantly to dress is unpatriotic" … angered us because they were so trivial … We *did not need* to be told not to dress extravagantly, not to do this, not to do that'.[174]

Perhaps most importantly, civilian men were keen to point out that prices themselves acted as a powerful inducement on middle-class households to economise. In March 1916 Robinson responded to a National Organising Committee for War Savings appeal by stressing that 'as far as this household is concerned, we are already complying … and have been doing so for some time'. The increased prices of items such as bread, butter, tea, cheese, beef and eggs illustrated 'the necessity for economy in consumption even to keep domestic expenditure down to pre-war totals much less to effect any savings'.[175] Writing at around the same time, Saunders pointed out that 'I don't know a single article that has not gone up in prices, so that it is a case of "Needs must" with many people over Economy'.[176] In October 1916, having received a National War Savings Committee appeal to use less coal, Clark observed that 'the price of coal ought of itself to be a sufficient deterrent against lavish use of it'.[177] A few days later he complained of the 'fatuous' material sent by 'people [The Duty and Discipline Movement] who think that a hard-working, poor country parish requires to give up "luxury"'.[178]

In February 1917 Lord Devonport, the Food Controller, responded to the continued price rises and shortages by calling on people to voluntarily limit their consumption of certain foodstuffs: meat, bread and sugar in particular. Civilians were put 'on their honour to cut down their consumption of food to an amount which he is satisfied is ample for all': 2½ lb of meat, 4lb of bread and flour, and ¾lb of sugar per person, per week.[179] The Cossins responded by making 'a study of our books'. They found that 'we have been consuming rather more than this on an average and it will be difficult to cut it down still further. However, we must see what can be done'.[180] Others responded in a similar fashion. 'From enquiries made of the cook' it was discovered that food consumption in the Robinson household, consisting of eight grown-up people, considerably exceeded the amounts set by Devonport. 'It therefore means cutting down our food, and this will apply to most people of a similar status in life, where there is plenty but no waste. However, better this than food tickets, so instructions have been given that the allowances are not to be exceeded'.[181] According to Cossins, 'people are trying to fall in with the Controller's restrictions of food supplies', adding that 'to some the restrictions must be very drastic indeed and it will probably take some time before we all get accustomed to the smaller supplies. But it brings the war home to everyone without a doubt'.[182]

In April 1917 Robinson noted that all their family meals were eaten with a sign 'always staring us in the face', stating: 'In honour bound we adopt the national scale of voluntary rations', a reference to the small placards distributed by the Ministry of Food to encourage voluntary rationing. 'And what is more', added Robinson, 'we conscientiously carry this out in practice, as indeed most persons of our acquaintance are doing'.[183] Others found such gimmicks irritating. Clark thought the placards 'silly, and yet the government, while wasting paper, makes a great to-do about shortage of paper'.[184] Yearsley expressed himself more forcefully, condemning 'another of the many foolishnesses', which he speculated might amount 'to some form of war hysteria': the practice of 'placing in windows … cards stating that "This house is pledging to eat less than its ration" … there was a "League" … to induce fools to sign a pledge to that effect and buy a purple ribbon to wear', all signs 'of that smug humility that goes with self-righteousness'.[185] Blumenfeld believed that there was 'a great deal of humbug underneath all this war-time economy'. Referring to comfortably-off middle-class individuals like himself, he considered that 'we' did not economise out of financial necessity, but 'largely because it is wise and patriotic to do so … and sometimes we economise for the purpose of posing to our friends and neighbours as extra-super patriots'.[186]

However, 'silly' gimmicks and 'humbug' were not the only problems with voluntary rationing. Much more significant was a belief that the system itself was unfair, disadvantaging the patriotic citizens who sought to adhere to the voluntary limits, while 'others' paid little heed to appeals to consume less. Robinson noted that in April 1917 a last attempt was being made to reduce consumption further by voluntary means. He believed that there was a general feeling that this was unfair, given that 'German prisoners, to say nothing of the … [conscientious objectors] at Princetown, are fed on a more liberal scale'.[187] Reflecting on the issue in later years, Yearsley thought that the mistake with voluntary rationing 'was in not remembering that all people have not the necessary sense of honour and it would have been better if the allowance had been obligatory from the first',[188] adding later that 'it was absurd to pretend to put people on their "honour" when so many had no conception of its meaning'.[189] Writing up his diary after the war, Cooper came to the conclusion that 'there is a difficulty in carrying out voluntary rationing', and placed the blame squarely on working-class shoulders: 'the servants resent it and generally the poorer people do not realise any necessity for it so long as they can buy all they want'.[190]

Complaints had been voiced as early as 1915 that those people who were doing well out of the conflict were spending their money freely, without any thought for the war effort. In January 1915 Robinson noted disapprovingly that the London sales were taking place as usual: 'they are crowded with anxious buyers who appear to have unlimited sums to spend, just as if nothing unusual were taking place in the world outside'.[191] The following Christmas Cossins thought that 'in spite of the war, perhaps because of it, there is a tremendous lot of money about and people are spending a great deal this Christmas … shopkeepers are lucky in finding plenty of full purses', adding that 'economists have a hard time in teaching people to be thrifty while they have easy money to spend'.[192]

By the second year of war, disquiet about the spendthrift ways of some people had solidified into an increasingly bitter resentment, as middle-class opinion turned against the section of the population that was suspected of having 'money to burn':[193] the working class. Although anger towards profligate capitalists and 'profiteers' was by no means spent, it was the (supposedly) newly affluent working class, spending its money extravagantly while the hard-pressed middle class suffered unprecedented hardships, which aroused the greatest indignation. In January 1916 Caldwell told Clark that 'in London the Christmas trade in the poor districts was exceptionally good. The working-classes being flush with money'.[194] According to Blumenfeld, 'the British piano dealers have never been so prosperous as they are to-day. You cannot buy a cheap piano for immediate delivery. They have all gone into the cottages of the workmen, who have never made so much money'.[195] A year later Hewish worried about the country's continued shipping losses. He noted that 'the cost of living is still rising, and the necessaries of life are at famine prices', but added that 'nobody seems in the least perturbed, there is so much money in the hands of the working people that they do not as a whole feel the pinch of the high prices'[196] (Figure 16).

As Caldwell told Clark in May 1915, 'the only people who are earning money now are people who are making "munitions"'. He lamented the fact that they were 'taking no heed' of Lloyd George's recommendation that people 'who are now making large money', should 'lay by for a bad time to come'.[197] A year later Lockwood poured scorn on the notion that munitions workers were motivated by patriotism. He described munitions factories as 'a modern Noah's Ark', adding that 'the patriotism of a large number of munitions workers is false'. Theirs was the 'patriotism to save their own skins and enrich their pockets'.[198] Saunders was also struck by the fact that 'many of the working classes were never so well off as they are now … not the country farm lads, but the people near the Munitions Works'. As a result, price rises did not 'affect them as much as the people with fixed incomes who are forced to economise'.[199] The following year he suggested that munitions workers actually bore some of the responsibility for the high prices, their spending habits having an adverse effect on middle-class salaried workers' standards of living: 'owing to the high wages secured by some families, especially munition workers, people pay any price rather than go without … the man who feels it the most is, of

16 'Blimey, Lizer, the war's over', *The Bystander*, 20 November 1918. Reproduced with permission of the Bodleian Libraries, University of Oxford, Per.2705 d.161, p. 322.

course, the one with the fixed salary'.[200] Most unforgivably, while middle-class civilians were doing their best to economise, both for patriotic and for financial reasons, 'the wage earners and especially of the munition workers ... seem to deny themselves nothing that they fancy'.[201]

Conclusion

Middle-class male consumers felt diminished by their wartime experiences. In some cases, this was a literal 'reduction'. In April 1917 Clark noted that he had lost a remarkable seven stones in weight in the previous year, from 18 stone 9lb to 11 stone 10lb.[202] Seven months later Cooper complained that 'very few here are in their usual health, I have probably lost two stones in weight owing to worry and rations I suppose but do not feel much the worse for it at present although I dread another cold winter like last'.[203] Writing a few days after the Armistice, Robinson observed that 'as a family we came out without loss, except that which affects the pocket and the disappearance of approximately ten per cent of one's adipose tissue'.[204] Back in April that year he had noted that he was 'now able owing to "shrinkage" (due to want of proper food)' to wear clothes that had not fitted him for the past ten or twelve years.[205]

Despite press and propaganda attempts to argue for the health benefits of cutting down food consumption, this was not felt to be the healthy weight loss that many pre-war doctors and 'reducing' manuals had recommended for middle-class men in sedentary occupations, 'whose sagging abdomens needed to be cultivated for the sake of health, aesthetics, and national efficiency'.[206] Indeed, the physical 'shrinkage' experienced by middle-class civilians was not the result of a manly regime of healthy exercise and dietary self-control, but of wartime scarcity: it was a 'bodily discipline'[207] imposed on them by forces over which they had little control, and which threatened to undermine their standard of living. By the final months of war, then, middle-class men's attitudes towards consumption had changed a great deal from the almost academic preoccupation of 1914, when the growing price of commodities such as bread was seen overwhelmingly as a working-class problem. By 1917, if not earlier, middle-class men were increasingly feeling that as they did their patriotic best to adapt to wartime circumstances, giving up many of the things that made life worthwhile, others – most notably, munitions workers – were taking advantage of wartime opportunities to spend their newly acquired wealth freely and without thought for the consequences.

Power relations, it was felt, had decidedly shifted in the course of the war: working-class people were not only still enjoying all their old consumer and leisure activities, but were increasingly impinging on and disrupting middle-class leisure sites, while even shopkeepers and shop assistants seemed to be sloughing off their accustomed deferential attitude. Most importantly, while the middle class faced unprecedented hardships, workers were believed to be indulging in extravagant expenditure, paying no attention to economy appeals. As early as January 1916, then, Joseph could be found lamenting that 'the situation at home seems to me deplorable. The Government have allowed thousands to wax fat on the war'. These were the 'thousands of semi-skilled men … earning £4' a week, as well as skilled men who 'in exceptional cases [could earn] even up to £20'. Infuriatingly, while the middle classes were feeling the squeeze, there was among such newly affluent workers 'a widespread' and culpable 'unwillingness to make sacrifices'.[208]

Notes

1 H. C. Cossins Diary, 1914–18 (hereafter Cossins Diary), 9 August 1914, PP/MCR/371, Department of Documents, Imperial War Museum (hereafter IWM Documents), London. Before the war, two-thirds of sugar consumed in Britain had been imported from Germany and Austria. A. Marwick, *The Deluge: British Society and the First World War* (Palgrave Macmillan, Basingstoke, second edition, 2006, first published 1965), p. 201.
2 A. Clark War Diary, 'Echoes of the 1914 War in an Essex Village' (hereafter Clark Diary), 21 August 1914, Ms Eng. Hist. e.88, Special Collections, Bodleian Library, University of Oxford (hereafter Bodleian Special Collections), Oxford.
3 Wartime Diaries of H. W. B. Joseph 1914–18 (hereafter Joseph Diaries), 4 August 1914, Ms. Top. Oxon. e.288, Bodleian Special Collections.
4 Diary of R. W. M. Gibbs, 1914–20 (hereafter Gibbs Diary), 20 September 1914, Ms Eng. misc. c.159, Bodleian Special Collections. A Cabinet Committee on Food Supplies was established soon after the outbreak of war. By mid-August it was 'purchasing large stocks of foodstuffs previously supplied by Germany, most notably sugar, of which £260,000 worth was bought in New York in one week alone'. G. J. DeGroot, *Blighty: British Society in the Era of the Great War* (Longman, Harlow, 1998, first published 1996), p. 58.
5 See, for example, L. Ugolini, *Men and Menswear: Sartorial Consumption in Britain, 1880–1939* (Ashgate, Aldershot, 2007); D. Cohen, *Household Gods: The British and their Possessions* (Yale University Press, New Haven, CT, 2006); K. Honeyman, 'Following suit: men, masculinity and gendered practices in the clothing trade in Leeds, England, 1890–1940', *Gender & History*, vol. 14, no. 3 (2002), pp. 426–46; M. Hilton, *Smoking in British Popular Culture 1800–2000: Perfect Pleasures* (Manchester University Press, Manchester, 2000); A. Kidd and D. Nicholls (eds), *Gender, Civic Culture and Consumerism: Middle-Class Identity in Britain, 1800–1940* (Manchester University Press, Manchester, 1999); C. Breward, *The Hidden Consumer: Masculinities, Fashion and City Life 1860–1914* (Manchester University Press, Manchester, 1995).
6 A. J. Coles, 'The moral economy of the crowd: some twentieth-century food riots', *Journal of British Studies*, vol. 18, no. 1 (1978), pp. 157–8.
7 Cossins Diary, 29 October 1916, PP/MCR/371, IWM Documents.
8 *Ibid.*, 27 February 1915. In 1914 almost 80 per cent of wheat consumed in Britain was imported. T. Bonzon and B. Davis, 'Feeding the cities', in J. Winter and J.-L. Robert (eds), *Capital Cities at War: Paris, London, Berlin 1914–1919* (Cambridge University Press, Cambridge, 1999, first published 1997), p. 309. For the political symbolism of the loaf of bread, see F. Trentmann, *Free Trade Nation: Commerce, Consumption, and Civil Society in Modern Britain* (Oxford University Press, Oxford, 2008), pp. 88–95.

9 F. A. Robinson, 'Diary of the Great War', 27 January 1916, vol. 2, P.401, IWM Documents.
10 Clark Diary, 7 November 1916, Ms Eng. Hist. e.138, Bodleian Special Collections.
11 Cossins Diary, 4 November 1916, PP/MCR/371, IWM Documents.
12 *Ibid.*, 7 February 1917.
13 M. Yearsley ('Eyewitness'), 'The Home Front, 1914–18', p. 210, DS/MISC/17, IWM Documents.
14 Clark Diary, 15 April 1915, Ms Eng. Hist. e.101, Bodleian Special Collections. See, for example, the description of how 'War hardship descends upon the poor' in E. S. Pankhurst, *The Home Front* (The Cresset Library, London, 1987, first published 1932), Chapter 2. Also R. Roberts, *The Classic Slum: Salford Life in the First Quarter of the Century* (Penguin, Harmondsworth, 1974, first published 1971), pp. 188–9.
15 Yearsley, 'The Home Front', p. 257, DS/MISC/17, IWM Documents.
16 Clark Diary, 22 September 1916, Ms Eng. Hist. e.135, Bodleian Special Collections.
17 *Ibid.*, 14 December 1916, Ms Eng. Hist. e.140.
18 For a revealing comparison of the food situation in London, Paris and Berlin, see Bonzon and Davis, 'Feeding the cities', pp. 305–41.
19 Cossins Diary, 27 May 1916, PP/MCR/371, IWM Documents.
20 Clark Diary, 20 September 1916, Ms Eng. Hist. e.134, Bodleian Special Collections.
21 R. Saunders to son, 23 December 1916, R. Saunders, Letters to Son in Canada, 1914–18 (hereafter Saunders Letters), 79/15/1, IWM Documents.
22 Gibbs Diary, 19 November 1916, Ms Eng. misc. c.183, Bodleian Special Collections.
23 J. M. Bourne, *Britain and the Great War 1914–1918* (Edward Arnold, London, 1989), pp. 68–70.
24 Cossins Diary, 23 February 1917, PP/MCR/371, IWM Documents.
25 J. Hollister to 'dad', 19 March 1917, J. Hollister Letter, 1917, 98/10/1, IWM Documents.
26 E. W. Hewish, 1917 Diary and Accounts (hereafter Hewish Diary), 10 March 1917, 02/43/1, IWM Documents.
27 *Ibid.*, 19 June 1917.
28 R. Saunders to son, 30 September 1917, Saunders Letters, 79/15/1, IWM Documents. See also Chapter 3 in this book for Caldwell's belief that 'Whitechapel Jews' were buying up all the supplies in Braintree market in November 1917.
29 Clark Diary, 18 October 1917, Ms Eng. Hist. e.155, Bodleian Special Collections.
30 Gibbs Diary, 27 October 1917, Ms Eng. misc. c.194, Bodleian Special Collections.

31 Joseph Diaries, 18 December 1917, Ms. Top. Oxon. e.288, Bodleian Special Collections. Although England did not see serious food protests like many other combatant nations, the potential dangers of long queues should not be underestimated. In one week in February 1918 the Metropolitan Police estimated that approximately 80,000 Londoners had queued for meat and 30,000 for other goods. J. M. Winter, *The Great War and the British People* (Palgrave Macmillan, Basingstoke, 2003, first published 1985), p. 216.

32 R. Saunders to son, 9 April 1917, Saunders Letters, 79/15/1, IWM Documents.

33 R. Briggs, Memoir, 1919, 01/59/1, IWM Documents.

34 Yearsley, 'The Home Front', p. 222, DS/MISC/17, IWM Documents. For the wartime supply and consumption of coal, see also A. Triebel, 'Coal and the metropolis', in Winter and Robert (eds), *Capital Cities at War*, especially pp. 357–61.

35 Robinson, 'Diary of the Great War', 6 August 1917, vol. 3, P.402, IWM Documents.

36 Clark Diary, 22 April 1918, Ms Eng. Hist. e.162, Bodleian Special Collections.

37 R. Saunders to son, 4 August 1918, Saunders Letters, 79/15/1, IWM Documents.

38 Clark Diary, 11 September 1918, Ms Eng. Hist. e.168, Bodleian Special Collections.

39 Yearsley, 'The Home Front', p. 57, DS/MISC/17, IWM Documents; DeGroot, *Blighty*, pp. 86–92; Marwick, *The Deluge*, pp. 218, 235. It should be noted that in 1917 there still did not seem to be a systematic food policy in operation: food control was still 'largely in the hands of local officials and structures, who were charged with managing the administration and enforcement of legislation that appeared piecemeal, confusing, and ill-considered'. A. R. Seipp, *The Ordeal of Peace: Demobilization and the Urban Experience in Britain and Germany, 1917–1921* (Ashgate, Farnham, 2009), p. 61. Also pp. 61–5.

40 Joseph Diaries, 20 January 1918, Ms. Top. Oxon. e.288, Bodleian Special Collections.

41 Gibbs Diary, 20 January 1918, Ms Eng. misc. c.197, Bodleian Special Collections.

42 Clark Diary, 20 January 1918, Ms Eng. Hist. e.159, Bodleian Special Collections.

43 *Ibid.*, 8 March 1918, Ms Eng. Hist. e.161.

44 Hewish Diary, 10 December 1917, 02/43/1, IWM Documents.

45 P. E. Dewey, 'Nutrition and living standards in wartime Britain', in R. Wall and J. Winter (eds), *The Upheaval of War: Family, Work and Welfare in Europe, 1914–1918* (Cambridge University Press, Cambridge, 1988), p. 210. Food shortages in Britain hardly compared with the 'chronic inequalities

and general malnourishment prevalent in Berlin [and presumably, Germany as a whole] from 1916 onwards'. Bonzon and Davis, 'Feeding the cities', p. 322. Declining mortality rates among the British civilian population between 1910–12 and 1921–23 also suggest that there was no serious erosion in home front nutrition during the war. Winter, *The Great War and the British People*, Chapters 4 and 7.

46 Robinson, 'Diary of the Great War', 15 February 1918, vol. 4, P.402, IWM Documents.

47 *Ibid.*, 6 February 1918. According to Arthur Bowley, 'at the date of the Armistice wholesale prices were 140 per cent above the pre-war level'. A. L. Bowley, *Some Economic Consequences of the Great War* (Thornton Butterworth, London, 1931, first published 1930), p. 69.

48 The Diary of Ernest R. Cooper, 'Nineteen Hundred and War Time', 28 July 1914 – 3 December 1918 (hereafter Cooper Diary), 9 November 1918, P.121, IWM Documents. For the wartime vicissitudes of menswear retailers unable to take advantage of government contracts, see Ugolini, *Men and Menswear*, Chapter 6.

49 Joseph Diaries, 8 October 1914, Ms. Top. Oxon. e.288, Bodleian Special Collections.

50 Cossins Diary, 29 November 1914, PP/MCR/371, IWM Documents.

51 *Ibid.*, 19 December 1914.

52 J. Burnett, *Plenty and Want: A Social History of Diet in England from 1815 to the Present Day* (Scolar Press, London, revised edition, 1979), pp. 232–9; D. J. Oddy, *From Plain Fare to Fusion Food: British Diet from the 1890s to the 1990s* (Boydell Press, Woodbridge, 2003), p. 68.

53 Cossins Diary, 14 November 1916, PP/MCR/371, IWM Documents.

54 Gibbs Diary, 27 October 1917, Ms Eng. misc. c.194, Bodleian Special Collections.

55 Robinson, 'Diary of the Great War', 16 November 1916, vol. 2, P.401, IWM Documents.

56 Clark Diary, 21 December 1916, Ms Eng. Hist. e.141, Bodleian Special Collections.

57 *Ibid.*, 2 August 1917, Ms Eng. Hist. e.151.

58 *Ibid.*, 3 August 1917.

59 F. T. Lockwood, 'Notes Written by F. T. Lockwood', 15 January 1917, 96/52/1, IWM Documents.

60 Cooper Diary, 7 January 1917, P.121, IWM Documents; Robinson, 'Diary of the Great War', 3 February 1918, vol. 4, P.402, IWM Documents.

61 J. Axton to P. Liddle, 19 April 1992, DF148, Liddle Collection (1914–18), Special Collections, Brotherton Library, Leeds University (hereafter Liddle Collection), Leeds.

62 C. H. Ward, 'Recollections of the First World War', 1971, DF148, Liddle Collection.

63 Robinson, 'Diary of the Great War', 28 February 1917, vol. 3, P.402, IWM Documents.
64 *Ibid.*, 1 July 1917.
65 *Ibid.*, 26 July 1917.
66 *Ibid.*, 6 October 1917.
67 *Ibid.*, 3 February 1918, vol. 4, P.402.
68 *Ibid.*, 6 February 1918.
69 J. Burnett, *England Eats Out: 1830–Present* (Pearson Longman, Harlow, 2004), pp. 75, 183–7.
70 Clark Diary, 16 May 1917, Ms Eng. Hist. e.148, Bodleian Special Collections.
71 Robinson, 'Diary of the Great War', 3 January 1917, vol. 3, P.402, IWM Documents.
72 *Ibid.*, 14 April 1917.
73 *Ibid.*, 15 February 1918, vol. 4, P.402.
74 *Ibid.*, 15 May 1918.
75 Yearsley, 'The Home Front', p. 243, DS/MISC/17, IWM Documents.
76 R. Saunders to son, 13 May 1917, Saunders Letters, 79/15/1, IWM Documents.
77 Clark Diary, 16 January 1917, Ms Eng. Hist. e.143, Bodleian Special Collections.
78 The largest fall in expenditure (at constant 1938 prices) was on alcoholic drinks (45 per cent), followed by expenditure on clothing (33 per cent). Expenditure on food fell by 11 per cent. C. H. Feinstein, *National Income, Expenditure and Output in the United Kingdom 1855–1965* (Cambridge University Press, Cambridge, 1972), table 25, pp. T65–6. See also P. Dewey, *War and Progress in Britain 1914–1918* (Longman, Harlow, 1997), pp. 31–2. See also P. Dewey, 'The new warfare and economic mobilisation', in J. Turner (ed.), *Britain and the First World War* (Unwin Hyman, London, 1988), p. 79.
79 Robinson, 'Diary of the Great War', 13 October 1917, vol. 3, P.402, IWM Documents.
80 *Ibid.*, 11 November 1917. On standard suits, see also Ugolini, *Men and Menswear*, pp. 162–3.
81 Yearsley, 'The Home Front', p. 217, DS/MISC/17, IWM Documents.
82 J. W. E. Cory, untitled, 20 February 1980, DF148, Liddle Collection. At the outbreak of war Cory was a schoolboy growing up in Epsom. His father died during the influenza epidemic in the final year of war.
83 Yearsley, 'The Home Front', p. 6, DS/MISC/17, IWM Documents.
84 Cooper Diary, 28 July 1914, P.121, IWM Documents. Although dated 28 July 1914, the entry was clearly written later.
85 J. H. Butlin to B. Burnett Hall, 16 August 1914, Letters of Lieutenant James H. Butlin (hereafter Butlin Letters), 67/52/1, IWM Documents.
86 Clark Diary, 24 October 1914, Ms Eng. Hist. e.90, Bodleian Special Collections.

87 Cossins Diary, 7 August 1915, PP/MCR/371, IWM Documents.
88 *Ibid.*, 13 January 1916.
89 *Ibid.*, 25 January 1916. The decision proved an unpopular one and museums were re-opened shortly after. G. Robb, *British Culture and the First World War* (Palgrave, Basingstoke, 2002), p. 137.
90 Robinson, 'Diary of the Great War', 15 October 1917, vol. 3, P.402, IWM Documents.
91 *Ibid.*, 9 May 1918, vol. 4, P.402.
92 Cossins Diary, 29 October 1914, PP/MCR/371, IWM Documents.
93 Yearsley, 'The Home Front', p. 42, DS/MISC/17, IWM Documents. Clearly, in Yearsley's eyes the thousands who 'flocked' to League matches did not count as part of 'public opinion'. For the football results depicted as 'The shirkers' war news' in January 1915, see *Mr. Punch's History of the Great War* (Cassell, London, 1919), p. 22. Professional football ceased with the Football Association 'Khaki Final' of April 1915. See A. Horrall, *Popular Culture in London, c.1890–1918: The Transformation of Entertainment* (Manchester University Press, Manchester, 1991), p. 198; C. Veitch, ' "Play up! Play up! And win the war!" Football, the nation and the First World War 1914–15', *Journal of Contemporary History*, vol. 20, no. 3 (1985), p. 370. But see also the continued popularity on both home and battle fronts of professional sports such as boxing. Horrall, *Popular Culture*, pp. 200–5. The 'cultural continuum' between home and battle fronts is also emphasised in J. Rüger, 'Entertainments', in J. Winter and J.-L. Robert (eds), *Capital Cities at War: Paris, London, Berlin 1914–1919 Volume 2: A Cultural History* (Cambridge University Press, Cambridge, 2007), pp. 116–25 and J. Winter, 'Popular culture in wartime Britain', in A. Roshwald and R. Stites (eds), *European Culture in the Great War: The Arts, Entertainment and Propaganda, 1914–1918* (Cambridge University Press, Cambridge, 1999), pp. 330–48.
94 R. D. Blumenfeld, *All in a Lifetime* (Ernest Benn, London, 1931), p. 27.
95 J. H. Butlin to B. Burnett Hall, 20 September 1914, Butlin Letters, 67/52/1, IWM Documents.
96 Yearsley, 'The Home Front', pp. 70–1, DS/MISC/17, IWM Documents.
97 Cossins Diary, 13 February 1915, PP/MCR/371, IWM Documents.
98 *Ibid.*, 19 December 1914. The importance of 'escapism' is stressed, for example, in I. F. W. Beckett, *The Great War 1914–1918* (Pearson Education, Harlow, 2001), pp. 340–1.
99 Lockwood, 'Notes', 19 February 1916, 96/52/1, IWM Documents. The men who feature in this book showed little interest in the many propagandist plays on offer on the London stage. L. J. Collins, *Theatre at War, 1914–18* (Macmillan Press, Basingstoke, 1998), Chapter 7.
100 Joseph Diaries, 26 June 1915, Ms. Top. Oxon. e.288, Bodleian Special Collections.
101 *Ibid.*, 31 August 1915.

102 Holcombe Ingleby to Clement, 15 September 1915, The First World War Letters of Holcombe Ingleby MP (hereafter Ingleby Letters), P.343, IWM Documents.
103 *Ibid.*, 23 November 1915.
104 *Ibid.*, 15 October 1914.
105 *Ibid.*
106 For images of the wartime 'nut', see for example *Punch*, 28 October 1914, p. 353; 24 May 1916, p. 344.
107 Ugolini, *Men and Menswear*, pp. 75–81.
108 Lockwood, 'Notes', 26 September 1914, 96/52/1, IWM Documents.
109 *Ibid.*, 7 September 1915, 15 November 1915.
110 *Ibid.*, 27 May 1916.
111 *Ibid.*, 29 July 1916.
112 *Ibid.*, 13 August 1916.
113 *Ibid.*, 2 September 1916.
114 *Ibid.*, 23 April 1917.
115 Gibbs Diary, 5 November 1915, Ms Eng. misc. c.172, Bodleian Special Collections.
116 See, for example, C. Sheridan Jones's sensational account of the way in which legislation had driven West End night-life underground. He condemned the 'puritans' who had transformed London from a 'bright, open place' into a 'dark and secretive' one. C. Sheridan Jones, *London in War-Time* (Grafton, London, 1917), pp. 1–23. Although see also pp. 116–17.
117 Cossins Diary, 27 August 1914, PP/MCR/371, IWM Documents.
118 Robinson, 'Diary of the Great War', 18 August 1916, vol. 2, P.401, IWM Documents.
119 Joseph Diaries, 29 May 1918, Ms. Top. Oxon. e.288, Bodleian Special Collections.
120 Cossins Diary, 7 February 1917, PP/MCR/371, IWM Documents.
121 See, for example, 'How to save and why', leaflet no. 4 (The National Organising Committee for War Savings, 1916), in A. Clark, 'Scrapbooks of leaflets, newspaper cuttings etc., illustrating aspects of the Great War', Bodleian Library, University of Oxford, Oxford.
122 Blumenfeld, *All in a Lifetime*, p. 9.
123 Cossins Diary, 27 August 1915, PP/MCR/371, IWM Documents.
124 R. Saunders to son, 8 August 1914, Saunders Letters, 79/15/1, IWM Documents.
125 G. B. Wood-Walker, 'Reminiscences 1914–18', not dated, DF148, Liddle Collection.
126 Joseph Diaries, 4 October 1917, Ms. Top. Oxon. e.288, Bodleian Special Collections.
127 Gibbs Diary, 5 August 1916, Ms Eng. misc. c.180, Bodleian Special Collections.

128 Cossins Diary, 22 April 1916, PP/MCR/371, IWM Documents.

129 R. Saunders to son, 12 August 1917, Saunders Letters, 79/15/1, IWM Documents.

130 The far from straightforward relationship between middle-class status and serious, 'respectable' leisure activities and behaviour is explored in M. Huggins and J. A. Mangan (eds), *Disreputable Pleasures: Less Virtuous Victorians at Play* (Frank Cass, Abingdon, 2004).

131 See, for example, '1915. Specimen advertisements. Foods Drinks Smokes', in Clark, 'Scrapbooks of leaflets, newspaper cuttings etc.'.

132 Lockwood, 'Notes', 22 December 1916, 96/52/1, IWM Documents.

133 Robinson, 'Diary of the Great War', 28 February 1917, vol. 3, P.402, IWM Documents.

134 Shopping – both for necessities and for luxuries – was also portrayed as a feminine preserve, for example, in Sheridan Jones, *London in War-Time*, Chapter 5. See also C. S. Peel, *How We Lived Then: A Sketch of Social and Domestic Life in England during the War* (John Lane The Bodley Head, London, 1929), Chapter 7.

135 Clark Diary, 31 March 1916, Ms Eng. Hist. e.123, Bodleian Special Collections.

136 Hewish Diary, 22 February 1917, 02/43/1, IWM Documents.

137 D. B. Skinner to P. Liddle, 5–8 March 1979, DF148, Liddle Collection. Skinner was eleven at the outbreak of war.

138 R. Saunders to son, 8 August 1914, Saunders Letters, 79/15/1, IWM Documents.

139 Cutting, *Evening News*, 18 January 1916, '1915. Miscellaneous notes as to newspapers and miscellaneous periodicals and some official notices in wartime', in Clark, 'Scrapbooks of leaflets, newspaper cuttings etc.'.

140 Clark Diary, 3 December 1916, Ms Eng. Hist. e.140, Bodleian Special Collections.

141 R. Saunders to son, 27 January 1917, Saunders Letters, 79/15/1, IWM Documents. As A. James Hammerton's study of nineteenth-century marriages show, men's involvement in household management was by no means always welcomed by their wives. A. J. Hammerton, *Cruelty and Companionship: Conflict in Nineteenth-Century Married Life* (Routledge, London, 1992), especially Part 2.

142 R. Saunders to son, 15 February 1917, Saunders Letters, 79/15/1, IWM Documents. It is worth noting that at this very time New York Jewish women were involved in a city-wide boycott of various foodstuffs, in protest at high prices. D. Frank, 'Housewives, socialists, and the politics of food: the 1917 New York cost-of-living protests', *Feminist Studies*, vol. 11, no. 2 (1985), pp. 255–85. Historians have stressed women's participation in the food politics of the First World War, both in Britain and in other combatant countries. See, for example, K. Hunt, 'The politics of food and

women's neighborhood activism in First World War Britain', *International Labor and Working-Class History*, no. 77 (2010), pp. 8–26; M. Healy, *Vienna and the Fall of the Habsburg Empire: Total War and Everyday Life in World War One* (Cambridge University Press, Cambridge, 2004), Chapter 1; B. Davis, *Home Fires Burning: Food, Politics and Everyday Life in World War One Berlin* (University of North Carolina Press, Chapel Hill, NC, 2000); B. Alpern Engel, 'Not by bread alone: subsistence riots in Russia during World War I', *The Journal of Modern History*, vol. 69, no. 4 (1997), pp. 696–721; J. Smart, 'Feminists, food and the fair price: the cost of living demonstrations in Melbourne, August–September 1917', in J. Damousi and M. Lake (eds), *Gender and War: Australians at War in the Twentieth Century* (Cambridge University Press, Cambridge, 1995), pp. 274–301; T. Kaplan, 'Female consciousness and collective action: the case of Barcelona, 1910–1918', *Signs*, vol. 7, no. 3 (1982), especially pp. 560–6.

143 F. Trentmann and F. Just, 'Introduction', in F. Trentmann and F. Just (eds), *Food and Conflict in Europe in the Age of the Two World Wars* (Palgrave Macmillan, Basingstoke, 2006), p. 3.

144 Gibbs Diary, 22 October 1916, Ms Eng. misc. c.182, Bodleian Special Collections.

145 G. Pember, 'Some Memories of the Great War', not dated, DF148, Liddle Collection.

146 Cooper Diary, 12 November 1917, P.121, IWM Documents.

147 Cossins Diary, 19 August 1916, PP/MCR/371, IWM Documents.

148 *Ibid.*, 20 December 1916.

149 *Ibid.*, 21 December 1916.

150 *Ibid.*, 23 December 1916.

151 *Ibid.*, 12 February 1917.

152 *Ibid.*, 17 February 1917.

153 Clark Diary, 17 September 1916, Ms Eng. Hist. e.134, Bodleian Special Collections.

154 Cossins Diary, 6 December 1916, PP/MCR/371, IWM Documents.

155 Robinson, 'Diary of the Great War', 17 January 1917, vol. 3, P.402, IWM Documents.

156 Cooper Diary, 12 November 1917, P.121, IWM Documents. For accusations of profiteering, see also Chapter 6.

157 R. Saunders to son, 1 September 1917, Saunders Letters, 79/15/1, IWM Documents.

158 *Ibid.*, 28 October 1917.

159 M. J. Winstanley, *The Shopkeeper's World, 1830–1914* (Manchester University Press, Manchester, 1983), p. 54.

160 R. Saunders to son, 7 September 1918, Saunders Letters, 79/15/1, IWM Documents. For the 'psychological toll' of 'powerlessness in consumer society' see also Seipp, *The Ordeal of Peace*, p. 65.

161 Robinson, 'Diary of the Great War', 23 July 1918, vol. 4, P.402, IWM Documents.
162 *Ibid.*, 26 August 1918.
163 Cossins Diary, 21 July 1915, PP/MCR/371, IWM Documents.
164 Robinson, 'Diary of the Great War', 31 July 1915, vol. 1, P.401, IWM Documents.
165 In February 1917 Lloyd George made an important speech in the House of Commons, telling 'the country plainly that much greater privations and discomfort must be suffered if we are to escape disaster'. Cossins Diary, 24 February 1917, PP/MCR/371, IWM Documents. See also Yearsley, 'The Home Front', p. 204, DS/MISC/17, IWM Documents.
166 Clark Diary, 28 August 1916, Ms Eng. Hist. e.132, Bodleian Special Collections.
167 Robinson, 'Diary of the Great War', 2 May 1916, vol. 2, P.401, IWM Documents.
168 Clark Diary, 21 June 1917, Ms Eng. Hist. e.149, Bodleian Special Collections.
169 *Ibid.*, 14 September 1918, Ms Eng. Hist. e.169.
170 *Ibid.*, 1 November 1915, Ms Eng. Hist. e.113.
171 Cossins Diary, 17 December 1915, PP/MCR/371, IWM Documents.
172 Clark Diary, 21 June 1917, Ms Eng. Hist. e.149, Bodleian Special Collections.
173 Robinson, 'Diary of the Great War', 2 March 1916, vol. 2, P.401, IWM Documents.
174 Yearsley, 'The Home Front', p. 166, DS/MISC/17, IWM Documents.
175 Robinson, 'Diary of the Great War', 6 March 1916, vol. 2, P.401, IWM Documents.
176 R. Saunders to son, 21 March 1916, Saunders Letters, 79/15/1, IWM Documents.
177 Clark Diary, 4 October 1916, Ms Eng. Hist. e.136, Bodleian Special Collections.
178 *Ibid.*, 19 October 1916, Ms Eng. Hist. e.137.
179 Cossins Diary, 3 February 1917, PP/MCR/371, IWM Documents.
180 *Ibid.*
181 Robinson, 'Diary of the Great War', 3 February 1917, vol. 3, P.402, IWM Documents.
182 Cossins Diary, 6 February 1917, PP/MCR/371, IWM Documents.
183 Robinson, 'Diary of the Great War', 26 April 1917, vol. 3, P.402, IWM Documents.
184 Clark Diary, 13 June 1917, Ms Eng. Hist. e.149, Bodleian Special Collections.
185 Yearsley, 'The Home Front', p. 218, DS/MISC/17, IWM Documents.
186 Blumenfeld, *All in a Lifetime*, p. 56.

187 Robinson, 'Diary of the Great War', 26 April 1917, vol. 3, P.402, IWM Documents.

188 Yearsley, 'The Home Front', p. 201, DS/MISC/17, IWM Documents.

189 *Ibid.*, p. 243.

190 Cooper Diary, 16 February 1917, P.121, IWM Documents. By the end of 1917 most middle-class observers thought that the imposition of some form of compulsory food rationing was inevitable. Its piecemeal introduction from December 1917, covering items such as meat, butter, margarine, tea and sugar provoked relatively little comment. See, for example, Hewish Diary, 22 February 1917, 02/43/1, IWM Documents; Cooper Diary, 9 June 1918, P.121, IWM Documents. Even Robinson, despite his dislike of regulation, eventually came to recognise the inevitability, and indeed advantages, of some form of compulsory rationing. See, for example, Robinson, 'Diary of the Great War', 20 January 1918, 3 March 1918, vol. 4, P.402, IWM Documents.

191 *Ibid.*, 14 January 1915, vol. 1, P.401.

192 Cossins Diary, 21 December 1915, PP/MCR/371, IWM Documents.

193 *Ibid.*, 19 October 1916.

194 Clark Diary, 1 January 1916, Ms Eng. Hist. e.118, Bodleian Special Collections. For complaints about working-class affluence and lack of patriotism, see also Chapter 3 of this book. Tales of the profligate spending habits of well-off workers were not an entirely new element in middle-class culture. See, for example, claims in 1899 that Coventry bicycle workers drank champagne with every meal. B. Beaven, *Leisure, Citizenship and Working-Class Men in Britain, 1850–1945* (Manchester University Press, Manchester, 2005), p. 49.

195 Blumenfeld, *All in a Lifetime*, p. 61.

196 Hewish Diary, 19 June 1917, 02/43/1, IWM Documents.

197 Clark Diary, 15 May 1915, Ms Eng. Hist. e.103, Bodleian Special Collections.

198 Lockwood, 'Notes', 15 March 1916, 96/52/1, IWM Documents.

199 R. Saunders to son, 21 March 1916, Saunders Letters, 79/15/1, IWM Documents.

200 *Ibid.*, 28 October 1917.

201 *Ibid.*, 7 September 1918.

202 Clark Diary, 21 April 1917, Ms Eng. Hist. e.147, Bodleian Special Collections.

203 Cooper Diary, 12 November 1917, P.121, IWM Documents

204 Robinson, 'Diary of the Great War', prefatory note, 15 November 1918, vol. 1, P.401, IWM Documents.

205 Robinson, 'Diary of the Great War', 29 April 1918, vol. 4, P.402, IWM Documents.

206 I. Zweiniger-Bargielowska, 'The culture of the abdomen: obesity and

reducing in Britain, circa 1900–1939', *Journal of British Studies*, vol. 44, no. 2 (2005), p. 244.

207 *Ibid.*, p. 267.

208 Joseph Diaries, 5 January 1916, Ms. Top. Oxon. e.288, Bodleian Special Collections.

8

Families and relationships

Introduction

In April 1918 Horace Joseph spent two days in Gloucester, visiting an uncle: 'it was a rest to be away … from the Bursary, and rationing, and the Volunteers'.[1] Networks of family and friends were extremely important to middle-class men, and became even more so during the war. It was within these networks that they often spent their working hours, as well as their leisure time. It was from these that they sought information, advice, solace in time of trouble and sometimes practical help. As Joseph found, family and friends could also provide a refuge, however temporary, from the pressures of war. And although middle-class men certainly did not lead their lives in a 'separate sphere' from their womenfolk, it was other men of a similar social background and often age, with whom they tended to develop the closest ties.[2]

As Reginald Gibbs's frequent disputes with friends, relatives and acquaintances indicate, conflict and disagreement were certainly not absent from middle-class men's circles.[3] However, wartime diaries and letters placed a much greater emphasis on supportive relationships and amicable exchanges, perhaps partly due to a reluctance to acknowledge and record conflict, but perhaps also to the likelihood of middle-class men surrounding themselves with like-minded people. Even Gibbs occasionally found individuals who shared his views, like 'the science master at the V.C.S. [who] … fully sympathises with my sentiments in abhorring war',[4] or the Mr Braisher who briefly took over the diary when Gibbs was called up in 1917.[5]

It is these networks of family and friendship, and civilian men's place within them, which are the focus here. The chapter begins by considering the disruption caused to such networks by the war, focusing particularly on the impact of relatives' and friends' absence while on active service, and questioning whether this led to a breakdown of relationships across a fault-line that separated civilians from servicemen. The chapter then turns to examine further the impact of war on family relationships, and assesses whether the conflict brought about changes – or indeed, challenges – to the established role and authority of the paterfamilias. Finally, the chapter concludes by focusing in greater detail on one particular relationship: that between fathers and sons, and particularly civilian fathers and combatant sons, questioning whether wartime experiences and events led to a renegotiation of roles and responsibilities across generations.

Disruptions

For the duration of the conflict, it was from the men (and some women) who wrote to him or visited the vicarage that Andrew Clark obtained much of the information and opinions that formed the basis of his wartime diary. The purpose of Dr Smallwood's visits, for example, was to see Clark's wife, already suffering from ill-health at the outset of war, but he rarely left without having a chat with Clark too,[6] while F. J. Cooper, an Inland Revenue and Old Age Pensions officer, regularly 'brought a bright budget of news'.[7] Clark also corresponded with a number of relatives and friends, including his gloomy brother-in-law, John Paterson – whom in November 1914 he found 'down-cast (as usual)'.[8] His most regular visitor, however, was James Caldwell, whose opinions he valued highly: he was 'a man of wide experience, industrial and military; very observant, and very just'.[9] He also clearly enjoyed his company, always finding him 'very talkative, very sarcastic, and (withal) very informative and amusing'.[10]

However, just as networks of family, friendship and sociability acquired a new importance in civilian men's lives, including as sources of news and information, many were disrupted by the war. Most notably, perhaps, as individuals left for the armed forces, the effects of their absence – even when only temporary – were often felt more widely than just within their immediate family circle. In September 1914 Ernest Cooper's solicitor's practice had to do without two of its workers, both of whom were Cooper's nephews: 'Stephen … was called up in the Suffolk Yeomanry and I sent Noel home in August to help his father through harvest'. While the latter was away, 'another nephew Claude … came and helped in the office for a few weeks', although he too left not long after, having enlisted in Kitchener's army.[11] Younger men were hit particularly hard by losses within their circle of friends, which were the most likely to be made up of young men of military age. For Leslie Craig, who came of age shortly before the Armistice, the war made it 'a lonelier world', as 'so many of my slightly senior friends (i.e. most of them) had not returned from France' at the end of the conflict.[12] The impact of losing friends to the armed forces, even when such a loss was only a temporary one, should not be underestimated. Before the war Frank Lockwood had spent a good deal of time with his friend Arthur Wood, and continued to do so after the outbreak of hostilities. In September 1914, for example, they spent the evening together, going 'as far as Leymoor Picture Palace',[13] while two months later they tried out the new 'Picturedrome' in nearby Slaithwaite.[14] Lockwood clearly missed him a great deal once Wood enlisted in the navy in November 1915[15] and it was not until an evening in April the following year that he 'had a pleasant surprise … Arthur Wood, my pal, was over on leave, and it seemed quite like old times, to be able to go for a walk together'.[16]

We do not know whether the young men's friendship was affected by their different experiences of war, although there is no indication that Wood's visit brought Lockwood anything other than pleasure at a time when he was unhappy and uncertain about his future. Indeed, it was certainly not a foregone conclusion that friendships between men in the armed forces and on the home front should founder, replaced by an exclusive comradeship between combatants on the one hand and civilians' complacent isolation from the realities of war on the other.[17] As a number of historians have observed, links between servicemen and civilians often remained strong, maintained through a constant flow of letters, parcels and leave visits.[18] Such relationships, furthermore, were not exclusively one-way, with civilians always being the ones to provide support, both moral and practical, to servicemen. The letters sent by Humphrey Gleave to his brother Edward in 1916, while the latter was on active service in France, for example, show that help could also flow the other way. In February 1916 Humphrey, at the time still living at home in Leeds, planned to appeal for exemption and asked his brother to write letters to confirm his ill-health, as well as the fact that he was the only one left at home to look after their mother, who was ill with bowel cancer. This was to be 'the second string so to speak, in case the doctors accept me for light duties … it is exceedingly unpleasant for me to be in a red tape machine but it is war and individuals suffer in all directions'.[19] Edward seems to have been quite willing to write the letters, apparently not finding anything objectionable in his brother's tone. On the contrary, another letter from

Humphrey a few days later suggests that he had been very helpful: 'You have done awfully well to get me the allowance and I am delighted at the thought of owning a first class microscope. Of course you shall have back what you gave me … If you want things I will send them when I get the money'. He concluded by stating that 'I really thought last week I was doomed to shoulder a gun, but I am more hopeful now'.[20]

Humphrey Gleave made no secret of his wish to stay out of the army, and expected – correctly, as it turned out – his brother to be sympathetic. However, not all civilians were as unselfconscious about their intention of avoiding military service (nor, no doubt, were all servicemen as helpful). Indeed, many felt guilty, particularly at the thought that they were still safe at home while friends or relatives were risking their lives on active duty. In spring 1917 Captain E. Hewish chafed at finding himself still stationed at home in Herne Bay, wishing to 'take a man's part in this show'.[21] The thought of his brother, then serving on the Western Front, made him feel particularly guilty. In July he received a letter from Alfred, who had just returned from a spell on the front line. While his brother was being shelled, he noted, 'I [was] sleeping soundly in my bed!! I feel a worm'.[22] Writing to Lieutenant Archie Steavenson, an old school-friend, in September 1916, 'Dudley', a schoolmaster, explained that 'I am still a civilian having been deferred till January 25th next'. Their friendship seems to have remained an affectionate one – Dudley, for example, addressed Steavenson as 'Dear Old Bottom', clearly an old nickname – but he worried that his continued civilian status might have alienated at least one of the friends they had in common: 'Robert[?] has not written for ages. I think he puts me down as a shirker'.[23]

A valuable insight into the nature of friendship between servicemen and civilians is provided by the 135 letters written during the conflict by Lieutenant James H. Butlin to his friend Basil Burnett Hall. By the outbreak of war, the friendship between the two young men, who had been to school together, was already a well-established one, based on a shared interest in various sporting and leisure activities, including the more or less serious pursuit of girls. In August 1914, for example, Butlin wrote in typical fashion: 'I am so glad you met the heavenly Edith. What do you think of her? Fancy Alfred in the Territorials … We had a tournament at the [tennis] club on Bank Holiday'.[24] A month later, after mentioning that he had been 'to see The Girl in the Taxi the other night. It was awfully good and the two leading girls were very pretty', he went on to discuss a variety of other topics, none of which had anything to do with the war, and which included Basil's recent horse-racing winnings.[25]

Butlin enlisted soon after the outbreak of war and by spring 1915 was serving with the British Expeditionary Force in France as a subaltern attached to the 2nd Battalion Yorkshire Regiment. Burnett Hall, on the other hand, did not enlist and remained a civilian throughout the conflict, medical examination having revealed that he suffered from a weak heart. He thus completed his university studies and in 1917 found work in the Foreign Office. However, the two men's diverging paths did not mean an end to their friendship: they remained in touch by letter and regularly met up during Butlin's periods of leave. That said, Burnett Hall's continued civilian status was clearly not entirely unproblematic, and Butlin's letters were peppered with humorous, yet pointed, references to it. In August 1914, in between references to his work for the National Reserve Offices in Weymouth and news about mutual friends, he asked: 'haven't you joined any regiment? You are a scoundrel'.[26] In December, having just enlisted, he concluded his letter with two PS: 'I have fallen in love with Madge Green or very nearly. She is jolly pretty' and 'When are you going to join the army? It is the duty of every able-bodied citizen to defend his country'.[27]

Butlin continued to ask such jokey questions, often couched in the language of contemporary recruiting propaganda, throughout the conflict, and regularly commented on their contrasting circumstances. In June 1915, having just seen action at Festubert, he complained: 'You have given yourself up to … enjoyment while your brothers in Flanders have been engaged in one of the most sanguinary battles of history. How wrong of you! … I am glad you were at "the top of your form" in tennis'.[28] Six months later he wrote:

> My dear old pal Basil, doubtless by this time you will be a conscript in his Majesty's army drawing the princely wage of 1/1 per diem. If however (which I hope is the case) you still succeed in hoodwinking the doctors that you are weak and puny, I take it that you will be in 42 Grosvenor Gardens by the side of a roaring fire. I, on the other hand, will be standing … shivering in a trench full of mud and water and cursing the Kaiser and his abominable hordes.[29]

As Burnett Hall's letters have not survived, we do not know his reaction to comments that hovered so uncertainly between resentment, irony and affection. However, there are indications that – unsurprisingly – he sometimes found them hurtful. In January 1916, referring to the introduction of conscription, Butlin asked: 'Is the compulsion for single men very terrifying to you? … I expect you've got wind up now the *Daily Mail* is hot on your track. You, remember, are one of the 400,000 (?) branded in the eyes of the world as a slacker'.[30] A fortnight later he responded to a letter from Burnett Hall by writing: 'you say that some letter I wrote to you appeared to you to be in rather bad taste. I don't know what the hell you mean, but I trust you are not really offended. However, I will not be deluded into continuing the discussion'.[31] In any case, his friend's remonstrance had little effect. Only a week later he was writing: 'your letter of 16 January 1916 reminded again me of the existence of a "slacker" who is still unstarred and at liberty'.[32]

Despite such taunts, Butlin and Burnett Hall remained close friends, keeping in touch throughout (and after the end of) the conflict. Burnett Hall not only wrote long letters, but also regularly sent parcels containing treats such as chocolates and chocolate biscuits,[33] as well as items that Butlin may not have been able to request from his parents or younger sister. In July 1915, for example, he mentioned that 'I could do with a magazine or two and any fruity publication your roving eye lights upon'.[34] The importance to Butlin of letters and parcels, as well as of Burnett Hall's congenial company while at home on leave, should not be underestimated. In October 1915 he wrote from France, planning his next period of leave: 'If you are at Oxford, say in November, you would have to get leave to meet me in London'. He was thankful for the latest parcel: the apples had been 'exceedingly good. I cannot thank you enough for your unfailing kindness to me dear Basil. At the same time I may mention that Oxford's famous chocolates would be very acceptable out here! Write me a nice bracy, breezy and saucy letter next time'.[35]

Most importantly, Butlin could confide in his friend in a way that was not possible with his family. It was not only the more shocking and bloody details of active service and of battle that he was able to impart – although these certainly featured in the letters too[36] – but also more intimate aspects of his life during the war. Thus, in October 1916, while at home on sick leave, he became friendly with a girl called Eileen, 'a topping girl and quite lady like, though between you and me and the brick wall … her people are nothing much'. He had travelled to Bournemouth to see her and they had been out for dinner and then to the theatre. They had met again the following day and gone out for a walk. 'Of course this information is for your ears only: please do not noise it abroad'.[37] The following March, back in France and waiting to be posted to the front, he met a girl named Juliette. She was 'most awfully pretty and looked different from the painted type with which we are all familiar'. He 'stayed the night with her … I am supremely happy. Of course you *must* never mention all that I have told you to a living soul: I have trusted you implicitly because I know I can'.[38]

In May, after his experiences at the battle of Arras left him 'a bit nervy',[39] Butlin found himself at Craiglockhart War Hospital in Midlothian, receiving treatment for neurasthenia. It was to Burnett Hall that he turned to, complaining that 'even a "complete and glorious loaf" palls after a few days ... Why the devil they can't send me home for a couple of months, but there you are'. He confided that he had got into trouble for bringing his girlfriend into the grounds of the hospital in the evening, adding that the 'incident ... is not known to my people'.[40] In one of the most telling passages in the correspondence, reflecting the continued importance of friendships established before the war, even when individuals' wartime experiences varied dramatically, Butlin acknowledged that 'I feel it a great joy that I can freely express my feelings to you: you are a safety valve so to speak'.[41]

Family and home

Throughout the war years, the extended family continued to play a central part in most civilian middle-class men's lives. Even when not living together, or even close, relatives often kept in touch, visited or spent holidays together: much of middle-class leisure time was spent with family members. Thus, when asked how he spent his time away from his work as a journalist during the war, Philip Ashton Murrray singled out 'family gatherings', adding that 'home life with a family of ten ... there was plenty of fun there'.[42] That said, family life and relations were not unaffected by the war. To some extent, the conflict saw middle-class women gain new roles and responsibilities – and presumably status – outside the home. According to Fredrick Robinson, writing soon after the end of the war, members of his family, including his wife and daughter, had 'done their "bit" in various ways, in the Civil service, VAD Nursing, bandage-making, etc.'[43] Many women became deeply involved in war charities and other 'war work'. In October 1914 Holcome Ingleby wrote to his son Clement that 'your mother is busy all day and every day with the Soldiers and Sailors' Association and is rapidly becoming a sort of Mrs Jellaby!'[44] For some middle-class women the war brought even more radical changes. In July 1916 Clark noted that the 'son in law of Mr Turnbull (who lives at Fairstead Hall) is manager and part-owner of Turnbull's a gentleman's outfitting shop, in Duke Street, London. He has just lost his last remaining salesman'. As a result, 'as a stop-gap, his wife ... has gone into the shop, leaving her infant son to be looked after by the grandmother at Fairstead Hall'.[45]

However, the extent to which the war upset conventional gender roles and husbands' position of ultimate authority within middle-class families should not be exaggerated.[46] Indeed, if there was a challenge to the authority of the paterfamilias, it did not come directly from wives' newfound status and responsibilities. Rather, it derived from the disruption to work and the economy caused by the war, threatening husbands' role as bread-winners and undermining the power and prestige that went with it. In February 1917, for example, Harold Cossins almost lost his job as his firm struggled to repay its loans,[47] while in January 1916 Alfred Bradburn explained to his brother that with 'Bis. … at a complete standstill',[48] his daughter would 'not return to school this term, the funds won't run to it … things are going to be very tight in the money line with me for the next 12 months or so. As my income will be mostly what I get from munitions my *average £2–15–0 a week*'. He was considering letting the lower part of their house, but wanted to be 'sure' of the people who had expressed an interest in renting it, otherwise 'the little money gained is not worth the discomfort of having any one undesirable in the house'.[49] Wartime pressures disrupted well-established domestic arrangements in other ways too. According to William McIvor, before the war his family had been strict in its Sunday observance, and decades later he could 'recall the quite un-holy joy we children got from the gradual relaxation of these restrictions because of the necessity to devote many Sundays or parts of Sundays to various forms of war effort in which in one way or another we all took part'. He was very pleased to say that 'things never reverted again to the pre-war type Sunday'.[50]

In some cases, it was the threat – and indeed, the reality – of enemy air- and sea-raids, which disrupted normal routines and arrangements. In 1916 the Copeman family was caught up in a naval bombardment while staying at their house in Caister, Norfolk. In a letter to his son, Charles Copeman explained that as a result they had decided not to send his brother Harry back to school in Yarmouth, 'as we think he might be nervous after our experiences last week', adding that 'I don't suppose we shall go back to Caister until the German cruisers are sunk'.[51] For some families the circumstances of war brought about long periods of separation, not only from fathers, sons or brothers on active duty, but also from other family members. In December 1915, for example, North Whitehead, a university professor, wrote to his wife to wish her 'many many happy returns of the day, sweet pet … It is not nice to be parted just at these dates … But everything is overridden by necessity just now … So I am not repining, but I am thinking of you lovingly'.[52]

In December 1914 Ernest Cooper explained that 'as things were looking lively in the North Sea' and as their baby had not been well, his wife had taken her to stay 'with Grannie at Sutton', Surrey.[53] They did not return home to Southwold until the following February, by which time Cooper found the baby 'much advanced, walking nicely and beginning to chatter'.[54] Two months later they experienced their first Zeppelin raid and having 'heard from the Mayor that it was expected a raid would be made by sea to burn murder and destroy within sixty days I thought it time to take precautions, so … we sent Nurse and baby up to Grannie', followed by his wife and maid, 'while the old Birds went to Wales for three week cure'. Cooper was 'left alone with a housekeeper', although he spent Whitsun at Sutton, which he found 'a most welcome rest'.[55] In November 1917 he decided that his wife and daughter should spend the winter in Southbourne, while he stayed on in Southwold. He explained that 'after three years of war alarms on the East Coast and the continued delicacy of the child I thought it well that they should both get away out of Air raids and far from Gunfire and Explosive Mines … I hope it may do them both good'.[56]

As in the Copeman family's case, the Coopers were able to make decisions (with Ernest, it seems, having the final say) in order to try and ensure the family's safety and well-being, even if this entailed long periods of separation. In other cases, however, middle-class men seem to have felt far less in control of events that affected their family, being reduced to the role of passive observers. In August 1918, for example, Robinson wrote of his family's distress at seeing ships being torpedoed while on holiday at the seaside. On one occasion, they 'saw the whole thing from the time the ship was struck until she disappeared … Watching through a powerful telescope we saw her gradually sinking … this is the fourth vessel which has been torpedoed before our eyes'.[57] A week later, having seen more boats being sunk, he added, rather infelicitously, that 'this sort of thing is getting on our nerves, and quite spoiling our holiday'.[58]

Not all disruptions to family life were caused by the war, although they were often exacerbated by it. By April 1916, for example, Andrew Clark's wife was already seriously ill. As he wrote to his friend William Redman, who had recently moved out of the village, 'she is very weak, and has not been out for many weeks, nor is able to see anyone'.[59] Four months later he wrote again, explaining that 'I have been, and still am, in great troubles. Mrs Clark is in the grip of a fatal disease, and is now in great weakness, and has to be dazed with drugs day and night to keep away the pain'.[60] Cossins' wife also suffered a long period of illness, made worse, it seems, by worries about the war. In October 1915 the doctor 'recommended Marjorie to spend the Winter at sea … four or five months … free from worries and anxieties, will I hope make Marjorie stronger than she has ever been since I knew her'.[61] A month later they moved to Brighton with their young son and their servant Mabel, where Cossins hoped that 'away from Zeppelin scares and household worries and [with] the sea air' Marjorie would be restored to health.[62] In December she spent some weeks at a nursing home for a period of complete rest,[63] emerging in the New Year, 'glad to be back in the world'.[64] She then slowly regained her strength, and in October they were able to return to their home in St Albans,[65] where they made 'a great effort to ensure her as calm and peaceful conditions as possible', although 'with a restless boy like John in the house this is far from easy'.[66]

Whatever the causes, disruptions to family life often left men feeling lonely and bereft, as well as powerless in the face of distressing circumstances. A few days after the death of his wife, Clark wrote to Redman: 'the last few years have been years of partings for me, and have left me a very lonely man, lingering behind my old friends'.[67] Even short separations could be trying. In June 1916 Cossins spent a very enjoyable weekend in Bury St Edmunds as a guest of Mr Hatton, the manager of the Alberta Land Company, 'but I am longing to be with Marjorie again; nothing seems much worthwhile without her'.[68] In January 1916 Joseph heard that one of the other New College fellows was to be married. He admitted in his diary that he 'couldn't be altogether glad' of the news. As two of the fellows had died while on active service and three had married since the start of the war, only five were left to live in college. This, he believed, was 'not enough for working the college properly', but most significantly, 'I begin to feel very lonely'.[69] A year later he suffered a further 'private grief': the death of his mother. He explained that in the twenty-six years since his father's death 'she and I had been very much together. But she was the same to us all: the centre of our home, to whom each brought our troubles … who helped all, and thought the best of all'. By 'home' he meant the family home near Wells, in Somerset, to which he returned at the end of each term. He reflected that 'I shall not realise till vacations come, and I have nowhere to turn to, what it is to have no longer a home'.[70] Four months later the siblings met 'to divide up things. When we clear out of the house, and cease to have a home, is not yet quite settled'.[71]

The pain caused by loss and absences from the family, even when only temporary, could be intense. According to McIvor his had been 'a typical compact family dealing with war time conditions as best we could'. In 1918, however, his brother reached military age and left home. To McIvor, 'as a boy, this was really the ultimate; war had come "home". I don't need to enlarge on the "empty chair at the table" and "stiff upper lip" themes; at that time they were commonplace'. He acknowledged that 'as a family, [we] were only one of hundreds of thousands' in the same position, but 'that fact didn't lessen the blow'.[72] It was such threats to the domestic fulcrum of middle-class life, as individuals were lost to illness, death, military service or other circumstances over which they had little control, which seem to have hit civilian men particularly hard.

Maintaining or restoring at least a semblance of 'home' – as an emotional, as well as a physical space – thus assumed a new urgency, although at times the task proved difficult, if not impossible. In 1917, for example, Richard Attwater's older brother was able to get leave just before Christmas, but in order to re-join his unit on time, was forced to leave straight after Christmas lunch. After he left, 'both father and mother tried to make the rest of the day like Christmas', but despite all their efforts, 'we spent an unhappy afternoon and evening and we were all glad when it was time for bed'.[73] In December 1915, having heard of the death in Flanders of his brother-in-law Mervyn, Cossins immediately travelled down to Minehead to stay with his aunt and sister Violet, whom he found 'bearing up better in their great trial than I had expected'.[74] He spent time with his sister, who told him more of Mervyn's life before coming to Minehead: 'it is dreadful to feel that he has risen superior to and triumphed over so many hardships only to be snuffed out like this'.[75] Following a practice common to many bereaved families, they looked through some of the dead soldier's belongings.[76] The sketches and postcards sent by Mervyn had acquired a new and painful significance: 'it is dreadful to think he will not be able to send any more nor even finish one sketch which he had begun of a farmhouse just behind the lines. I am glad she is able to talk of them with me'. The subject of Violet's future 'home' soon came up, although her response was telling and to Harold, worried that his sister was now left alone, perhaps surprising: 'everything associated with … [Mervyn] bring pleasant memories, not painful ones, so she does not wish to go away from home just yet'.[77]

Fathers and sons

Speaking in August 1914 at a meeting in Great Leighs to enrol volunteers as special constables, Sir Richard Pennefather made clear the role expected of fathers and sons in wartime: 'young men who are eligible for army-service should enlist, and their fathers and mothers should encourage them to seek training to fit them, if need be, to fight for the safety of their country'.[78] Pennefather did not go so far as to suggest that parents should put pressure on their sons to join up, but – most would have agreed – it was certainly not their role to try and dissuade them or place any obstacles in their path.[79] Indeed, it is often assumed that middle-class fathers were only too keen for their sons to do their patriotic duty and join up. In reality, however, attitudes were rarely so straightforward.

As is well-known, a central element of Edwardian middle-class manliness was the support and protection of the family, a concern that did not lose any of its potency during the war: indeed, many of the actions and decisions made by the men who feature in this book were influenced (and justified) by this very imperative. In October 1914, for example, George Murray wrote to Clark from the coastal town of Deal. He explained that 'if things get any worse here, I think it very likely that my wife and Janice may go to America while Gerty and myself will remain here, as long as it is safe, simply to preserve our belongings'. He was particularly worried about 'bombs and airships. I scarcely think they will invade England, but one never knows: and it is my place to make everything as secure as I can for my wife and children'.[80] Taking action that ranged from buying respirators for the whole household[81] to having an extra exit added to the cellar,[82] it was the role of the paterfamilias to take all possible precautions to ensure his family's safety.[83] Significantly, furthermore, fathers' protective role often blended into a nurturing one. H. Maingay was the son of a GP and surgeon in Scarborough. During the war he and his three siblings had 'tried doing without sugar in our tea. Father, however, decided that we were not getting enough sugar and made us eat a lump after tea'.[84]

It has been suggested that by the end of the nineteenth century 'men's emotional involvement with child rearing declined as their role in transmitting skills was taken over by formal education and professional qualifications ... leaving some virtually to abdicate from child rearing'.[85] However, this did not stop middle-class men such as Cossins from being both affectionate and attentive fathers: the reality of Victorian and Edwardian fatherhood was a good deal more complex than 'the caricature of the Victorian paterfamilias whose cold and forbidding presence still touches the popular imagination'.[86] Cossins noted in his diary significant landmarks and 'firsts' in his son's life, making clear his own active involvement in his upbringing. In June 1915, for example, he returned early from work to attend 'an open air concert and fete … at which John made his first appearance in public – as a lamb in a pastoral dance. He was quite a success and too interested to appear to be nervous'.[87] In January 1916 John lost his first tooth,[88] and a month later Cossins took him to see 'his first pantomime, "Cindarella"'.[89] The following October it was time for John to begin school, and Cossins went to speak to the Headmaster of a new prep school in St Albans. He concluded that 'it seems very nice but I fear that it may be rather a shock to John after his sheltered life, fussed over by so many anxious relatives'.[90] He clearly found his son's first day at school rather a trial and was relieved to discover that all had gone well.[91]

It was not unheard of, furthermore, for middle-class fathers to take their responsibilities further, and become involved in the day-to-day care of their children, as well as in the special occasions.[92] In the (unexplained) absence of his wife Gibbs took over at least some of the routine care of his children, particularly that of his youngest son Bob. In January 1917 he noted that 'Bob has been sleeping in my bed for some time now … In the morning he comes trotting in the bathroom behind me and religiously washes his hands and face and brushes his teeth'.[93] Six months later he had 'a terrible fright'. Early in the morning Bob had 'asked for his morning sweet, which I always put under the pillow ready for him'. A little later Gibbs was woken up 'by a terrible cry'. Bob 'had nearly choked … He might have died by my side, in which case I should have offered myself for the firing line at once'.[94] Having received his call-up papers in November, he admitted that 'I hate leaving poor little Bob. I know he cries for me at night. I always give him sweets and biscuits and attend to him'. He now 'sleeps with —, who is very deaf … When she and — get together in the kitchen with the door shut, the two babies might yell themselves hoarse for all they would hear'.[95]

It is unsurprising, then, that there should have been a tension between fathers' protective – and indeed nurturing – roles, and the expectation that they should be content to see their sons risking their lives and limbs on active service.[96] That said, many men certainly wished to see their sons do their patriotic duty at a time of national emergency. Gibbs and his father, for example, disagreed profoundly about the war and about the justice of the British cause.[97] While he does not seem to have put any explicit pressure on his son to enlist, Gibbs felt that he, together with his headmaster, William Tinniswood, and another old friend, General

Christopher, were 'determined to "fight to the death" to the last drop of *my* blood. Young men go with the war, exhilarated by their illusions, and old men, secure in their immunity, drum them on'.[98] For his part, Ingleby was suspicious of any hint that his son's role in the war might be anything less than exemplary. In July 1915 he was surprised to hear that Clement was stationed in Alexandria, something that was 'very difficult to explain to one's friends … when every hand is wanted at the pumps in the Dardanelles'. He added that 'it is glorious to read of the bravery of our chaps and their recent successes … and I should like to feel that you are sharing the honour'.[99] He returned to this theme a few days later, his tone now brusque: 'What I want to know is why you are stowed away in Alexandria when everyone else is fighting. Have you annoyed your senior officers by grumbles or criticism or something? We are a little anxious about you'.[100] His next letter, clearly written after receiving an indignant reply from his son, was more conciliatory, but hardly apologetic. He pointed out that he had not known that Clement was 'engaged on any work' in Egypt. 'I assumed that you were simply a gentleman at large … Honestly I am glad you are in Alexandria, provided of course that you are there without loss of honour'.[101] Honour, valour, bravery and other martial qualities were important to Ingleby as, no doubt, they were to many other civilian fathers[102] (Figure 17).

Nevertheless, middle-class fathers did not always act as unofficial recruiting sergeants, enthusiastically embracing and policing their sons' adherence to the dominant rhetoric of patriotic service and sacrifice, perhaps in the belief that even in the case of young men unsuited to military life, 'the adventure of the battlefield might be the making of [them]'.[103] Peter Barham suggests that this was the attitude taken by the father of George Major Gomm, a gentleman's hosier in a London department store, who suffered a mental breakdown after enlisting. According to Barham, 'we may surmise that [Gomm] … was bolstered by his father's patriotic ardour, and his desire to live up to the standards of manliness his father extolled'.[104] In reality, Gomm's father's feelings or attitudes have left no trace in the historical record and it is equally possible that he did his best to dissuade his son from enlisting.

The writer W. J. Dawson's reaction on hearing that his three sons wished to enlist, for example, was one of fear: 'the occasion crushed me and drew forth no answering courage'. It was only as he worried that 'if I allowed my fear for them to interfere with the natural energy of their desires, and if their affection for me induced them to submit to my wishes, was I not guilty of the emasculation of their manhood which must ensue?', that he

SON-WORSHIP

17 ‘Son-worship’, *The Bystander*, 28 June 1916. Reproduced with permission of the Bodleian Libraries, University of Oxford, Per.2705 d.161, p. 585.

gave his grudging consent to their enlistment.[105] The exchange between Arthur Burge and his father was thus probably fairly typical. Burge told his father: '"Look here, Father, I must enlist at once". He said, "Don't be silly, boy, you are not fit to be a soldier". I replied "Don't forget, Father, I went to Malvern College where they were very keen on the army". We were in the Officer Training Corps and if I didn't join up my name would be mud … He said, "I can't stop you but I think you're silly", so I said, "Well, I'm going to be silly then"'.[106]

While holding deeply conventional views on patriotism and manly conduct in wartime, Robinson was nevertheless a staunch defender of his civilian son's wartime record. In November 1914 he complained that 'there is a sort of persecution going on, and young men (who may have excellent reasons for not enlisting) are subject to reproaches and insults'. Writing in generalities, but obviously thinking of specific individuals, he was infuriated by 'girls [who] go about offering young men *white* feathers, and they write letters to their young men friends urging them to enlist and wanting to know the reasons for *not* doing so. These are the women, or some of them, who up till quite recently claimed equality with man, and who by their outrageous conduct and their immodest fashions in dress have done their utmost to bring themselves into contempt'.[107]

Robinson stressed his son's difficult position: although 'ready to go' he was repeatedly told by the Board of Trade that 'he could not be spared'.[108] At the end of 1915, again clearly thinking of his son, he was angry about the young men who, although 'indispensable', had nevertheless attested under the Derby scheme. There was no chance that they would be called up, but 'had the distinction of wearing one of the khaki armlets, and so … [saved themselves] from being regarded as … social pariah'.[109] The following year he was irritated by calls for 'comb-outs' of government departments: 'the people who make this suggestion are the first to complain of "inefficiency" of the Government offices', but the situation would hardly be helped 'if a lot of ignorant people are to replace officials who at least have been trained for their particular jobs'.[110] In April 1917, clearly exasperated by the mixture of personal and press attacks directed at young men like his son, he claimed that 'no one can say now, that he has not done his bit, and he has probably run greater risk of his life than if he were in the trenches'.[111]

By the time he was called up in April 1917 Lockwood felt thoroughly beleaguered, probably rather like Robinson's son. He wrote: 'the wishes of our good friends have been gratified for I received my papers this morning. I have to report on Saturday so I am sorry that I shall not be able to take part in the general rejoicing'.[112] That said, his father seems to have been unwavering in his support. Their relationship had been a close one even before the war, but his father's companionship clearly became increasingly important as the conflict went on, especially after his friend Arthur Wood joined up. They thus spent more and more time together, going for walks or to see 'shows' in nearby music-halls, at least until fears of police 'comb-outs' deprived Lockwood of any taste for such amusements. Even this did not mean an end to all outings. In March 1917, for example, 'Father and I went up to Mr and Mrs Baxter's tonight and I spent the most enjoyable evening I have had for a long time. Mr and Mrs Baxter are good company and their daughters entertained us with the piano and songs'.[113] His father's support was also important beyond his companionship during leisure hours: in June 1916 he accompanied Lockwood on a trip to Leeds to enquire about the possibility of enlisting with the Ordnance Survey Department.[114] The evening he finally received his call-up papers, Lockwood and his father went to 'the Palace' together for the first time in months, where they enjoyed 'a fairly good programme'.[115]

Even among men who would have found it more difficult than Lockwood's father to condone such reluctance to enlist on the part of their sons, the expression of conventional patriotic sentiments did not always entirely conceal the underlying ambivalence about sons' military service. Even Ingleby admitted in October 1914 that when he and his wife received the news that Clement was due to the Front, they found that 'hopes and fears alternate with us'. On the one hand, they hoped that 'you will bear yourself like a man', but on the other, they could hardly avoid 'the fear that anything may happen to you'.[116] Such ambivalence was also clear in a joint family letter sent in March 1915 to H. Carter, then serving in France with the Liverpool Regiment: 'We wish you to do your duty, but be careful, run no great risks'.[117]

A year later Charles Copeman had some advice for his son, steering a difficult course between caution and manly duty. He acknowledged that 'naturally we shall feel more anxious about you when you go abroad but you will I know do what you think right on the matter, but I suppose you need not go to the length of declining a job if offered simply because you think it a "soft job", although it would be different if you tried for one on that ground, but I suppose as a matter of fact you will not have much choice'.[118] After his son's death during the battle of the Somme, Roy Benson's father responded to a letter of condolence by making reference to conventional patriotic sentiments, stressing that 'grief is tempered by the knowledge that he willingly gave his young life, bravely fighting for the dear old country he loved so well'. Turning to write about his other son, however, the letter abruptly shifted away from the high diction of patriotic rhetoric. He too was 'a good lad, but as he was severely wounded in the jaw at Gallipoli, I sincerely trust that the war may be over before it again becomes his turn to face the bullets'.[119]

While adhering to the idea that it was the patriotic duty of every fit young man to volunteer his services to the armed forces, the reality of sons leaving for military service hit many middle-class (and no doubt other) fathers hard. In the village of Great Leighs in May 1916 Harry Taylor was on his last leave before 'going out'. His father, 'now a very old man, is very tender-hearted about his going'.[120] In November 1917 Gibbs finally received his call-up papers and found that for all his patriotic bluster, his father was hardly happy about his imminent departure: 'the poor old man is very worried about my going'.[121] Working as a chemist for a colliery firm, George Wilkinson was exempted from military service, but felt that he was not doing 'his bit', or at least that he was not doing 'enough', especially after the death of his brother, and joined up in January 1918. His parents 'didn't take very kindly' to the news. His mother had been 'broken-hearted' after 'losing' his brother and had broken down and cried when the time had come for his own departure. His father, on the other hand, had maintained a stoic front as he walked him to the station to see him off.[122]

The expectation of stoicism and strength from middle-class fathers was a powerful one. Robert Saunders, for example, sought to live up to such expectations when his son Ron enlisted in September 1914, implying that his attitude was different to that of his wife: 'Ma ... is very upset ... She doesn't understand what a sacrifice it is on his part and doesn't feel proud to have all her sons doing something for their country'.[123] In the following months he made frequent references to 'ma' being worried about their sons.[124] Behind this façade, however, Saunders had his own fears. In June 1915 he admitted that now that Ron was at the Front 'we are all very anxious as the fighting is now continuous and the losses simply appalling'.[125] Four months later he wrote that the 'terrible lists of casualties' made them all fear for Ron: 'you can't help feeling, sometimes that Ron's turn may come as well as others'.[126] In July 1916, a fortnight into the battle of the Somme, 'we are dreading the telegram that so many have received lately'.[127] By then Saunders was no longer making a secret of the fact that he was just as fearful and anxious as his wife: 'shan't we appreciate the peace when it comes and be able to go to bed without worrying about the boys'.[128]

The absence of the four adult sons left a significant and painful gap in the Saunders household. In January 1915 Saunders admitted that he was relieved when Christmas was over: 'of the many I remember it has been one of the least enjoyable … no boys for the first Christmas. What a difference it made you can imagine'.[129] Almost two years later he concluded a letter by wondering: 'shall we ever see you all home together. I do miss the Boys'.[130] Faced with a new distance between themselves and their sons, middle-class fathers could adopt a variety of strategies to narrow the gap. In some cases they sought to bridge the distance physically. Thus, in July 1917 Canon Gilpin told Clark 'that he was presently taking his holiday at Lowestoft to be near his "flying boy"'. He did not expect to have any difficulty finding accommodation, 'as that town (like other east coast towns) was deserted by visitors because of the air-raids': clearly this did not deter him from his desire to be near his 'boy'.[131]

However, such physical proximity to combatants was rarely an option and many middle-class fathers sought alternative ways of maintaining meaningful links with their sons. Periods of leave, marked by a son's brief return to the family fold, acquired a heightened significance for all involved. In December 1915 Saunders's son Ron was home on leave for the first time since seeing active service. Saunders observed that 'whatever newspaper writers may say you may take my word for it no one can ever look the same again after seeing the awful slaughter of a modern battle field, hearing the noise of a 1,000 guns firing high explosives, and living in the trenches'. Assuming the mantle of a slightly detached (but certainly not unfeeling) observer, Saunders 'sat and watched Ron when he first came home and tried to note the change in him … it made me feel awfully sad to note many things none of the others would notice in their delight in seeing him'. He was particularly moved by the fact that Ron spent a good deal of time in the attic, 'trying to reconstruct some of the scenes he had played there with Bob and Wally … I know he was always trying to form a mental picture of home to carry back with him'.[132]

In the bustle of a brief homecoming, with various claims made on the returning serviceman's attention, middle-class fathers such as Saunders could find themselves side-lined: it was the moment of arrival, or more often the moment of departure, which seems to have provided the best opportunity for closeness between fathers and sons. In January 1917 Saunders was touched by Ron's new 'freedom from shyness in showing his affection … When Ron arrived he put his arms right round me and hugged me and did the same when he left'.[133] The journey to and from the station or the bus stop at the start or the end of leave had especial significance for fathers: this was often the only moment when they had their son to themselves. Thus, the only diary entry marking Rory Macleod's son's leave in May 1915 was: 'to station to meet Jack (four days home)'.[134] One of George Cole's brothers spent the war in the Royal Field Artillery. Writing in 1990 Cole recalled that after periods of leave at home in Clapham, 'his return train always seemed to leave in the early hours of the morning when the only way to get to Victoria station (about four miles away) was to walk. My father used to accompany him'.[135]

Correspondence provided another important way of maintaining strong links with sons on active service, letters and parcels often accomplishing a good deal more than simply enabling fathers and sons to keep in touch.[136] Michael Roper notes that among family members, fathers were by far the least frequent recipients of letters from servicemen: in most cases, mothers were the main correspondents. However, as Roper points out, citing the example of Arnold Hooper's father's habit of sending copies of *The Architect* magazine to his son in Mesopotamia, lack of letters did not necessarily imply a distant or unloving relationship.[137] Furthermore, where fathers did write regularly to their sons on active service, the correspondence played an important part in cementing their relationship. It was through his letters – as well as, it seems, through conversations while his son was on leave – that Ingleby repeatedly sought to assert his continued (if relatively benign) paternal authority over Clement. In September 1914, having dealt with some business matters, he concluded a letter by telling his son: 'please don't send me to Amy for news. The idea of a fond father rushing off for news of his son to an unrelated family … is to place him in a lower position than that to which he is entitled or has a right to claim … if [Amy] … had the most interesting news in the world … I should not stoop to what would be an insult to myself to ask her to produce it'.[138]

Later the same month, following Clement's announcement that he wanted to get married, Ingleby reminded him of 'that talk we had at Dinner one night when you were most emphatic in your opinion that it was a shabby trick of a man to marry a girl and then [go] off to the war … Well. I won't bind you to your opinion'. However, he asked his son to 'turn over in your mind two other considerations'. Firstly, there was the possibility that the war might end quickly, and 'you will find yourself married to a girl without having any sufficient means to keep her'. Secondly, 'suppose you fall by the way – as I devoutly hope you won't – Then I shall have made over to a young woman whom I barely know a portion of the family property'. He stressed that 'I do not want to influence you against your own wishes, provided that you have looked at all contingencies in the face', although he could not help adding that 'I think this hurry to put your head in the noose has very little to recommend it', before acknowledging that 'I am not the chief actor – only adviser-in-chief, and you will now take your own course'.[139]

Ingleby did not hesitate to reprimand, as well as advise, when he thought the circumstances warranted it. In December 1914 he thus noted that 'you wrote to me some time ago saying you did not want money – and I am sorry to hear from the enclosed that you are not paying your way. We can all be rich men … if we don't pay our bills'. He had also received a letter from the bank: 'Is it a fact that you drew a cheque … after you had closed your account? … It is one thing to get into difficulties – such things are not unknown! It is another thing to do something … dishonourable … and which might bring you within the law'.[140] Most often, however, he sought to guide and influence Clement's behaviour in a more subtle way. In July 1915, for example, he tried to dissuade his son from returning to the navy, while assuring him (not entirely convincingly) that 'in all these matters you are old enough to judge for yourself, and you will act on your own after careful consideration'.[141] Clement's own marriage and fatherhood did not serve to demote Ingleby from his position as 'adviser-in-chief'. On the contrary, issues such as 'the question of the name for your boy', which in February 1916 was 'exercising the minds of the family', provided him with new opportunities to assert his fatherly wisdom and experience: 'it is recognised that your word is law in the matter, but I should like to take counsel with you so that you may give it further consideration … .'[142]

Not all fathers were as determined as Ingleby to use their correspondence to assert their paternal authority. Indeed, although the extent to which the notion of 'companionate fatherhood' had gained acceptance by 1914 should not be exaggerated, the final two decades of the nineteenth century had seen 'a shift towards more interactive and less authoritarian patterns of fatherhood'.[143] According to G. S. Street, 'the domestic authority enjoyed by parents and guardians … had been toppling for a long time', but the war had given this trend a further impulse: 'the young men are performing a man's task and a most vital one: who can forbid them to order their lives … in their own way?'[144] It is certainly the case that men such as Whitehead seem to have enjoyed a close and loving relationship with their sons, in ways far removed from the stereotypical image of the stern, unbending Edwardian paterfamilias.[145] In December 1915 he thus wrote to his wife that the previous day he had suffered from 'some twinges of rheumatism in my shoulder', but 'Eric looked after me like an angel'. Both their son and their daughter had been 'so kind', but it was Eric who was 'a genius at nursing', which was 'just like him'.[146] This affectionate relationship seems to have continued after Eric left for active service, fostered by news-filled letters to 'darling Eric' from 'your loving daddy'.[147] Indeed, alongside such expressions of love and concern, which suggest that emotional constraint was not always a feature of middle-class fatherhood,[148] the main thrust of fathers' letters seems to have been not an assertion of paternal authority, but an unhappy feeling of helplessness.

It had long been an expectation, for example, that middle-class fathers would use their resources and connections to help their sons establish their career, even to the extent of ensuring their placement in a business or a profession.[149] However, such networking and nepotism became a good deal more difficult, if not impossible, once sons entered the armed forces. Even Ingleby, despite his connections as an MP, found himself stymied. In October 1915 he responded to a request from Clement to help him get transferred to the navy by explaining that 'it is rather a curious circumstance, seeing that I have a large number of friends at the War Office, that I have none at the Admiralty. I am sending a line to Admiral Noel to see if he can help you'.[150] A month later he wrote that 'you mustn't think I neglect your naval … interests'. He had 'tried to get Admiral Noel to say a word for you, but the crusty old beggar wouldn't!'[151] Even for the minority of middle-class fathers who had the necessary connections to influential individuals, the problem was that attempts to secure favours for sons in the armed forces were increasingly frowned upon, in a significant reversal of pre-war practice. Thus, in January 1916 Ingleby assured Clement that 'I won't lose a chance of furthering your interests if it comes in my way', but added that 'I can't exactly hawk you about, for this scarcely comports with my dignity and might not help you'.[152] He returned to this theme a month later, explaining that although 'if I get the opportunity on my return to town I will not fail to push it home in your interests', this was not a straightforward matter: 'people are apt to look askance at a request to draw a comparatively young fellow from the fighting front unless there is some active reason for it'.[153]

As middle-class fathers found it increasingly difficult to pull strings or use their 'connections' in order to influence their sons' fates, many sought to find alternative ways of helping, or at least of ameliorating their circumstances: the practice of sending parcels of food, clothing, reading matter, cigarettes and other 'comforts' was perhaps the most important. Thus, H. Carter's parents asked their son in March 1915: 'is there anything you want in the way of underclothing, if so, perhaps we could get something to you, or any other thing'.[154] In October 1914 Ingleby asked his son, then interned in Holland, 'do you want cash or comforts? Let us know'.[155] Perhaps influenced by the many examples advertised in the press, including the 'Chemico' body shield, which promised protection against shrapnel, as well as against bayonet, lance or sword thrusts,[156] in November 1915 Ronald Craigie's father offered to send his son a 'shield'.[157] Macleod's diary was peppered with references to the purchase of various items for his two sons, including 'to Boots re Jack's field glasses',[158] 'ordered spurs for Rory',[159] 'to lamp shop and garage re registration for Rory's motorbike',[160] 'to Bacon's for cigarettes for Jack and his men'[161] and 'Boot's razor blades, for Jack 2/-'.[162]

However, the opportunities to help their sons provided by 'comforts' and other commodities were never entirely sufficient to counter many fathers' feelings of powerlessness, particularly when their sons were in trouble. Thus, there was little Thomas Stoddart could do when he and his wife heard that 'our dear son Arthur', had been wounded in the thigh and was 'seriously ill' in hospital in France. His health had slowly improved, which 'we were very pleased to hear as we have had quite an anxious time'.[163] However, the inaction clearly proved intolerable, particularly once the Stoddarts received the news that Arthur's leg was to be amputated, and they decided to travel to France and stay near his hospital 'till he is out of danger'.[164] Perhaps partly in unconscious acknowledgement of their own inability to ensure their son's safety, in March 1915 the Carters, a strongly religious family, ended a letter by entrusting his safety with God: 'good luck so good night and *God bless* you and keep you safe to return home'.[165]

In November 1915, after five weeks without receiving any news of their son's fate, the Goodwins finally heard that Walter ('Wallie') was in hospital in Egypt with an infected hand, which he had contracted at Gallipoli. During the time without any news Goodwin's father had kept busy on his son's behalf, but with little success: he had 'written everywhere but no one would, or could not tell us anything'.[166] Writing shortly after they had finally heard from Wallie, his father worked hard to re-establish meaningful links: not only by making arrangements for parcels of food and other 'comforts' to be sent to Egypt, but also in less obviously practical ways, by inviting his son to look back to a shared past and forward to a possible (and better) future. Thus, Wallie's father could 'well I remember twenty-three years ago today, when your mother presented me with a red haired rascal, but little did I think then that I should be writing, exactly twenty-three years after to that same red haired rascal, who had become a soldier in the greatest (and I hope last) war in the history of the world'.[167] A few days later he wrote that 'we are looking forward to your homecoming … when you will have a real good time'. Perhaps in response to a query he added that 'your ma says she will have a good meat pudding ready for you as soon as she knows you are coming home' and suggested that 'perhaps we will go and sample one of the famous 2/- portions of the "Cheshire cheese" Fleet Street made famous by the jovial spirits in Dr Johnson's time'.[168]

Throughout the conflict, middle-class fathers generally responded to fears for their sons' safety by *doing* something: in Goodwin's father's case, for example, by writing scores of letters to anybody he could think of. When Joyce Crow's family heard that her brother was 'missing, presumed killed', her 'father, because he was a journalist, pulled every string to try and find out whether he might still be alive'.[169] Bereaved middle-class fathers were also active in trying to find out more about the circumstances of their sons' deaths, seeking out, organising and passing on as much information as they could, from as many different sources as they could gather.[170] However, this tendency to take action should not obscure the helplessness many of them felt and the emotional impact of their inability to protect or help their sons. In October 1916 R. D. Blumenfeld, whose own son was in the military, stressed 'the anxiety, the tension, the feeling of helplessness that possesses those that are left behind merely to await the dreaded telegram'.[171] In response to his son's exhortation 'to be cheerful and keep my pecker up', Goodwin's father explained that 'I am not worrying about things at home, I can fight those as long as I have good health', but admitted that 'it is only natural … for your ma and myself, to feel ourselves so helpless, on your account, and as soon as we hear that you are homeward bound and in good health a great load will be taken off our minds'.[172]

The Goodwins's ordeal ended happily, with their son's recovery, but in other cases fathers' helplessness and realisation there was nothing they could *do* was further magnified, sometimes unbearably, by bereavement. As David Cannadine and other historians have shown, in the years following the end of the conflict many middle-class men, including bereaved fathers, were actively involved in the creation of war memorials and the development of Armistice Day rituals, as well as being among the proponents of a newly revitalised spiritualist movement.[173] However, for most fathers faced with the news of the death of their son (or, in some cases, sons), such actions – and any solace they may have brought – lay in the future.[174] Their immediate reaction seems often to have been one of helpless despair.[175] Thus, in November 1917 Saunders heard that one of their acquaintances had died: 'he has never been the same since his youngest son was killed and when Lu went to say goodbye he gave her the impression he had no wish to live and expected the end soon'.[176] Six months earlier, the Saunders's butcher had received an official envelope among the post. 'This he put down thinking it was from the War Office about sheep and cattle as he had had several'. He finally opened the letter at dinner time 'and found it was a notice to say Harry, the youngest boy, was killed in France'. His response was one of utter helplessness, for which no solace was possible: 'poor old Grover was so upset and can't seem to get over it, if any one tries to sympathise he stands and cries'.[177]

Conclusion

In December 1914 Butlin was training with the 3rd Battalion Dorsetshire Regiment, based at Wyke Regis. He looked forward to a visit from Burnett Hall, writing that 'I long to see you', particularly as 'most of the subalterns at Wyke are pretty boring fools and they doubtless think the same of me'.[178] It is difficult to believe that Butlin can have gone through his three-year military career without making any friends among his fellow junior officers, and yet this does not mean that the relationships he had formed before the war became any less important. For their part, despite heavy-handed jokes about 'shirking', middle-class civilians like Burnett Hall also seem to have valued and worked hard at maintaining links with those friends or relatives who had left to join the military. In fact, Burnett Hall and Butlin's friendship continued after the war. Having recently become engaged, in 1923 Butlin wrote to his mother that although Basil did not yet know the news, he had 'met Sarah out with me once and liked her very much'.[179] That his best friend should like his future wife clearly mattered to him.

If links between friends remained important during the war, those between family members were even more so, even as they came under increasing pressure. Of course, not all middle-class men fitted the mould of a responsible, family-loving husband or father. Frank Dawkins's father, 'full of beer and bounce' enlisted at the outbreak of war, despite being over age. He had 'decided that the war would only last three months and would be over by Christmas', unforgivably – in his son's eyes – leaving his family 'home on their own'.[180] Plenty of other men, however, were very conscious of the impact of the war on their families and were troubled by the disruption to established routines and practices, by the threats to the ability of the paterfamilias to support their family and by the sometimes long and painful periods of separation from loved ones. Indeed, it was not only sons who were an object of concern during the war. In August 1916, for example, William Hay Aitken, canon of Norwich cathedral, received a wire to say that his daughter Evelyn, at the time working as a nurse in Egypt, had been admitted to hospital. He worried that she 'would not have wired had she not been extremely and seriously unwell',[181] and waited anxiously for wires in the days that followed, unsure of the nature of the illness.[182] She seems to have recovered fairly quickly, and two months later was back in England. Aitken went up to London to see her: 'such a hug! She is looking wonderfully well. But oh how near we have been to losing her!'[183]

However, it was perhaps inevitable that as increasing numbers of young men were absorbed into the armed forces, the relationship between civilian fathers and combatant sons should acquire new meaning and significance. Middle-class men's pride in seeing their sons do their patriotic duty should not be underestimated, but it is clear that this was often accompanied by a deep unease, as fathers' protective and nurturing roles were undermined by the knowledge of the hardships and dangers that their sons were enduring. The prickly, undemonstrative father in J. M. Barrie's 1918 short story, who assured his son, about to leave for the front, that he would not be 'a funk', then blurted out: 'Mind you don't be rash my boy; and for God's sake, keep your head down in the trenches', seems to have reflected the reality of many fathers' feelings.[184] Opportunities to take action in order to assist their sons, furthermore, were felt to be limited and inadequate. Indeed, just as bereavement and the break-up of relationships led many middle-class men to acknowledge feelings of loneliness, highlighting further the importance of 'home' just as this was under threat, fathers like Grover the butcher were all too often forced to admit their utter powerlessness. At least for the time being, contrary to widely shared understandings of middle-class fatherhood and its responsibilities, there was nothing they could *do*.

Notes

1 Wartime Diaries of H. W. B. Joseph 1914–18 (hereafter Joseph Diaries), 21 April 1918, Ms. Top. Oxon. e.288, Special Collections, Bodleian Library, University of Oxford (hereafter Bodleian Special Collections), Oxford.
2 Of course, there are exceptions to this generalisation, such as the close and loving relationships that men like Harold Cossins had with their wives. Late Victorian male homosocial networks are considered in J. Tosh, *A Man's Place: Masculinity and the Middle-Class Home in Victorian England* (Yale University Press, New Haven, CT, 1999), pp. 186–90.
3 See Chapter 1 in this book.
4 Diary of R. W. M. Gibbs, 1914–20 (hereafter Gibbs Diary), 7 November 1914, Ms Eng. misc. c.161, Bodleian Special Collections.
5 *Ibid.*, 28 August 1917, Ms Eng. misc. c.192; 21 November 1917, Ms Eng. misc. c.195.
6 A. Clark War Diary, 'Echoes of the 1914 War in an Essex Village' (hereafter Clark Diary), 29 January 1915, Ms Eng. Hist. e.97, Bodleian Special Collections.
7 *Ibid.*, 28 September 1914, Ms Eng. Hist. e.89.
8 *Ibid.*, 9 November 1914, Ms Eng. Hist. e.91.
9 *Ibid.*, 15 May 1915, Ms Eng. Hist. e.103.
10 *Ibid.*, 25 December 1915, Ms Eng. Hist. e.116.
11 The Diary of Ernest R. Cooper, 'Nineteen Hundred and War Time', 28 July 1914 – 3 December 1918 (hereafter Cooper Diary), 3 September 1914, P.121, Department of Documents, Imperial War Museum (hereafter IWM Documents), London.
12 C. L. Craig (Revd), untitled, 16 November 1979, DF148, Liddle Collection (1914–18), Special Collections, Brotherton Library, Leeds University (hereafter Liddle Collection), Leeds.
13 F. T. Lockwood, 'Notes Written by F. T. Lockwood', 26 September 1914, 96/52/1, IWM Documents.
14 *Ibid.*, 21 November 1914.
15 *Ibid.*, 15 November 1915.
16 *Ibid.*, 29 April 1916.
17 The importance (and limitations) of 'bonding' and comradeship between servicemen is explored in J. Bourke, *Dismembering the Male: Men's Bodies, Britain and the Great War* (Reaktion Books, London, 1996), Chapter 3. See also J. Meyer, *Men of War: Masculinity and the First World War in Britain* (Palgrave Macmillan, Basingstoke, 2009), especially Chapters 2 and 5. Accounts of the relationship between combatants and civilians have often been influenced by post-war combatant memoirs and novels, particularly their portrayal of home leave as a moment of realisation of the new separation of servicemen from civilian life. See, for example, R. H. Mottram, *Sixty-four, Ninety-four!* (Chatto & Windus, London, 1925), Chapter 9.

Literary combatants' changing conceptions of friendship are explored in M. Saunders, 'Friendship and enmity in First World War literature', *Literature & History*, vol. 17, no. 1 (2008), pp. 62–77.

18 See, for example, M. Roper, *The Secret Battle: Emotional Survival in the Great War* (Manchester University Press, Manchester, 2009).

19 H. Gleave to E. Gleave, 12 February 1916, E. T. Gleave Letters, 78/31/1, IWM Documents.

20 *Ibid.*, 21 February 1916.

21 E. W. Hewish, 1917 Dairy and Accounts (hereafter Hewish Diary), 6 May 1917, 02/43/1, IWM Documents. See also Chapter 4 in this book.

22 *Ibid.*, 9 July 1917. Alfred Hewish was killed at the end of 1917.

23 'Dudley' to 'Dear Old Bottom' (A.G. Steavenson), 10 September 1916, A. G. Steavenson Letters, 86/77/1, IWM Documents.

24 J. H. Butlin to B. Burnett Hall, 10 August 1914, Letters of Lieutenant James H. Butlin (hereafter Butlin Letters), 67/52/1, IWM Documents.

25 *Ibid.*, 20 September 1914.

26 *Ibid.*, 10 August 1914.

27 *Ibid.*, 13 December 1914.

28 *Ibid.*, 23 June 1915.

29 *Ibid.*, 9 December 1915.

30 *Ibid.*, 1 January 1916.

31 *Ibid.*, 15 January 1916.

32 *Ibid.*, 20 January 1916.

33 *Ibid.*, 7 May 1915. The importance to servicemen of food sent from home is emphasised, for example, in Roper, *The Secret Battle*, pp. 125–30.

34 J. H. Butlin to B. Burnett Hall, 19 July 1915, Butlin Letters, 67/52/1, IWM Documents.

35 *Ibid.*, 23 October 1915.

36 See, for example, *ibid.*, 22 May 1915; 19 April 1917.

37 *Ibid.*, 8 October 1916.

38 *Ibid.*, 21 March 1917.

39 *Ibid.*, 16 April 1917.

40 *Ibid.*, 11 May 1917; 26 June 1917.

41 *Ibid.*, 11 May 1917.

42 P. Ashton Murray interview, 14 October 1985, 9114, reel 1, Department of Sound, Imperial War Museum (hereafter IWM Sound), London. Of course, there were also middle-class men who neglected or mistreated their families. See, for example, J. Benson, *The Wolverhampton Tragedy: Death and the 'Respectable' Mr Lawrence* (Carnegie, Lancaster, 2009).

43 F. A. Robinson, 'Diary of the Great War', 'Prefatory note', 15 November 1918, vol. 1, P.401, IWM Documents.

44 Holcombe Ingleby to Clement, 15 October 1914, The First World War Letters of Holcombe Ingleby MP (hereafter Ingleby Letters), P.343, IWM

Documents. See also the rather scathing comments about the new opportunities provided by the war to 'women of means' and the general 'rushing about on war work' in E. S. Pankhurst, *The Home Front* (The Cresset Library, London, 1987, first published 1932), pp. 38–9. The notions of 'service' embraced by the various members of one well-to-do middle-class family, the Beales of Standen, are explored by J. S. K. Watson, *Fighting Different Wars: Experience, Memory and the First World War in Britain* (Cambridge University Press, Cambridge, 2004), Chapter 4.

45 Clark Diary, 7 July 1916, Ms Eng. Hist. e.128, Bodleian Special Collections.

46 For husbands' power within the middle-class family, see A. J. Hammerton, *Cruelty and Companionship: Conflict in Nineteenth-Century Married Life* (Routledge, London, 1992), especially Chapter 5. The impact of war on 'authority' within working-class families is considered briefly in R. Wall, 'English and German families in the First World War', in R. Wall and J. Winter (eds), *The Upheaval of War: Family, Work and Welfare in Europe, 1914–1918* (Cambridge University Press, Cambridge, 1988), pp. 93–8. See also C. Rollet, 'The home and family life', in J. Winter and J.-L. Robert (eds), *Capital Cities at War: Paris, London, Berlin 1914–1919 Volume 2: A Cultural History* (Cambridge University Press, Cambridge, 2007), pp. 315–53 and S. Pedersen, *Family, Dependence, and the Origins of the Welfare State: Britain and France, 1914–1945* (Cambridge University Press, Cambridge, 1993), Chapter 2.

47 H. C. Cossins Diary, 1914–18 (hereafter Cossins Diary), 2 February 1917, PP/MCR/371, IWM Documents.

48 A. Bradburn to S. Bradburn, 14 December 1915, Letters from Alfred Bradburn to his brother Samuel (hereafter Bradburn Letters), 95/16/1, IWM Documents.

49 *Ibid.*, 16 January 1916.

50 W. L. McIvor, Recollections, October 1978, DF148, Liddle Collection.

51 C. Copeman to T. Copeman, 30 April 1916 [the letter mistakenly gives the date as 1915], Letters to Tom Copeman from Family Members, 1916 (hereafter Copeman Letters), MC81/26/405–8, Norfolk Record Office, Norwich.

52 N. Whitehead to wife ('Darling'), 15 December 1915, N. Whitehead, Letters, DF141, Liddle Collection.

53 Cooper Diary, 11 December 1914, P.121, IWM Documents.

54 *Ibid.*, 22 February 1915.

55 *Ibid.*, May 1915. For a description of the Zeppelin raid, see *ibid.*, 15–16 April 1915.

56 *Ibid.*, 12 November 1917.

57 Robinson, 'Diary of the Great War', 26 August 1918, vol. 4, P.402, IWM Documents.

58 *Ibid.*, 3 September 1918.
59 J. Munson (ed.), *Echoes of the Great War: The Diary of the Reverend Andrew Clark 1914–1919* (Oxford University Press, Oxford, 1985), p. 122.
60 *Ibid.*, p. 147. She died two months later, in October 1916. See p. 164.
61 Cossins Diary, 31 October 1915, PP/MCR/371, IWM Documents.
62 *Ibid.*, 10 November 1915.
63 *Ibid.*, 10 December 1915.
64 *Ibid.*, 1 January 1916.
65 *Ibid.*, 9 October 1916.
66 *Ibid.*, 11 November 1916.
67 Munson (ed.), *Echoes of the Great War*, p. 167.
68 Cossins Diary, 18 June 1916, PP/MCR/371, IWM Documents.
69 Joseph Diaries, 5 January 1916, Ms. Top. Oxon. e.288, Bodleian Special Collections.
70 *Ibid.*, 7 February 1917.
71 *Ibid.*, 25 June 1917.
72 McIvor, Recollections, October 1978, DF148, Liddle Collection. Women's relationships with combatant brothers are explored in A. Woollacott, 'Sisters and brothers in arms: family, class, and gendering in World War One Britain', in M. Cooke and A. Woollacott (eds), *Gendering War Talk* (Princeton University Press, Princeton, NJ, 1993), pp. 128–47.
73 T. R. Attwater, 'A Civilian Remembers', not dated, DF005, Liddle Collection.
74 Cossins Diary, 28 December 1915, PP/MCR/371, IWM Documents.
75 *Ibid.*, 30 December 1915.
76 J. Winter, *Sites of Memory, Sites of Mourning: The Great War in European Cultural History* (Cambridge University Press, Cambridge, 1995), p. 51.
77 Cossins Diary, 31 December 1915, PP/MCR/371, IWM Documents.
78 Clark Diary, 31 August 1914, Ms Eng. Hist. e.88, Bodleian Special Collections.
79 For 'patriotic motherhood' and the ambivalent responses it evoked, see N. F. Gullace, *'The Blood of our Sons': Men, Women and the Renegotiation of British Citizenship during the First World War* (Palgrave Macmillan, Basingstoke, 2002), Chapter 3.
80 Clark Diary, 19 October 1914, Ms Eng. Hist. e.90, Bodleian Special Collections. It is worth noting that Murray also wanted to get his daughter 'Gerty away for a time, but she won't go'.
81 Cossins Diary, 16 June 1915, PP/MCR/371, IWM Documents.
82 Cooper Diary, 3 May 1917, P.121, IWM Documents. Cooper had the exit added 'so that in the event of another bombardment we could get down there safely without running so much risk of being buried alive'.
83 For fathers' protective role see also, for example, M. Doolittle, 'Fatherhood, religious belief and the protection of children in nineteenth-century English

families', in T. L. Broughton and H. Rogers (eds), *Gender and Fatherhood in the Nineteenth Century* (Palgrave Macmillan, Basingstoke, 2007), pp. 31–42.

84 H. Maingay (Dr), untitled, not dated, DF148, Liddle Collection. Maingay was born in 1906.

85 M. Daunton, *Wealth and Welfare: An Economic and Social History of Britain 1851–1951* (Oxford University Press, Oxford, 2007), pp. 339–40. See also C. Nelson, *Invisible Men: Fatherhood in Victorian Periodicals, 1850–1910* (University of Georgia Press, Athens, GA, 1995), especially Chapter 2; S. Humphries and P. Gordon, *A Labour of Love: The Experience of Parenthood in Britain 1900–1950* (Sidgwick and Jackson, London, 1993), pp. 92, 175; A. A. Jackson, *The Middle Classes 1900–1950* (David St John Thomas Publisher, Nairn, 1991), pp. 154, 171, 173.

86 T. L. Broughton and H. Rogers, 'Introduction: the empire of the father', in Broughton and Rogers (eds), *Gender and Fatherhood*, p. 5. The relationship between Victorian fathers and their children is explored in Tosh, *A Man's Place*, Chapter 4.

87 Cossins Diary, 24 June 1915, PP/MCR/371, IWM Documents. John was then five years old.

88 *Ibid.*, 14 January 1916.

89 *Ibid.*, 5 February 1916.

90 *Ibid.*, 17 October 1916.

91 *Ibid.*, 23 October 1916.

92 Fathers' adoption of a more hands-on, nurturing role with their children was not unproblematic. See T. Sabatos, 'Father as mother: the image of the widower with children in Victorian art', in Broughton and Rogers (eds), *Gender and Fatherhood*, pp. 71–84. See also M. Marwick, 'Hands-on fatherhood in Trollope's novels', in Broughton and Rogers (eds), *Gender and Fatherhood*, pp. 85–95; Tosh, *A Man's Place*, p. 87.

93 Gibbs Diary, 31 January 1917, Ms Eng. misc. c.185, Bodleian Special Collections. Gibbs rarely mentioned his wife, although he regularly wrote about his children.

94 *Ibid.*, 5 July 1917, Ms Eng. misc. c.191.

95 *Ibid.*, 9 November 1917, Ms Eng. misc. c.195. The impact on children of fathers leaving for the front is vividly illustrated in R. Van Emden and S. Humphries, *All Quiet on the Home Front: An Oral History of Life in Britain during the First World War* (Headline, London, 2003), pp. 30–2.

96 Fathers' ambivalent attitudes towards their sons' enlistment is a theme explored in a number of the novels written during the war by civilian authors. See, for example, H. A. Vachell, *The Soul of Susan Yellam* (Cassell and Co., London, 1918), which was dedicated 'to the memory of my son, Richard Tanfield Vachell captain, fifth fusiliers'; H. G. Wells, *Mr Britling Sees it Through* (The Hogarth Press, London, 1985, first published 1916).

97 Gibbs Diary, 9 November 1917, Ms Eng. misc. c.173, Bodleian Special Collections.
98 *Ibid.*, 26 May 1916, Ms Eng. misc. c.177. It is worth noting that Tinniswood had just made an application for exemption on Gibbs's behalf. See 18 May 1916.
99 Holcombe Ingleby to Clement, 1 July 1915, Ingleby Letters, P.343, IWM Documents.
100 *Ibid.*, 5 July 1915.
101 *Ibid.*, 9 July 1915.
102 See also, for example, *ibid.*, 3 June 1916.
103 P. Barham, *Forgotten Lunatics of the Great War* (Yale University Press, New Haven, CT, 2004), p. 15.
104 *Ibid.*, pp. 15, 178–80.
105 W. J. Dawson, *The Father of a Soldier* (John Lane, The Bodley Head, London, 1918), pp. 78, 93. The book follows Dawson's growing acceptance of his sons' military service as 'the highest duty which the soul can recognise'. See pp. 196–7.
106 Quoted in Emden and Humphries, *All Quiet on the Home Front*, p. 24. Burge was rejected as physically unfit for military service. See also p. 25.
107 Robinson, 'Diary of the Great War', 10 November 1914, vol. 1, P.401, IWM Documents.
108 *Ibid.*, 26 October 1915.
109 *Ibid.*, 29 December 1915.
110 *Ibid.*, 20 September 1916, vol. 2, P.401. See also *ibid.*, 29 January 1917, vol. 3, P.402.
111 *Ibid.*, 23 April 1917.
112 Lockwood, 'Notes', 23 April 1917, 96/52/1, IWM Documents.
113 *Ibid.*, 10 March 1917.
114 *Ibid.*, 1–2 June 1916.
115 *Ibid.*, 23 April 1917.
116 Holcombe Ingleby to Clement, 4 October 1914, Ingleby Letters, P.343, IWM Documents.
117 Father, mother, brother and sisters to H. Carter, 13 March 1915, H. Carter Collection, 86/8/1, IWM Documents.
118 C. Copeman to T. Copeman, 30 April 1916 [the letter mistakenly gives the date as 1915], Copeman Letters, MC81/26/405–8, Norfolk Record Office.
119 Quoted in F. Meeres, *Norfolk in the First World War* (Phillimore, Chichester, 2004), p. 39.
120 Clark Diary, 16 May 1915, Ms Eng. Hist. e.103, Bodleian Special Collections.
121 Gibbs Diary, 9 November 1917, Ms Eng. misc. c.195, Bodleian Special Collections.
122 G. D. Wilkinson interview, 9104, reel 4, IWM Sound.

123 R. Saunders to son, 7 September 1914, R. Saunders, Letters to Son in Canada, 1914–18 (hereafter Saunders Letters), 79/15/1, IWM Documents. The importance of self-control in defining nineteenth-century middle-class male gentility is discussed in L. Young, *Middle-Class Culture in the Nineteenth Century: America, Australia and Britain* (Palgrave Macmillan, Basingstoke, 2003), especially Chapter 4.
124 See, for example, R. Saunders to son, 27 February 1915, Saunders Letters, 79/15/1, IWM Documents.
125 *Ibid.*, 14 June 1915.
126 *Ibid.*, 17 October 1915.
127 *Ibid.*, 16 July 1916.
128 *Ibid.*, 11 March 1917. For the wartime challenge to the 'rigid stoicism' of 'Victorian fatherhood', see J. Damousi, *The Labour of Loss: Mourning, Memory and Wartime Bereavement in Australia* (Cambridge University Press, Cambridge, 1999), pp. 46–64.
129 R. Saunders to son, 11 January 1915, Saunders Letters, 79/15/1, IWM Documents.
130 *Ibid.*, 18 November 1916.
131 Clark Diary, 30 July 1917, Ms Eng. Hist. e.151, Bodleian Special Collections. By 'flying boy' he meant a son in the Royal Flying Corps.
132 R. Saunders to son, 12 December 1915, Saunders Letters, 79/15/1, IWM Documents.
133 *Ibid.*, 27 January 1917.
134 R. H. Macleod Diary, 21 May 1915, R. H. Macleod Papers, DF087, Liddle Collection.
135 G. W. Cole, 'Some Recollections of the 1914–18 War', January 1990, DF148, Liddle Collection.
136 Meyer, *Men of War*, p. 15.
137 Roper, *The Secret Battle*, pp. 60–3.
138 Holcombe Ingleby to Clement, 8 September 1914, Ingleby Letters, P.343, IWM Documents.
139 *Ibid.*, 29 September 1914.
140 *Ibid.*, 17 December 1914.
141 *Ibid.*, 23 July 1915.
142 *Ibid.*, 14 February 1916.
143 Tosh, *A Man's Place*, p. 163.
144 G. S. Street, *At Home in the War* (William Heinemann, London, 1918), p. 78.
145 Tosh, *A Man's Place*, pp. 162–8.
146 N. Whitehead to wife ('Darling'), 15 December 1915, N. Whitehead, Letters, DF141, Liddle Collection.
147 N. Whitehead to E. Whitehead, 28 February 1918, N. Whitehead, Letters, DF141, Liddle Collection.

148 Damousi, *The Labour of Loss*, p. 48.
149 J. M. Quail, 'From personal patronage to public school privilege: social closure in the recruitment of managers in the United Kingdom from the late nineteenth century to 1930', in A. Kidd and D. Nicholls (eds), *The Making of the British Middle Class? Studies of Regional and Cultural Diversity since the Eighteenth Century* (Sutton Publishing, Stroud, 1998), pp. 169–85.
150 Holcombe Ingleby to Clement, 1 October 1915, Ingleby Letters, P.343, IWM Documents.
151 *Ibid.*, 6 November 1915.
152 *Ibid.*, 21 January 1916.
153 *Ibid.*, 11 February 1916.
154 Father and mother to H. Carter, 6 March 1915, H. Carter Collection, 86/8/1, IWM Documents.
155 Holcombe Ingleby to Clement, 4 October 1914, Ingleby Letters, P.343, IWM Documents.
156 L. Ugolini, *Men and Menswear: Sartorial Consumption in Britain, 1880–1939* (Ashgate, Aldershot, 2007), p. 162.
157 R. Craigie to mother, 28 November 1915, R. Craigie Letters, BT92/49, Herefordshire Record Office, Hereford.
158 R. H. Macleod Diary, 29 August 1914, R. H. Macleod Papers, DF087, Liddle Collection.
159 *Ibid.*, 29 May 1915.
160 *Ibid.*, 15 June 1915.
161 *Ibid.*, 3 August 1915.
162 *Ibid.*, 20 September 1915.
163 Clark Diary, 17 October 1917, Ms Eng. Hist. e.155, Bodleian Special Collections.
164 *Ibid.*, 30 November 1917, Ms Eng. Hist. e.156. For the arrangements to travel to France, see 4 December 1917, Ms Eng. Hist. e.157. Arthur Stoddart survived the operation and in May 1918 was back at home with his parents. See 15 May 1918, Ms Eng. Hist. e.163.
165 Father, mother, brother and sister to H. Carter, 13 March 1915, H. Carter Collection, 86/8/1, IWM Documents. Carter was killed a month later.
166 'Ma' to 'Wallie', 4 November 1915, W. A. Goodwin Collection, Con Shelf, IWM Documents.
167 'Dadd' to 'Wallie', 4 November 1915, W. A. Goodwin Collection, Con Shelf, IWM Documents.
168 *Ibid.*, 7 November 1915.
169 Quoted in Emden and Humphries, *All Quiet on the Home Front*, p. 94.
170 Work on the Australian experience of the First World War is especially illuminating. P. Jalland, *Australian Ways of Death: A Social and Cultural History 1840–1918* (Oxford University Press, Melbourne, 2002), pp. 322–5; Damousi, *The Labour of Loss*, p. 60. See also the 'consolation of knowledge'

provided by letters of condolence sent by the military, examined in Meyer, *Men of War*, pp. 84–95.

171 R. D. Blumenfeld, *All in a Lifetime* (Ernest Benn, London, 1931), p. 63.

172 'Dadd' to 'Wallie', 7 November 1915, W. A. Goodwin Collection, Con Shelf, IWM Documents. Goodwin survived the war and was demobilised in 1919.

173 D. Cannadine, 'War and death, grief and mourning in modern Britain', in J. Whaley (ed.), *Mirrors of Mortality: Studies in the Social History of Death* (Europa Publications, London, 1981), pp. 187–242. See also A. Carden-Coyne, *Reconstructing the Body: Classicism, Modernism and the First World War* (Oxford University Press, Oxford, 2009), p. 127; S. Goebel, *The Great War and Medieval Memory: War, Remembrance and Medievalism in Britain and Germany, 1914–1940* (Cambridge University Press, Cambridge, 2007), pp. 188–9; Damousi, *The Labour of Loss*, pp. 52–64; P. Jalland, *Death in the Victorian Family* (Oxford University Press, Oxford, 1996), pp. 372–81; J. Winter, *Sites of Memory, Sites of Mourning: The Great War in European Cultural History* (Cambridge University Press, Cambridge, 1995), especially Chapters 3 and 4.

174 See also the often overlooked post-war 'silent' grief identified in Jalland, *Australian Ways of Death*, pp. 320–2.

175 For the loneliness of many fathers' grief, see also Roper, *The Secret Battle*, pp. 219–20. See also J.-M. Strange, '"Speechless with grief": bereavement and the working-class father, c. 1880–1914', in Broughton and Rogers (eds), *Gender and Fatherhood*, pp. 138–49. Jay Winter also stresses the solace of action. Winter, *Sites of Memory, Sites of Mourning*, p. 34. The 'suppression' of emotion is emphasised in Van Emden and Humphries, *All Quiet on the Home Front*, pp. 104–7.

176 R. Saunders to son, 16 November 1917, Saunders Letters, 79/15/1, IWM Documents. See also Meeres, *Norfolk*, p. 36.

177 R. Saunders to son, 20 May 1917, Saunders Letters, 79/15/1, IWM Documents.

178 J. H. Butlin to B. Burnett Hall, 27 December 1914, Butlin Letters, 67/52/1, IWM Documents.

179 J. H. Butlin to mother, 4 October 1923, Butlin Letters, 67/52/1, IWM Documents.

180 F. Dawkins to P. Liddle, 16 March 1986, DF148, Liddle Collection.

181 Canon W. Hay Aitken Diary, 8 August 1916, MC2165/1/25, Norfolk Record Office, Norwich.

182 *Ibid.*, 9 August 1916; 10 August 1916.

183 *Ibid.*, 14 October 1916.

184 J. M. Barrie, 'The new word', in T. Tate (ed.), *Women, Men and the Great War: An Anthology of Stories* (Manchester University Press, Manchester, 1995), p. 237.

Conclusion

Writing in 1940, Robert Graves and Alan Hodge asserted that at the Armistice 'there were no scenes in the trenches even remotely resembling those that took place at home. There the lighter-hearted part of the population ran mad … There were extraordinary scenes of joviality. Guns captured in battle were pulled in procession round the towns to which they had been officially presented and pushed off bridges or quays. Sexual affairs between perfect strangers took place promiscuously in parks, shop entrances and alleyways'.[1] Later historians have concurred with this image of unrestrained celebration on the home front. According to John Bourne, for example, the end of the war was greeted on the home front 'with ecstatic relief. Factories stopped work. Children were sent home from school. Crowds spilled on to the streets. Social inhibitions were cast aside. Sexual restraint collapsed … it was time to rejoice'.[2] At the same time, accounts of the Armistice also stress the presence on the home front of bereaved individuals (mostly women) who 'unable to forget the ubiquitous tragedy of the war, found it impossible to share in celebration', and for whom 11 November 1918 was a day of isolation and grief.[3]

Neither the extremes of unrestrained celebration nor of lonely sorrow seem to have been the experience of Armistice of most middle-class civilian men. They must, of course, have formed at least a proportion of the people who travelled to town and city centres across the country immediately or soon after hearing the news of the end of the war: it is estimated, for example, that around 100,000 people 'flocked to London upon the news of the Armistice in 1918, and continued to do so for several subsequent days'.[4] Many, no doubt, behaved less than impeccably. And yet most middle-class men tended to portray themselves as *spectators* to the celebrations, rather than as active participants. Shifting attention for a moment north of the border, for example, Thomas Livingstone noted in his diary that on 11 November there were 'Great scenes in Glasgow. Took Agnes and Tommy [his wife and young son] into town to see the sights. City packed'.[5] Others too emphasised their role as observers rather than as contributors to the mayhem. According to Frank Dawkins 'the end of the war came without warning'. Shouts were heard through the office window that the Armistice had been signed and 'everyone just left work and went mad'. His own behaviour seems to have been remarkably sedate: 'I went home and after a meal sallied off down to the west to see the excitement and buy the special editions of midday papers confirming it was all over'.[6] Fourteen-year-old George Cole was among those who thought 'it would be fun to go up to Buckingham Palace to see what was happening there and I was one of a huge crowd standing outside the Palace when the Royal Family came out onto the balcony'. Equally memorable, however, was the fact that 'I then had to walk back to Clapham in the pouring rain arriving home soaked to the skin'.[7]

It was often servicemen, rather than civilians, who were perceived as indulging in the wildest celebrations on the home front. In the Suffolk town of Southwold the first sign of the Armistice was the arrival of a noisy car 'full of mad officers, cheering, waving flags and blowing trumpets', while later 'some soldiers came up on a wagon with the Kaiser in effigy, which they tied to the town pump and burnt amidst cheers'.[8] Not everywhere, furthermore, were celebrations unrestrained. Andrew Clark noted the joy and 'excitement' with which the news of the Armistice was greeted in Great Leighs and surrounding towns and villages: schools (the ones that were not closed because of the influenza epidemic) were given a holiday, work was interrupted, flags were hung out and church bells rung. Felsted, where 'the schoolboys paraded the village with their band and a very large flag, cheering', and 'nearly every house had hung out a flag', seems to have been typical of local celebrations.[9]

Although the Armistice appears to have come as a surprise to some on the home front, by the end of October 1918 the continued Allied advances on the Western Front had already begun to give people hope that the war would end soon. However, as Horace Joseph observed: 'last year we rang the bells for the … victory at Cambrai – it taught us a lesson'. He added that in Oxford 'there seems to be singularly little sign of elation now. One feels relief, and a sense of difficult days impending. Partly it may be that there is so much illness at home just now'. The mortality rates in Oxford, he pointed out, were the highest 'of any provincial town in the country. But I think it is chiefly because men feel so deeply how great has been the … sacrifice'.[10] The impact of the influenza epidemic on the mood on the home front during the last month of war should not be underestimated: by May 1919 the death-toll in Britain had reached approximately 200,000.[11] In October 1918 Clark was among those who noted that many people in the nearby villages had fallen ill, some of them seriously.[12] Frederick Robinson observed that 'our [war] casualties for many weeks past have been enormous … The hospitals are full to overflowing', and 'to crown it all there is a very serious outbreak of influenza which is claiming thousands of victims, and which is probably due to insufficient food and warmth'.[13]

In Southwold the epidemic reached its peak during late October and early November 1918: 'several deaths occurred … whole families were in bed at once and it spread in the most wholesale manner'. Ernest Cooper's wife and daughter caught it, although Cooper himself 'had one day in bed but escaped the real thing'.[14] Thus, on 9 November he noted that 'it is strange how quietly everyone here is taking the sudden prospect of an early peace, either owing to the sickness everywhere or to the people having steeled themselves to another and harder winter of war and not wishing to shout until well outside the wood'.[15] He was at work on 11 November when the County Adjutant called him to say that the Armistice had been signed. 'I did not take it in at first and could hear him shouting "War is Over" at the other end … the bells began to ring and a few of us adjourned to the Mayor's house and cracked some bottles of fizz … we went to a short thanksgiving service at the church and nearly all work was knocked off for the day, but the town took it very quietly on the whole'.[16]

Images of middle-class men indulging in ridiculous acts, such as the 'men wearing silk hats and frock coats' marching in fours, 'headed by a "band" whose instruments consisted of tin-kettles containing stones … these men – one can hardly believe – were members of the Stock Exchange, the most cautious and crafty of beings', spotted by the journalist Michael McDonagh in London,[17] should not obscure the complexity of feelings with which news of the Armistice was greeted. McDonagh himself was shocked by his own response. He felt no upsurge of joy, but rather 'a melancholy took possession of me when I came to realise … that a great and unique episode in my life was past and gone … to-morrow we return to the monotonous and the humdrum'.[18] Many recorded a sense of disbelief that the war might really be over. Writing on the day of the Armistice, Robinson found it 'impossible to realise that we are … at peace at last',[19] while Joseph used very similar words: he 'could hardly realise' that the war had finally ended, 'and I felt as ready to weep as to cheer'.[20]

As Adrian Gregory points out, most families were able greet the news of the Armistice with the relief of knowing that loved ones *would* be returning home from the war.[21] 'Mr Sam. Woodirvin, Great Waltham', who happened to be in Great Leighs Post Office when news of the end of hostilities came through, 'said he might now hope to have back undamaged his son who had been at the front in France for four years'.[22] According to Cyril Winchcombe, on the evening of 11 November his family was 'sitting happily by the fireside when the doorbell rang': it was his brother Fred, who had been demobilised early that very morning from the Curragh camp in Ireland.[23] Not all families were quite so lucky, but those like Richard Attwater's could nevertheless be 'very relieved … to know that in due time … [his brothers] Harry and John would come home'.[24] Even those like Cooper who had no immediate relatives in the armed forces felt it a 'happiness to go to bed at night without any dread of what might happen before morning'.[25]

However, it is not surprising that in the days that followed the Armistice thoughts should turn to wartime losses. On 25 November Clark wrote to the Bodleian librarian, informing him that 'not many of the lads who went out from this district are left to come back. The Flanders campaign was very deadly this year to our lads, and Palestine and Salonika have also taken victims on the field or in hospital'.[26] News of deaths on or close to the Armistice acquired new and painful meaning, even when they did not involve close relatives. Cooper was much struck by the contrast between the general jubilation and the 'only sad event' on the day of the Armistice: the funeral of a fellow Volunteer Training Corps (VTC) member, a well-liked man who had died of the influenza, aged only thirty-seven.[27] On the afternoon of 11 November Clark heard that 'young Louis Wright, aet. 19', had just died in hospital at Sheerness of double pneumonia.[28] He had been home on leave only a few days earlier, when Clark had observed that 'in his khaki he looks very diminutive'.[29] He was, he added, the Wrights' 'only son'.[30] Sadness and grief, however, were by no means middle-class civilian men's only response to the end of hostilities. In December 1918 Cooper decided to put his war diary away: 'I think I may well bring this record to a close here with a heartfelt thankfulness at being spared to see so glorious a finish to such a stupendous war and such grand prospects for a great future for the British Empire'.[31] There is no doubt that Cooper, like many others, had thought the war an 'awful nightmare' and a 'dreadful thing',[32] but in the immediate aftermath of the conflict it was widely felt that far from having been tarnished, patriotic values had in fact been vindicated by victory.

That said, the cultural primacy of values associated with patriotism and the military had not been an inevitable outcome of the conflict. Indeed, as this book has argued, the majority of middle-class men who did *not* volunteer their services to the armed forces in 1914 or 1915, or who applied for exemption after the introduction of conscription, justified their decision by reference to an alternative notion of manliness, one that stressed the link between masculinity, work and family responsibilities. It was only in 1916 that the climate of opinion seems to have decisively shifted, and the claims of patriotism, country and military comradeship proved more powerful than those of hearth, home and family. Far from having become 'disillusioned', by the end of the war most middle-class men had come to accept and even embrace a notion of manliness that placed a high value on military service and patriotism. However, this was no longer the muscular, adventurous and sporting manliness that had been endorsed by so many public schools and other voluntary organisations before the war.[33] Rather, as Ana Carden-Coyne suggests, the notion of manliness to emerge from the conflict was one that had been 'reframed … around pain and sacrifice'.[34] Indeed, it was to such an understanding of manliness, linked to unselfish service and suffering, which middle-class civilian men sought to stake their claim.

As many middle-class civilians saw it in 1918, a disproportionate amount of wartime pain and sacrifice had been theirs. They felt that they had been compelled to shoulder much of the regulatory and financial burdens of the war, enduring an unprecedented loss of income and erosion to their standard of living, while 'others' had not only made little contribution to the war effort, but had either undermined or taken advantage of it to enrich themselves. The sincerely held middle-class belief in a nation united against a common enemy was thus constantly undermined by a wide range of unpatriotic and unscrupulous 'others', who could range from profiteering capitalist magnates to (working-class) soldiers' wives. A good deal of anger was also directed at young unmarried men who were thought to be avoiding doing their 'bit'. All too easily, furthermore, criticism of 'some' young 'shirkers' who lounged about at their leisure, having somehow managed to avoid military service or other war work, could slip into a condemnation of the youth of the country, who, it was complained, left the older generation to shoulder most of the burden of war. However, the most significant of middle-class wartime *bêtes noires* were 'millionaire' munitions workers, who – it was thought – not only benefited from munificent wages, but also spent their money freely on scarce commodities, blithely ignoring economy appeals, while most middle-class incomes declined and middle-class families faced unprecedented hardships.[35]

Middle-class civilian men may truly have truly believed that they had been forced to bear more than their fair share of the burdens of war, but their efforts to stake a claim for wartime manliness based on notions of suffering and sacrifice rarely paid off. Part of the problem was that in a context where sacrifice was the ultimate virtue, civilian suffering was hardly comparable to that of combatants. As Jay Winter points out, during the war 'all other social questions were measured, in part, by reference to … the harsh realities faced by the men at the front'. Given the comparison, people on the English home front, whatever the hardships they may have faced, would always be in a 'privileged' position, at least 'as long as the killing went on'.[36] In August 1916 the gloomy man who complained in a *Punch* cartoon: 'shocking business this rise in food-prices', was dismissed as a 'professional grievance-monger'. As the 'British mother' pointed out: 'all I know is they're feeding my boys at the front all right, and that's good enough for me'. Indeed, as the title of the cartoon put it, the well-being of combatants was 'The thing that matters' (Figure 18). As Robinson observed six months later, the average 'John Jones' was 'not even allowed to grumble'. If he did, he was soon told 'to think of the sacrifices of the men in the trenches and be ashamed. To this argument there is no answer and it is being freely used'.[37]

The comparison with combatants was not the only weakness in middle-class civilians' claims to wartime manliness. Perhaps most importantly, their sacrifices did not bring about a bolstered self-esteem and sense of pride, but rather a leaching away of power and authority. The effects were felt in a variety of ways. Employers, for example, considered that labour shortages were forcing them to accede to their increasingly confident workers' every demand. As the complaints of farmers in the Great Leighs area suggest, what aroused their ire was not only having to bow to demands for higher wages or shorter hours, but also the loss of deference seen even among 'the old hands'. Workers, at least according to one tenant farmer, now had the upper hand: 'If you find fault, he will tell you he is master now, and you cant [*sic*] do without him'.[38] In the consumer arena, furthermore, high prices and the scarcity of many commodities also ensured that the balance of power swung decisively in favour of retailers and shop assistants, from whom middle-class consumers could no longer be certain of receiving the respectful behaviour that they were accustomed to. Not only were shopkeepers widely suspected of profiteering, to the detriment of their customers, but had also become

THE THING THAT MATTERS.

PROFESSIONAL GRIEVANCE-MONGER. "SHOCKING BUSINESS THIS RISE IN FOOD-PRICES."

BRITISH MOTHER. "THAT'S AS MAY BE. ALL I KNOW IS THEY'RE FEEDING MY BOYS AT THE FRONT ALL RIGHT, AND THAT'S GOOD ENOUGH FOR ME."

18 'The professional grievance-monger', *Punch*, 30 August 1916.

'a thousand times more independent'. In a topsy-turvy wartime world, it was now up to the customer to approach them deferentially, 'with his cap in his hand'.[39]

Wartime challenges to middle-class men's authority also went beyond interactions at work or in the marketplace, and were felt to have reached even into the private arena of the home. Domestic arrangements were thus disrupted in a variety of ways. Not only did billeted soldiers represent an alien presence in civilian homes, but their behaviour all too often showed a distinct lack of respect for the authority of the paterfamilias, while householders' justified reprimands were met with 'sulky, or even uncivil, looks and language'.[40] Established roles and places within the home were also undermined not – as one might expect, given the contemporary emphasis on women's contribution to the war effort – by a new independence among middle-class women, but by the more general economic and social vicissitudes of war. Thus, when in October 1917 Robinson wondered whether as a result of the new coal regulations the family were 'to sit shivering in the cold, or are we to sit and have our meals in the kitchen with the servants?'[41] he was fearing a greater breakdown in domestic arrangements than any caused by his wife and daughter's 'VAD Nursing, bandage-making, etc.'[42] Significantly, furthermore, the loss of male servants and domestic 'handymen' to the armed forces or to munitions factories meant that many middle-class men were forced to take over much of the physical labour involved in running and maintaining middle-class houses and grounds. While most resisted committing themselves to the National Service scheme, refusing to labour at poorly paid work they thought unsuited to educated, professional men, many found themselves forced to undertake just such hard, menial and, it was felt, demeaning work around their own homes – for no pay. Such work, furthermore, was thought unsuited not only to their status, but also to their physical capabilities. As Clark pointed out, some of the work, which included 'heaving wood – cutting grass – sawing wood – mending fence – piling-up rubbish on bonfire-heaps',[43] was 'disagreeable' and 'much of it trialsome for a sedentary student' in his sixties.[44]

Whether at work, home or in the marketplace, wartime vicissitudes thus tended to undermine, rather than to bolster middle-class men's identities as manly citizens. In addition, just when new doubts were cast on the 'value' of much middle-class and white-collar work in wartime, reduced incomes, new regulations, restrictions on consumption and seemingly never ending demands on their pockets, all meant that many men found it increasingly hard to maintain their own and their families' accustomed standard of living.[45] At the same time, far from arousing admiration, their attempts to contribute to the war effort by undertaking volunteer activities on the home front as special constables, as members of a VTC unit or in other capacities, were met with official snubs and public contempt and ridicule. In Keble Howard's 1917 novel *The Smiths in Wartime*, a VTC colonel speaks at a dinner held in honour of seventy-year-old Mr Smith. He tells his audience, amid applause: 'they may smile at our enthusiasm; they may call us "Gorgeous Wrecks" (much cheering and laughter); but ... we strive every minute of the day to do our duty'.[46] Howard's image was one of Volunteers rising above snubs and ridicule. In reality, these left a considerable legacy of bitterness. Writing in 1920, Cooper was still angry about what he saw as the shabby way in which VTC members had been treated during and in the immediate aftermath of the war. He complained that despite their 'tenacity and pluck during the most gravely dangerous period our England has ever known', they had been 'the only Branch of the Services unrepresented in the Victory Parades and even the Special Service men who threw up everything and proceeded voluntarily on active service in the dark days of 1918 remain without any adequate acknowledgement of their patriotism'.[47]

Not only did home front volunteers not live up to the standard of manliness set by combatants, but their activities also seemed to highlight their lack of competence and – arguably most importantly – their physical frailties. Indeed, wartime notions of manliness involved elements of physical fitness and youthful strength that middle-class civilian men frequently seemed to fall short of, whether as rejects from military service because of physical unfitness, as gardeners unable to keep up with the physical labour involved in tending allotments or growing vegetables, or as volunteers who found the demands of drill, route marches or night-time patrols too much for them. Cartoons that portrayed special constables as puny, ineffectual weaklings or the taunts and catcalls directed at VTC members as 'Grandpapa's Regiment'[48] or 'England's last hope',[49] all made clear the low esteem in which physically unimposing home front volunteers were held.

A couple of weeks after the Armistice, Clark wrote to the Bodleian librarian, apologising for the delay in sending the recent volumes of his diaries. He explained that 'the work of the garden and the grounds has kept me busy all year, every minute of daylight that I could spare from my ordinary duties'. As a consequence he was 'very tired and limp when I leave off each night, and let all things slide'. Despite the extra labour, he acknowledged that 'I have been for me very well'.[50] This was as close as

Clark ever came to suggesting that the outdoor, physically demanding work he was being forced to undertake might actually have been beneficial to his health. Much more commonly, Clark and men like him felt that together with food shortages and changes to their diets – particularly the introduction of unpalatable and supposedly indigestible items like 'war bread' – unaccustomed labour was taking its toll on their bodies: by 1918 many middle-class men were feeling weaker, thinner and literally 'diminished' by their war experiences.

Civilian middle-class men's loss of power and control, however, was felt to be at its sharpest when faced with threats to the safety and well-being of their families, whether caused by the financial pressures and shortages of war, by enemy bombardments, or by enforced separations. This helplessness was further magnified in the relationship between civilian fathers and combatant sons, as middle-class men often found themselves unable to fulfil the protective – and indeed to some extent nurturing – roles expected of them. Five days after the Armistice Robert Saunders tried to describe the psychological toll of this helplessness. He suspected that the war had 'pressed more heavily on us than is generally thought, even by ourselves, and I am afraid has aged us more than then 4½ years warrant as regards time'. He thought that this was 'especially true with those whose friends were fighting, or in a position of danger'. No doubt drawing upon his own experiences, he explained that 'the first thing on waking and the last thing at night, and often in the night when unable to sleep one's thoughts naturally turned to those in peril and try as you would you could not help worrying. The coming of post though eagerly looked for was always tinged with dread of the news it might bring, and when no news was received the suspense of waiting was a sore trouble'. By the end of the war, he concluded, 'it certainly appeared as though our feelings were blunted as regards those not directly connected with us, but specially sharpened as far as those near and dear to us were concerned'.[51] All Saunders's sons survived the conflict, but for fathers like Grover, the Fletching village butcher, the immediate reaction to bereavement seems to have been one of paralysing helplessness, the consolation of action not yet a possibility.[52]

Middle-class men may have claimed their share – or, as they argued, more than their 'fair' share – of patriotic suffering and sacrifice, but this ultimately only served to undermine their claims to manliness: overwhelmingly, their war experiences involved a loss of power and authority, as well as physical diminishment and a new sense of helplessness, particularly in their relationship with their families and with combatant sons. It is perhaps not surprising, then, that at the Armistice middle-class civilian men should have looked back on the war years with more anger and resentment, particularly directed at the working class, than satisfaction, and forward into the future with a mixture of apprehension and uncertainty. As Joseph put it, expressing the feelings of many: 'August 4 1914 to November 11 1918 – what losses, changes, heroism, blunders, hopes and fears. And the future for us all – ?'[53]

Notes

1 R. Graves and A. Hodge, *The Long Weekend: A Social History of Great Britain* (Abacus, London, 1995, first published 1940), p. 17.

2 J. M. Bourne, *Britain and the Great War 1914–1918* (Edward Arnold, London, 1989), p. 241. See also A. Gregory, *The Last Great War: British Society and the First World War* (Cambridge University Press, Cambridge, 2008), p. 250–2; G. J. DeGroot, *Blighty: British Society in the Era of the Great War* (Longman, Harlow, 1998, first published 1996), pp. 249–51; A. Marwick, *The Deluge: British Society and the First World War* (Palgrave Macmillan, Basingstoke, second edition, 2006, first published 1965), pp. 299–301.

3 DeGroot, *Blighty*, pp. 251–2.

4 Gregory, *The Last Great War*, p. 14.

5 T. Livingstone, *Tommy's War: The Diaries of a Wartime Nobody* (HarperPress, London, 2008), p. 359.

6 F. Dawkins to P. Liddle, 16 March 1986, DF148, Liddle Collection (1914–18), Special Collections, Brotherton Library, Leeds University (hereafter Liddle Collection), Leeds. See also the scenes in London described by M. MacDonagh, *In London during the War: The Diary of a Journalist* (Eyre and Spottiswoode, London, 1935), pp. 332–3 and by F. A. Robinson, 'Diary of the Great War', 11 November 1918, vol. 4, P.402, Department of Documents, Imperial War Museum (hereafter IWM Documents), London.

7 G. W. Cole, 'Some Recollections of the 1914–18 War', January 1990, DF148, Liddle Collection.

8 The Diary of Ernest R. Cooper, 'Nineteen Hundred and War Time', 28 July 1914 - 3 December 1918 (hereafter Cooper Diary), 11 November 1918, P.121, IWM Documents.

9 A. Clark War Diary, 'Echoes of the 1914 War in an Essex Village' (hereafter Clark Diary), 11 November 1918, Ms Eng. Hist. e.171, Special Collections, Bodleian Library, University of Oxford (hereafter Bodleian Special Collections), Oxford. See also the very similar description of the celebrations in the village of Amesbury in Wiltshire. T. R. Attwater, 'A Civilian Remembers', not dated, DF005, Liddle Collection.

10 Wartime Diaries of H. W. B. Joseph 1914–18 (hereafter Joseph Diaries), 31

October 1918, Ms. Top. Oxon. e.288, Bodleian Special Collections. See also 24 October 1918.

11 J. Williams, *The Home Fronts: Britain, France and Germany 1914–1918* (Constable, London, 1972), p. 259.

12 Clark Diary, 20 October 1918, Ms Eng. Hist. e.171, Bodleian Special Collections.

13 Robinson, 'Diary of the Great War', 28 October 1918, vol. 4, P.402, IWM Documents.

14 Cooper Diary, 20 October 1918, P.121, IWM Documents.

15 *Ibid.*, 9 November 1918.

16 *Ibid.*, 11 November 1918. See also Robinson, 'Diary of the Great War', 11 November 1918, vol. 4, P.402, IWM Documents.

17 MacDonagh, *In London during the War*, pp. 332–3.

18 *Ibid.*, pp. 327–8. Don Todman emphasises that reactions to the Armistice varied according to 'location, role and personal experience'. D. Todman, *The Great War: Myth and Memory* (Hambledon, London, 2005), p. 49.

19 Robinson, 'Diary of the Great War', 11 November 1918, vol. 4, P.402, IWM Documents.

20 Joseph Diaries, 12 November 1918, Ms. Top. Oxon. e.288, Bodleian Special Collections.

21 Gregory, *The Last Great War*, p. 251.

22 Clark Diary, 11 November 1918, Ms Eng. Hist. e.171, Bodleian Special Collections.

23 C. D. Winchcombe, 'The Great War of 1914–1918: Memories of an Octogenarian', not dated, DF148, Liddle Collection.

24 Attwater, 'A Civilian Remembers', not dated, DF005, Liddle Collection.

25 Cooper Diary, 3 December 1918, P.121, IWM Documents.

26 Clark Diary, A. Clark to F. Madan, 25 November 1918, Ms Eng. Hist. e.171, Bodleian Special Collections.

27 Cooper Diary, 11 November 1918, P.121, IWM Documents.

28 Clark Diary, 11 November 1918, Ms Eng. Hist. e.171, Bodleian Special Collections.

29 *Ibid.*, 26 October 1918.

30 *Ibid.*, 11 November 1918.

31 Cooper Diary, 3 December 1918, P.121, IWM Documents.

32 Robinson, 'Diary of the Great War', 13 October 1918, vol. 4, P.402, IWM Documents.

33 J. A. Mangan, '"Muscular, militaristic and manly": the British middle-class hero as moral messenger', *The International Journal of the History of Sport*, vol. 13, no. 1 (1996), pp. 28–47; A. Woollacott, *Gender and Empire* (Palgrave Macmillan, Basingstoke, 2006), Chapter 3.

34 A. Carden-Coyne, *Reconstructing the Body: Classicism, Modernism and the First World War* (Oxford University Press, Oxford, 2009), p. 15. See also G.

L. Mosse, *The Image of Man: The Creation of Modern Masculinity* (Oxford University Press, Oxford, 1998), p. 105. The reconstruction of conceptions of citizenship around notions of 'sacrifice' is also explored in N. F. Gullace, *'The Blood of our Sons': Men, Women and the Renegotiation of British Citizenship during the First World War* (Palgrave Macmillan, Basingstoke, 2002), especially Chapter 7.

35 For the post-war legacy of middle-class bitterness and hostility towards the working class and towards organised labour, see R. McKibbin, *Classes and Cultures: England 1918–1951* (Oxford University Press, Oxford, 2000, first published 1998), pp. 57–9, 89–105. See also C. F. G. Masterman, *England after War: A Study* (Hodder and Stoughton, London, 1923), pp. 54–5.

36 J. Winter, 'Paris, London, Berlin 1914–1919: capital cities at war', in J. Winter and J.-L. Robert (eds), *Capital Cities at War: Paris, London, Berlin 1914–1919* (Cambridge University Press, Cambridge, 1999, first published 1997), pp. 13–14.

37 Robinson, 'Diary of the Great War', 24 February 1917, vol. 3, P.402, IWM Documents.

38 Clark Diary, 6 July 1915, Ms Eng. Hist. e.107, Bodleian Special Collections. See chapter 6.

39 Robinson, 'Diary of the Great War', 26 August 1918, vol. 4, P.402, IWM Documents. See Chapter 7.

40 Clark Diary, 10 July 1915, Ms Eng. Hist. e.107, Bodleian Special Collections. See chapter 2.

41 Robinson, 'Diary of the Great War', 13 October 1917, vol. 3, P.402, IWM Documents. See Chapter 7.

42 *Ibid.*, 15 November 1918, vol. 1, P.401. See Chapter 5.

43 Clark Diary, 11 May 1916, Ms Eng. Hist. e.125, Bodleian Special Collections.

44 *Ibid.*, 16 January 1917, Ms Eng. Hist. e.143. See Chapter 6.

45 Many sections of the middle class continued to experience straitened circumstances in the immediate post-war period, although by 1923 losses in real income 'had … for most been more than made up'. McKibbin, *Classes and Cultures*, p. 53. Also pp. 50–4.

46 K. Howard, *The Smiths in Wartime* (John Lane The Bodley Head, London, 1917), p. 74.

47 E. R. Cooper, 'The 3rd Volunteer Battalion Suffolk Regiment', June 1920, p. 16, P.121, IWM Documents.

48 M. Yearsley ('Eyewitness'), 'The Home Front, 1914–18', p. 77, DS/MISC/17, IWM Documents.

49 Cooper, 'The 3rd Volunteer Battalion Suffolk Regiment', June 1920, p. 2, P.121, IWM Documents. See Chapter 5.

50 A. Clark to F. Madan, Clark Diary, 25 November 1918, Ms Eng. Hist. e.171, Bodleian Special Collections. See Chapter 6.

51 R. Saunders to son, 16 November 1918, R. Saunders, Letters to Son in Canada, 1914–18, 79/15/1, IWM Documents.

52 *Ibid.*, 20 May 1917.

53 Joseph Diaries, 12 November 1918, Ms. Top. Oxon. e.288, Bodleian Special Collections. McKibbin notes that 'it is impossible not to be struck … by the precariousness of life as much of the middle class saw it at the end of the First World War; by the sense of helplessness with which many contemplated the future'. McKibbin, *Classes and Cultures*, p. 50.

Bibliography

Archives

Special Collections, Bodleian Library, University of Oxford, Oxford

A. Clark War Diary, 'Echoes of the 1914 War in an Essex Village', Ms Eng. Hist. e.88–171.

Diary of R. W. M. Gibbs, 1914–20, Ms Eng. misc. c.159–97.

Wartime Diaries of H. W. B. Joseph 1914–18, Ms. Top. Oxon. e.288.

Department of Documents, Imperial War Museum, London

Anon., Diary of a London Lady, Misc. 29, Item 522.

Letters from Alfred Bradburn to his Brother Samuel, 95/16/1.

R. Briggs, Memoir, 1919, 01/59/1.

Letters of Lieutenant James H. Butlin, 67/52/1.

H. Carter Collection, 86/8/1.

The Diary of Ernest R. Cooper, 'Nineteen Hundred and War Time', 28 July 1914 – 3 December 1918, P.121.

E. R. Cooper, 'The 3rd Volunteer Battalion Suffolk Regiment', June 1920, P.121.

H. C. Cossins Diary, 1914–18, PP/MCR/371.

E. T. Gleave Letters, 78/31/1.

W. A. Goodwin Collection, Con Shelf.

E. W. Hewish, 1917 Diary and Accounts, 02/43/1.

J. Hollister Letter, 1917, 98/10/1.

The First World War Letters of Holcombe Ingleby MP, P.343.

F. T. Lockwood, 'Notes Written by F. T. Lockwood', 96/52/1.

F. A. Robinson, 'Diary of the Great War', 1914–16, P.401; 1917–18, P.402.

R. Saunders, Letters to Son in Canada, 1914–18, 79/15/1.

A. G. Steavenson Letters, 86/77/1.

M. Yearsley ('Eyewitness'), 'The Home Front, 1914–18', DS/MISC/17.

P. M. Yearsley Collection, 71/11/1.

Department of Sound, Imperial War Museum, London

P. Ashton Murray interview, 14 October 1985, 9114.
P. Attwood interview, 9559.
L. F. Friswell interview, 8774.
G. Hyam interview, 9567.
W. G. Ostler interview, 21 March 1973, 39.
G. D. Wilkinson interview, 9104.
Mr Wilson interview, 1963 BBC recording, 4261.

Liddle Collection (1914–18), Special Collections, Brotherton Library, Leeds University, Leeds

F. Ashe Lincoln, Interview, 1993, DF148.
T. R. Attwater, 'A Civilian Remembers', not dated, DF005.
J. Axton to P. Liddle, 12 January 1992, DF148.
G. W. Cole, 'Some Recollections of the 1914–18 War', January 1990, DF148.
J. W. E. Cory, untitled, 20 February 1980, DF148.
C. L. Craig (Revd), untitled, 16 November 1979, DF148.
J. F. Crowder, Reminiscences, August 1991, DF148.
F. Dawkins to P. Liddle, 16 March 1986; 26 March 1986, DF148.
F. W. M. Drew, Recollections, not dated, DF148.
G. Edinger, Memoirs, not dated, DF148.
A. D. Gardner, Reminiscences, not dated, DF148.
A. E. J. Hepworth to P. Liddle, 18 September 1981, DF148.
H. J. Kitchener to P. Liddle, not dated, DF148.
R. H. Macleod Papers, DF087.
H. Maingay (Dr), untitled, not dated, DF148.
D. J. Martin, Reminiscences, not dated, DF148.
W. L. McIvor, Recollections, October 1978, DF148.
G. Pember, 'Some Memories of the Great War', not dated, DF148.
E. K. Quick, '1914–1918', not dated, DF148.
K. A. Scott-Moncrieff, General Manager, Electrical Supply Company, DF115.
D. B. Skinner to P. Liddle, 5–8 March 1979, DF148.
D. Toomey, 'Recollections of the 1914–1918 War', not dated, DF148.
C. H. Ward, 'Recollections of the First World War', 1971, DF148.
N. Whitehead, Letters, DF141.
C. D. Winchcombe, 'The Great War of 1914–1918: Memories of an Octogenarian', not dated, DF148.
G. B. Wood-Walker, 'Reminiscences 1914–18', not dated, DF148.
E. Yates, Correspondence, 1914, DF146.

Herefordshire Record Office, Hereford

R. Craigie Letters, BT92/49.

Norfolk Record Office, Norwich

Canon W. Hay Aitken Diary, MC2165/1/25.
Letters to Tom Copeman from Family Members, 1916, MC81/26/405–8.

Manuscripts Reading Room, Cambridge University Library, Cambridge

Kennet Papers, Part 1. Papers of Rt. Hon. Edward Hilton Young (1879–1960), first Lord Kennet of Dene, 66/119.

Ephemera

'Miscellaneous papers relating to the Great War, 13 volumes', Bodleian Library, University of Oxford, Oxford.
A. Clark, 'Scrapbooks of leaflets, newspaper cuttings etc., illustrating aspects of the Great War', Bodleian Library, University of Oxford, Oxford.

Articles

Adams, R. J. Q., 'Asquith's choice: the May coalition and the coming of conscription', *Journal of British Studies*, vol. 25, no. 3 (1986), pp. 243–63.
Alpern Engel, B., 'Not by bread alone: subsistence riots in Russia during World War I', *The Journal of Modern History*, vol. 69, no. 4 (1997), pp. 696–721.
Ashplant, T. G., G. Dawson and M. Roper, 'The politics of war memory and commemoration: contexts, structures and dynamics', in T. G. Ashplant, G. Dawson and M. Roper (eds), *The Politics of War Memory and Commemoration* (Routledge, London, 2000), pp. 3–85.
Badsey, S., 'Press, propaganda and public perceptions', in M. Howard (ed.), *A Part of History: Aspects of the British Experience of the First World War* (Continuum, London, 2008), pp. 27–35.
Beckett, I. F. W., 'The nation in arms, 1914–18', in I. F. W. Beckett and K. Simpson (eds), *A Nation in Arms: A Social History of the British Army in the First World War* (Manchester University Press, Manchester, 1985), pp. 1–35.
Benson, J., 'Domination, subordination and struggle: middle-class marriage in early twentieth-century Wolverhampton, England', *Women's History Review*, vol. 19, no. 3 (2010), pp. 421–33.
Birley, D., 'Sportsmen and the deadly game', in J. A. Mangan (ed.), *A Sport-Loving Society: Victorian and Edwardian Middle-Class England at Play* (Routledge, Abingdon, 2006, article first published 1986), pp. 274–96.

Bonzon, T., 'Transfer payments and social policy', in J. Winter and J.-L. Robert (eds), *Capital Cities at War: Paris, London, Berlin 1914–1919* (Cambridge University Press, Cambridge, 1999, first published 1997), pp. 286–302.

Bonzon, T. and B. Davis, 'Feeding the cities', in J. Winter and J.-L. Robert (eds), *Capital Cities at War: Paris, London, Berlin 1914–1919* (Cambridge University Press, Cambridge, 1999, first published 1997), pp. 305–41.

Boswell, J. S. and B. R. Johns, 'Patriots or profiteers? British businessmen and the First World War', *The Journal of European Economic History*, vol. 11, no. 2 (1982), pp. 423–45.

Broughton, T. L. and H. Rogers, 'Introduction: the empire of the father', in T. L. Broughton and H. Rogers (eds), *Gender and Fatherhood in the Nineteenth Century* (Palgrave Macmillan, Basingstoke, 2007), pp. 1–28.

Bryder, L., 'The First World War: healthy or hungry?', *History Workshop Journal*, no. 24 (1987), pp. 141–57.

Cannadine, D., 'War and death, grief and mourning in modern Britain', in J. Whaley (ed.), *Mirrors of Mortality: Studies in the Social History of Death* (Europa Publications, London, 1981), pp. 187–242.

Coles, A. J., 'The moral economy of the crowd: some twentieth-century food riots', *Journal of British Studies*, vol. 18, no. 1 (1978), pp. 157–76.

Constantine, S., 'Amateur gardening and popular recreation in the 19th and 20th centuries', *Journal of Social History*, vol. 14, no. 3 (1981), pp. 387–406.

Cronier, E., 'The street', in J. Winter and J.-L. Robert (eds), *Capital Cities at War: Paris, London, Berlin 1914–1919 Volume 2: A Cultural History* (Cambridge University Press, Cambridge, 2007), pp. 57–104.

Derez, M., 'The flames of Louvain: the war experience of an academic community', in H. Cecil and P. H. Liddle (eds), *Facing Armageddon: The First World War Experienced* (Leo Cooper, London, 1996), pp. 617–29.

Dewey, P., 'The new warfare and economic mobilisation', in J. Turner (ed.), *Britain and the First World War* (Unwin Hyman, London, 1988), pp. 70–84.

Dewey, P. E., 'Nutrition and living standards in wartime Britain', in R. Wall and J. Winter (eds), *The Upheaval of War: Family, Work and Welfare in Europe, 1914–1918* (Cambridge University Press, Cambridge, 1988), pp. 197–220.

Dewey, P. E., 'British farming profits and government policy during the First World War', *Economic History Review*, second series, vol. 37, no. 3 (1984), pp. 373–90.

Dintenfass, M., 'Service, loyalty and leadership: the life tales of British coal masters and the culture of the middle class, c. 1890–1950', in A. Kidd and D. Nicholls (eds), *The Making of the British Middle Class? Studies of Regional and Cultural Diversity since the Eighteenth Century* (Sutton Publishing, Stroud, 1998), pp. 214–27.

Doolittle, M., 'Fatherhood, religious belief and the protection of children in nineteenth-century English families', in T. L. Broughton and H. Rogers (eds), *Gender and Fatherhood in the Nineteenth Century* (Palgrave Macmillan, Basingstoke, 2007), pp. 31–42.

Englander, D., 'Police and public order in Britain 1914–1918', in C. Emsley and B. Weinberg (eds), *Policing Western Europe: Politics, Professionalism and Public Order 1850–1940* (Greenwood Press, New York, 1991), pp. 90–138.

Fordham, E., 'Universities', in J. Winter and J.-L. Robert (eds), *Capital Cities at War: Paris, London, Berlin 1914–1919 Volume 2: A Cultural History* (Cambridge University Press, Cambridge, 2007), pp. 235–79.

Frank, D., 'Housewives, socialists, and the politics of food: the 1917 New York cost-of-living protests', *Feminist Studies*, vol. 11, no. 2 (1985), pp. 255–85.

French, D., 'Spy fever in Britain, 1900–1915', *The Historical Journal*, vol. 21, no. 2 (1978), pp. 355–70.

Garrard, J. and V. Parrott, 'Craft, professional and middle-class identities: solicitors and gas engineers, c. 1850–1914', in A. Kidd and D. Nicholls (eds), *The Making of the British Middle Class? Studies of Regional and Cultural Diversity since the Eighteenth Century* (Sutton Publishing, Stroud, 1998), pp. 148–68.

Garton, S., 'Return home: war, masculinity and repatriation', in J. Damousi and M. Lake (eds), *Gender and War: Australians at War in the Twentieth Century* (Cambridge University Press, Cambridge, 1995), pp. 191–204.

Gilbert, S. M., 'Soldier's heart: literary men, literary women, and the Great War', in M. Randolph Higgonet, J. Jenson, S. Michel and M. Collins Weitz (eds), *Behind the Lines: Gender and the Two World Wars* (Yale University Press, New Haven, 1987), pp. 197–226.

Goebel, S., 'Exhibitions', in J. Winter and J.-L. Robert (eds), *Capital Cities at War: Paris, London, Berlin 1914–1919 Volume 2: A Cultural History* (Cambridge University Press, Cambridge, 2007), pp. 143–87.

Gray, R., 'The platform and the pulpit: cultural networks and civic identities in industrial towns, c. 1850–70', in A. Kidd and D. Nicholls (eds), *The Making of the British Middle Class? Studies of Regional and Cultural Diversity since the Eighteenth Century* (Sutton Publishing, Stroud, 1998), pp. 130–47.

Gregory, A., 'Lost generations: the impact of military casualties on Paris, London, and Berlin', in J. Winter and J.-L. Robert (eds), *Capital Cities at War: Paris, London, Berlin 1914–1919* (Cambridge University Press, Cambridge, 1999, first published 1997), pp. 57–103.

Gullace, N. F., 'White feathers and wounded men: female patriotism and the memory of the Great War', *Journal of British Studies*, vol. 36, no. 2 (1997), pp. 178–206.

Hammerton, A. J., 'The English weakness? Gender, satire and "moral manliness" in the lower middle class, 1870–1920', in A. Kidd and D. Nicholls (eds), *Gender, Civic Culture and Consumerism: Middle-Class Identity in Britain, 1800–1940* (Manchester University Press, Manchester, 1999), pp. 164–82.

Honeyman, K., 'Following suit: men, masculinity and gendered practices in the clothing trade in Leeds, England, 1890–1940', *Gender & History*, vol. 14, no. 3 (2002), pp. 426–46.

Hosgood, C., 'Mrs Pooter's purchase: lower middle-class consumerism and the sales, 1870–1914', in A. Kidd and D. Nicholls (eds), *Gender, Civic Culture and Consumerism: Middle-Class Identity in Britain, 1800–1940* (Manchester University Press, Manchester, 1999), pp. 146–63.

Hosgood, C. P., '"Mercantile monasteries": shops, shop assistants and shop life in late-Victorian and Edwardian Britain', *Journal of British Studies*, vol. 38, no. 3 (1999), pp. 322–52.

Huggins, M. J., 'More sinful pleasures? Leisure, respectability and the male middle classes in Victorian England', *Journal of Social History*, vol. 33, no. 3 (2000), pp. 585–600.

Hunt, K., 'The politics of food and women's neighborhood activism in First World War Britain', *International Labor and Working-Class History*, no. 77 (2010), pp. 8–26.

Kaplan, T., 'Female consciousness and collective action: the case of Barcelona, 1910–1918', *Signs*, vol. 7, no. 3 (1982), pp. 545–66.

Kidd, A. and D. Nicholls, 'Introduction: the making of the British middle class?', in A. Kidd and D. Nicholls (eds), *The Making of the British Middle Class? Studies of Regional and Cultural Diversity since the Eighteenth Century* (Sutton Publishing, Stroud, 1998), pp. xv–xl.

Lawrence, J., 'Material pressures on the middle classes', in J. Winter and J.-L. Robert (eds), *Capital Cities at War: Paris, London, Berlin 1914–1919* (Cambridge University Press, Cambridge, 1999, first published 1997), pp. 229–54.

Leon, C., 'Special constables in the First and Second World Wars', *Police History Society Journal*, vol. 7 (1992), pp. 1–41.

Mangan, J. A., '"Muscular, militaristic and manly": the British middle-class hero as moral messenger', *The International Journal of the History of Sport*, vol. 13, no. 1 (1996), pp. 28–47.

Manning, J., 'Wages and purchasing power', in J. Winter and J.-L. Robert (eds), *Capital Cities at War: Paris, London, Berlin 1914–1919* (Cambridge University Press, Cambridge, 1999, first published 1997), pp. 255–85.

Marwick, M., 'Hands-on fatherhood in Trollope's novels', in T. L. Broughton and H. Rogers (eds), *Gender and Fatherhood in the Nineteenth Century* (Palgrave Macmillan, Basingstoke, 2007), pp. 85–95.

McDermott, J., '"A needless sacrifice": British businessmen and business as usual in the First World War', *Albion*, vol. 21, no. 2 (1989), pp. 263–82.

Morton Osborne, J., 'Defining their own patriotism: British Volunteer Training Corps in the First World War', *Journal of Contemporary History*, vol. 23, no. 1 (1988), pp. 59–75.

Quail, J. M., 'From personal patronage to public school privilege: social closure in the recruitment of managers in the United Kingdom from the late nineteenth century to 1930', in A. Kidd and D. Nicholls (eds), *The Making of the British Middle Class? Studies of Regional and Cultural Diversity since the Eighteenth Century* (Sutton Publishing, Stroud, 1998), pp. 169–85.

Reid, A., 'The impact of the war on British workers', in R. Wall and J. Winter (eds), *The Upheaval of War: Family, Work and Welfare in Europe, 1914–1918* (Cambridge University Press, Cambridge, 1988), pp. 221–33.

Robert, J.-L., 'The image of the profiteer', in J. Winter and J.-L. Robert (eds), *Capital Cities at War: Paris, London, Berlin 1914–1919* (Cambridge University Press, Cambridge, 1999, first published 1997), pp. 104–32.

Rollet, C., 'The home and family life', in J. Winter and J.-L. Robert (eds), *Capital Cities at War: Paris, London, Berlin 1914–1919 Volume 2: A Cultural History* (Cambridge University Press, Cambridge, 2007), pp. 315–53.

Roper, M., 'Between manliness and masculinity: the "war generation" and the psychology of fear in Britain, 1914–1950', *Journal of British Studies*, vol. 44, no. 2 (2005), pp. 343–62.

Rüger, J., 'Entertainments', in J. Winter and J.-L. Robert (eds), *Capital Cities at War: Paris, London, Berlin 1914–1919 Volume 2: A Cultural History* (Cambridge University Press, Cambridge, 2007), pp. 105–40.

Sabatos, T., 'Father as mother: the image of the widower with children in Victorian art', in T. L. Broughton and H. Rogers (eds), *Gender and Fatherhood in the Nineteenth Century* (Palgrave Macmillan, Basingstoke, 2007), pp. 71–84.

Saunders, M., 'Friendship and enmity in First World War literature', *Literature & History*, vol. 17, no. 1 (2008), pp. 62–77.

Silbey, D., 'Bodies and cultures collide: enlistment, the medical exam, and the British working class, 1914–1916', *Social History of Medicine*, vol. 17, no. 1 (2004), pp. 61–76.

Simkins, P., 'Soldiers and civilians: billeting in Britain and France', in I. F. W. Beckett and K. Simpson (eds), *A Nation in Arms: A Social History of the British Army in the First World War* (Manchester University Press, Manchester, 1985), pp. 165–91.

Smart, J., 'Feminists, food and the fair price: the cost of living demonstrations in Melbourne, August–September 1917', in J. Damousi and M. Lake (eds), *Gender and War: Australians at War in the Twentieth Century* (Cambridge University Press, Cambridge, 1995), pp. 274–301.

Strange, J.-M., '"Speechless with grief": bereavement and the working-class father, c. 1880–1914', in T. L. Broughton and H. Rogers (eds), *Gender and Fatherhood in the Nineteenth Century* (Palgrave Macmillan, Basingstoke, 2007), pp. 138–49.

Summers, A., 'Militarism in Britain before the Great War', *History Workshop Journal*, vol. 2 (1976), pp. 104–23.

Tosh, J., 'Hegemonic masculinity and the history of gender', in S. Dudnik, K. Hagemann and J. Tosh (eds), *Masculinities in Politics and War: Gendering Modern History* (Manchester University Press, Manchester, 2004), pp. 41–58.

Trentmann, F. and F. Just, 'Introduction, in F. Trentmann and F. Just (eds), *Food and Conflict in Europe in the Age of the Two World Wars* (Palgrave Macmillan, Basingstoke, 2006), pp. 1–12.

Triebel, A., 'Coal and the metropolis', in J. Winter and J.-L. Robert (eds), *Capital Cities at War: Paris, London, Berlin 1914–1919* (Cambridge University

Press, Cambridge, 1999, first published 1997), pp. 342–73.

Veitch, C., '"Play up! Play up! And win the war!" Football, the nation and the First World War 1914–15', *Journal of Contemporary History*, vol. 20, no. 3 (1985), pp. 363–78.

Waites, B., 'The government of the home front and the "moral economy" of the working class', in P. H. Liddle (ed.), *Home Fires and Foreign Fields: British Social and Military Experience in the First World War* (Brassey's, London, 1985), pp. 175–93.

Wall, R., 'English and German families in the First World War', in R. Wall and J. Winter (eds), *The Upheaval of War: Family, Work and Welfare in Europe, 1914–1918* (Cambridge University Press, Cambridge, 1988), pp. 43–106.

Wild, J., '"A merciful, heaven-sent release"? The clerk and the First World War in British literary culture', *Cultural and Social History*, vol. 4, no. 1 (2007), pp. 73–94.

Winter, J., 'Popular culture in wartime Britain', in A. Roshwald and R. Stites (eds), *European Culture in the Great War: The Arts, Entertainment and Propaganda, 1914–1918* (Cambridge University Press, Cambridge, 1999), pp. 330–48.

Winter, J., 'Paris, London, Berlin 1914–1919: capital cities at war', in J. Winter and J.-L. Robert (eds), *Capital Cities at War: Paris, London, Berlin 1914–1919* (Cambridge University Press, Cambridge, 1999, first published 1997), pp. 3–24.

Winter, J., 'Some paradoxes of the First World War', in R. Wall and J. Winter (eds), *The Upheaval of War: Family, Work and Welfare in Europe, 1914–1918* (Cambridge University Press, Cambridge, 1988), pp. 9–42.

Woollacott, A., 'Khaki fever and its control: gender, class, age and sexual morality on the British homefront in the First World War', *Journal of Contemporary History*, vol. 29, no. 2 (1994), pp. 325–47.

Woollacott, A., 'Sisters and brothers in arms: family, class, and gendering in World War One Britain', in M. Cooke and A. Woollacott (eds), *Gendering War Talk* (Princeton University Press, Princeton, NJ, 1993), pp. 128–47.

Zweiniger-Bargielowska, I., 'The culture of the abdomen: obesity and reducing in Britain, circa 1900–1939', *Journal of British Studies*, vol. 44, no. 2 (2005), pp. 239–73.

Books

H. W. B. Joseph 1867–1943: An Address Delivered in Chapel by the Sub-warden of New College (A. H. Smith) 23 November 1943 (University Press, Oxford, not dated).

Acton, C., *Grief in Wartime: Private Pain, Public Discourse* (Palgrave Macmillan, Basingstoke, 2007).

Anderson, B., *Imagined Communities: Reflections on the Origin and Spread of Nationalism* (Verso, London, 1983).

Bibliography

Anon., *The Volunteer Force and the Volunteer Training Corps during the Great War: Official Record of the Central Association of Volunteer Regiments* (P. S. King and Son, London, 1920).

Ashplant, T. G., G. Dawson and M. Roper (eds), *The Politics of War Memory and Commemoration* (Routledge, London, 2000).

Barham, P., *Forgotten Lunatics of the Great War* (Yale University Press, New Haven, CT, 2004).

Beaven, B., *Leisure, Citizenship and Working-Class Men in Britain, 1850–1945* (Manchester University Press, Manchester, 2005).

Beckett, I. F. W., *Home Front 1914–1918: How Britain Survived the Great War* (The National Archives, London, 2006).

Beckett, I. F. W., *The Great War 1914–1918* (Pearson Education, Harlow, 2001).

Beckett, I. F. W. and K. Simpson (eds), *A Nation in Arms: A Social History of the British Army in the First World War* (Manchester University Press, Manchester, 1985).

Beddoe, D., *Back to Home and Duty* (Pandora, London, 1989).

Bennett, A., *The Pretty Lady: A Novel* (Cassell, London, not dated, *c.* 1918).

Benson, J., *The Wolverhampton Tragedy: Death and the 'Respectable' Mr Lawrence* (Carnegie, Lancaster, 2009).

Benson, J., *Affluence and Authority: A Social History of Twentieth-Century Britain* (Hodder Arnold, London, 2005).

Bibbings, L. S., *Telling Tales about Men: Conceptions of Conscientious Objectors to Military Service during the First World War* (Manchester University Press, Manchester, 2009).

Blake, G., *Returned Empty* (Faber and Faber, London, 1931).

Blumenfeld, R. D., *All in a Lifetime* (Ernest Benn, London, 1931).

Bourke, J., *Dismembering the Male: Men's Bodies, Britain and the Great War* (Reaktion Books, London, 1996).

Bourne, J. M., *Britain and the Great War 1914–1918* (Edward Arnold, London, 1989).

Bowley, A. L., *Some Economic Consequences of the Great War* (Thornton Butterworth, London, 1931, first published 1930).

Bracco, R. M., *Merchants of Hope: British Middlebrow Writers of the First World War, 1919–1939* (Berg, Oxford, 1993).

Braybon, G., *Women Workers in the First World War* (Routledge, London, 1989).

Breward, C., *The Hidden Consumer: Masculinities, Fashion and City Life 1860–1914* (Manchester University Press, Manchester, 1995).

Broughton, T. L. and H. Rogers (eds), *Gender and Fatherhood in the Nineteenth Century* (Palgrave Macmillan, Basingstoke, 2007).

Burnett, J., *England Eats Out: 1830–Present* (Pearson Longman, Harlow, 2004).

Burnett, J., *Plenty and Want: A Social History of Diet in England from 1815 to the Present Day* (Scolar Press, London, revised edition, 1979).

Bush, J., *Behind the Lines: East End Labour 1914–1919* (Merlin Press, London, 1984).

Carden-Coyne, A., *Reconstructing the Body: Classicism, Modernism and the First World War* (Oxford University Press, Oxford, 2009).

Cartmell, H., *For Remembrance: An Account of some Fateful Years* (George Toulmin & Sons, Preston, 1919).

Cecil, H. and P. H. Liddle (eds), *Facing Armageddon: The First World War Experienced* (Leo Cooper, London, 1996).

Chapman, H. B., *Home Truths about the War* (George Allen & Unwin, London, 1917).

Cohen, D., *Household Gods: The British and their Possessions* (Yale University Press, New Haven, CT, 2006).

Cohen, D., *The War Come Home: Disabled Veterans in Britain and Germany, 1914–1939* (University of California Press, Berkeley, CA, 2001).

Collins, L. J., *Theatre at War, 1914–18* (Macmillan Press, Basingstoke, 1998).

Connell, R., *Masculinities* (Polity, Cambridge, second edition, 2005, first published 1995).

Connell, R., *Gender and Power: Society, the Person and Sexual Politics* (Polity Press, Cambridge, 1987).

Connelly, M., *The Great War, Memory and Ritual: Commemoration in the City and East London, 1916–1939* (The Boydell Press for the Royal Historical Society, Woodbridge, 2002).

Constantine, S., M. W. Kirby and M. M. Rose (eds), *The First World War in British History* (Edward Arnold, London, 1995).

Cooke, M. and A. Woollacott (eds), *Gendering War Talk* (Princeton University Press, Princeton, NJ, 1993).

Damousi, J., *The Labour of Loss: Mourning, Memory and Wartime Bereavement in Australia* (Cambridge University Press, Cambridge, 1999).

Damousi, J. and M. Lake (eds), *Gender and War: Australians at War in the Twentieth Century* (Cambridge University Press, Cambridge, 1995).

Das, S., *Touch and Intimacy in First World War Literature* (Cambridge University Press, Cambridge, 2005).

Daunton, M., *Wealth and Welfare: An Economic and Social History of Britain 1851–1951* (Oxford University Press, Oxford, 2007).

Davidoff, L. and C. Hall, *Family Fortunes: Men and Women of the English Middle Class, 1780–1850* (Hutchinson, London, 1987).

Davis, B., *Home Fires Burning: Food, Politics and Everyday Life in World War One Berlin* (University of North Carolina Press, Chapel Hill, NC, 2000).

Dawson, G., *Soldier Heroes: British Adventure, Empire and the Imagining of Masculinities* (Routledge, London, 1994).

Dawson, W. J., *The Father of a Soldier* (John Lane, The Bodley Head, London, 1918).

DeGroot, G. J., *Blighty: British Society in the Era of the Great War* (Longman, Harlow, 1998, first published 1996).

Dewey, P., *War and Progress in Britain 1914–1918* (Longman, Harlow, 1997).

Dudnik, S., K. Hagemann and J. Tosh (eds), *Masculinities in Politics and War: Gendering Modern History* (Manchester University Press, Manchester, 2004).

Egremont, M., *Siegfried Sassoon: A Biography* (Picador, London, 2005).

Emsley, C., *The English Police: A Political and Social History* (Longman, Harlow, 1996, first published 1991).

Emsley, C. and B. Weinberg (eds), *Policing Western Europe: Politics, Professionalism and Public Order 1850–1940* (Greenwood Press, New York, 1991).

Feinstein, C. H., *National Income, Expenditure and Output in the United Kingdom 1855–1965* (Cambridge University Press, Cambridge, 1972).

French, D., *Military Identities: The Regimental System, the British Army and the British People, c.1870–2000* (Oxford University Press, Oxford, 2005).

Fussell, P., *The Great War and Modern Memory* (Oxford University Press, Oxford, 1977, first published 1975).

Goebel, S., *The Great War and Medieval Memory: War, Remembrance and Medievalism in Britain and Germany, 1914–1940* (Cambridge University Press, Cambridge, 2007).

Graves, R. and A. Hodge, *The Long Weekend: A Social History of Great Britain* (Abacus, London, 1995, first published 1940).

Gray, J., *Gin and Bitters* (Jarrold Publishers, London, not dated, *c.* 1938).

Grayzel, S. R., *Women's Identities at War: Gender, Motherhood, and Politics in Britain and France during the First World War* (The University of North Carolina Press, Chapel Hill, NC, 1999).

Gregory, A., *The Last Great War: British Society and the First World War* (Cambridge University Press, Cambridge, 2008).

Gregory, A., *The Silence of Memory: Armistice Day 1919–1946* (Berg, Oxford, 1994).

Grieves (ed.), K., *Sussex in the First World War*, Sussex Record Society vol. 84 (Sussex Record Society, Lewes, 2004).

Grieves, K., *The Politics of Manpower, 1914–18* (Manchester University Press, Manchester, 1988).

Gullace, N. F., *'The Blood of our Sons': Men, Women and the Renegotiation of British Citizenship during the First World War* (Palgrave Macmillan, Basingstoke, 2002).

Gunn, S. and R. Bell, *Middle Classes: Their Rise and Sprawl* (Phoenix, London, 2003, first published 2002).

Gwynn, S. (ed.), *The Anvil of War: Letters between F. S. Oliver and his Brother 1914–1918* (Macmillan and Co., London, 1936).

Hall, L. A., *Hidden Anxieties: Male Sexuality, 1900–1950* (Polity Press, Cambridge, 1991).

Hammerton, A. J., *Cruelty and Companionship: Conflict in Nineteenth-Century Married Life* (Routledge, London, 1992).

Healy, M., *Vienna and the Fall of the Habsburg Empire: Total War and Everyday Life in World War One* (Cambridge University Press, Cambridge, 2004).

Hilton, M., *Smoking in British Popular Culture 1800–2000: Perfect Pleasures* (Manchester University Press, Manchester, 2000).

Holt, T. and V., *'My Boy Jack?' The Search for Kipling's Only Son* (Leo Cooper, Barnsley, 1998).

Hoover, A. J., *God, Germany and Britain in the Great War: A Study of Clerical Nationalism* (Praeger, New York, 1989).

Horn, P., *Rural Life in England in the First World War* (Gill and Macmillan, St Martin's Press, New York, 1984).

Horne, J. N., *Labour at War: France and Britain 1914–1918* (Clarendon Press, Oxford, 1991).

Horrall, A., *Popular Culture in London, c.1890–1918: The Transformation of Entertainment* (Manchester University Press, Manchester, 1991).

Howard, K., *The Smiths in Wartime* (John Lane The Bodley Head, London, 1917).

Huggins, M. and J. A. Mangan (eds), *Disreputable Pleasures: Less Virtuous Victorians at Play* (Frank Cass, Abingdon, 2004).

Humphries, S. and P. Gordon, *A Labour of Love: The Experience of Parenthood in Britain 1900–1950* (Sidgwick and Jackson, London, 1993).

Hynes, S. L., *The Soldiers' Tale: Bearing Witness to Modern War* (Pimlico, London, 1998).

Jackson, A. A., *The Middle Classes 1900–1950* (David St John Thomas Publisher, Nairn, 1991).

Jalland, P., *Australian Ways of Death: A Social and Cultural History 1840–1918* (Oxford University Press, Melbourne, 2002).

Jalland, P., *Death in the Victorian Family* (Oxford University Press, Oxford, 1996).

James, L., *The Middle Class: A History* (Little, Brown, London, 2006).

Keohane, N., *The Party of Patriotism: The Conservative Party and the First World War* (Ashgate, Farnham, 2010).

Kidd, A. and D. Nicholls (eds), *Gender, Civic Culture and Consumerism: Middle-Class Identity in Britain, 1800–1940* (Manchester University Press, Manchester, 1999).

Kidd, A. and D. Nicholls (eds), *The Making of the British Middle Class? Studies of Regional and Cultural Diversity since the Eighteenth Century* (Sutton Publishing, Stroud, 1998).

King, A., *Memorials of the Great War in Britain: The Symbolism and Politics of Remembrance* (Berg, Oxford, 1998).

Koditschek, T., *Class Formation and Urban Industrial Society: Bradford, 1750–1850* (Cambridge University Press, Cambridge, 1990).

Kramer, A., *Dynamics of Destruction: Culture and Mass Killing in the First World War* (Oxford University Press, Oxford, 2008, first published 2007).

Leed, E., *No Man's Land: Combat and Identity in World War One* (Cambridge University Press, Cambridge, 1979).

Liddle, P. H., *Voices of War: Front Line and Home Front* (Leo Cooper, London, 1988).

Liddle (ed.), P. H., *Home Fires and Foreign Fields: British Social and Military Experience in the First World War* (Brassey's, London, 1985).

Litman, S., *Prices and Price Control in Great Britain and the United States during the World War* (Oxford University Press, New York, 1920).

Livingstone, T., *Tommy's War: The Diaries of a Wartime Nobody* (HarperPress, London, 2008).

Lowerson, J., *Sport and the English Middle Classes 1870–1914* (Manchester University Press, Manchester, 1993).

Lucy, H., *The Diary of a Journalist*, vol. 1 (J. Murray, London, 1920).

MacDonagh, M., *In London during the War: The Diary of a Journalist* (Eyre and Spottiswoode, London, 1935).

Mangan, J. A. (ed.), *A Sport-Loving Society: Victorian and Edwardian Middle-Class England at Play* (Routledge, Abingdon, 2006).

Mann, F. O., *Grope Carries On: Being the Further Adventures of Albert Grope during the War* (Faber and Faber, London, 1932).

Marrin, A., *The Last Crusade: The Church of England in the First World War* (Duke University Press, Durham, NC, 1974).

Marwick, A., *The Deluge: British Society and the First World War* (Palgrave Macmillan, Basingstoke, second edition, 2006, first published 1965).

Marwick, A., *Women at War* (Fontana, London, 1977).

Masterman, C. F. G., *England after War: A Study* (Hodder and Stoughton, London, 1923).

McCartney, H., *Citizen Soldiers: The Liverpool Territorials in the First World War* (Cambridge University Press, Cambridge, 2005).

McGeown, P., *Heat the Furnace Seven Times More* (Hutchinson, London, 1967).

McIvor, A. J., *A History of Work in Britain, 1880–1950* (Palgrave Macmillan, Basingstoke, 2008, first published 2001).

McKibbin, R., *Classes and Cultures: England 1918–1951* (Oxford University Press, Oxford, 2000, first published 1998).

McPhail, H., *The Long Silence: Civilian Life under the German Occupation of Northern France, 1914–1918* (I. B. Tauris, London, 1999).

Meeres, F., *Norfolk in the First World War* (Phillimore, Chichester, 2004).

Meyer, J., *Men of War: Masculinity and the First World War in Britain* (Palgrave Macmillan, Basingstoke, 2009).

Miles, H. E., *Untold Tales of War-Time London: A Personal Diary* (Cecil Palmer, London, 1930).

Morris, R. J., *Class, Sect and Party: The Making of the British Middle Class, Leeds, 1820–1850* (Manchester University Press, Manchester, 1990).

Morton, J., *Spies of the First World War: Under Cover for King and Kaiser* (The National Archives, Richmond, 2010).

Mosse, G. L., *The Image of Man: The Creation of Modern Masculinity* (Oxford University Press, Oxford, 1998).

Mottram, R. H., *Sixty-four, Ninety-four!* (Chatto & Windus, London, 1925).
Mr. Punch's History of the Great War (Cassell, London, 1919).
Munsom, J. (ed.), *Echoes of the Great War: The Diary of the Reverend Andrew Clark 1914–1919* (Oxford University Press, Oxford, 1985).
Nelson, C., *Invisible Men: Fatherhood in Victorian Periodicals, 1850–1910* (University of Georgia Press, Athens, GA, 1995).
Oddy, D. J., *From Plain Fare to Fusion Food: British Diet from the 1890s to the 1990s* (Boydell Press, Woodbridge, 2003).
O'Donovan, G., *How they Did It* (Methuen & Co., London, 1920).
Panayi, P., *Immigration, Ethnicity and Racism in Britain, 1815–1945* (Manchester University Press, Manchester, 1994).
Panayi, P., *The Enemy in our Midst: Germans in Britain during the First World War* (Berg, Oxford, 1991).
Pankhurst, E. S., *The Home Front* (The Cresset Library, London, 1987, first published 1932).
Pedersen, S., *Family, Dependence, and the Origins of the Welfare State: Britain and France, 1914–1945* (Cambridge University Press, Cambridge, 1993).
Peel, C. S., *How We Lived Then: A Sketch of Social and Domestic Life in England during the War* (John Lane The Bodley Head, London, 1929).
Pendlebury, A., *Portraying 'the Jew' in First World War Britain* (Vallentine Mitchell, London, 2006).
Perkin, H., *The Rise of Professional Society: England since 1880* (Routledge, London, revised edition, 2002, first published 1989).
Playne, C. E., *Britain Holds on 1917, 1918* (George Allen & Unwin, London, 1933).
Playne, C. E., *Society at War 1914–1916* (George Allen & Unwin, London, 1931).
Randolph Higgonet, M., J. Jenson, S. Michel and M. Collins Weitz (eds), *Behind the Lines: Gender and the Two World Wars* (Yale University Press, New Haven, CT, 1987).
Reeves, N., *Official British Film Propaganda during the First World War* (Croom Helm in association with the Imperial War Museum, London, 1986).
Reid, F., *Broken Men: Shell Shock, Treatment and Recovery in Britain, 1914–1930* (Continuum, London, 2010).
Robb, G., *British Culture and the First World War* (Palgrave, Basingstoke, 2002).
Roberts, R., *The Classic Slum: Salford Life in the First Quarter of the Century* (Penguin, Harmondsworth, 1974, first published 1971).
Roper, M., *The Secret Battle: Emotional Survival in the Great War* (Manchester University Press, Manchester, 2009).
Roshwald, A. and R. Stites (eds), *European Culture in the Great War: The Arts, Entertainment and Propaganda, 1914–1918* (Cambridge University Press, Cambridge, 1999).
Rowbotham, S., *Hidden from History: 300 Years of Women's Oppression and the Fight Against it* (Pluto, London, 1973).

Sainsbury, J. D., *Herts Volunteer Regiment* (Hart Books, Welwyn, 2005).
Sanders, M. L. and P. M. Taylor, *British Propaganda during the First World War, 1914–18* (Macmillan, Basingstoke, 1982).
Seipp, A. R., *The Ordeal of Peace: Demobilization and the Urban Experience in Britain and Germany, 1917–1921* (Ashgate, Farnham, 2009).
Shanks, E., *The Old Indispensables: A Romance of Whitehall* (Martin Secker, London, 1919).
Sheridan Jones, C., *London in War-Time* (Grafton, London, 1917).
Silbey, D., *The British Working Class and Enthusiasm for War, 1914–1916* (Frank Cass, London, 2005).
Simmonds, A. G. V., *Britain and World War One* (Routledge, Abingdon, 2011).
Stevenson, D., *1914–1918: The History of the First World War* (Allen Lane, London, 2004).
Street, G. S., *At Home in the War* (William Heinemann, London, 1918).
Tate, T. (ed.), *Women, Men and the Great War: An Anthology of Stories* (Manchester University Press, Manchester, 1995).
Thom, D., *Nice Girls and Rude Girls: Women Workers in World War I* (I. B. Tauris, London, 1998).
Thompson, E. P., *The Making of the English Working Class* (Penguin Books, London, 1988, first published 1963).
Todman, D., *The Great War: Myth and Memory* (Hambledon, London, 2005).
Tosh, J., *A Man's Place: Masculinity and the Middle-Class Home in Victorian England* (Yale University Press, New Haven, CT, 1999).
Trentmann, F., *Free Trade Nation: Commerce, Consumption, and Civil Society in Modern Britain* (Oxford University Press, Oxford, 2008).
Trentmann, F. and F. Just (eds), *Food and Conflict in Europe in the Age of the Two World Wars* (Palgrave Macmillan, Basingstoke, 2006).
Turner, J., *British Politics and the Great War: Coalition and Conflict, 1915–1918* (Yale University Press, New Haven, CT, 1992).
Tylee, C. M., *The Great War and Women's Consciousness: Images of Militarism and Womanhood in Women's Writings, 1914–64* (Macmillan, Basingstoke, 1990).
Ugolini, L., *Men and Menswear: Sartorial Consumption in Britain, 1880–1939* (Ashgate, Aldershot, 2007).
Vachell, H. A., *The Soul of Susan Yellam* (Cassell and Co., London, 1918).
Van Emden, R. and S. Humphries, *All Quiet on the Home Front: An Oral History of Life in Britain during the First World War* (Headline, London, 2003).
Wahrman, D., *Imagining the Middle Class: The Political Representation of Class in Britain, c. 1780–1840* (Cambridge University Press, Cambridge, 1995).
Waites, B., *A Class Society at War: England 1914–1918* (Berg, Leamington Spa, 1987).
Wall, R. and J. Winter (eds), *The Upheaval of War: Family, Work and Welfare in Europe, 1914–1918* (Cambridge University Press, Cambridge, 1988).

Watson, J. S. K., *Fighting Different Wars: Experience, Memory and the First World War in Britain* (Cambridge University Press, Cambridge, 2004).

Wells, H. G., *Mr Britling Sees it Through* (The Hogarth Press, London, 1985, first published 1916).

Whaley, J. (ed.), *Mirrors of Mortality: Studies in the Social History of Death* (Europa Publications, London, 1981).

Wilkinson, A., *The Church of England and the First World War* (SCM Press, London, 1996, first published 1978).

Williams, J., *The Home Fronts: Britain, France and Germany 1914–1918* (Constable, London, 1972).

Wilson, T., *The Myriad Faces of War: Britain and the Great War, 1914–1918* (Polity Press, Cambridge, 1986).

Winstanley, M. J., *The Shopkeeper's World, 1830–1914* (Manchester University Press, Manchester, 1983).

Winter, J. M., *The Great War and the British People* (Palgrave Macmillan, Basingstoke, 2003, first published 1985).

Winter, J., *Sites of Memory, Sites of Mourning: The Great War in European Cultural History* (Cambridge University Press, Cambridge, 1995).

Winter, J. and A. Prost, *The Great War in History: Debates and Controversies, 1914 to the Present* (Cambridge University Press, Cambridge, 2005).

Winter, J. and J.-L. Robert (eds), *Capital Cities at War: Paris, London, Berlin 1914–1919* (Cambridge University Press, Cambridge, 1999, first published 1997).

Winter, J. and J.-L. Robert (eds), *Capital Cities at War: Paris, London, Berlin 1914–1919 Volume 2: A Cultural History* (Cambridge University Press, Cambridge, 2007).

Wohl, R., *The Generation of 1914* (Weidenfeld and Nicolson, London, 1980).

Woollacott, A., *Gender and Empire* (Palgrave Macmillan, Basingstoke, 2006).

Woollacott, A., *On Her Their Lives Depend: Munitions Workers in the Great War* (University of California Press, Berkeley, CA, 1994).

Wrigley (ed.), C., *Challenges of Labour: Central and Western Europe 1917–1920* (Routledge, London, 1993).

Young, L., *Middle-Class Culture in the Nineteenth Century: America, Australia and Britain* (Palgrave Macmillan, Basingstoke, 2003).

Zweiniger-Bargielowska, I., *Managing the Body: Beauty, Health and Fitness in Britain, 1880–1939* (Oxford University Press, Oxford, 2010).

Periodicals

The Bystander, 1914–18

Punch, 1914–18

The Sketch, 1914–18

Theses

Cullen, S. M., 'Gender and the Great War: British Combatants, Masculinity and Perceptions of Women, 1918–1939' (Unpublished DPhil thesis, University of Oxford, 1998).

McDermott, J., 'The Work of the Military Service Tribunals in Northamptonshire, 1916–1918' (Unpublished PhD thesis, University of Northampton, 2009).

Index

Milton Keynes UK
Ingram Content Group UK Ltd.
UKHW031522050224
437298UK00003B/646

9 781526 116666